The Practical Guide to Experience Design

A guidebook for passionate, curious, and intentional people who enjoy designing for humans.

Shannon E. Thomas

Published by Artificial Publishing, Amsterdam

https://practical.guide

GIRL FRIDAY PRODUCTIONS

Edited and designed by Girl Friday Productions

www.girlfridayproductions.com

Cover design: Paul Barrett

Interior design: Shannon E. Thomas

Project management: Sara Addicott

ISBN (paperback): 9789083041407

ISBN (ebook): 9789083041414

First edition

Table of Contents

Preface

Let me introduce myself. I'm Shannon. I've had a passion for design for as long as I can remember—not just the product of design, but the actual thinking and doing of design. It stems from the insatiable curiosity that most of us have as children and was nurtured by my family, who encouraged me to always be drawing, making, and inventing. Resisting the urge to grow up completely, I channeled this energy into a fine arts degree and eventually into a career in design.

I've bounced around a lot. I've been in-house at start-ups and at large corporations. I've worked in a small ad agency and in one of the world's most well-known design consultancies. I've worked at the strategic beginnings of projects and at the tactical finales, pushing to get products ready for market and iterating for later releases. I've even worked with companies to design the process of design itself. Throughout all of this, my curiosity, passion, and intention led me to seek and understand new experiences. Eventually, across the ocean from where I started, I founded my own boutique UX agency. As an agency, we worked with clients that were both large and small, near and far, rigid and flexible. Along with my partner and a small group of talented designers, I used the work as a vehicle to teach both designers and clients about the value of experience design. As we all learned together, I began writing this book.

When I began writing, I knew that I wanted to highlight the patterns of design processes. Rather than focus only on the more traditional aspects of design, I wanted to show how projects are structured, how design teams integrate into larger organizations, and how teams work together to deliver experiences to users. I wanted to cover popular methodologies, but also to show how they work within the larger context of a project.

I knew that I wanted *The Practical Guide to Experience Design* to be for designers while also speaking to audiences beyond designers. Because I believe that great experience designers can come from any background, this book aims to guide anyone who is curious and passionate about the subject. It avoids jargon and tries to explain things in as straightforward a way as possible.

While I started with a clear goal for the book, it wasn't until the writing was well underway that I realized how important realistic and detailed examples were to teaching anyone the process of design. I asked myself how a design book could be as easy to follow as a well-designed cookbook. Like a cookbook visualizing ingredients and final products, this book will show the steps as well as the output of design processes. Also like a cookbook, this book provides room and suggestions for variation within each process. And so the five sample projects woven throughout this book became core to its purpose. For this I owe many thanks to the talented women of The Artificial who helped in the design of so many artifacts.

With these intentions, *The Practical Guide to Experience Design* was born. This book does not seek to provide answers but rather to give perspective. As you read, I hope you find your own patterns and inspirations. Adopt those processes that are helpful for your team or client, and change what doesn't work to fit your needs. Try, learn, iterate, and try again.

"If you can design one thing, you can design everything."

Massimo Vignelli

Introduction

Hello. Welcome to *The Practical Guide to Experience Design*. Before you get started, there are a few things worth knowing about this book.

What is *experience*?

Experience is a person's perception of an interaction. This interaction could be internal or external, with the environment or with other people, and solo or shared. Experiences happen all of the time and often with very little intention.

The design of experiences focuses on first determining the desired experience of a person or user and then on curating, creating, and refining a system of interactions that will facilitate that outcome. Of course human behavior and perception are unpredictable, so the process of designing experiences often feels like a science experiment, where hypotheses are repeatedly made, tested, and either proven or disproven.

Who is this book for?

Design is broad, often spanning and ideally bridging multiple disciplines. Within design, there are industrial designers, graphic designers, interaction designers, visual designers, UI (user interface) designers, UX (user experience) designers, service designers, design researchers, information architects, art directors, and copywriters, to name a few. Add to that list everyone involved in the creation of an experience: business strategists, marketers, technologists, architects, developers, engineers, manufacturers, and so on. With so many roles, each with their own needs and goals, bringing an experience to life can be a challenge. By providing a common language and structure for exploring and evaluating the different aspects of an experience, designers can drive toward alignment and increase efficiency within a team.

Regardless of what is being designed—whether a physical thing, a digital product, a human service, or even an organization—the ways of thinking, methodologies around collaboration, and means of communication are key to bringing an idea to life. And despite having many distinct disciplines, the different types of design have a good deal of overlap when it comes to their processes.

This book aims to distill these patterns in a simple way that can be a reference for anyone, designer or otherwise, working to create great experiences.

How should you read this book?

How you read the book depends, of course, on what you need from it. If you're seeking a general overview of the processes used in designing experiences, you might read it from cover to cover. If you're looking for inspiration for how to approach a specific problem within a project, you might skim the table of contents for the chapters that are most relevant to that. If you're more interested in the examples, you could follow the individual projects within this book to see how they evolve over time through different activities. In short, there is no wrong way to read this book.

What should you expect?

This book is a practical guide. This means it focuses on the application of design processes. It provides guidance for approaching, thinking about, and framing problems and solutions. You'll find descriptions of collaborative workshops and instructions for producing artifacts that drive toward decisions. At the end of almost every chapter there are examples that can be used as inspiration for your own projects.

This book is not about design theory. Anecdotes are used sparingly, and case studies are used only for the five sample projects within the book. While some chapters use history to explain how a process came to be, this is not a history book. It is also not a book about business methodologies or development approaches like Lean or Agile. If you're looking for more on these subjects, the end of this book has some suggestions for additional reading.

The Processes of Design

When approaching any overwhelming problem, it's best to break it into smaller, more manageable pieces. Experience design is the same way. Rather than approaching all aspects of design and communication at once, it's best to break them into phases. Each phase has multiple activities that seek to dispel ambiguity and align stakeholders and artifacts that capture and communicate findings and decisions.

Activities are the actions the design team takes toward understanding. These could be actions undertaken alone by the designer or opportunities for collaboration with the broader team. They could be actions that require outside input from users or experts, or they could aim to facilitate communication internally. For any given project, there are countless activities that might be applicable, so it's important to determine which are most appropriate for the desired outcome.

Artifacts are the things that the design team produces to communicate what was learned or made through a process's activities. While the design of the product or service itself is an artifact, so are the many insights, decisions, and specifications around the product or service. Depending on the artifact's purpose, it might need only to communicate something at a single point in time, or it may need to be maintained for the duration of the project.

Phases group similar activities together and usually focus on outcomes. When and how these phases occur depend on how your extended team is working together. For example, up-front approaches like waterfall might have a design team completing activities and artifacts through the refine and build phases before engaging implementation, while more integrated processes might have designers working alongside developers much earlier. Your approach determines how the activities of phases feed into one another, as well as how artifacts are structured for stakeholder review.

Every company organizes activities and artifacts a little differently and calls these phases by different names, but they generally come down to the same steps: understand the context of your problem, generate possible solutions, refine a single solution, and then execute that solution considering all necessary details. This book calls these phases discover, define, refine, and build.

> *"Good process serves you so you can serve customers. But if you're not watchful, the process can become the thing. This can happen very easily in large organizations. The process becomes the proxy for the result you want. You stop looking at outcomes and just make sure you're doing the process right."*
>
> Jeff Bezos

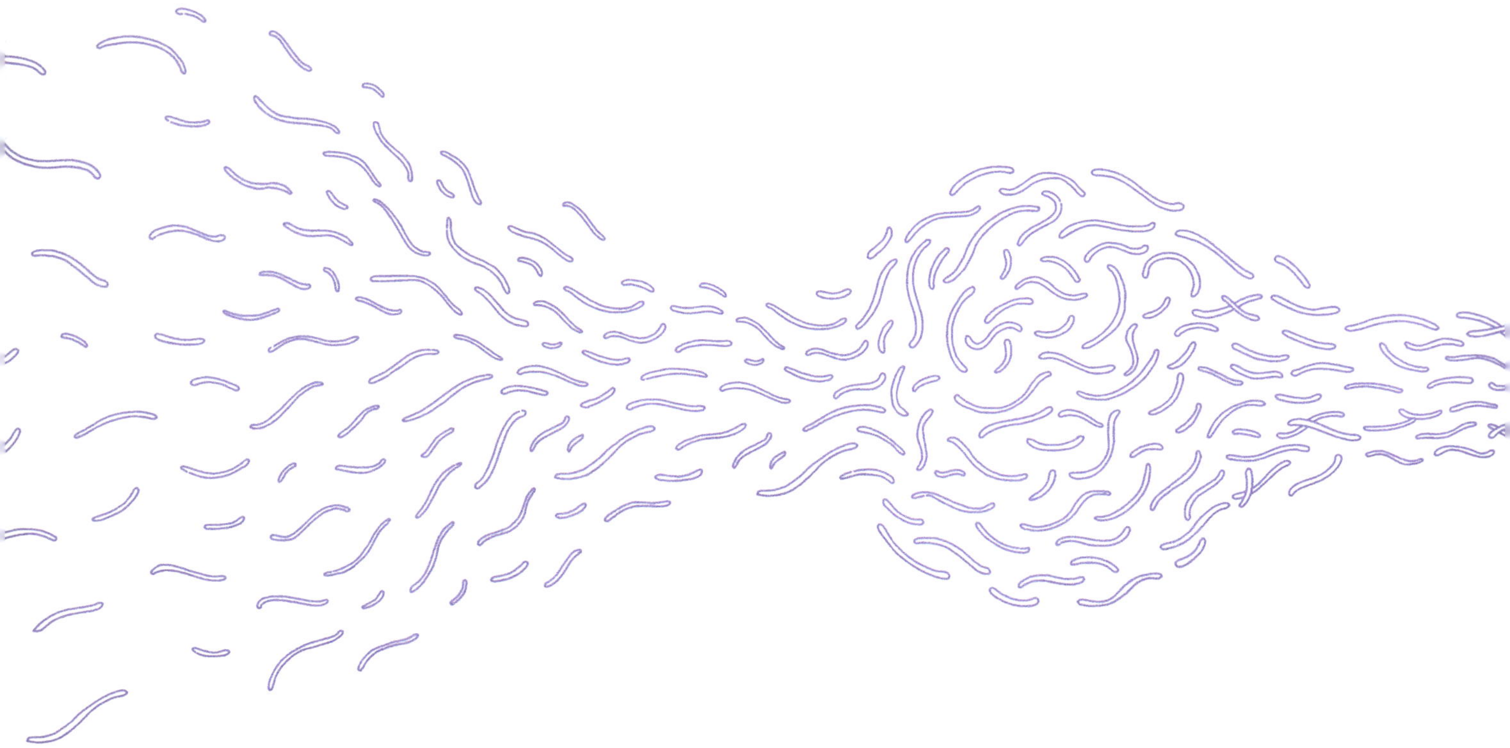

The Discover Phase

Traditionally the first part of a project, the discover phase uses research to understand the problem and its context. This might consist of desk research or field research. It could include surveys or interviews. Discovery almost always results in a large number of sticky notes that need to be sorted through to make sense of it all. At the end of the discover phase, you should understand the market you're designing for and what technological constraints you'll need to design around. You should also understand your stakeholders, along with any other organizational risks.

The Define Phase

Typically following the discover phase, the define phase makes sense of and synthesizes raw notes, ideas, and observations into a series of concepts that will be further synthesized and iterated upon until a clear idea of the product or service emerges. The define phase usually begins with ambiguity and ends with a clear understanding of what the company will do to appeal to the user and meet their needs.

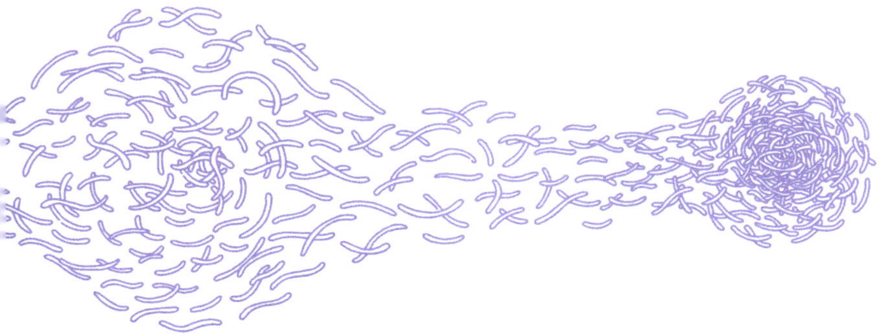

The Refine Phase

The refine phase takes the general direction established with the define phase and transforms it into a single cohesive design. Refinement starts with more focused explorations of potential executions at a low fidelity and ends with the execution of a single design solution. Focusing on perfecting the key moments that determine the overall experience for the user, the refine phase stops short of designing all of the details. By the end of the refine phase, the design system should be comprehensive, even though the design is not yet complete.

The Build Phase

Often done alongside those implementing the experience, the build phase focuses on details, communication, and validation. In this final phase, designers flesh out the many intricacies of the design system, create and maintain documentation that communicates design decisions, and validate the design with users and stakeholders. The build phase of experience design is typically the longest phase of work, extending not only through implementation but often through subsequent iterations as well.

Designing the Project Plan

A good project plan will weave together multiple activities and artifacts to drive understanding and alignment while ensuring the quality of the experience being designed. Not every chapter in this book will be necessary for every project, and it's likely that what you think a project needs at the start will change as you learn more about the experience you're designing. Many projects will use only a fraction of what's listed here, and some will use methods beyond those contained in this book. Most projects will require more activities than they'll represent in artifacts.

When creating a project plan, start with a brief. What are the desired outcomes of the project? Are there deadlines or constraints that need to be considered? If the outcomes are too broad and the deadlines too far out, try breaking the project into smaller, less risky chunks. There are countless approaches to project planning. Here are two possibilities:

If you're working with timing constraints that you don't control, you might start by defining milestones. What goals need to be achieved by when? Perhaps you're working with a development team that's starting sprints in a month or with a manufacturer that needs specifications in six weeks to make a holiday product launch date. Start with the immovable dates, and then work backward and into more detail. Choose the activities you'll need for each milestone, the artifacts you'll use to communicate, and then estimate what's possible. For each milestone, document what's necessary and what's only nice to have. Then build your timeline.

The second approach is more relevant when you have fewer constraints. Rather than working backward from imposed deadlines, choose the most effective activities and artifacts for your organization and establish your own milestones. Define reviews and check-ins based on what you've planned. Plan a regular rhythm for meeting with stakeholders to ensure that the design stays aligned with the organization. This will also keep commitment, motivation, and enthusiasm for the work you're doing high.

As you design your project plan, keep in mind that success should be focused on the experience being designed. Your activities might be creative and collaborative and your artifacts beautiful and useful, but none of this matters if they don't provide meaningful contributions to the product or service being built. Always keep outcomes top of mind when planning.

Regardless of how well your project is planned, it is likely that the plan will be disrupted. Immovable dates will move and stakeholders will change. Feedback will go beyond the scope of the project, and new requests will derail old ones. It's important to stay flexible in what you do while also staying committed to the goals you set out with originally. Perhaps you aren't able to do formal user interviews because of timing and budget, but you can still understand the friction a user has with an experience by informally polling friends and family, approaching strangers on the street, or doing surveys. Plan for the ideal, and stay focused on goals when things change.

Five Projects

This book uses five projects with four fictional clients to provide examples of activities and artifacts. These samples represent a variety of project types done by experience designers. While the work in these examples is only speculative, the plans on the following pages are based on actual projects with real clients.

The first project, Future of Boats, seeks to illustrate a long-term vision for urban waterways. This project focuses on research and concept generation, defining the many possible experiences that future users might have. It does not get into the details of executing those experiences.

The Connected Bicycle project aims to create an experience that encompasses a bike, an on-bike display, and a user's mobile app. While a rough version of the experience already exists, it needs improvement before being launched in multiple countries.

Ambience Mirror is a project seeking to create a new experience for users based on emerging technologies. Some research has been done, but decisions around technology and design have not yet been made. Similar products exist, but none have been widely adopted, so there's a lot of opportunity to succeed or to fail.

Observations Suite is a product for companies in the hospitality industry to improve how they do business. With a market full of competition, design is seen as an opportunity for differentiation. Like many real-world projects, the scale and variety of what needs to be done requires two projects, each with its own approach and outcomes. The first project seeks to lay out an overall vision for the suite of tools and services, focusing on discover and refine activities. The second project focuses on designing a single tool to get to market quickly, briefly revisiting some define-phase activities before diving into refine and build phases.

“A goal without a plan is just a wish.”

Antoine de Saint-Exupéry

European Waterworks / **Future of Boats**

Project Plan

Future of Boats

Cities like Hamburg, Venice, and Amsterdam have an abundance of water, with canals making up a vital part of their structure. All of this water demands unique infrastructure beyond boats and bridges. We were approached by European Waterworks to imagine how new technologies might enable boats to more significantly contribute to a functioning city.

Because this project is focused on generating possibilities rather than implementing solutions, it will focus primarily on the discover and define phases. The first part of the project needs to be research focused, with activities to identify the problems that cities, and specifically cities with extensive networks of waterways, face, and then to uncover existing solutions and upcoming technologies that are relevant to those problems. With this foundation, the team can generate and then refine concepts on a strategic roadmap.

This project proposes a timeline of four weeks, with the first two weeks reserved for research and the last two weeks focused on concept generation, refinement, and presentation. The final deliverable will be a future roadmap of boat concepts aimed to inspire the organization to develop the infrastructure, laws, and technology necessary to bring water-oriented cities into the coming decades.

CityBike / **Connected Bicycle**

Project Plan

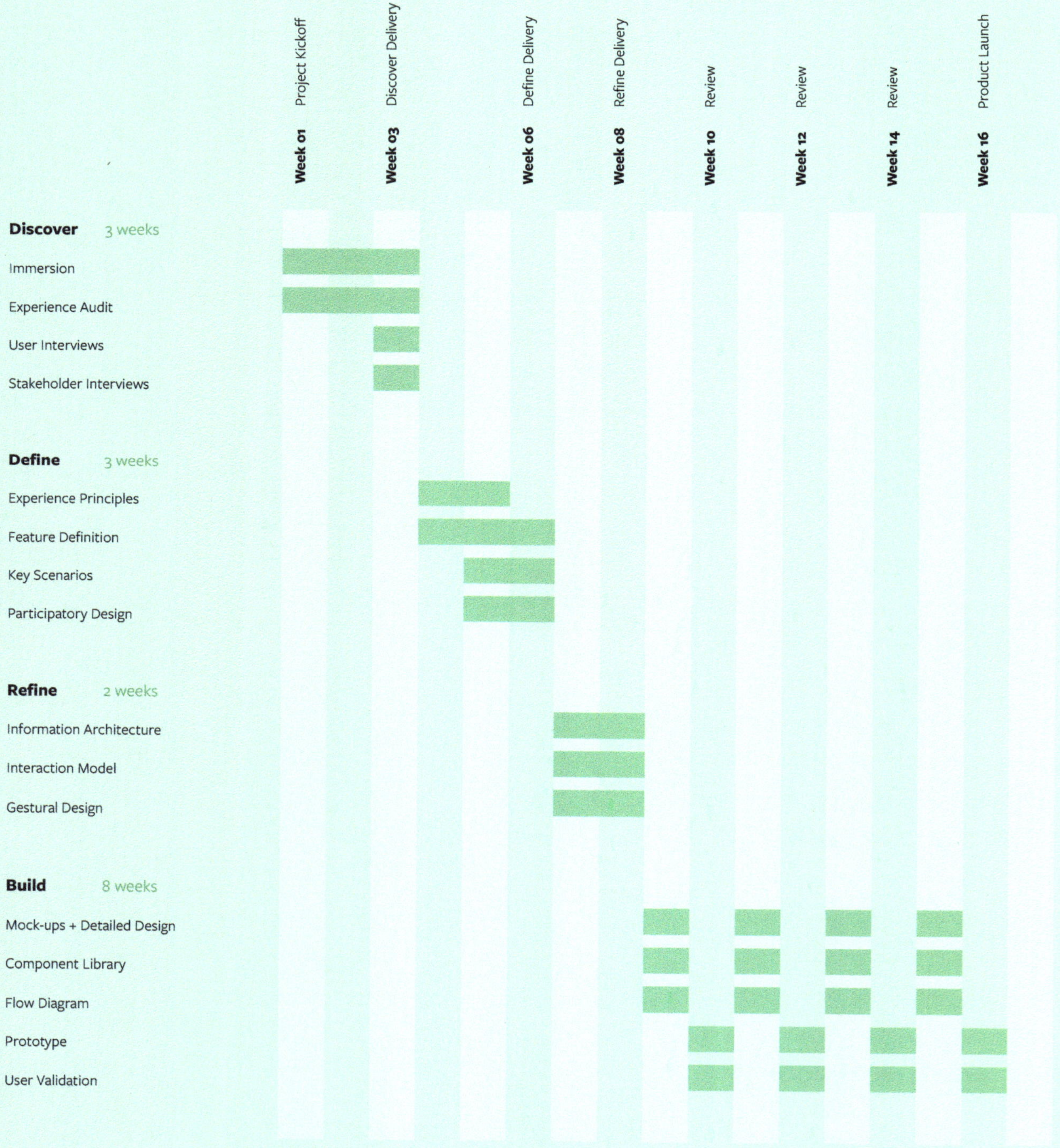

Connected Bicycle

CityBike is a company focused on making accessible commuter bikes. Last year they created a proof of concept for their Connected Bicycle, and they are now seeking to refine the bike, on-bike display, and app for launch across Europe, Asia, and North America. We were approached by CityBike six months prior to launch to refine the rough design and to choreograph the experience of riding Connected Bicycles through the city.

This project has a tight timeline and will cover all four phases of experience design. Fortunately, because CityBike already has a proof of concept, a good deal of thinking already exists. The first part of this project will focus on understanding urban cyclists as well as uncovering existing decisions and problems with the current product. Immersing the team in an urban commuting culture and conducting an experience audit will provide firsthand experience, while user and stakeholder interviews will provide insight into specific needs of users and constraints of the product. From here, the team can get started on foundational design work like experience principles, feature definition, and key scenarios. Then design can work with users to refine the feature set and to define the ideal on-bike experience. The team can create an information architecture and multiple design variations before locking down on a single solution for implementation. For the last eight weeks of the project, the design team will integrate with implementation in two-week sprints to design, document, prototype, and test with users.

This project proposes a timeline of sixteen weeks, with the first half focused on discovering and defining, and the last half focused on refining and building. Checkpoints occur throughout the project timeline to ensure that all stakeholders stay aligned.

Personal Intelligence / **Ambience Mirror**

Project Plan

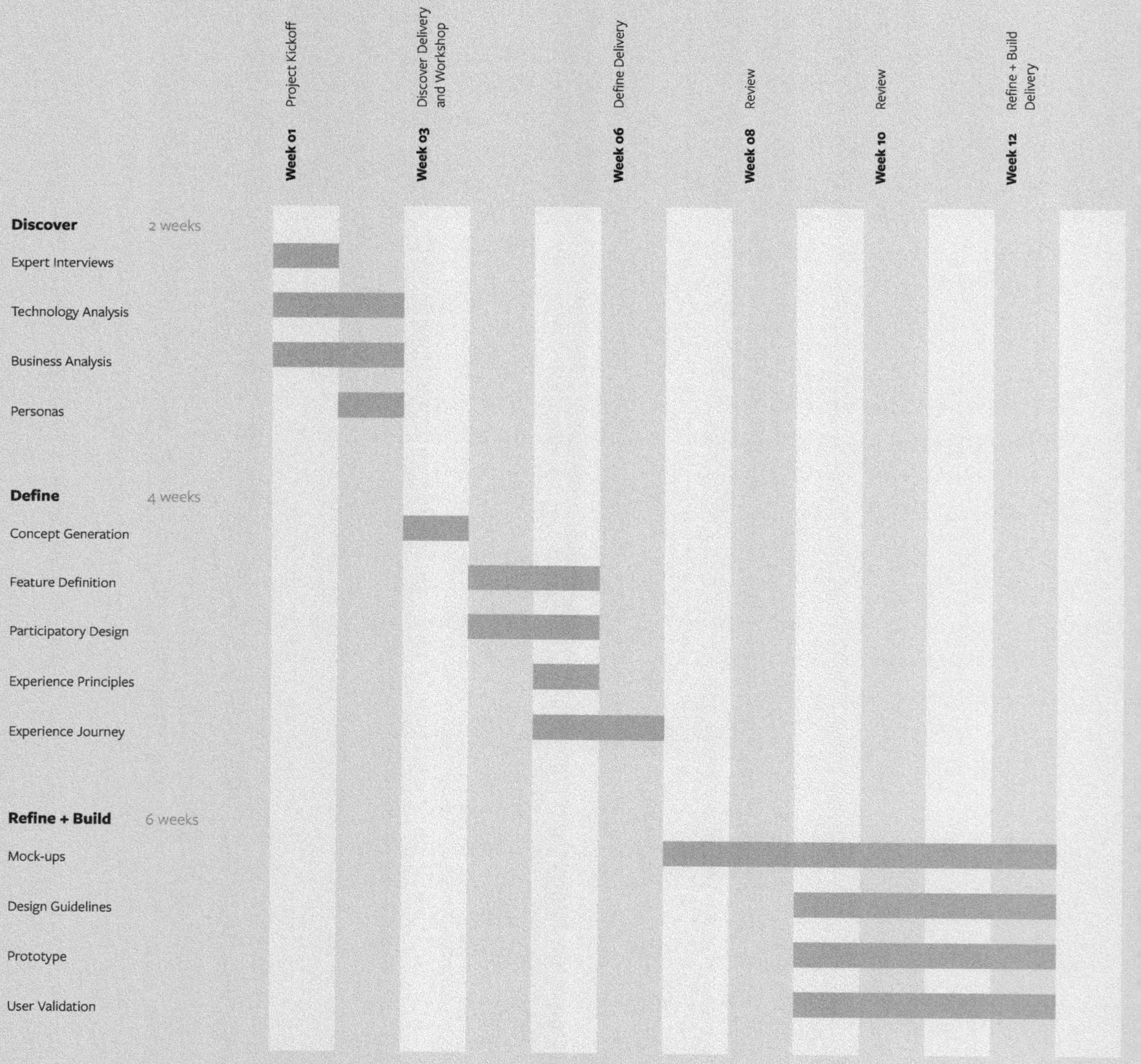

Ambience Mirror

In a world where connected products and digital interfaces consume our undivided attention, Personal Intelligence seeks to provide users with data and information through ambient experiences. While their sensors don't require extra effort from users, their apps require focus in a way that's inconsistent with their brand messaging. We were engaged to develop an ambient smart-mirror concept capable of providing users with information in ambient and less attention-grabbing ways. Once complete, our work will be handed off to production designers and engineers to build and implement.

With a project focused on concept development, discover and define activities are important to set a solid foundation. This project will start with expert interviews and technology and business analysis to determine likely users and user needs. These findings will be summarized in personas and then used to generate concepts with the client. Concepts will be refined into features, with users providing input via participatory design. Experience principles will guide future design, and an experience journey will provide a summary of how the team expects users to engage with the features of the Ambience Mirror. From here, the design team will create mock-ups, design guidelines, and a prototype to be tested and refined with users.

The proposed project will take twelve weeks with heavy user involvement. Two weeks will be committed to research and persona creation, followed by four weeks to develop and test concepts and features with users. The last half of the project is for refining the design with prototypes and user validation and creating light documentation for the internal design and development teams to use as they take the design forward.

Omniscient / **Observations Suite**

Project Plan

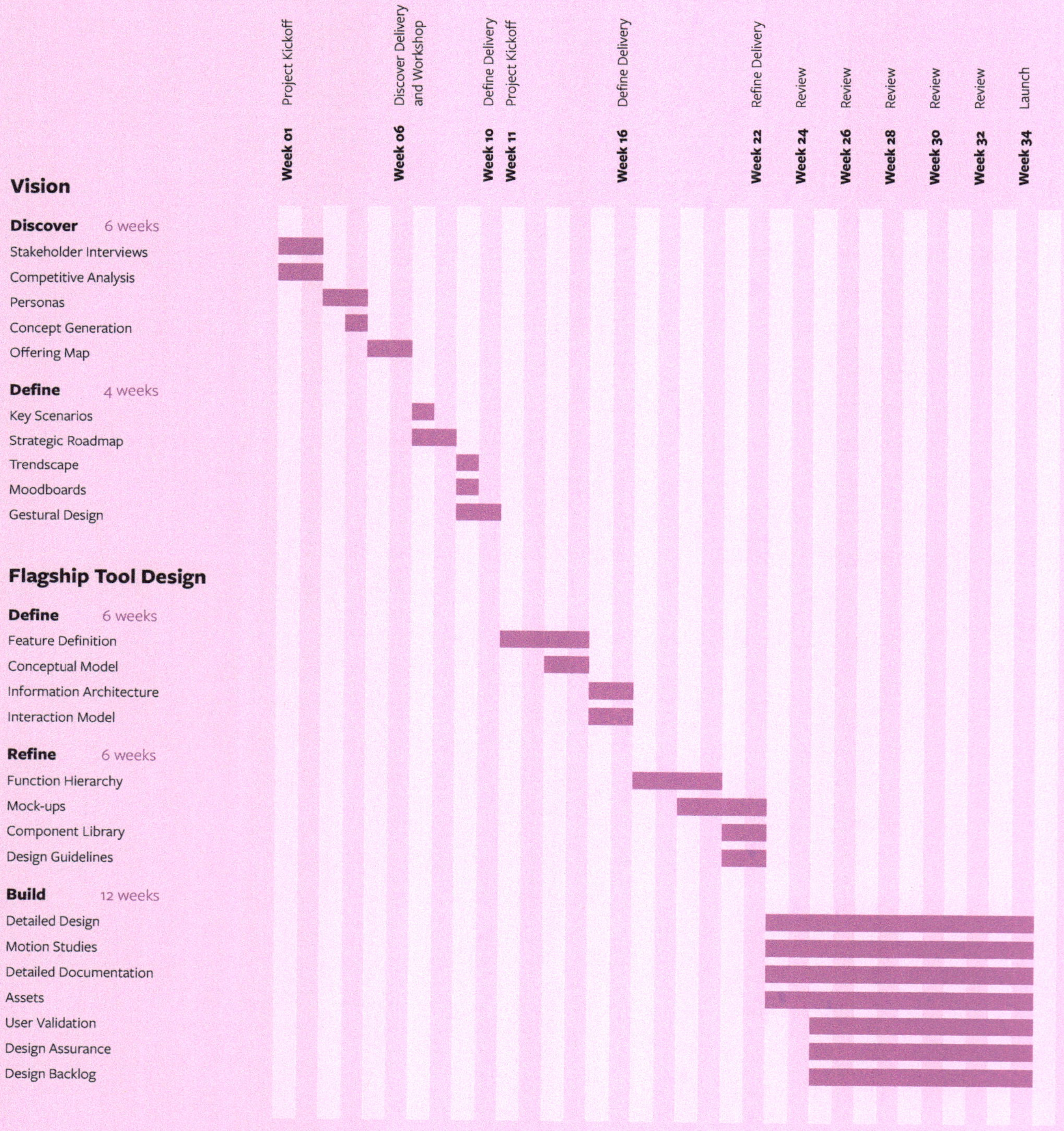

Observations Suite

Omniscient, an established company in the world of business analytics software, is looking to move beyond digital and into physical spaces. They hope to disrupt the service industry and plan to perfect their product with restaurants before selling to bigger targets like hotels, resorts, and other tourist destinations. They approached us to determine what tools will meet their new customers' needs and then to create a flagship product.

This project requires significant effort from discovery through build, and by breaking it into two smaller projects, we reduce the risk. The first and more strategic project focuses on the discover and define phases, heavy with research, exploration, and synthesis activities. The outcome of the first project is a series of possible design directions and tools Omniscient might provide to their new users.

For the second project, stakeholders will select a single design direction and tool for their flagship product. The second project will start with a handful of define-phase activities, now looking specifically at the flagship tool rather than at the market. Refine and build phases will follow, ending with a close integration between the design and development teams.

The first project's timeline spans ten weeks and involves several big presentations to high-level stakeholders. In the second project, the design team spends twenty-four weeks designing the tool and then working with development to bring it to life.

Discover

The discover phase of work provides clarity for later phases by seeking to understand the culture a product or service will live in, the stakeholders who will influence it, the constraints of the technologies relied upon, and the needs of the users who will buy it. Most projects benefit from having a discover phase, but projects seeking to design experiences around new technologies or behaviors will benefit most. When working with a new client, discover-phase activities are useful for getting to know their organization, though artifacts might be less important.

At the end of the discover phase, the experience designer should understand the context of the experience they're building and have a loose understanding of what success should look like throughout the following phases. They should also be able to balance the many priorities of the business, the constraints of the technology, and the needs of the user.

The discover phase of a project is often more focused on the activities of discovery and less on making and building artifacts. To do this, a designer might collect information by reading, researching, interviewing, listening, and experiencing. They'll build a complete picture by speaking with stakeholders, experts, and users. To be most effective, the designer may need to travel to understand the world their users live in, to visit stakeholders in their day-to-day contexts, or to visit factories to better understand the constraints of their implementation technologies.

The artifacts that emerge from the discover phase play a valuable role in establishing a foundation for the experience, surfacing new ideas, exposing perspectives, and creating alignment among team members. It's important to selectively maintain some artifacts in subsequent phases so that early discoveries and decisions don't get lost through execution.

If you happen to enter a project after the discover phase has already occurred, set aside some time to catch up. Even if you were unable to influence this phase of work, it's still important to understand the findings of it so that you can make informed design decisions moving forward.

In This Section:

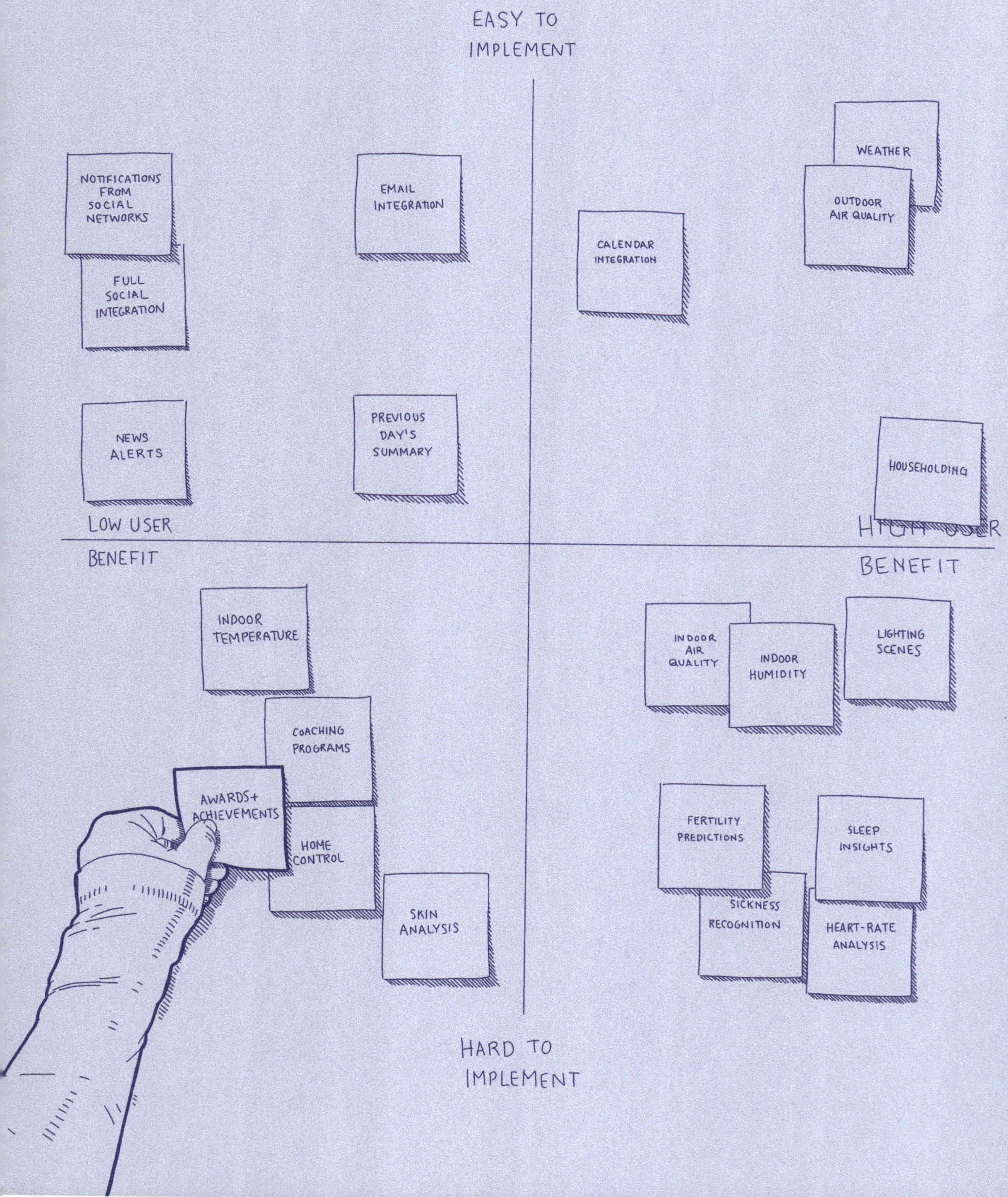
EASY TO IMPLEMENT
NOTIFICATIONS FROM SOCIAL NETWORKS
FULL SOCIAL INTEGRATION
EMAIL INTEGRATION
NEWS ALERTS
PREVIOUS DAY'S SUMMARY
CALENDAR INTEGRATION
WEATHER
OUTDOOR AIR QUALITY
HOUSEHOLDING
LOW USER BENEFIT
BENEFIT
INDOOR TEMPERATURE
COACHING PROGRAMS
AWARDS+ ACHIEVEMENTS
HOME CONTROL
SKIN ANALYSIS
INDOOR AIR QUALITY
INDOOR HUMIDITY
LIGHTING SCENES
FERTILITY PREDICTIONS
SLEEP INSIGHTS
SICKNESS RECOGNITION
HEART-RATE ANALYSIS
HARD TO IMPLEMENT

Business Analysis

Business analysis identifies and assesses product and service opportunities by comparing a company's capabilities to the demands of the market. Looking externally, the process determines if people will buy the product, how much they will spend, and what barriers exist for adoption. Internally, the process determines if the company can deliver on a viable proposition that can be produced for a cost that customers are willing to pay.

Business analysis may not be a traditional design practice; however, it is a practice that is useful for designers to be acquainted with. If you're new to business analysis, find opportunities to observe business team members to better understand their process, priorities, and communication. Seek to support business strategists by visualizing output. Sometimes these visualizations will even highlight new opportunities or areas of inquiry.

If you join a project in later phases, it's likely that business analysis has shaped many of the decisions made before your arrival. Reviewing business-analysis artifacts can help you understand prior decisions and make better decisions going forward. For projects aiming to create something similar to a successful product that already exists or to iterate on an already-successful experience, you might not even need business analysis.

Activities

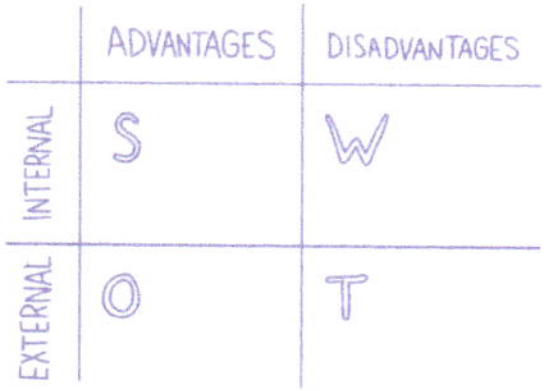

SWOT is one framework for mapping advantages and disadvantages.

Business strategists and analysts spend much of their time using quantitative data to make recommendations and justify decisions. They use specific formulas to understand markets and rigorous processes to identify opportunities. While many of their findings may seem intuitive, the thoroughness of the approach and the power of their numbers provide confidence in their conclusions. Rather than seeking a deep understanding of the processes that business analysts and strategists use, it's important for a designer to understand what they aim to achieve, how their outcomes affect design, and the best way to communicate results to influence stakeholders.

Business analysis studies a product or service and its context to ensure that it's a good fit for the market and for the company. The goal is to predict, prior to serious investment, how successful a product or service will be. For this, success should be measurable—in profit, customers reached, adoption rates, etc. While you may not be able to match the level of detail and certainty of a full-fledged business analysis, there are some activities that can help deepen your understanding.

SWOT analysis is a popular technique for determining a company's ability to deliver by analyzing strengths, weaknesses, opportunities, and threats. Strengths and weaknesses reflect the internal advantages and disadvantages the organization has when it comes to delivery, while opportunities and threats capture the external forces that could either help or hinder the product or service. Completing a lightweight SWOT analysis ensures that designers will be more prepared to make and empathize with business decisions.

If you already have an idea of what features your product should have, try mapping impact against effort. Build a two-by-two matrix with benefit to the user on one axis and effort on the other. Then for each feature consider benefit and effort. Easy-to-implement features with high user benefit should be the focus of your experience, while features providing little to no benefit can be safely ignored. If a high-benefit feature is difficult for your company to implement, assess what partners you might enlist to get what you need. Consider what your company could offer these partners in exchange.

Once you have loosely defined your product or service, try to determine if there is a market and how big that market might be. To do this you might look at how similar and competing products are doing. Try to find actual numbers. Depending on what value your product provides to users, often captured in a value proposition, relevant figures might focus on profit, engagement, social impact, etc.

The outcomes of business analysis affect everything from what value the product or service seeks to deliver to users to how it's marketed to them. Broadly, a business analysis should be able to determine if the company is capable of pulling off the product or service as imagined. It might map which parts of the organization are necessary for achieving the design, or it might recommend acquiring new competencies if those within the organization are insufficient. It might recommend changing the pricing model or prioritizing a target audience. A business analysis might also recommend completely pivoting the concept or killing off a product or service. From discover to build, each of these recommendations affects the design process, so it's important to have confidence in this early work.

Not all projects seek to establish this kind of certainty or even strong opinions from the beginning. Designers on these types of projects should be prepared to change direction in significant ways as the organization uncovers how its product or service fits into the market.

Artifacts

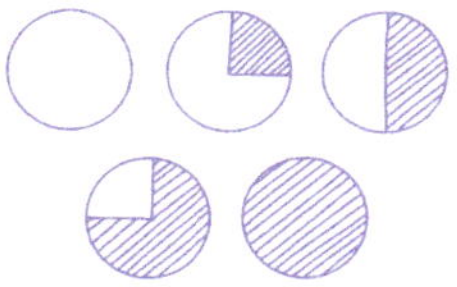

Harvey balls are useful for making multiple comparisons across offerings or features.

A continuum shows how multiple competitors or features compare.

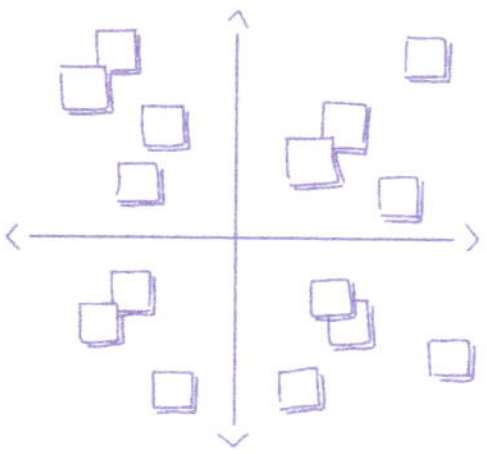

Combine continuums to create a 2x2. Positive outcomes traditionally sit in the upper right.

Business analysis is often summarized in a presentation or paper, with key points highlighted in some sort of executive summary. An executive summary highlights the most important points and recommendations concerning the product or service, target audience, partnerships, and so on, usually in a single page or value proposition.

A value proposition defines your users and describes what needs your product or service fulfills. Consider emotional as well as functional needs. If you have obvious competitors, describe why your product is better. Summarize this in just a few sentences. Additional details about individual feature recommendations help a busy executive understand where to invest and what the next steps for the project are. The details of the research supporting those recommendations are outlined in the rest of the presentation.

The design team can contribute to this process by ensuring that data is communicated clearly, concisely, and in a way that supports the team's recommendations. Aside from highlighting findings and pulling out surprising facts and figures, you might use charts and graphs to help stakeholders get a quick understanding of distribution, saturation, trends, and more. For this type of dense reading, familiarity is key to ensuring quick comprehension. Here are a few common ways of representing the findings of a business analysis:

Harvey Balls

Harvey balls provide a simple way to compare data points, filling circles in quarter intervals from empty to full. These visualizations reduce complexity and imply precision by rounding data to the nearest quarter. This is perfect if you're working with a small sample size or with inexact data but not for communicating precise amounts, such as 82%.

Continuum

A continuum chooses one aspect for comparing different entities against each other and then lays out entities in a visual list. A continuum could map quantitative measures such as cost or engagement, or qualitative measures like delight or public versus private engagement. If your continuum is vertical, place the more desirable trait at the top, and if it's horizontal, place it on the right.

2X2

A 2x2 matrix is a combination of two continua—one vertical and one horizontal. Choose your axes carefully! Try different combinations of traits to find which highlight the most interesting and compelling aspects of your data. The desirable traits should be listed in the upper right quadrant.

Speculative Reviews

Writing speculative reviews of the product or service as if you're a customer can help to highlight the value the team should expect users to get from the experience and can help to uncover potential pitfalls. These reviews might be used to make business analysis feel more human or to reinforce the value proposition.

The outcomes from business analysis can be helpful in identifying competitors worth researching for competitive analysis and identifying target markets for inspiring personas. It can also be useful for prioritizing features and determining how to monetize the experience.

Speculative reviews can humanize data and findings.

Business analysis activities for the Ambience Mirror look to establish a timeline for rolling out the product across different markets, to plan integrations, and to create an initial prioritization of potential features.

Business Analysis

The Ambience Mirror will provide our customers with a simple way to review data from their connected health products and services.

The mirror will promote the sales of products in the Ambience line and will serve as the flagship channel for our new Personal Intelligence Insights subscription service.

The revenue for Ambience Mirror will come from Ambience Mirror sales, subscription services, and associated Ambience products.

Speculative Positive Review

★★★★★

The Ambience Mirror is a big success in our house. My entire family uses it, and it's helped us all break our morning phone addictions. We get just enough information to know what to expect of our days without getting distracted by games or social media.

My only complaint is that I still need my phone for reading and replying to emails. Maybe that could be done with the voice interface, like Siri?

Speculative Negative Review

★★

I installed Ambience Mirror three weeks ago, and so far the only benefit I get out of it is the weather. My calendar is too complicated for the simplistic interface, and the integration of other services like Withings and Samsung leaves a lot to be desired. I can see the data from those services, but there's no real meaning to it.

I would give a second-generation product a chance but wouldn't recommend this one.

Target Audience

We will target current users of Ambience products and similar demographics. Over a year we will release in different markets, reaching global availability in early 2021.

April 2020	July 2020	October 2020	January 2021
United States	Canada UK Australia	China EU Brazil	Global

Ambience Ecosystem

The Ambience Mirror is a hub for the things our users most need to know. It replaces users' phones in the morning and before bed, ensuring a great start and end to the day.

Optimized

Ambience products
Weather and air data
Calendar
Amazon Alexa

Integrated

Health (Apple)
Samsung Health
Withings products
Xiaomi products
Philips products

Limited

Facebook
Twitter
Email

Feature Prioritization

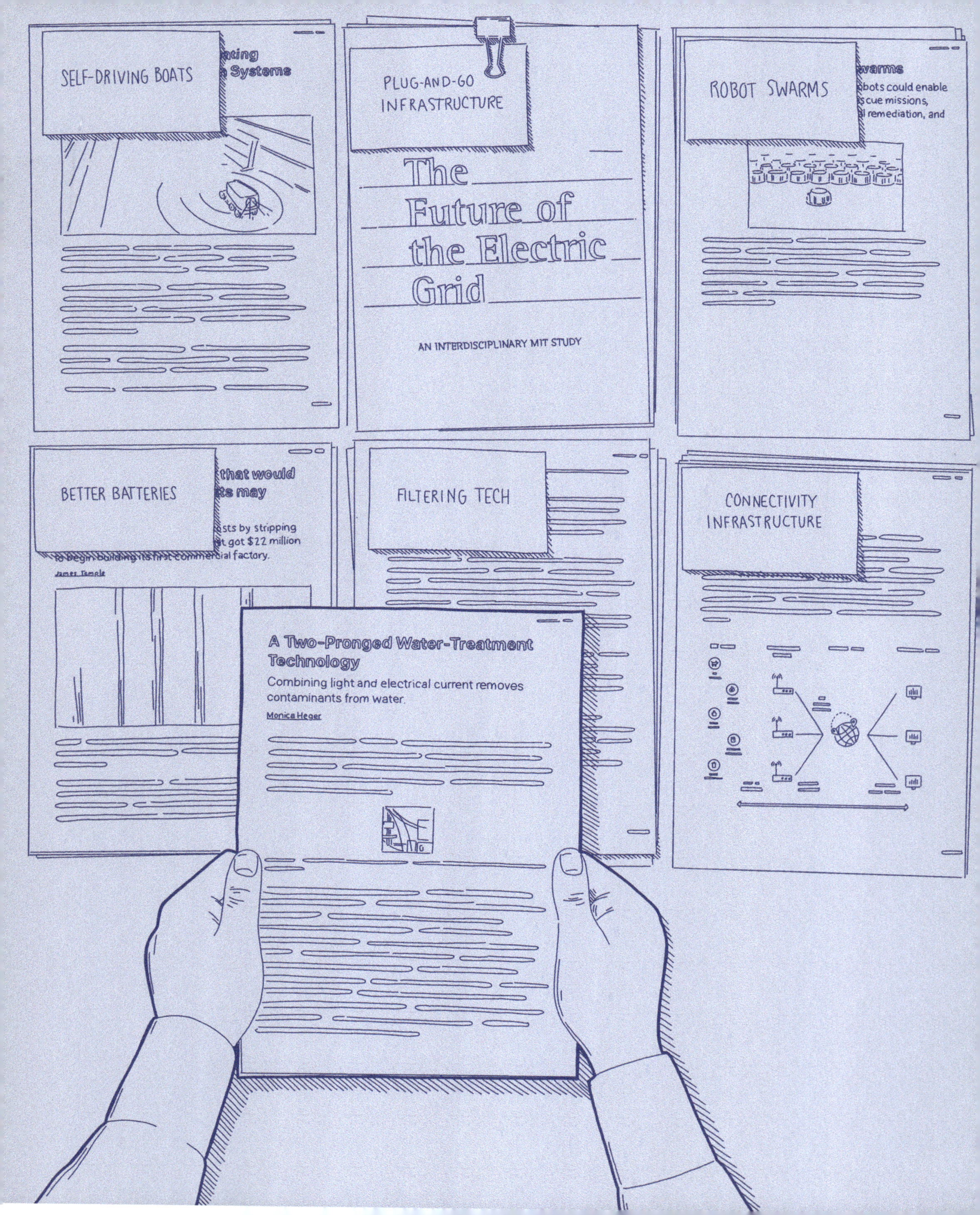
SELF-DRIVING BOATS
ating
Systems
PLUG-AND-GO INFRASTRUCTURE
The Future of the Electric Grid
AN INTERDISCIPLINARY MIT STUDY
ROBOT SWARMS
warms
bots could enable
scue missions,
l remediation, and
BETTER BATTERIES
that would
ts may
sts by stripping
t got $22 million
to begin building its first commercial factory.
James Temple
FILTERING TECH
CONNECTIVITY INFRASTRUCTURE
A Two-Pronged Water-Treatment Technology
Combining light and electrical current removes contaminants from water.
Monica Heger

Technology Analysis

Technology analysis is a broad term for the strategic analysis of technology that should be done before undertaking the production of any new product or service. Even lacking a background in technology, an experience designer should be able to work with tech strategists to understand the basics of the technology required to enable a product or service. With experience, a designer should be able to make recommendations for, follow the patterns of, and identify common problems with various technologies.

A technology analysis seeks to discover what technological constraints exist and what enablers can support in fulfilling user needs or business desires. Of course this means that user needs and business desires should be at least loosely defined. Before you dive into researching various technologies, you should be able to describe your users, the value you're providing to those users, and the general problems you're seeking to solve.

Activities

Start by understanding the type of analysis that will benefit your project. Are you looking to understand what technologies will disrupt the industry in the coming years, to find specific technologies that will enable a solution that's already underway, or to uncover the patterns of a technology to inform the design of a product or service? The needs of the project should dictate the scale and focus of the technology analysis.

For the Love of Technology

Organizations can easily become enamored with a new technology and will seek a user need or problem for that new technology to solve. As an experience designer, it's important to keep your feet firmly planted, insisting that the need precede the technology in priority, even if not in time. In situations where a new technology exists without a clear user need, experimentation is called for. It's not uncommon for business and tech strategists to work together to rapidly prototype and test value propositions for a given technology, throwing away hypothesis after hypothesis until a viable need-solution match is found.

After establishing a scale, begin your research. Similar to business analysis, a technology analysis often looks for insights both internal and external to the organization. Start within your company to understand what currently exists and how things are done. Stakeholder and expert interviews can be helpful in uncovering unfamiliar processes and understanding any unique technological advantages or constraints your company has and can establish the basic understanding necessary to do productive desk research. If you have more open-ended research goals and don't know where to begin, try skimming recent articles with lists of technologies. Not all will be relevant, but those technologies that are can provide a starting point for deeper research.

As you research the benefits and problems of specific technologies, also seek understanding about how your users relate to those technologies. What are users familiar with? What platforms do they engage with? What technologies are they likely to adopt in the next few years? What benefits do your users expect from the technologies they engage with? Focusing on the answers to these questions will help ensure that design solutions use technology to empower users.

Once you understand your users' relationships with different technologies, you're ready to dive into more detail. Depending on the type of project you're doing, you may need to look at technology in different layers. General technologies, such as heart-rate sensors or hosting services, are useful for determining which capabilities a product or service can have by when. Similarly, the availability of specific manufacturing techniques might place limitations on the design of a product, the timeline for shipping, or the ability to scale quickly.

For some strategic projects, this high-level view might be enough; however, if you're creating a product or service, you'll need to make recommendations. First, you'll need to understand if your organization is already using a specific heart-rate sensor or hosting service. For the technology decisions that have already been made, document the unique constraints and opportunities that will affect the user's experience. In the event that these decisions change, it'll be easier to see where the design needs adjusting.

For the technology decisions that have not been made, you'll need to research the available options. These choices can often affect what benefits you're able to provide and how your users engage with your product. Even if the user might not be able to tell the difference between one manufacturer's sensor and another's, these technologies often have so many downstream effects in terms of integration that making good recommendations for technology partners is essential.

If you're working with software, you'll also need to make choices around operating systems and platforms. These tend to vary more and change frequently with time. The user probably understands the different options available, likely even having loyalty to one operating system or platform over another.

Software products and services also mean your team will need to decide which tools, libraries, and services it will use. Choices at this level are the most variable, volatile, and abundant. Sometimes the

When documentation isn't enough, prototype to better understand the limitations of a technology.

choice isn't even between providers but rather between using someone else's creation versus building your own. Because tools, libraries, and services change frequently and vary significantly, it's important to avoid getting too reliant on any individual partner.

The ultimate outcomes of a technology analysis are decisions around what technologies to invest in. Decisions of this scale need buy-in from the team, so finding the most persuasive arguments for your recommendations is a must. Along with stakeholder interviews, you might also read reviews of competitors' products and services to better understand what technologies users appreciate, or read competitors' case studies about how they built their products or services and how they've changed over time. You might peruse white papers to find opportunities for cutting-edge technologies or explore the update history of a specific tool or library. You might even work with a technologist to prototype with different technologies, uncovering their limitations through actual use.

“Any sufficiently advanced technology is indistinguishable from magic.”

Arthur C. Clarke

Artifacts

Similar to business analysis, the findings of a technology analysis are often summarized as a series of findings and recommendations in an executive summary. A more detailed presentation or paper supports the recommendations made, often with statistics, data visualizations, quotes from expert interviews, or competitor information.

Because the output of a technology analysis is often succinct, it's worth sharing all of the effort that went into the decisions you're about to present. How many interviews did you do? How many white papers did you read? Quantifying the input that went into your recommendations can help others trust them more.

If you're designing a product or service within an ecosystem where decisions have already been made about technology, it can be helpful to start by presenting the current state of that ecosystem. Visualize complex relationships between different systems, parts of the organization, and partners to help make them easier to understand. Highlight not only how things work, but also what's working well and what's not working at all. This establishes a common understanding of what exists and can be useful in supporting any changes you recommend.

If your technology analysis will feed into a strategic roadmap, present important dates for the development of the product or service. On a timeline, show when new technologies will be released, platforms updated, and partnerships formed. Document what effects these will have on the development of the design or service.

As you make recommendations, remember that decisions surrounding technology often change as new requirements are discovered. It's likely that you'll want to present a top choice and also an alternative. This provides potential backup plans in case a technology changes or becomes unsupported or in the event that the execution of a chosen technology tests poorly. Keep the technology-analysis artifact handy throughout the project. It can also be helpful to reevaluate old decisions when new technologies inevitably emerge.

The technology analysis for the Future of Boats takes input from stakeholder and expert interviews as well as desk research to make predictions about the future, outlining which technologies will become relevant and when.

Ambience Mirror's technology analysis focuses on finding which of the available technology options will provide the best user experience by addressing a series of specific concerns. This technology analysis also looks across the ecosystem to determine how the Ambience Mirror will share data with third parties.

Technology Analysis

Process Overview

We started by understanding the current uses and state-of-the-art technology around boats and then explored enablers likely to affect what we can do with boats in the near future. Likely enablers were curated and synthesized for this presentation.

Activities

6
Stakeholders Interviewed

12
Experts Interviewed

72
White Papers Read

47
Technologies Researched

Technologies Researched

3-D printing
Air-pollution sensors
Aquatic plants
Augmented reality
Autonomous navigation
Batteries
Biometric materials
Biological filtration
Biorefinement
Blockchain
Carbon-dioxide batteries
Carbon filters
Data platforms
Desalinization
Drones
Dynamic positioning functionality
Electric-charging infrastructure
Grid management
Groundwater mapping
Solar energy
Holographic displays
Hybrid boat engine
Hydroponic gardening
Hydroelectric engine
Hyperloop
Inboard performance system
Infrared water filters
Light sensors
LoRaWAN
Machine learning
Membrane filtration
Nanotechnology water filtration
New sanitation
NB-IoT
Quantum computing
Rainwater harvesting
Reverse-osmosis filtering
Robotics
Self-docking
Sewage infrastructure
Swarming drones
Traffic sensors
Trash-skimming boats
Underwater cameras
UV water filters
Water-pollution sensors
Virtual reality

Summary of Findings

PRESENT

Augmented and Virtual Reality

Augmented reality provides users with information overlaid on reality. Augmentation can be visual or can apply to the other senses. Virtual reality provides users with low-cost, low-risk experiences via sight, sound, and spatial awareness.

Applications	Related
Wayfinding	Ubiquitous sensing
Professional interfaces	Holographic displays
Virtual tourism	Remote-controlled drones

NEAR FUTURE

Machine Learning

Machine learning analyzes data to provide optimal results. More advanced machine learning seeks relevance by combing through data sets unprompted.

Applications	Related
Traffic management	Ubiquitous sensing
Pollution management	Aggregated data platforms

NEAR FUTURE

Ubiquitous Sensing

With the proliferation of connected objects and smart things with sensors, everything that can be measured is, usually on a hyperlocal scale.

Applications	Related
Data collection	Aggregated-data platforms
Safety reports	Connectivity infrastructure

FUTURE

Better Battery Technology

Better batteries ensure vehicles can go longer and do more before needing to recharge. Batteries on boats could be used to provide temporary or mobile energy for nonboat purposes.

Applications	Related
Charging stations	High-efficiency solar
Drone boats	Plug-and-go infrastructure

FUTURE

Advanced Filtering Technology

From acoustic to biofiltration, new methods of filtering water allow for portable, low-energy solutions to remove pollutants from the water.

Applications	Related
Recreation (swimming)	Ubiquitous sensing
Drinking water	Nanotechnology water filtration

FAR FUTURE

Widespread Plug-and-Go Infrastructure

Standard ports make electricity, water, and sewage easily accessible for temporary structures.

Applications	Related
Houseboats	Grid management
Mobile businesses	New sanitation
Docking drones	

Technology Analysis

Open Questions

How can we ensure the user's privacy?

How should the user interact with the Ambience Mirror, and what level of interaction can we provide?

What are sensor shortcomings, and how do we compensate for them?

Summary of Considerations

Technology	Drawbacks and Risks	Recommendation
Amazon Alexa integration provides a VUI without cameras or physical interaction	• Microphone always listening	Recommended
Touch interface provides interaction without microphones or cameras	• Fingerprints reduce mirror visibility	Not recommended
Mirror is read only, relying on an app for its interface	• Requires the use of a phone	Not recommended
Google Assistant integration provides a VUI without cameras or physical interaction	• Microphone always listening • Privacy concerns	Not recommended
A gestural interface uses cameras and facial recognition to provide interaction	• Cameras pose serious privacy concerns	Not recommended
Use infrared camera plus voice recognition to identify users	• Less accurate than traditional camera facial detection	Recommended
Facial detection to identify users	• Cameras pose serious privacy concerns	Not recommended
A combination of a near-infrared camera plus a liquid crystal tunable filter measure hydration	• The user needs to be close to the mirror to take a measurement	Recommended
An infrared camera measures flushness and skin irritation	• Measurements should not be taken after strenuous activity or after showering	Recommended
A camera measures skin hydration and flushness	• Cameras pose serious privacy concerns	Not recommended
An external product measures skin hydration	• Not marketable as a stand-alone product	Not recommended
In-mirror sensors measure temperature, air quality, and humidity	• Data will fluctuate, with bathroom use (primarily showers) creating anomalies	Recommended
The Personal Intelligence Insights Engine collects data and provides insights to use	• Requires setup with an app • Essential to the business model	Recommended

Partnerships and Integrations

ANALYTICS
FLOOR PLAN
MARKETING + CAMPAIGNS
CRM
RESERVATIONS + BOOKINGS
EMPLOYEE MANAGEMENT
POS
INVENTORY
CENTRAL HOME
AVERO
EPOS NOW
HCS
ORACLE
SEVENROOMS
SQUARE
TOAST
TOUCHBISTRO

Competitive Analysis

A competitive analysis provides the team with an understanding of how other companies are solving similar problems. While business analysis looks inward to determine if the company can deliver on the needs and demands of users, competitive analysis looks outward at the decisions other companies have made about similar products and services. A more business-oriented competitive analysis might look more at what features competitors are using to reach their users, while a design-oriented analysis might focus on a product's or service's architecture, design, and execution.

A competitive analysis will help you to understand what's common and therefore necessary for your product or service to do in order to be successful while also highlighting opportunities for differentiation. Because every experience competes for users' attention, the competitive analysis is always important. Even if you don't do a formal competitive analysis, take the time to make yourself aware of the competition before moving into the define or refine phases of work.

Activities

Comprehensively compare features and offerings across the competition.

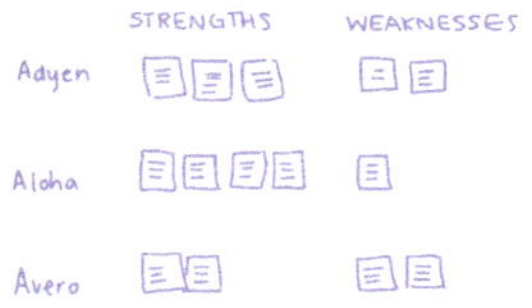

Or focus on where each competitor is strongest and weakest.

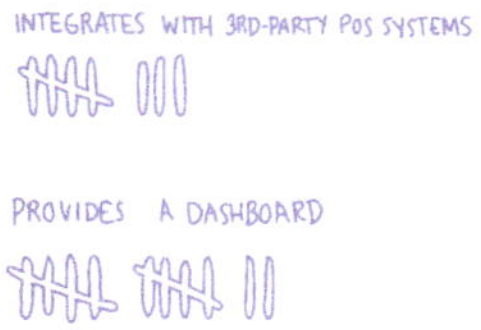

Seek patterns across competitors' offerings.

The first step in a competitive analysis is to identify the competition. Some competitors are more obvious than others. For example, if you're building a suite of analytics tools enabled by camera technology, it's obvious that you should look at other systems that track and diagnose customer movement through space. What's less obvious is that you should expand your search to other tools that restaurants and hotels use to capture and analyze guest behavior. Consider not only the products and services that provide a similar value, but also those that have the attention of your target audience.

If you're struggling to understand who your competition is, try using the internet to search for products or browse the similar-product recommendations provided by online retailers. User interviews can also be used to better understand what alternatives exist, as well as how your target audience spends their attention and their money.

Once you've loosely identified your competition, you'll need to define some structure. You might take a feature-first approach, selecting a handful of the most important features to compare between competitors, or you might lead with the strengths and weaknesses of each of your curated competitors. Less rigorous but equally valid techniques include highlighting common patterns across competitors and capturing quotes from ratings and reviews. Whatever method or methods you choose for your competitive analysis, make sure you're consistent across competitors. If you're working with a team, you may even want to make sure everyone does a small part of each competitor to ensure that personal opinions don't end up creating a bias in your results.

Compare the Most Important Features

Make a list of features that are most important to the experience. Try to keep this list below twelve items. Look across the competitors you've identified to see which do these things very well and which do them poorly or not at all. Working with multiple team members and deciding on a consistent scale for rating or ranking experiences will help analysis be less subjective.

Highlight Strengths and Weaknesses

Looking through each competitive experience, what are the one or two things that stand out as being very thoughtful and well executed? What are the one or two things that feel neglected? Compare these across all experiences. The things that are universally done well set a bar for what your experience needs to achieve. The things that are poorly done might represent opportunities, or they might highlight universal challenges that the market has not yet found a way to overcome. Make sure to research any technical, legal, or other barriers behind these challenges before recommending them as opportunities.

Seek Patterns

When quickly experiencing multiple competitors' products or services in succession, it's easy to observe patterns. Some might be experiential patterns, like how digital drawing tools are more robust on larger screens. Others might be based on interaction, like the way long lists of album covers typically use a long-looping scroll. Still others might be visual, like the way financial apps are very monochromatic except for using green to indicate good and red to indicate bad. Like strengths and weaknesses, patterns can represent standard ways of doing things that should be followed, or they might highlight an opportunity for differentiation.

See What People Are Saying

Look at users' reviews of the competition. Users often spend more time with a product or service than we're able to in the brief time allotted for a competitive analysis. While users do have the advantages of being less biased about the experience and more focused on real goals, those that post reviews are often the most pleased or the most frustrated with the experience they're posting about. Nonetheless, it's helpful to understand which features and executions users most appreciate and which they most despise.

Any time you identify an anomaly that you believe might be an opportunity, dig deeper. Try to find additional examples that support the opportunity. If you can't find what you're looking for with competitors, try other research activities, like user interviews, expert interviews, a trendscape, or immersion, to support your point.

Read customer reviews to see what people actually use and enjoy.

Artifacts

A competitive analysis should provide your team with a clear list of recommendations for your experience. It should also establish where your company will compete with existing products or services to provide similar offerings to users and where you will pursue new opportunities, differentiating the experience from users' existing choices.

Back up these assertions in consumable and memorable ways. Use Harvey balls to compare the strength of specific features across multiple products, or show how well competitors provide a specific value to consumers by positioning them on a continuum of weak to strong. To highlight patterns in competitors' offerings, call out the pattern and then the percentage of competitors who provide it. Try using pie or doughnut charts to make the presentation more visual or to call attention to the most valuable figures.

To help team members understand the competition in a richer way, highlight strengths and weaknesses by calling out best-in-class or worst-in-class experiences with photos, short videos, or screenshots. To make the data more human, highlight quotes or product reviews as they pertain to a specific feature or aspect of the experience.

When working on a competitive analysis of digital experiences, capture version or release numbers or, if this is unavailable, links and dates. For any future work with the competitive analysis, this ensures that you're using information from the most current iteration of your competition's product or service.

The competitive analysis for Observations Suite highlights a series of features across key competitors and then establishes best-in-class practices with digital sketches for how features work, how they're organized, and how they're presented.

Omniscient / **Observations Suite Vision**

Competitive Analysis

Process Overview

We analyzed over twenty-four potential competitors and narrowed our selection to the eight most relevant. Then we looked in detail at the product and service offerings, marketing, and differentiating elements for each company.

Features

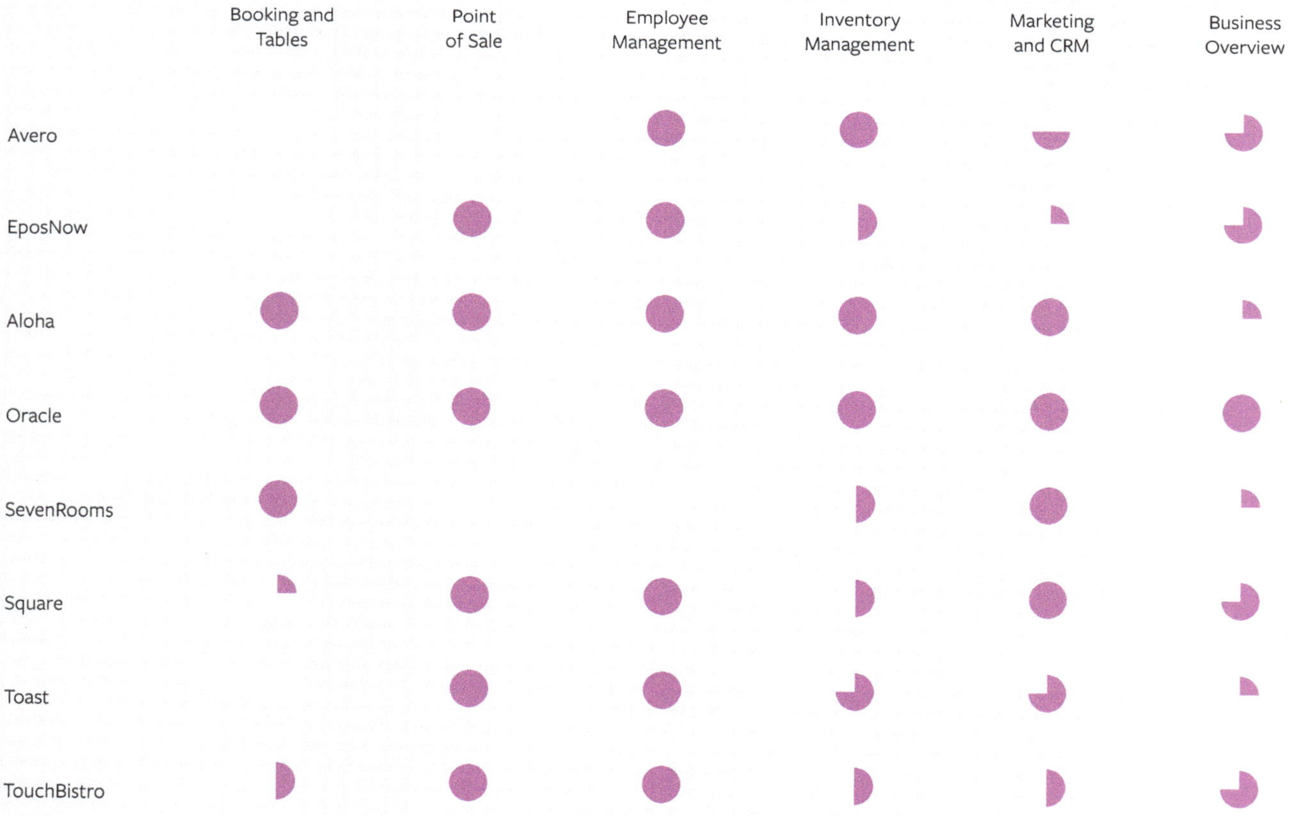

Summary of Findings

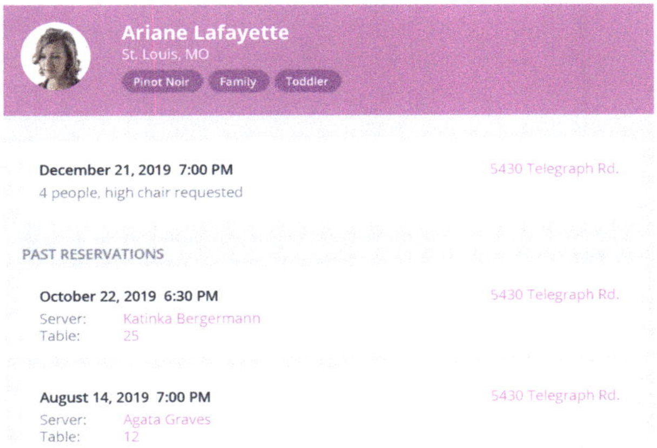

Customer Relationships

Put the customer at the center of every engagement. Understand customer types through segmentation, preferences through tagging and notes, and behaviors through observation. Aggregate information to provide easy access and to prioritize employee action.

Glanceable Dashboard

Aggregate information from all touchpoints into a single customizable dashboard that can be used as a launchpad to individual products within the Observations Suite. Include data from outside sources, such as weather and holidays.

Ingredient	Stock	Cost	Order Quantity	Total
Eggs	36	$ 0.08	400	$ 32.00
Basil	2	$ 0.96	72	$ 69.12
Heavy Cream	20	$ 0.48	0	
Garlic	18	$ 0.24	80	$ 19.20
Summer Squash	27	$ 0.88	0	
Pumpkin	4	$ 2.12	0	
EVOO	11	$ 4.68	0	

Inventory Management

Combine observations about trends and patterns with an understanding for specific consumers' needs to maintain inventory at any scale. Integrate where possible to provide single-interaction restocking.

Hardware and Software

Provide solutions that work with Omniscient hardware, integrate with off-the-shelf hardware, and provide value even if the user has no hardware yet.

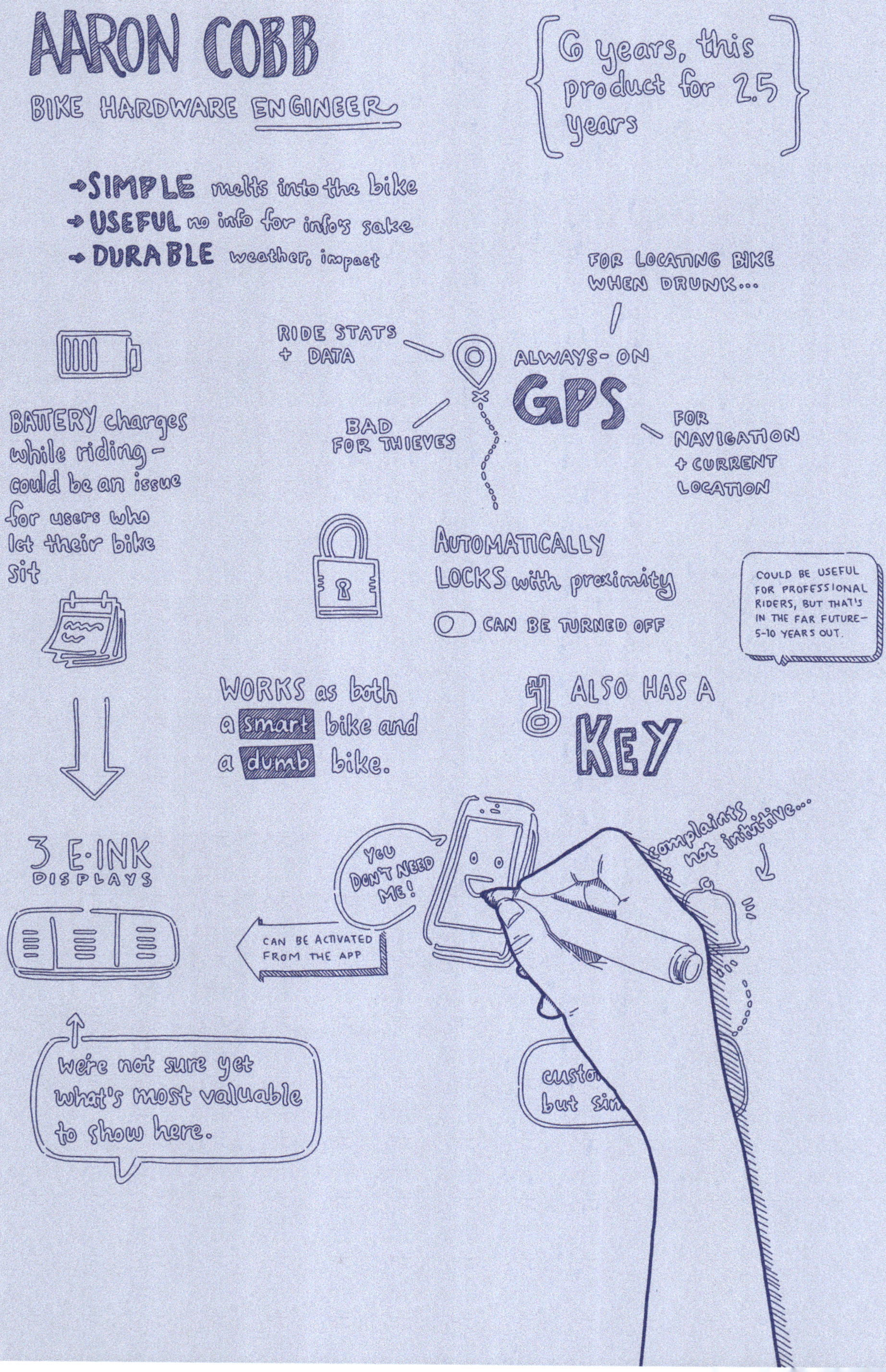
AARON COBB
BIKE HARDWARE ENGINEER
6 years, this product for 2.5 years
→ SIMPLE melts into the bike
→ USEFUL no info for info's sake
→ DURABLE weather, impact
FOR LOCATING BIKE WHEN DRUNK...
RIDE STATS + DATA
ALWAYS-ON GPS
BAD FOR THIEVES
FOR NAVIGATION + CURRENT LOCATION
BATTERY charges while riding - could be an issue for users who let their bike sit
AUTOMATICALLY LOCKS with proximity
CAN BE TURNED OFF
COULD BE USEFUL FOR PROFESSIONAL RIDERS, BUT THAT'S IN THE FAR FUTURE- 5-10 YEARS OUT.
WORKS as both a smart bike and a dumb bike.
ALSO HAS A KEY
3 E-INK DISPLAYS
YOU DON'T NEED ME!
CAN BE ACTIVATED FROM THE APP
complaints not intuitive...
we're not sure yet what's most valuable to show here.

Stakeholder Interviews

Ensuring that any concept or idea makes its way to market means enlisting the support of multiple stakeholders. Stakeholders are individuals who make decisions concerning and affecting the product or service that you're designing. This could include direct team members as well as outsiders who will contribute to or guide the project. Gaining broad support from stakeholders requires understanding what each of these influential people know about and want out of the project, what their teams contribute to the process, and how they will be involved throughout. Stakeholder interviews might also uncover business, technology, and competitor insights that can be useful in those analyses.

Formal stakeholder interviews are most useful when you're working with unfamiliar groups—usually in large organizations or as a consultant with smaller organizations. In these settings, interviews will not only provide valuable insight into how the company and team work but will also ensure that design is positioned as a curious collaborator in stakeholders' minds. Even if stakeholder interviews are not an explicit part of your project plan, consider doing them informally over a coffee or tea to get some of the same benefits.

Activities

Before conducting interviews, you need to understand who your stakeholders are and how they relate to each other. What is the organizational structure? Who is a part of the core team, those you meet with regularly, and who is a part of the extended team, those you meet with only for large group check-ins? Are there any stakeholders outside the extended team you should be aware of? (There usually are.) What part of the organization do people belong to, and what ranks do individuals have? Ensure you balance your interviews, collecting input from business, technology, and design. It's not necessary to interview every stakeholder in a project, so prioritize those who are most removed from, yet have the most influence over, the project or project team.

Be aware of politics. If certain stakeholders have reputations for causing problems, you may want to go out of your way to include them and get their input early on. If you have stakeholders that are likely to disagree with each other, you'll want to make sure you interview both, even if they're at different levels of the organization. Be prepared to add to your list of relevant stakeholders, as new names are bound to pop up as you make your way through the interviews.

Once you know who you're going to interview, make an interview plan. Depending on how close you are to the company, the questions will vary. If you're working with someone you're unfamiliar with, you'll want to ask basic questions about the stakeholder and their company, such as:

More Stakeholders than Time

It's likely that you'll want to gather input from more people than time allows. While surveys can be valuable in getting quick answers from large groups, it's also likely that they will go unanswered by busy executives. As an alternative, consider getting a large group into a room together for a collaborative exercise around project hopes and fears. With careful moderation to ensure that all voices are heard, these conversations can yield insights quickly and with very little effort.

* What is your role and what are you responsible for within your company?
* What is your role on this specific project?
* What processes and methodologies do you use?
* What are your company's strengths and weaknesses?
* What are your company's long-term goals?
* Who are you competing with and why are you better?

If you're working in house or if you're familiar with the company, you may want to skip these questions entirely and start with a more specific set:

* What do you hope to get out of this project?
* What trends (technology, business, etc.) do you think will be relevant to this product?
* Are there other projects, past or concurrent, that we should be paying attention to?
* What challenges do you foresee us facing with this project?
* Who else should we be talking to about this project?

Unlike users, stakeholders have specific roles and responsibilities. Take this into consideration as you choose which questions to ask each individual. If you're not sure what to ask, start with generic questions and develop follow-up questions as you go to get into the details around a stakeholder's specific responsibilities or passions. Always be prepared for your interview subject to want to talk about something that isn't directly relevant to their title.

A stakeholder interview can be as helpful to the stakeholder as it is to the design team. By asking the right questions, you may be able to help a stakeholder uncover new ideas, better understand their priorities, or determine what they can do to best support the project.

Once you have a plan, you're ready to conduct the interviews. Because it's likely that the most important stakeholders also

Capture the organization in a chart for easy reference later.

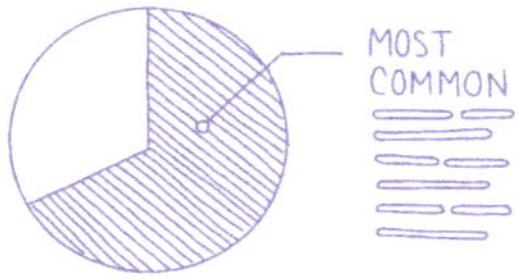

Focus on strong agreement and disagreement among stakeholders.

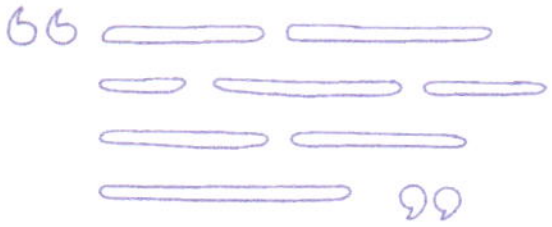

Use quotes to back up findings.

have the busiest schedules, you'll want to make the best use of their limited time. Do a test run of the interview with someone in your core team to get a feel for timing and interview priorities before setting up official interviews—especially with executives. If you find a stakeholder outside of your project team particularly interesting or helpful, ask if it's all right to contact them later. You may want to ask follow-up questions or even run work in progress by them for feedback.

After each interview reflect on your findings. Is there anything you should have asked that you didn't? Did you discover a new stakeholder that you should interview? Were any concerns brought up that need to be checked by other stakeholders? Every interview is an opportunity to improve your interview plan.

Artifacts

Once you've completed your interviews, you'll need to synthesize the findings into something that can be used by the core team. Your insights from stakeholder interviews will likely fall into two buckets: insights about the structure and politics of the organization and insights into the expectations and constraints of the project.

Some political insights tend to be more delicate and should be handled with care. It's not unusual to discover through interviews that stakeholders are leaving their positions, teams are being shuffled, or the organization is shifting strategies. If a stakeholder says, "This is not yet public," make sure you consider the inevitable, but don't make it a part of the official report.

What you do want to document are the places where stakeholders are in strong agreement and disagreement. Places where stakeholders agree are useful for defining success, while places where they disagree are indicative of risk.

When highlighting opportunities and risks, consider the source. Sometimes what was said will be taken in different ways depending on who said it. Use quotes to back up your findings, and remember who said what. This can help you navigate the politics of an organization later.

For internal team use, consider creating an organizational chart to capture who is involved in your project and at what level. This provides not only an overview of the team but also a quick reference for whom to talk to when someone is on holiday or whose attention to get when there's a problem with the project. RACI diagrams are also useful for this purpose, capturing roles and tasks, along
with who is responsible, accountable, consulted, and informed for each.

When deciding what stakeholder insights are important to share in terms of expectations and constraints, think about what's important from design, business, and development perspectives. Aside from calling out the most important insights, you'll also want to capture insights that will directly affect the design, such as features demands, technology constraints, and existing design guidelines.

> *"I sometimes find that in interviews you learn more about yourself than the person learned about you."*
>
> **William Shatner**

Stakeholder interviews for CityBike focus on getting to know team members' priorities and understanding all of the work and input that's been done to date. The output highlights priorities for design backed by quotes from stakeholders, as well as risks to the project.

Observations Suite stakeholder interviews focus on getting to know the team and its structure, while also uncovering individuals' biggest concerns and priorities.

CityBike / **Connected Bicycle**

Stakeholder Interviews

Stakeholders Interviewed

Core Team

Theresa Stevens
Software Product Manager

Alex Walker
Bike Software Engineer

Tina Fowler
iOS Developer

Extended Team

Janice Johns
Customer Support

Robert Petrov
Brand Manager

Aaron Cobb
Bike Hardware Engineer

Alice Bennett
Industrial Designer

Jeremy Bertolino
Marketing Director

Max Williams
Online Support

Priorities

Create a mechanical backup mechanism for the lock.

“ *The number one problem we get from beta testers is that they're locked out of their bike.”*

– Janice Johns

“ *We've done some research around a mechanical backup mechanism for the lock, but it's a lot of work to implement.”*

– Aaron Cobb

Create a best-in-class navigation experience.

“ *Online, our customers always complain about navigation features.”*

– Max Williams

“ *We're aware that nobody's happy with the navigation, but this isn't a problem unique to CityBikes.”*

– Theresa Stevens

Make sure stats take a back seat to other features.

“ *We've built some really awesome things around ride stats that will help set us apart from the competition.”*

– Tina Fowler

“ *The stats are a cool add-on, but nobody is buying the bike for them.”*

– Jeremy Bertolino

Risks

- Android development is understaffed and struggling to keep up with iOS.
- Early versions were designed with cyclists in mind.
- Battery limitations affect the overall bike experience. Current provider isn't working out.
- Accessibility studies have been limited.
- Privacy studies have been limited.
- Marketing is pushing bike-sharing features that are a long way from ready.
- Manufacturing has fallen behind, and important functionality is being cut.
- The marketing team is using mock-ups to sell the app, while the development team has deprioritized app aesthetics.

Make sure bike sharing is simple and foolproof.

" *There are still a lot of edge cases around bike sharing that cause errors and privacy concerns.*"

– Theresa Stevens

" *Bike sharing is a really big deal to a lot of our corporate clients, so we have to get this right.*"

– Jeremy Bertolino

Make the app feel authentic to CityBike.

" *Our brand is at the core of who we are. Everything needs to just feel like CityBike.*"

– Robert Petrov

" *We're really focusing on functionality before any of the superficial stuff.*"

– Tina Fowler

Provide riders with sensible options for the handlebar displays.

" *We decided to keep things simple and to avoid customization of the handlebar displays.*"

– Alex Walker

" *Our users are constantly asking to be able to customize the on-bike displays—especially if they're left-handed.*"

– Max Williams

Stakeholder Interviews

Introduction

We interviewed eight stakeholders from across the organization to better understand Observations Suite's unique opportunities and challenges. We synthesized perspectives from development, business, research, sales, and marketing into a series of insights to inform the project's next steps.

Stakeholder Map

Interview participants are highlighted.

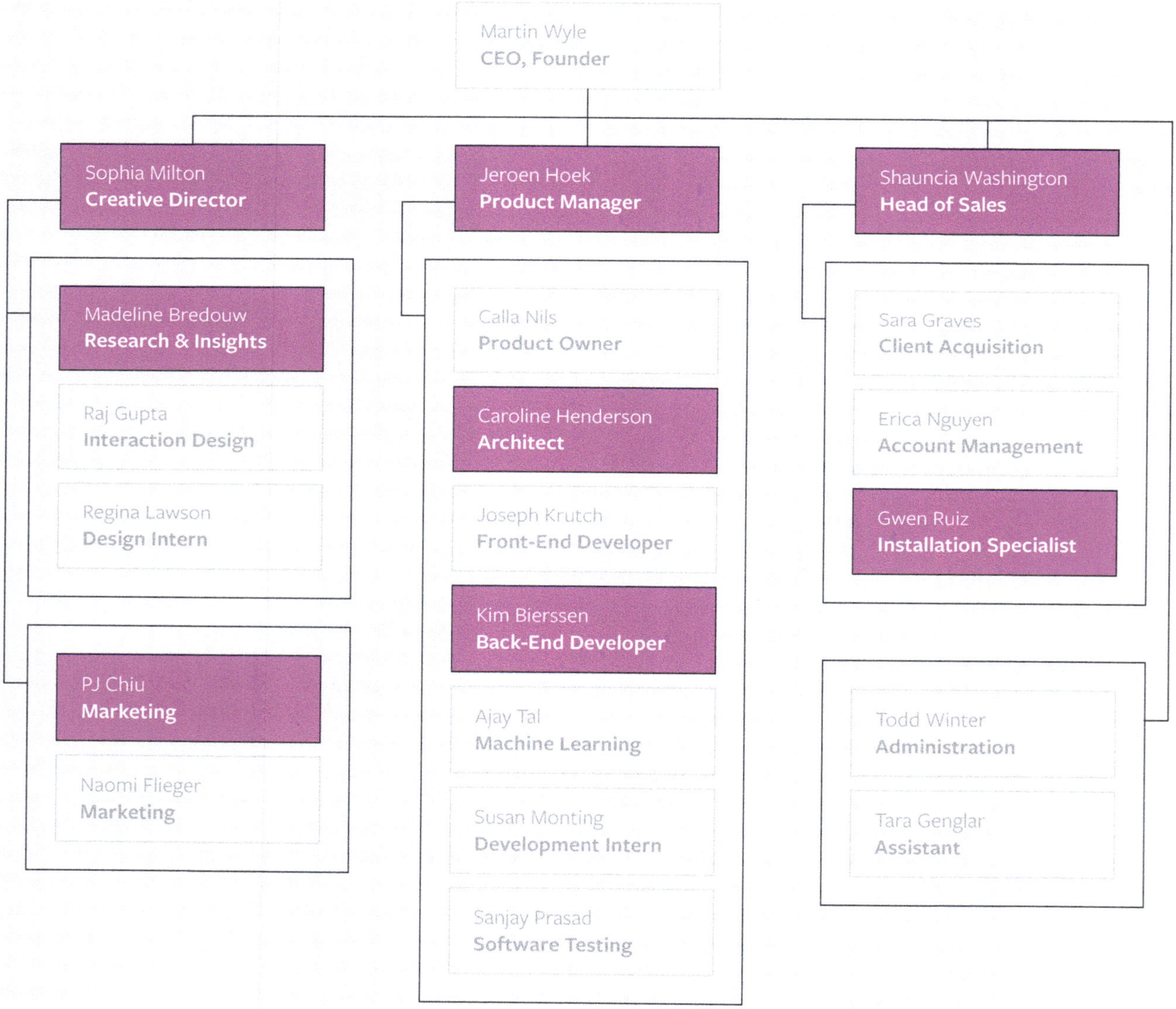

Interview Highlights

Feature the Cameras

Camera technology is what sets Observations Suite apart from other competitors, so whatever launches for MVP (minimum viable product) should feature that data.

This project should look deeper into how we can make the raw data collected from cameras into something valuable to businesses.

Get to Market in Nine Months

Investors want something in the market within nine months to confirm that the information collected from cameras is as valuable to restaurants as we all think it is.

Create Many Solutions

While business customers talk about what's useful to them, it's not entirely clear what types of insights will convince businesses to switch to Omniscient and which will keep them there. This needs to be tested, so multiple solutions are a must.

Don't Rely on the Insights Engine

While the timeline for Omniscient's insights engine shows a beta launching in three months, development is behind, and it's not certain that there will be anything ready for integration with Observations Suite by launch time.

Create a strong design that doesn't rely on insights to provide value to businesses but that can scale to accommodate insights when they're ready.

Don't Ignore Ugly Tools

Design partners in the past have ignored the established tools because they're ugly and feel outdated; however, these tools have been refined with user input over time. Observations Suite should look contemporary but should also avoid the oversimplification common to consumer experiences.

Keep the Future in Mind

While the initial launch will need to be limited in scope and focused on learning from MVP, the big picture should not be forgotten. Consider what the complete Observations Suite could be before scaling back to a focused first release.

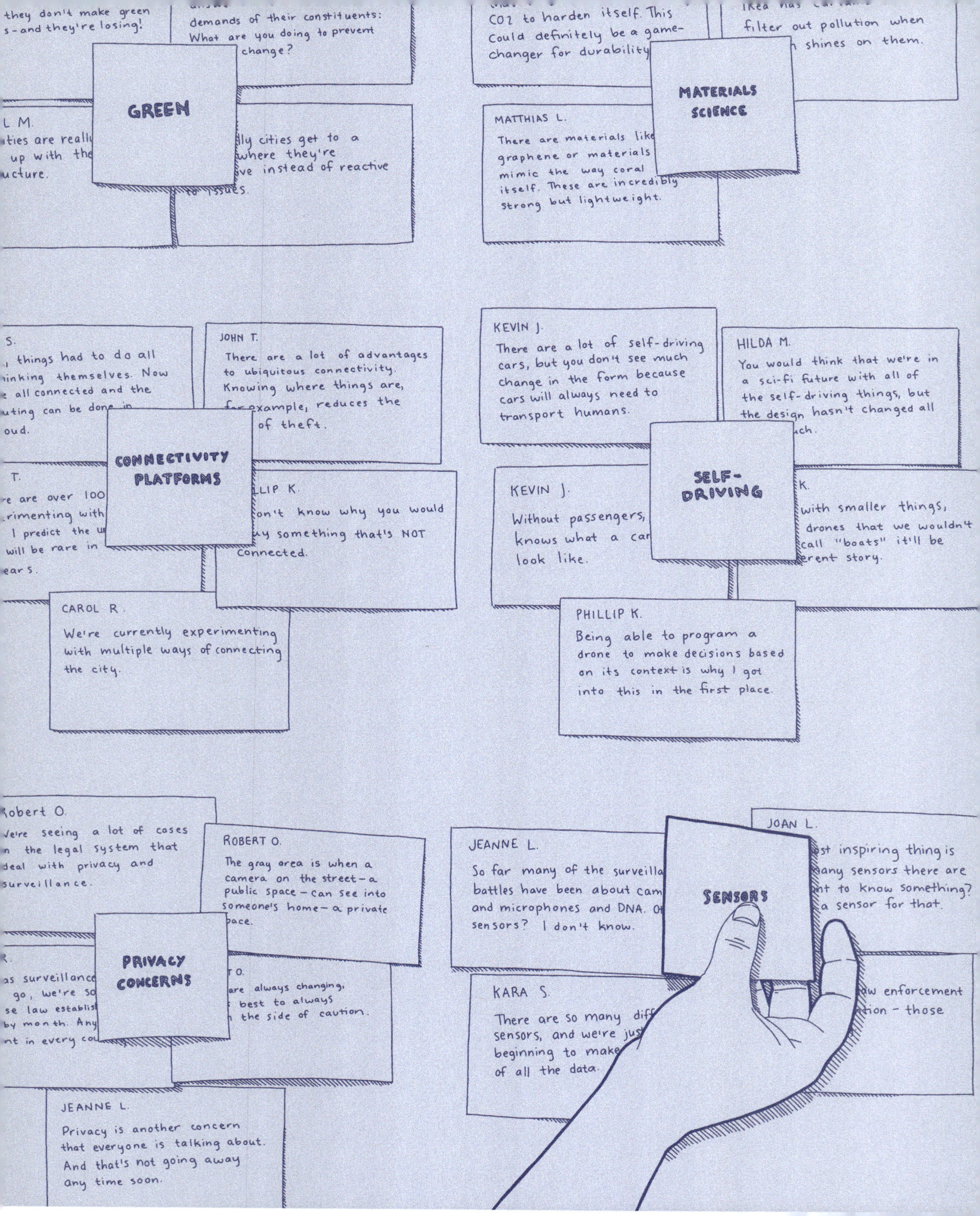
they don't make green
s-and they're losing!
demands of their constituents: What are you doing to prevent
change?
CO2 to harden itself. This could definitely be a game-changer for durability
filter out pollution when
shines on them.
GREEN
L M.
ties are reall
up with the
ucture.
lly cities get to a
where they're
ve instead of reactive
to issues.
MATERIALS SCIENCE
MATTHIAS L.
There are materials like graphene or materials
mimic the way coral
itself. These are incredibly strong but lightweight.
S.
things had to do all
hinking themselves. Now
all connected and the
uting can be done in
oud.
JOHN T.
There are a lot of advantages to ubiquitous connectivity. Knowing where things are,
example, reduces the
of theft.
KEVIN J.
There are a lot of self-driving cars, but you don't see much change in the form because cars will always need to transport humans.
HILDA M.
You would think that we're in a sci-fi future with all of the self-driving things, but the design hasn't changed all
ch.
CONNECTIVITY PLATFORMS
T.
re are over 100
rimenting with
I predict the
will be rare in
ears.
LLIP K.
on't know why you would
y something that's NOT connected.
KEVIN J.
Without passengers,
knows what a car
look like.
SELF-DRIVING
K.
with smaller things,
drones that we wouldn't
call "boats" it'll be
erent story.
CAROL R.
We're currently experimenting with multiple ways of connecting the city.
PHILLIP K.
Being able to program a drone to make decisions based on its context is why I got into this in the first place.
Robert O.
We're seeing a lot of cases
n the legal system that
deal with privacy and surveillance.
ROBERT O.
The gray area is when a camera on the street—a public space—can see into someone's home—a private
pace.
JEANNE L.
So far many of the surveilla
battles have been about cam
and microphones and DNA.
sensors? I don't know.
SENSORS
JOAN L.
st inspiring thing is
any sensors there are
nt to know something?
a sensor for that.
PRIVACY CONCERNS
as surveillance
go, we're so
se law establis
by month. Any
nt in every co
O.
are always changing,
best to always
the side of caution.
KARA S.
There are so many diff
sensors, and we're jus
beginning to make
of all the data.
w enforcement
tion - those
JEANNE L.
Privacy is another concern that everyone is talking about. And that's not going away any time soon.

Expert Interviews

It's not unusual for design teams to take on projects that fall outside their areas of expertise. In these situations, expert interviews can help to develop a fast and specific understanding of an industry, technology, or company, providing design teams insight into both its challenges and opportunities. Even if a design team is generally familiar with a topic, it can still be useful to do expert interviews to get a more nuanced understanding of the client's specific challenges.

Aside from a better understanding of a subject, expert interviews support the design process by reducing the number of assumptions involved when the design team is making decisions. If you are unable to discuss your project with experts, you'll likely need to do significant desk research to avoid making assumptions and uninformed design decisions. Of course, if you're doing a project with a familiar company using familiar technology, expert interviews might not reveal much that you didn't already know.

Activities

Start with a plan to make sure the entire team gets what they need.

The first step in conducting expert interviews is to identify what you know and what you need to know, and then to find experts. Aim for too many experts to interview, expecting that a number of them will decline. Clients are usually happy to supply reliable experts. Client-provided experts are often the most useful, as they understand the client's specific take on a topic and will be able to provide more than general industry expertise. It's also valuable to find experts outside of the client's network, as their perspectives can provide alternative ways of looking at the industry or technology. While one or two experts might be enough to glean a general understanding, it's better to talk to a greater number of experts from a variety of backgrounds to better understand the patterns and nuances that exist.

Before you start interviewing, have a plan. Collect input from your team to ensure that all members get what they need out of the expert interviews, and then formulate a series of questions and follow-on questions.

Here are some things to consider to ensure that your questions get you the most insightful responses:

* Ask questions even if they seem dumb. The answers to dumb questions are often the foundation to understanding more complex questions and answers.

* Confirm what you think you know. Different perspectives can shed new light or complexity on the things you think you understand. It's not unusual for the most useful bits of information to lie in the places where an expert

Visual Note-Taking

While the most important findings should be synthesized into an artifact for later reference, there's often value in the details of expert, stakeholder, and user interviews that can provide insight throughout the design process. Visual notes are a great way to preserve the content of these original conversations in a format that's easy to reflect on throughout the design process. When done in a large format, visual notes can be hung on the wall of the project room and will continue to inform throughout later phases of work.

holds an unorthodox opinion or in the places where experts disagree with each other.

* Avoid closed questions with simple yes or no answers. Open questions are more likely to yield surprising results and expand your understanding of a topic.

* Ask your expert to make decisions. Asking your expert to choose between options can help you understand priorities for later design exercises.

When you interview your subject, it's most convenient to have two people in the room—one to ask questions and one to take notes. If you can't have a second person present, ask if you can record the conversation so that you can stay focused on the interview instead of on note-taking.

Between interviews, reflect on how each went. Especially in your first few sessions, it's likely you'll realize that your interview plan needs some revising. Maybe you need to ask more questions about a specific topic, or maybe you need to extend the length of the interviews to accommodate all of your questions. For this reason, it's wise to save your most interesting interview subjects until later in the process, when you can be sure your plan is at its best.

Once you've completed your expert interviews, you'll need to synthesize what you heard into findings worth sharing with the team.

> *"The more things you're interested in, the better your work will be."*
>
> **Michael Beirut**

Artifacts

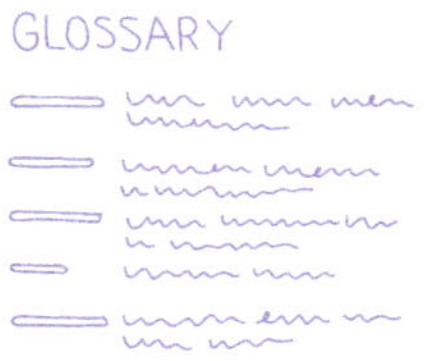

Create a glossary of terms to ensure a common understanding.

When communicating the findings from expert interviews, aim to create more clarity and insight within your team. Start by establishing a common understanding, and then get into details that will affect the design of your product or service.

To establish a general understanding of a topic, call out important statistics or figures. Rather than sharing every detail, aim for superlatives—the biggest misconception about a technology or the three biggest problems facing an industry. Give your team information in small, memorable chunks.

Help align your team's vocabulary and way of talking about the topic by creating a glossary of terms. Some experts will use general terms in ways that are specific to their company or methodology, so some desk research may be necessary to ensure that your glossary is accurate.

Call out any insights that are likely to affect design decisions, and then support them. This is especially important in cases where expert opinions diverged from the team's existing understanding. You might highlight insights on slides supported by experts' quotes or in videos with actual clips of experts sharing their thoughts.

Especially if you had access to only a limited number of experts, expert interviews might be combined with other discover-phase artifacts to increase their credibility. Depending on the nature of your experts, you may look to the technology, business, or competitive analyses to support findings. Stakeholder interviews can also prove useful, as stakeholders often interact regularly with experts and sometimes have an understanding of the same topics.

Expert interviews for Future of Boats captured broad insights from experts across many relevant fields. Each insight has associated outcomes that are important for generating and refining concepts for the strategic roadmap.

Ambience Mirror interviewed engineers and health experts to better understand the technology behind and the current ecosystem around smart mirrors. The artifact highlights opportunities for the development of the product and service.

European Waterworks / **Future of Boats**

Expert Interviews

Process Overview

We interviewed twelve experts across three continents about the future of the world's waterways, seeking input about advances in relevant technology, industry demands, and government regulation.

Experts Interviewed

4
Government Officials and Regulators

4
Boat Designers and Engineers

1
Automotive Engineer

3
Enthusiastic Hobbyists

Interview Insights

INFRASTRUCTURE

Cities are investing in connectivity platforms.

Connectivity will be consistent and ubiquitous, so boats will be able to rely on the cloud for tasks that require heavy computing. This means fewer sensitive parts on boats, which means fewer design constraints and more durable vehicles.

Outcomes

- Automated fleets will be able to take advantage of cloud computing to optimize efficiency on the scale of cities
- Theft and sabotage, especially when it comes to smaller crafts, will be reduced

DESIGN + ENGINEERING

Automation means new opportunities for boat designers.

Boats can increasingly navigate without humans, which means they no longer need to be built to human scale. This creates opportunties for smaller autonomous boats that can get into places that larger boats can't. It also means that boats can be completely submerged without having to carry an oxygen supply.

Outcomes

- Boats will become much smaller than we're used to, so there will be more of them, likely with more specialized purposes
- Boats will take forms (including swarms) unique to their functions

REGULATION + INFRASTRUCTURE

Cities are increasingly regulating carbon emissions.

Many cities are adopting aggressive plans to reduce the amount of carbon they emit, aiming for zero carbon emmissions in the coming decade. Many governments already have initiatives to encourage consumers to invest in green transportation options and have internal policies to invest in the same.

Outcomes

- Governments will buy electric vehicles for fleets
- Charging infrastructure will become more robust
- Charging infrastructure will use electricity from renewable sources or else will apply carbon offsets

ENGINEERING

Cheaper and more effective sensors are increasingly available.

Sensors used to require a lot of computing power and energy to measure their surroundings. Now we're seeing sensors get not only smaller and more efficient but also more effective. We can measure pollution in many forms, including pH, salinity, nitrates, dissolved oxygen, and at least a dozen other elements and compounds.

Outcomes

- Governments will be able to better detect and assign responsibility for chemical leaks at a consumer scale
- Water can be tested and determined safe for swimming or even drinking
- Fish farming and aquaculture can be used to greater effect

REGULATION

Governments are increasingly concerned about citizens' privacy.

As governments become increasingly aware about the ways that tech companies infringe on consumers' privacy, regulations will come into place to protect customers from inadvertently being spied on.

Outcomes

- The use of traditional cameras on boats will be limited, resulting in challenges, especially for police operations
- Governments will struggle with regulation, making what's legal something that's always in flux

DESIGN + ENGINEERING

More lightweight pollution-filtering materials are readily available.

Materials science is making fast advances in the creation of lightweight and durable technologies. Some even have unique features, like IKEA's new material that filters out pollution with sunlight. These and other material breakthroughs mean boats can be smaller and more effective and also have a longer life span.

Outcomes

- Boats will use materials that give them benefits beyond their original purpose
- Boats will be able to withstand more turbulent waters

Expert Interviews

Overview

Five engineers and three consumer-health experts provided insights into the technologies behind and the barriers to consumer adoption of a smart mirror.

Glossary of Terms

AVS	An acronym for Alexa Voice Service; provides automatic speech recognition and natural language processing
Flushness	The measurement of heat in the user's face; often appears as redness
Gestural Interface	Uses a depth sensor to read and interpret users' motions; also referred to as a natural user interface or NUI
Hydration	Skin hydration; used as a proxy for overall hydration
Infrared Camera	Also known as a thermal-imaging camera; a camera that creates images from infrared radiation
LCTF	An acronym for liquid crystal tunable filter; combines with the infrared camera to measure skin hydration
PIIE	An acronym for the Personal Intelligence Insights Engine; the insights engine used across all Personal Intelligence products to provide users with meaningful feedback based on their data
TVOC	An acronym for total volatile organic compounds; what is used to measure indoor air quality
Voice Authentication	A technology that uses a person's voice to authenticate their identity
VUI	An acronym for voice user interface; an interface that uses voice controls rather than tapping or touching

Opportunities

To gain users' trust, avoid using a camera.

" Many existing smart-mirror implementations use a camera, and we're seeing that customers aren't comfortable with that. So the products end up outside of the dressing room or outside of the bathroom."

" The main thing companies are using cameras for is authentication. There are some things you can sense with it as well, but almost all of those have alternatives."

Prioritize user needs over technical capabilities.

" Most of the smart mirrors we've seen are still in the proof-of-concept phase, focusing more on what can be done than on what should be done. We still need to show consumers how these things can benefit them, rather than just making another tech demo."

Take advantage of the Personal Intelligence and Ambience brands.

" Most people don't trust the tech giants with their personal information, so it'll be hard for companies like Amazon or Google or even Apple to get into a space as private as people's bathrooms."

Users are ready to engage with voice.

" We've seen a shift over the past five years where VUIs have gone from being a novelty to being mainstream."

Keep an open mind about pricing models.

" We've seen a lot of failed business models around health-information aggregators. Some people want to use the health hub as a way to sell more products, and others see it as an opportunity to sell subscriptions."

" Consumers just don't know what to think of these kinds of services yet, so it's important to keep an open mind and to learn what's valuable, rather than dictating it."

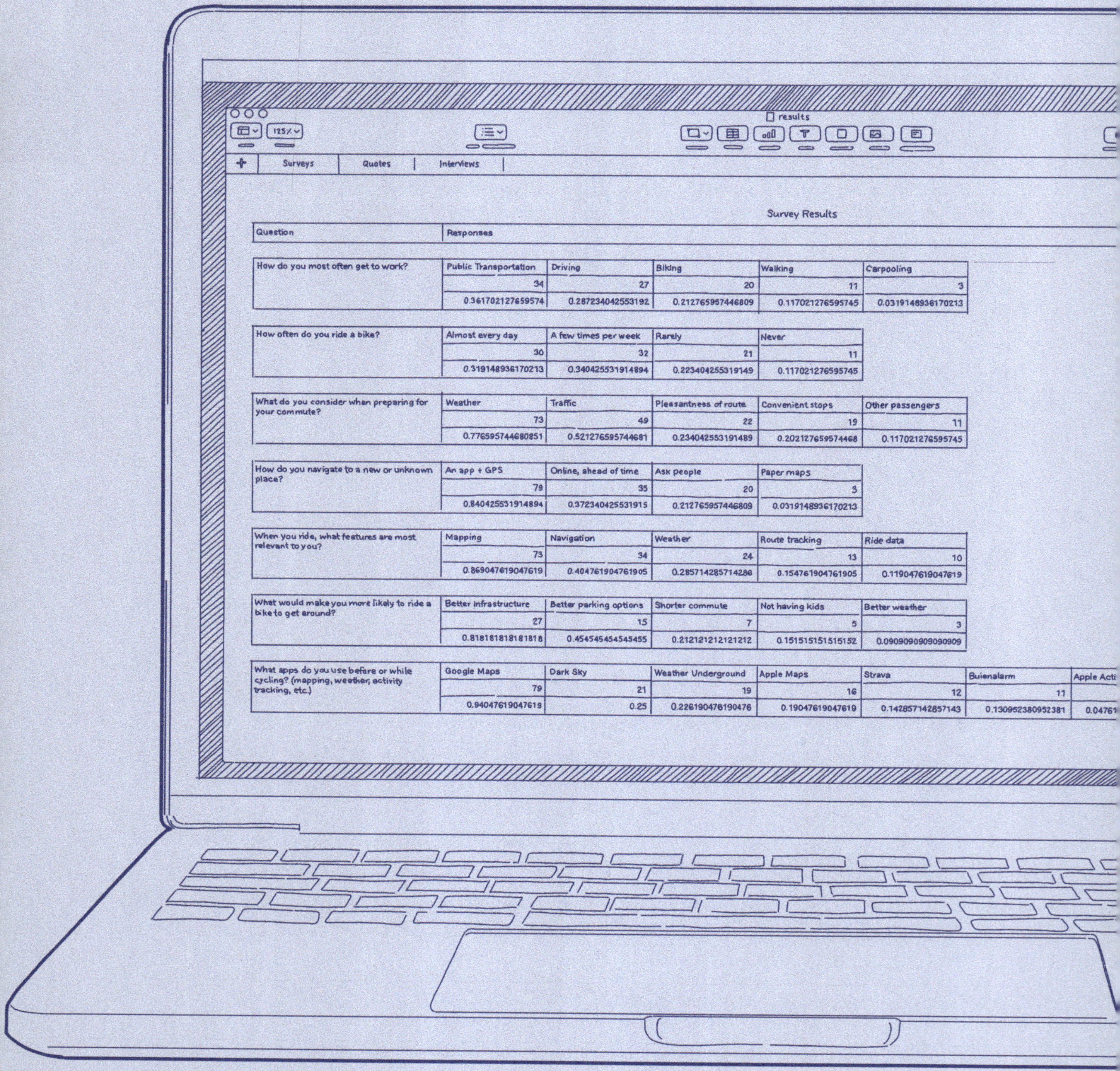
results
Surveys
Quotes
Interviews
Survey Results
Question
Responses
How do you most often get to work?
Public Transportation 34 0.361702127659574
Driving 27 0.287234042553192
Biking 20 0.212765957446809
Walking 11 0.117021276595745
Carpooling 3 0.0319148936170213
How often do you ride a bike?
Almost every day 30 0.319148936170213
A few times per week 32 0.340425531914894
Rarely 21 0.223404255319149
Never 11 0.117021276595745
What do you consider when preparing for your commute?
Weather 73 0.776595744680851
Traffic 49 0.521276595744681
Pleasantness of route 22 0.234042553191489
Convenient stops 19 0.202127659574468
Other passengers 11 0.117021276595745
How do you navigate to a new or unknown place?
An app + GPS 79 0.840425531914894
Online, ahead of time 35 0.372340425531915
Ask people 20 0.212765957446809
Paper maps 3 0.0319148936170213
When you ride, what features are most relevant to you?
Mapping 73 0.869047619047619
Navigation 34 0.404761904761905
Weather 24 0.285714285714286
Route tracking 13 0.154761904761905
Ride data 10 0.119047619047619
What would make you more likely to ride a bike to get around?
Better infrastructure 27 0.818181818181818
Better parking options 15 0.454545454545455
Shorter commute 7 0.212121212121212
Not having kids 5 0.151515151515152
Better weather 3 0.0909090909090909
What apps do you use before or while cycling? (mapping, weather, activity tracking, etc.)
Google Maps 79 0.94047619047619
Dark Sky 21 0.25
Weather Underground 19 0.226190476190476
Apple Maps 16 0.19047619047619
Strava 12 0.142857142857143
Buienalarm 11 0.130952380952381
Apple Acti 0.04761

User Interviews

Creating an experience requires understanding the users of that experience. If you're designing an experience to fulfill your own needs, you probably already have a pretty good understanding of the user. If not, user interviews can help to determine who your users are, as well as their motivations, attitudes, struggles, and needs. For this reason, it's important to talk to users early in the process so that the foundational decisions are made with actual humans in mind.

Because user interviews are such a powerful tool in guarding against the team's biases in the decision-making process, they should be conducted thoroughly and documented in a way that's easily shared, consumed, and referenced throughout the design of the experience. They might be used to guide design decisions or to balance the demands from business and technology stakeholders. You might continue to conduct user interviews throughout the design process, rather than just at the beginning, so that your understanding of the user evolves alongside the refinement of your product or service.

Activities

Use surveys to get input from a lot of people with little effort.

Remote interviews are useful when participants are far flung or when travel isn't an option.

Observation sessions are useful when an experience is uncommon or unfamiliar to the design team.

In order to conduct meaningful user interviews, you need to have some idea of what you want to learn from your users and/or potential users. Work with your team to identify the who, where, what, and how.

Whom do you want to interview? Depending on the product or service you're designing, your target group could be a broad spectrum of users or it might be incredibly specific. Where are your participants? Your audience won't always be one that you have access to or that you can communicate with easily. In some circumstances, you may need to enlist the help of someone who shares your users' context (language, location, etc.) to get meaningful findings from user interviews.

What do you hope to learn from user interviews? Are you looking for general beliefs or personal ideologies? Are you seeking information about individuals that's delicate and private or easily shared? Are you asking the user how they feel about an experience or to describe the experience itself? The nature of the information you're seeking determines how you should seek it.

How will you interview participants? You'll need to create a plan that's appropriate to the information you're seeking. This goes beyond obtaining the right questions to ask to finding the right setting to establish trust and solicit honesty. For example, inquiring about a participant's personal health history might require a different method than asking about their behavior on social media.

Once you know the who, where, what, and how—you're ready to start recruiting. Regardless of whether you're seeking participants in a foreign market or in your own neighborhood, it's likely that you'll need to enlist a recruiting agency to find a sample that is both specific and diverse enough to yield meaningful insights. If you're doing your own recruiting, make sure to have more participants than you need—people will inevitably cancel at the last minute.

If you don't have the time or budget for recruiting, enlist the help of friends and family. While this approach should not be presented as formal user interviews, it can still provide valuable input in the design process.

Surveys

While surveys are the least personal method of interviewing users, they are useful when quantity is a priority. When creating surveys to understand users, be sure to ask enough open questions to learn things you might not expect. At the end of your survey, ask your survey taker if they're open to further conversation, and capture the contact information if they say yes. It's always useful to have a list of users available for further questioning, participatory design, and usability testing.

Remote Interviews

Remote interviews are real-time interviews held in video, audio, or even text format. These types of interviews are more useful than surveys for getting to know a person and are useful if the person you're interviewing isn't available for an in-person session. When holding remove interviews with video or audio, make sure you're in a space without distractions so that you can keep your interview participant focused and at ease.

In-Person Interviews

A sit-down conversation with your user allows for the most natural conversation and also creates the opportunity to observe the user's behavior. With in-person interviews, it's also important to have a comfortable environment free of distraction so that the participant can stay focused on the conversation.

Observation Sessions

Pairing an interview with an observation session can be useful when designing everyday products and services that relate to existing experiences. Not only do observation sessions provide you with the opportunity to see actual behavior, but they can be a helpful way to prime your user so that their memories are fresh for the interview.

Group Interviews

Group interviews allow teams to gather more input in less time.

Group interviews usually involve somewhere between four and ten people and are typically longer than individual interviews. While group interviews provide the opportunity to observe the dynamics of individual participants reacting to each other, the peer pressure of groups can also lead to misleading results. Consider having short follow-ups with participants of group interviews to avoid this.

> *"If I had asked people what they wanted, they would have said faster horses."*
>
> **Henry Ford (allegedly)**

The interview method you choose will influence how you establish trust with the participant, how active your role is in the interview, and how explicit your questions need to be. If your interview follows an observation session, you'll want a structure that adapts to the experience you observed; if your interview is with a group, your role is more that of a moderator than an interviewer; and if your interview is in person, you'll likely want to be less formal and more conversational than you would be with a phone or text interview.

Regardless of interview method, a few good questions can go a long way. Don't ask users what they want. Focus instead on understanding their experiences. Avoid asking leading questions that suggest a particular emotion, experience, or response. Try to replace simple yes-or-no questions with those that inspire a conversation. Plan a small number of questions, and always be prepared to ask *why?*

Depending on the subject matter and the participant, interviews can range from relaxed to stressful. Try to think of the interview as a conversation to keep things relaxed for both you and your participant. Start the interview by asking some general questions, and even by answering some of the participant's questions about you. Do open up to help your participant trust you, but beware of oversharing anything that's under a nondisclosure agreement or NDA. Balance being professional with being human. Allow yourself to diverge from your plan, but don't lose sight of your interview goals. Be prepared to have at least one terrible interview. Never be afraid to end an interview early if the participant makes you uncomfortable or even if you're just not getting anything out of it.

Especially when conducting in-person interviews, beware of distracting participants by taking notes. Consider recording the interviews so that you can review them later. This will also give you the opportunity to reflect on your own performance as an interviewer. Always ask permission before recording.

Five Whys

Five Whys is an interrogative and diagnostic technique developed within Toyota. This technique helps uncover the root cause of a problem. Start with the problem and ask why. Based on that answer, ask why again. Repeat.

In user interviews, it's common for participants to make general statements about what they want or how they feel. By asking why, we can discover what's at the root of the user's feelings and inclinations.

Artifacts

By conducting user interviews, you should have a better idea of who your users are and what they need from your product or service. If you've done user interviews for an existing experience, you'll have a better idea of what you need to improve to satisfy your users. All of this should be captured in an easy-to-scan report that can be used to inform later activities like personas and feature definition.

The presentation of findings will depend on what methods you used to interview users, as well as whether you were seeking to discover or to confirm or reject a hypothesis. To present more exploratory findings with a large sample group, try using charts and ordered lists to highlight patterns among the users interviewed. Use quotes from users to make the data more human. For smaller groups, quotes can also be useful, but be careful not to pick and choose those that support only your existing opinions.

If you were seeking to confirm or reject a hypothesis, focus on user feedback relevant to that goal. For example, if your hypothesis is that users don't ride bikes because they lack the navigation tools, and user interviews show that's not true, this should be made immediately clear in your presentation. Seek to support the outcome with visualizations and quotes that inform the next step in either refining the existing hypothesis or taking on a new one. For that same example, you might show statistics and quotes relating to transportation preferences and reasoning, navigation use and favorite apps, and so on.

CityBike user interviews look at commuting behavior in general via surveys and bike commuting specifically through in-person interviews. Output highlights current user behaviors alongside users' stated needs.

User Interviews

Approach

We conducted ninety-four surveys with urban commuters and twenty interviews with bike commuters across Seattle, Amsterdam, Paris, and New York.

Insights

Most people use map features regularly and navigation features when they're taking an unfamiliar route.

Being prepared is important and usually requires too many apps.

Infrastructure, not bike technology, prevents people from seeing biking as a viable commuting option.

A small subset of riders use apps for tracking their rides. Usually those people track other physical activities as well.

Many riders are interested in reviewing past routes but won't download an app just for that.

User Needs

"I need to know where I'm going and the basics of how to get there."

"I need to be aware of construction and other obstacles to my commute."

"I always check to make sure the weather doesn't catch me by surprise."

"I like knowing how far and how fast I went."

"I like seeing past routes so I can decide which routes to repeat and which to avoid."

"I need an app that doesn't take my attention away from the ride."

"I want to see all of my rides in one place so I can compare them and see my progress."

Survey Results

How do you normally get to work?

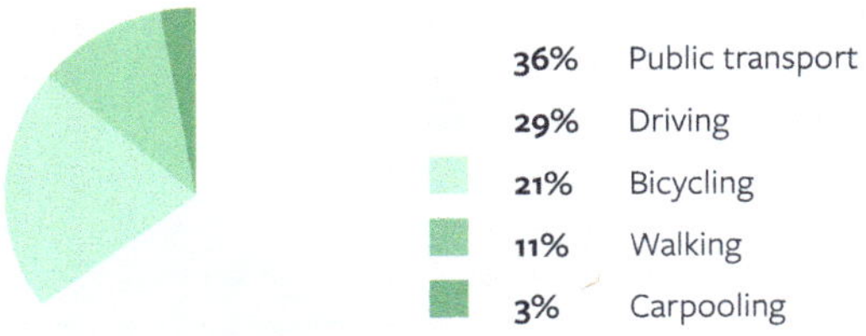

How often do you ride a bike?

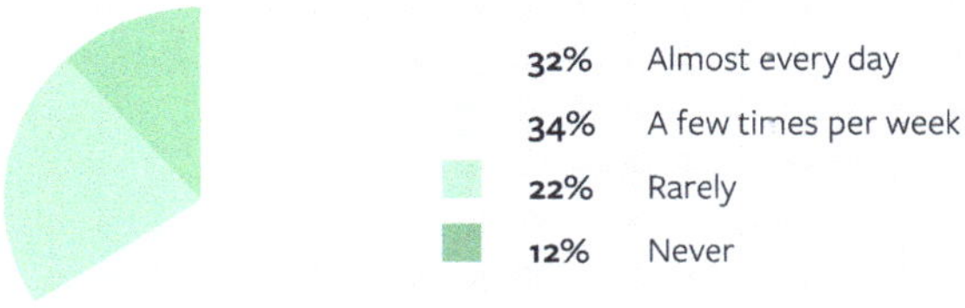

What do you consider before your commute?

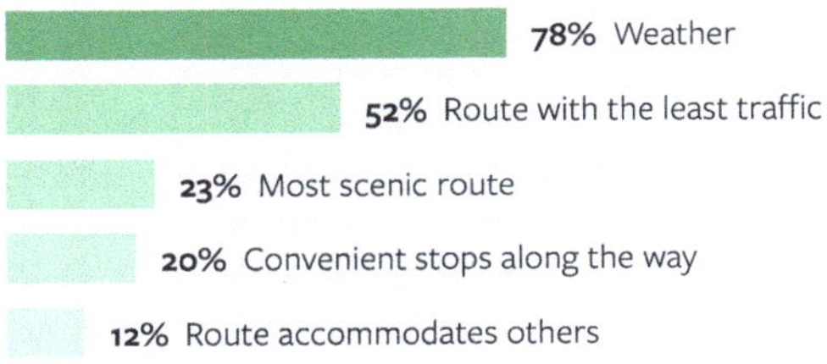

How do you navigate a new or unknown place?

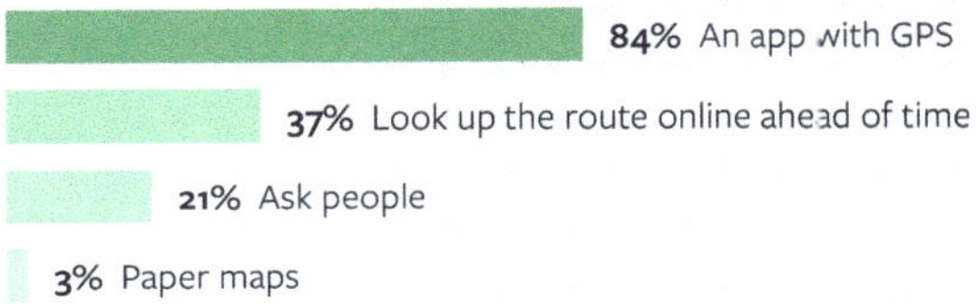

When you ride, what features are most relevant to you?

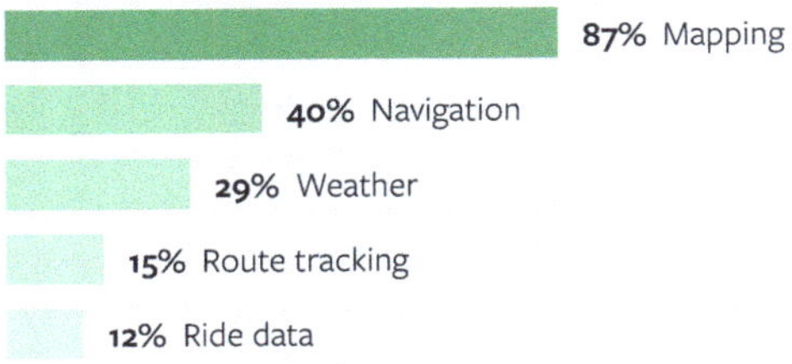

What would make you more likely to ride a bike to get around?

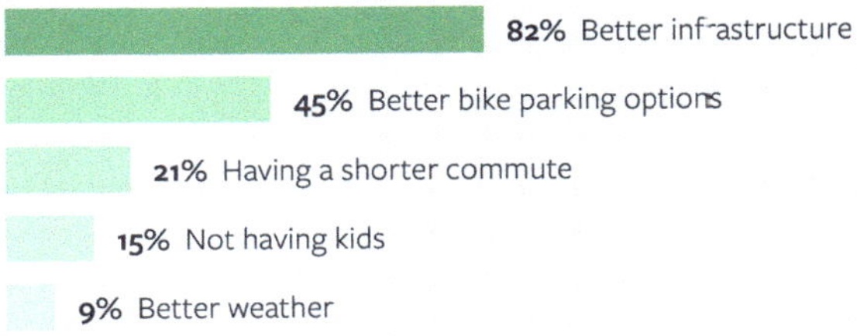

What apps do you use when cycling?

Maps & Navigation
Google Maps
MapOut
Apple Maps

Tracking
Strava
Cyclemeter
Komoot
Apple Activity

Weather
Dark Sky
Buienalarm
Weather Underground

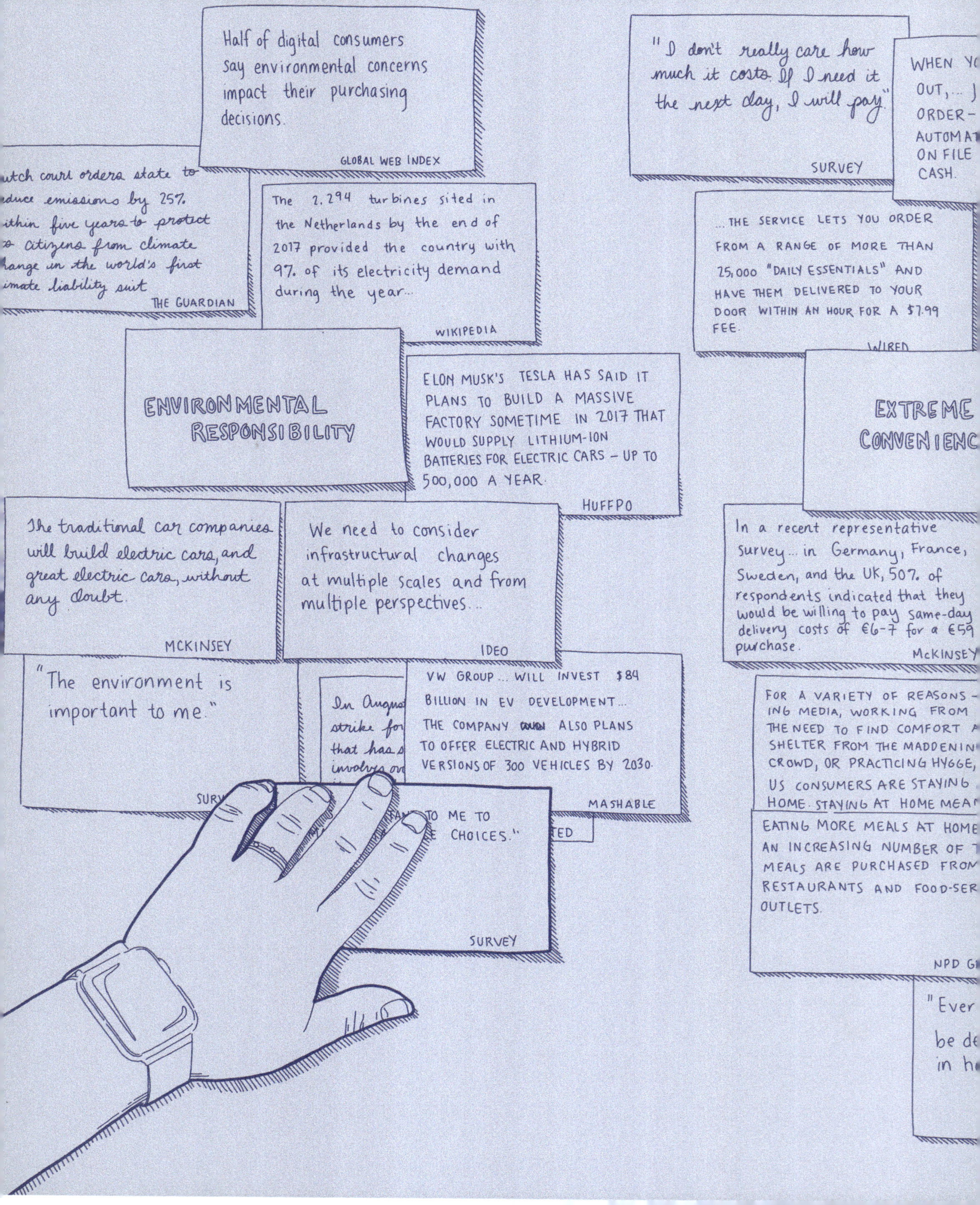
Half of digital consumers say environmental concerns impact their purchasing decisions.
GLOBAL WEB INDEX
utch court orders state to educe emissions by 25% ithin five years to protect s citizens from climate hange in the world's first imate liability suit
THE GUARDIAN
The 2,294 turbines sited in the Netherlands by the end of 2017 provided the country with 9% of its electricity demand during the year...
WIKIPEDIA
ENVIRONMENTAL RESPONSIBILITY
ELON MUSK'S TESLA HAS SAID IT PLANS TO BUILD A MASSIVE FACTORY SOMETIME IN 2017 THAT WOULD SUPPLY LITHIUM-ION BATTERIES FOR ELECTRIC CARS – UP TO 500,000 A YEAR.
HUFFPO
The traditional car companies will build electric cars, and great electric cars, without any doubt.
MCKINSEY
We need to consider infrastructural changes at multiple scales and from multiple perspectives...
IDEO
"The environment is important to me."
SURV
In Augus strike fo that has s involves ov
VW GROUP... WILL INVEST $84 BILLION IN EV DEVELOPMENT... THE COMPANY ALSO PLANS TO OFFER ELECTRIC AND HYBRID VERSIONS OF 300 VEHICLES BY 2030.
MASHABLE
TED
TO ME TO E CHOICES."
SURVEY
"I don't really care how much it costs. If I need it the next day, I will pay."
SURVEY
WHEN YO OUT, ... ORDER – AUTOMAT ON FILE CASH.
... THE SERVICE LETS YOU ORDER FROM A RANGE OF MORE THAN 25,000 "DAILY ESSENTIALS" AND HAVE THEM DELIVERED TO YOUR DOOR WITHIN AN HOUR FOR A $7.99 FEE.
WIRED
EXTREME CONVENIENC
In a recent representative survey ... in Germany, France, Sweden, and the UK, 50% of respondents indicated that they would be willing to pay same-day delivery costs of €6-7 for a €59 purchase.
MCKINSEY
FOR A VARIETY OF REASONS – ING MEDIA, WORKING FROM THE NEED TO FIND COMFORT A SHELTER FROM THE MADDENIN CROWD, OR PRACTICING HYGGE, US CONSUMERS ARE STAYING HOME. STAYING AT HOME MEA
EATING MORE MEALS AT HOME AN INCREASING NUMBER OF T MEALS ARE PURCHASED FROM RESTAURANTS AND FOOD-SER OUTLETS.
NPD G
"Ever be de in h

Trendscape

A trendscape is similar to a competitive analysis in that it looks to solutions in the market for inspiration; however, it is not limited only to similar experiences. A trendscape looks across experiences to see what users are familiar with. Varying in resolution and in formality, trendscapes might be as general as trends in user behavior and expectations or as specific as trends in colors used for health and wellness visualizations.

Along with immersion, trendscapes can be especially helpful when designing for unfamiliar cultures. They can help designers set aside their personal experiences to make more culturally appropriate decisions around functionality, form, color, and more.

Aside from being helpful in predicting what users will want and expect based on familiar experiences, whether adjacent or unrelated, trendscapes are also helpful in providing designers with common ways of explaining interactions in the define or refine phases. Rather than communicating the nuance of how a specific element works through long text descriptions, hand gestures, or motion studies, you can point to another product and say, "like that."

Activities

Understand what users are engaging with and how.

Look broadly at what users expect from the experiences they engage with.

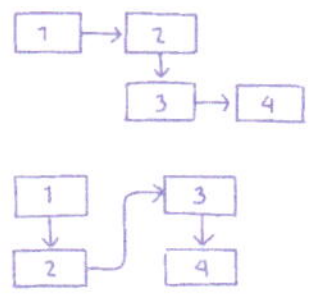

Look at architectures to uncover what patterns will be intuitive to users.

The type of project and how far along you are in the design process will determine how focused your trendscape should be. If you're still early in the discover phase, a broad trendscape looking across many experiences for general trends might be more appropriate; however, if you're in the define or refine phases, a trendscape looking at specific technologies, behaviors, and executions will probably lead to more applicable insights.

Regardless of what phase you're in, start your trendscape by understanding generally what products and services your audience is engaging with. Stakeholders and experts will be able to provide insights here and will likely already have favorite examples. If you're designing a familiar experience, trends might be obvious, but if you're designing for an unfamiliar market, experience, or culture, especially one where you don't speak the language, you may need immersion and user interviews to understand what's relevant.

The goal of trendscape activities is to determine which patterns are worth integrating or copying and which are worth improving or ignoring completely. To do this with confidence, you'll need to consider different things depending on the type of pattern you're searching for:

Market

What new experiences are your users engaging with? How have their behaviors and expectations changed over time? Can you learn anything from early adopters? A market trendscape provides insights into how your product or service fits into a user's existing lifestyle. If you're creating a new product or service, consider behaviors that are not yet mainstream. Use the trendscape to uncover patterns and to establish a hypothesis about what will become popular. When designing for next year's users, it's important to check in regularly to confirm that your hypothesis is still aligned with reality.

Functionality

What common features or functions should you anticipate users will expect of your experience? How have users' expectations changed over time? Are there any disrupters that could affect the expectations of users? A functionality trendscape ensures that your product or service delivers on users' basic needs while also identifying ways for you to differentiate the product or service.

Architecture

How do users navigate similar experiences? What platforms do they engage with for which functions? How have these behaviors changed with the introduction of new technologies? Designing an experience to a common architecture ensures familiarity, and anticipating how your users will engage with your product or service across multiple channels and touchpoints will ensure better adoption rates.

Aesthetics

What do users see? How do they expect an experience to make them feel? Look at color, material, typography, proportion and density, and shape and form to discover what your users are likely to be familiar with. Meeting users' aesthetic expectations will ensure that your experience feels appropriate to the time and place you're designing for. An aesthetic trendscape might also provide insights for how you can differentiate your product or service from the competition.

Uncover aesthetic patterns to inform future design decisions.

Artifacts

The trendscape should help drive alignment around patterns that will be familiar to users and opportunities for exploration. The goals of the trendscape will dictate the types of opportunities you uncover and share. While a market trendscape might uncover patterns and opportunities around user behavior, a functionality trendscape will reveal what features you need to deliver to match and then to surpass the competition.

If you are synthesizing opportunities for presentation, aim to curate them down to only the most relevant. Combine similar opportunities, and consider moving opportunities that cannot realistically be fulfilled to the appendix. Once you have a short selection of relevant and memorable opportunities, summarize them into a list with examples. Strengthen the trendscape by adding statistics and quotes from experts, or humanize the data with quotes and photos from users.

Trends might not be presented on their own but used instead to inform and support other activities. Opportunities from the trendscape might be useful for creating provocations for concept generation. For example, a trend like sharing economy could result in the provocation: *How might we provide boats to individuals who don't want to own their own boat?*

Photos and screenshots from the trendscape, especially aesthetic variations, can also be useful in establishing directions, inspiring interaction models, and populating moodboards. In the define or refine phase, consider using the trendscape to rationalize design decisions. Try presenting similar experiences alongside features or mock-ups, rationalizing decisions by pointing out already-existing best practices.

> *"Be culturally literate, because if you don't have any understanding of the world you live in and the culture you live in, you're not going to express anything to anybody else."*
>
> Paula Scher

The Future of Boats uses a market trendscape to better understand users' demands on infrastructure. Research for the trendscape looks at the needs of cities, as well as how users are engaging with their environment to fulfill their transportation, health, social, and lifestyle needs.

The trendscape for Observations Suite focuses both on architecture and aesthetics, showing how users interact with professional and personal tools. It highlights patterns in navigation, visualizations, product promotion, and communication.

European Waterworks / **Future of Boats**

Trendscape

Environmental Responsibility

"It's important to me to make sustainable choices."

"Dutch court orders state to reduce emissions by 25 percent within five years to protect its citizens from climate change in world's first climate liability suit."

- *The Guardian*

"VW Group, parent of European automakers like Volkswagen, Audi, and Porsche, will invest $84 billion in EV development. Roughly $60 billion of the total will be dedicated to battery production, but the company also plans to offer electric and hybrid versions of three-hundred vehicles by 2030."

- Mashable

Extreme Convenience

"Everything I need can be delivered to my door within hours."

"When you're ready to check out, you'll see your address, an estimated delivery time, and the price of the order, including tax and booking fee. When everything looks right, just tap Place Order—and that's it. We'll automatically use the card on file, so you never need cash."

- Uber Eats

"Available to those with Amazon Prime memberships and provided through a smartphone app, the service lets you order from a range of more than twenty-five thousand 'daily essentials' and have them delivered to your door within an hour for a $7.99 fee. And if you're OK with a two-hour window, the company waives this delivery fee."

- *Wired*

Sharing Economy

"Why buy and store things when I can just rent them when I need them?"

"The sharing economy is estimated to grow from $14 billion in 2014 to $335 billion by 2025."

- Brookings

"The number of public-use bicycles available around the world has more than tripled between 2013 and 2016. By the end of 2016, nearly 2.3 million bikes were available to the public around the world, with 1.9 million of these located in China alone."

- Statista

Urban Density

"Living in the city is so convenient—everything is just outside your door."

"Today, 55 percent of the world's population lives in urban areas, a proportion that is expected to increase to 68 percent by 2050."

- United Nations

"The data is eye opening. The United Nations, in 2009, and the International Organization for Migration, in 2015, both estimated that around 3 million people are moving to cities every week. Approximately 54 percent of people worldwide now live in cities, up from 30 percent in 1950. Sources estimate this will grow to 2/3 of world population in the next fifteen-thirty years."

- Grayline Group

Experience Economy

"We try to spend more time and money on experiences with each other than on stuff."

"In 2017, international tourist arrivals reached a new record high at over 1.3 billion, according to the latest UNWTO Tourism Highlights. The sector has now seen uninterrupted growth in arrivals for eight straight years. It also represents 10.4 percent of GDP, and in 2017 the tourism industry supported 313 million jobs or one in ten jobs globally."

- World Bank

"In fact, over the past few years, personal-consumption expenditures (PCE) on experience-related services—such as attending spectator events, visiting amusement parks, eating at restaurants, and traveling—have grown more than 1.5 times faster than overall personal-consumption spending and nearly 4.0 times faster than expenditures on goods."

- McKinsey

Smart-City Platforms

"My city government is always making improvements based on the data they collect."

"By providing easy access to data—free of charge—we aim to help you put them to innovative use and unlock their economic potential. The portal is also designed to make the EU institutions and other bodies more open and accountable."

- EU Open Data Portal

"The widespread availability of low-cost sensors and advanced networking technologies is fueling the IoT [internet of things] phenomenon and helping shape the smart-, connected-city market. Gartner, the research and advisory firm, projects that by 2020, 9.7 billion devices—including buildings, cars, streetlights, and parking meters—will be connected in smart cities around the globe."

- *MIT Technology Review*

Overwhelmed Infrastructure

"Getting through the city during rush hour is a nightmare."

"According to the municipality of Amsterdam, the last fifteen years has become busier on the canals. There are about eighteen thousand pleasure boats in the capital."

- NOS Journaal

"With 5 million people commuting each day and more bicycles than their population, the country simply doesn't have the infrastructure to accommodate the high and growing demand for bicycling."

- ZDNet

Clean Water

"Swimming in the canals shouldn't feel like a risk."

"Of the 912 million people living in the WHO European Region, in 2015 more than 62 million lack access to an adequate sanitation facility and 14 million do not use a basic drinking-water source."

- World Health Organization

"New technologies are promising to transform wastewater into a resource for energy generation and a source of drinking water. Modular hybrid activated sludge digesters, for instance, are now removing nutrients to be used as fertilizers and are, in turn, driving down the energy required for treatment by up to half."

- *The Guardian*

Trendscape

Links across Products

Quick navigation to other apps, sections, or functions is available from the top level of navigation. This also serves to market apps that the user might not have yet.

Graphy Photo Management (Mac OS), My Social Portal (iOS), Make Suite (web), CirclePlace (web)
January 2020

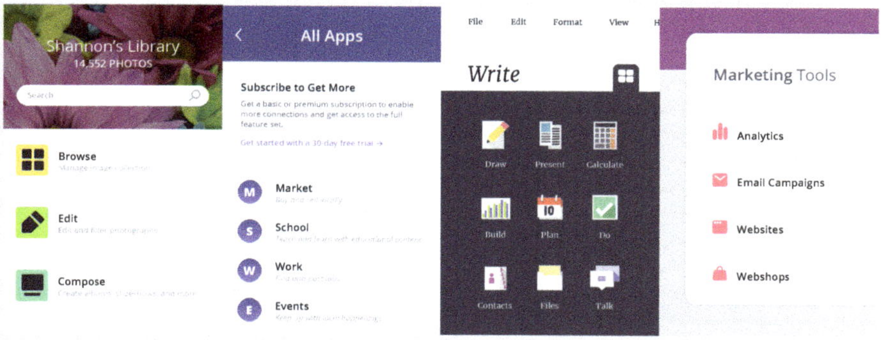

Previews in Navigation

Previews of information appear in lists of content, guiding the user's eye to the items that matter most.

DevPlaats (web), Weathere (iOS app), Health Daily (iOS app), Budgetary (iOS app)
January 2020

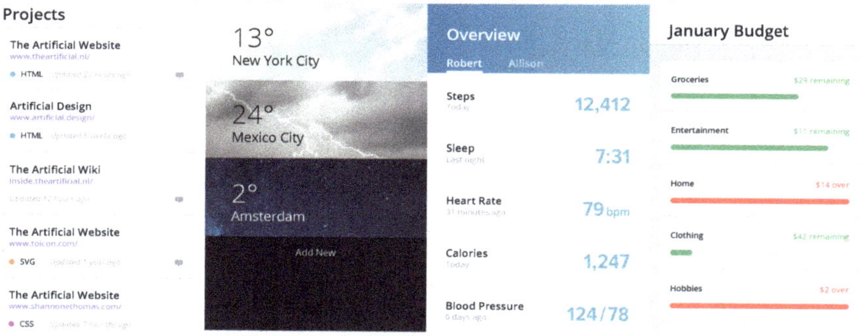

Out-of-the-Way Navigation

Navigation can be minimized or moved so that it's out of the way and not distracting from whatever's on the canvas.

HuisVinder (Mac OS), Make Suite (Mac OS), Tiger Management (web), CCalendar (web)
January 2020

Action Buttons

A single button is used for adding many types of information.

Imposter (web), CirclePlace (web), Ducky Calendar (web), Me Measure (web)
January 2020

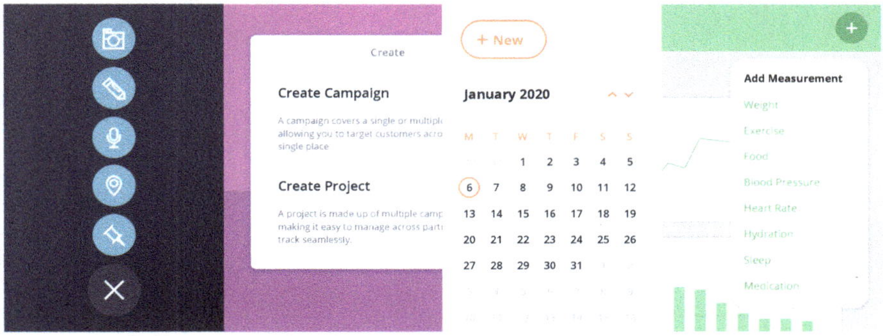

Positives and Negatives Highlighted

Color guides the eye to positive and negative trends and outliers across all visualizations.

Health Daily (app), Chirp Chirp (web), Million (web), FSI Pro (web)
January 2020

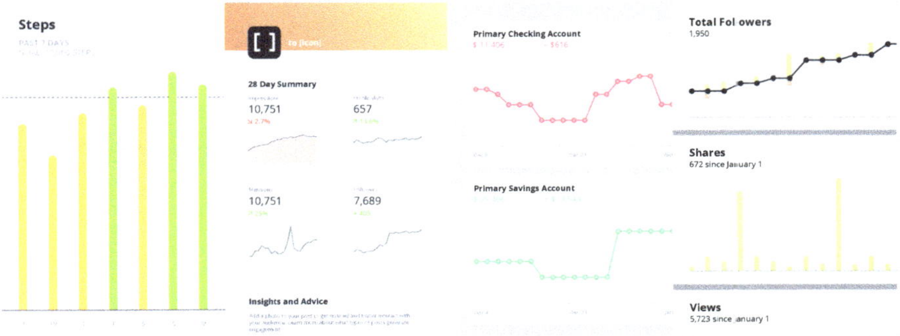

Weekly Email Updates

Weekly updates ensure that users don't go too long without checking in on status. Emails contain a combination of data, insights, and inspiration.

MiSyte Analytics (email), Going Dutch (email), Zorging (email), WriteWell (email)
January 2020

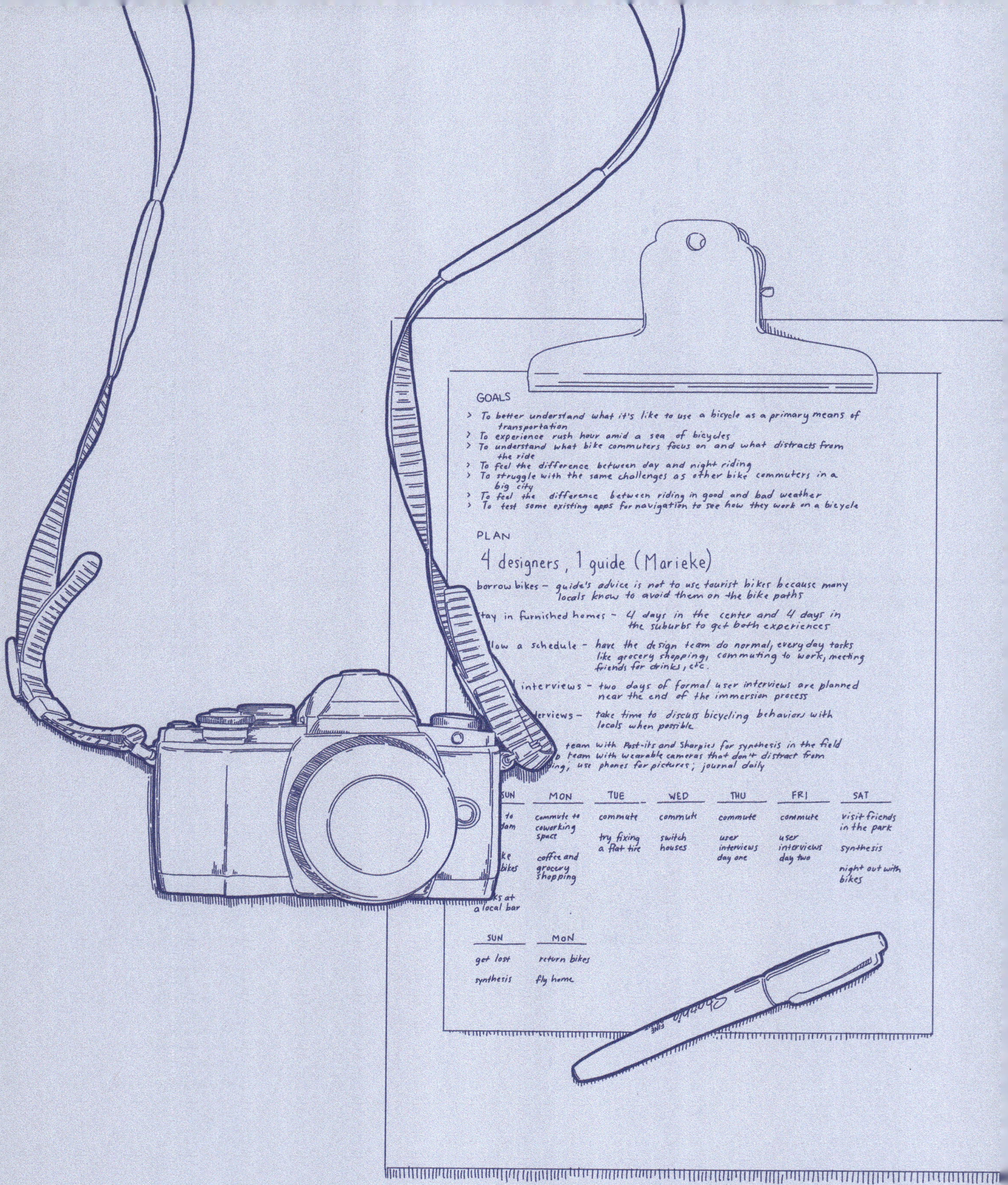

GOALS
› To better understand what it's like to use a bicycle as a primary means of transportation
› To experience rush hour amid a sea of bicycles
› To understand what bike commuters focus on and what distracts from the ride
› To feel the difference between day and night riding
› To struggle with the same challenges as other bike commuters in a big city
› To feel the difference between riding in good and bad weather
› To test some existing apps for navigation to see how they work on a bicycle
PLAN
4 designers, 1 guide (Marieke)
borrow bikes – guide's advice is not to use tourist bikes because many locals know to avoid them on the bike paths
in furnished homes – 4 days in the center and 4 days in the suburbs to get both experiences
a schedule – have the design team do normal, everyday tasks like grocery shopping, commuting to work, meeting friends for drinks, etc.
interviews – two days of formal user interviews are planned near the end of the immersion process
take time to discuss bicycling behaviors with locals when possible
team with Post-its and Sharpies for synthesis in the field
team with wearable cameras that don't distract from
use phones for pictures; journal daily
MON
commute to coworking space
coffee and grocery shopping
TUE
commute
try fixing a flat tire
WED
commute
switch houses
THU
commute
user interviews day one
FRI
commute
user interviews day two
SAT
visit friends in the park
synthesis
night out with bikes
a local bar
SUN
get lost
synthesis
MON
return bikes
fly home

Immersion

Designing for a different culture or market is always a challenge. Immersion is a useful research method that can help a team more thoroughly understand the context of users in unfamiliar situations by having team members experience those contexts firsthand. Immersion is most useful when creating products for unfamiliar cultures, professions, or experiences, and it is most influential when the same people who are designing the product or service are immersed in the foreign experience. In addition or as an alternative to immersion, you might bring designers native to a given context into the team. This ensures a deeper understanding than can be gathered from just a week or two in the field.

While it's most commonly done at the beginning of a project, immersion can be useful throughout the design process. As a design team moves from the discover phase into the define and, later, refine phases, immersion can be used to seek answers to more specific questions and to inform potential solutions. So, as a team continues to engage with users through participatory design and user validation, it makes sense to also continue engaging with their context.

Activities

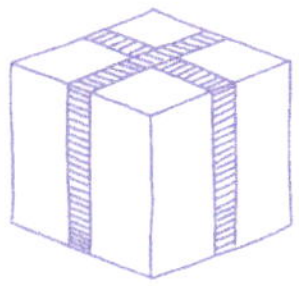

Bring a small gift from your culture as a way to break the ice.

The point of immersion is to understand an unfamiliar situation by experiencing that context, and so it's imperative that the designers of a product or service are the ones participating in immersion. Outsourcing this activity to a team of researchers who provide summary feedback may help designers make better decisions, but it won't help them intrinsically understand the people and contexts they're designing for.

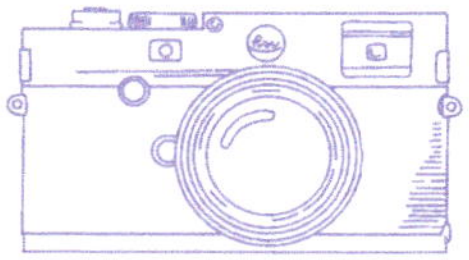

Take a lot of photos, but not at the expense of the experience.

There are certain barriers to experiencing an unfamiliar culture. Language and customs can be more than intimidating; they can prevent teams from getting any meaningful understanding out of an immersive experience. Whether you're discovering the intricacies of life as a trader on the floor of the New York Stock Exchange or learning about education systems in Bangladesh, finding a local guide or guides you can trust is key. Guides will help you with everything from understanding the language to finding the local spots to eat and drink.

As much as possible, live as your users live.

With a good guide, immersion is equal parts planning and spontaneity. Some planned activities you might try include visiting a user's home or workplace, accompanying a user through a relevant experience, or simulating a day in the life of your user.

Home visits are useful for understanding how people of a different culture or lifestyle live. Visiting a person's home can help you understand a person's day, the dynamics of the interactions between different people in the home, and the priorities of the individuals who dwell there. Home visits usually include observing these details, as well as interviewing the participant. If you're doing cultural immersion, you might even consider living with a host family instead of lodging in a hotel.

Workplace visits offer similar opportunities for observation as home visits. You'll be able to understand the type of environment a participant spends their day in, whom they engage with and how, and what sorts of tools they need for their trade.

You may interview the participant in their workplace, observe them as they do their work, or even join alongside to experience a day in their job.

Accompanying your user through an experience can help provide insight into struggles and delights that might not naturally come up in an interview setting. Going shopping with your participant might provide insight into their decision-making process, traveling with your participant might reveal new pain points, or sharing a workout with your user might highlight surprising behaviors.

Without needing to recruit participants, you might learn by re-creating a day in the life of your user. Eat, sleep, shop, dress, and commute as your users might. Observe your own behaviors as well as the behaviors of those around you. What do you interact with in a day? How do others react to you? What's normal and what's not normal?

Here are a few tips to ensure you get the most immersive experience:

* Make sure to treat your participants as fellow humans rather than research subjects. If you're researching a different culture, consider bringing something from your own culture as a gift to break the ice.

* Take a lot of photos, but don't let yourself experience everything from behind the lens. Cameras can be obtrusive when you're interacting with other humans in both interviews and on the streets. See how people's reactions change when you're not capturing every single moment.

* Plan your travel so that you can experience how people live. For example, stay in a five-star hotel with a personal driver only if you're researching that type of user.

* Respect the culture. It's unlikely that you'll learn how people behave naturally if you're acting out of place. Finding the boundaries between normal and not normal can be educational.

Remember that your presence might affect the behavior of people and users you're observing.

* Plan for your safety. Structure immersion activities for learning without putting yourself or your team in high-risk situations. Sometimes this might mean taking a guided tour instead of wandering off on your own or using a simulated experience rather than an actual one.

* Understand that your presence affects the behavior of those around you. As you formulate opinions about a context, consider the effect you have upon it.

> *"There's a whole load of stuff in life that is worth documenting. You see it every day but don't even notice."*
>
> **Jan Chipchase**

Artifacts

The purpose of immersion is not to create an artifact but rather to establish a foundational understanding that provides a better context for decision-making around the product or service. It's important to help team members and stakeholders who weren't a part of immersion get a taste of that foundational understanding.

Start by synthesizing observations from the field into a series of insights. Curate the list to those that are most relevant to the project, considering which are most likely to affect design decisions down the road. Work together with the team and with local experts to confirm your understanding and refine insights into something actionable for later phases of work.

While a list of insights might communicate important decision-making factors, communicating the actual experience is much more difficult. Photography and video are helpful tools in distilling an experience into something that stakeholders can see and feel with little effort. Consider making a short slideshow or video to accompany your insights and stories from the field.

Immersion for CityBike covers ten days of getting to know one of the busiest bicycling cities in the world—Amsterdam. Insights cover experiencing bicycling in both known and unknown terrain.

Immersion

Approach

We bicycled on the world's busiest bike paths in Amsterdam. We also ferried, parked, got lost, and talked to the locals along the way.

Insights

The busier the cycle path, the harder it is to stop to look up directions.

Getting distracted, even for a moment, can result in chaos.

Easy access to the bell is a must.

It's hard to find a parking spot for your bike and easy to lose it in the sea of other bicycles.

Almost everyone has had a bike stolen.

Even in bad weather, everyone cycles.

Biking is the default form of transportation, and you can find people of all ages on bikes.

Using a phone while riding isn't only frowned upon—it's illegal.

Navigation rarely provides instruction with enough foresight for a rider to react.

Sometimes understanding where you are in relation to where you're going is better than having navigation.

Opportunities

Provide on-bike displays that provide information without requiring interaction while riding.

Provide the rider with confidence that they'll always be able to find their bike, even when it's stolen.

Provide the rider with what they need to know to be prepared for the journey ahead.

Support both the native who knows where they're going and the visitor who needs more help getting to their destination.

Balance showing the rider what's most relevant in the moment with the big picture.

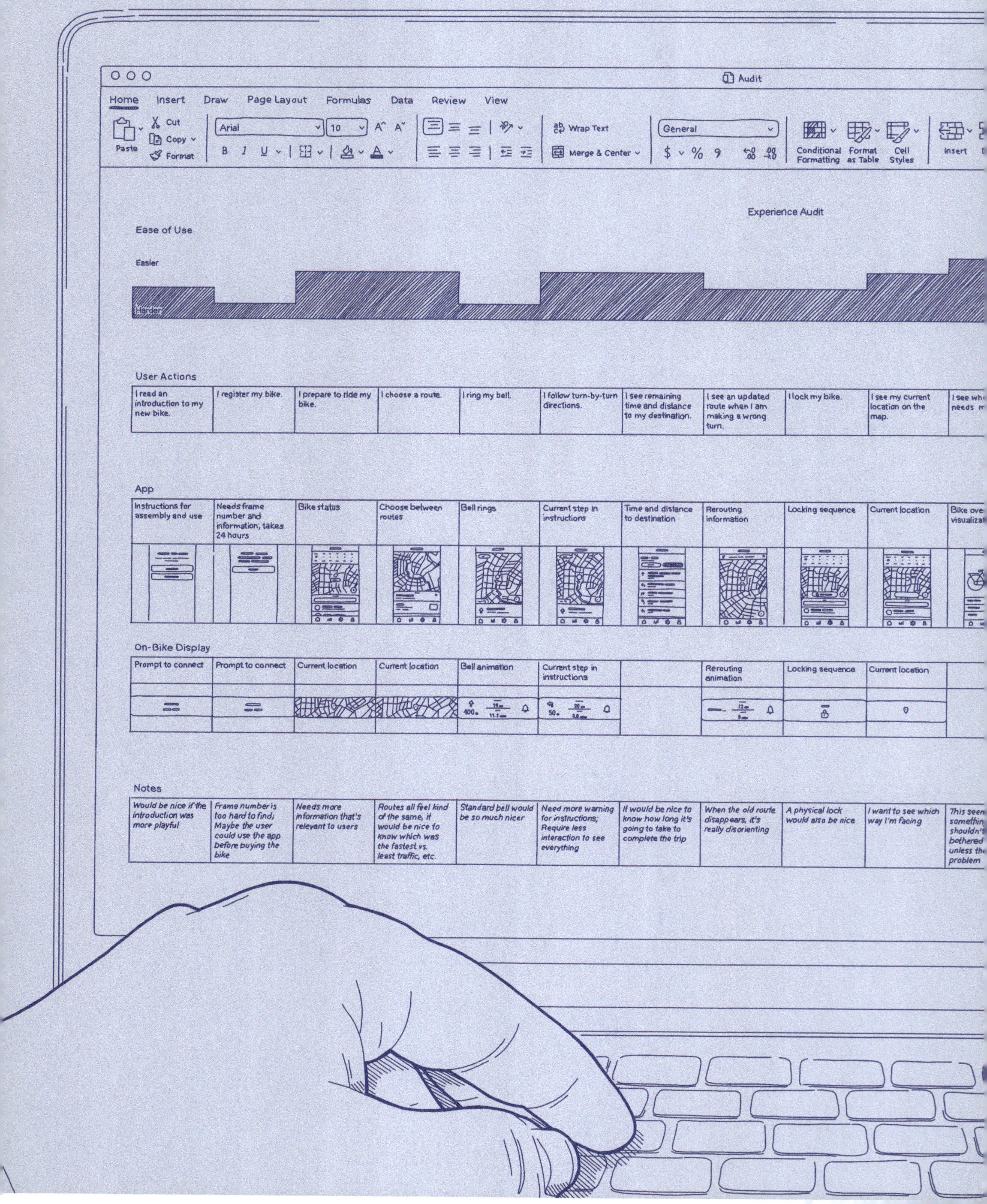
Audit
Home
Insert
Draw
Page Layout
Formulas
Data
Review
View
Paste
Cut
Copy
Format
Arial
10
Wrap Text
Merge & Center
General
Conditional Formatting
Format as Table
Cell Styles
Insert
Experience Audit
Ease of Use
Easier
Harder
User Actions
I read an introduction to my new bike.
I register my bike.
I prepare to ride my bike.
I choose a route.
I ring my bell.
I follow turn-by-turn directions.
I see remaining time and distance to my destination.
I see an updated route when I am making a wrong turn.
I lock my bike.
I see my current location on the map.
App
Instructions for assembly and use
Needs frame number and information; takes 24 hours
Bike status
Choose between routes
Bell rings
Current step in instructions
Time and distance to destination
Rerouting information
Locking sequence
Current location
On-Bike Display
Prompt to connect
Prompt to connect
Current location
Current location
Bell animation
Current step in instructions
Rerouting animation
Locking sequence
Current location
Notes
Would be nice if the introduction was more playful
Frame number is too hard to find; Maybe the user could use the app before buying the bike
Needs more information that's relevant to users
Routes all feel kind of the same, it would be nice to know which was the fastest vs. least traffic, etc.
Standard bell would be so much nicer
Need more warning for instructions; Require less interaction to see everything
It would be nice to know how long it's going to take to complete the trip
When the old route disappears, it's really disorienting
A physical lock would also be nice
I want to see which way I'm facing

Experience Audit

Not all experience-design projects focus on new experiences. Often, experience designers are enlisted in improving an existing experience or determining how multiple experiences might integrate into one. Other projects might be fast-follower experiences seeking to disrupt the front-runner in the field. In any of these situations, an experience audit can be helpful to dissect and analyze the existing experience.

An experience audit is a systemic way of analyzing experiences with the purpose of uncovering opportunities for improvement. For fast-follower or redesign projects, the audit can establish a baseline experience or minimum-requirement set. Input from a competitive analysis and feedback from user validation can further support opportunities, while concept generation can use outputs as prompts for generating possible solutions.

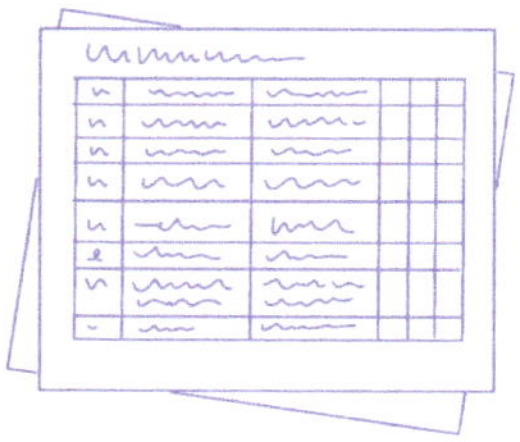

Start by reading existing documentation.

Experience audits are based on the heuristic evaluation, a methodology established in the software world by Jakob Nielsen. While they can be informal in practice, heuristic evaluations aim to quantify feedback through numeric ratings on specific chunks of functionality, often use cases. In order to more consistently quantify an experience, many differing sets of criteria have been established—including those by Jakob Nielsen. Because most of these criteria are heavily aimed at software experiences, they require a bit of evolution to also be relevant more broadly across experiences.

Collecting Data

When executing a heuristic evaluation, it's likely that you'll have questions about how specific pieces of the interface perform. If you're working on a new product or if your team doesn't already have analytics in place, consider making requests for them to be in place for future iterations.

Activities

Experience audits can be as simple as a heuristic evaluation and can expand to include layers of analytics and sales figures where the data is available. Experience audits might also make use of user validation to ensure the output isn't just the opinion of a single auditor. Working together, these layers help to create a holistic picture about where an existing experience is succeeding or has room for improvement.

Beginning a heuristic evaluation of an already-established product or service can be daunting. Start by skimming any existing documentation, from technical artifacts, like user stories, to design artifacts, like experience journeys and key scenarios, to better understand the experience's purpose and context. If you don't have original documentation, consider creating a lightweight experience journey or key scenarios to provide a framework for the experience.

Once you have the user's goals or experience in a linear form, you're ready to evaluate. Here are nine questions to get you started. Not all of these metrics will apply to all products, and there may be additional brand- or experience-specific metrics that are important to include in your audit. As you evaluate, consider when your experience is at its best for each metric as well as when it's at its worst.

Does the experience prepare the user? Does the experience provide the user with what they need to know to use the product or service? Are the user's expectations appropriately set? The experience should provide the user with everything they need to understand the product or service and use it successfully.

Is the experience predictable? Does the user encounter the experience in a form and place that they expect? Is the experience easy to understand based on what the user already knows? The experience should be in a form the user expects and/or it should exist within touchpoints the user is comfortable with. When it comes to metaphors, the experience should use those the user is already familiar with.

Is the experience consistent? Does the user engage with similar elements similarly? Is the user experience cohesive over time? The experience should look and behave consistently. Similar controls should have similar functions, and aesthetic cues should be used to convey similar meanings.

Is the experience efficient? Does each moment of the experience appropriately focus the user? Can the user accomplish their goals with minimal effort? The user should be able to find what they need in the experience without searching or wading through irrelevant information. They should be able to accomplish their goals with a reasonable amount of effort and within an expected time frame.

Does the experience react to the user? Does the experience provide appropriate feedback? Does the feedback provided help the user better understand their actions? Experiences should be responsive, providing the user with positive and negative feedback so that they understand what consequences their actions have.

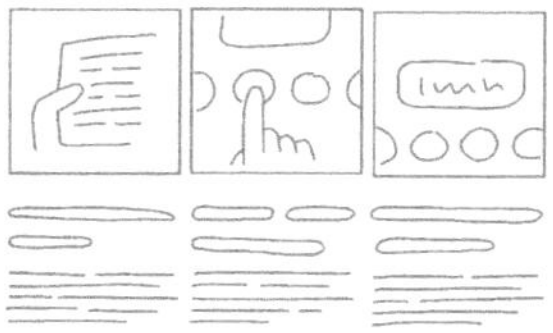

Photograph or take screenshots of the experience to show what's happening.

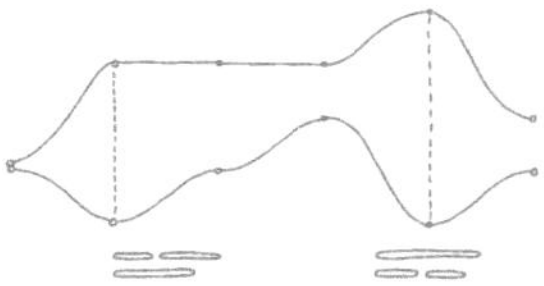

An experience journey can highlight differences between the actual and desired experiences.

Does the experience put the user in control? Does the user feel in control of their experience? Does the user get trapped in flows they cannot escape? The user should feel confident in the consequences their actions will have, just as they should feel confident in their ability to reverse or modify an action. In social experiences, the user should feel in control of their persona.

Does the experience support the user? Does the experience avoid creating situations where the user will likely fail? Does the experience fail gracefully? The experience should guide the user down a positive path and should support the user when errors do occur.

Does the experience support different types of users? Does the experience meet the various necessary cultural expectations? Does the experience accommodate a variety of user needs? Does the experience scale to accommodate different users' attention levels? The experience should provide appropriate experiences to the different cultures within the target market; it should scale to accommodate users with various accessibility needs; and it should meet the needs of both occasional and superusers.

Does the experience leave the user with an appropriate emotion? Does the experience leave the user with the desired emotion? Not all products are delightful, and not all services are fulfilling. Determine what emotion is appropriate throughout the experience, and consider how well the experience is delivering.

Artifacts

The most important outputs of an experience audit are the opportunities that were identified and, if applicable, the definition of the baseline experience. While the baseline experience might be presented as a list of required features, opportunities should be curated or prioritized so that the company can focus its efforts where they'll have the greatest effect.

It's also helpful to present the context of opportunities. Consider capturing in photos, screenshots, or text the different states of the user's engagement with the product or service. What is the user trying to achieve, and with what or whom are they interacting? Show the actual experience alongside the analysis of it.

Add layers of data to support your findings. Engagement analytics and sales figures can help convince skeptical stakeholders and can lead to better informed solutions in future phases.

Opportunities might be presented on their own, or they might be highlighted within the context of another artifact. For example, the experience journey can be an effective format for showing the current experience or capturing a baseline experience, while also highlighting opportunities within the same context. Personas might also be used to highlight how opportunities will affect specific users. If opportunities from the heuristic evaluation are used to generate concepts, the best concepts might be presented within the experience audit to provide more concrete examples of how opportunities might be addressed within the product or service.

CityBike's experience audit takes the experience journey and maps its strengths and weaknesses. Opportunities for improvement are called out as they relate to the journey, while specific areas for improvement are called out below.

Experience Audit

Opportunity Areas

Use the introductory experience to establish the brand and voice of CityBike.

Use the nonriding state to provide relevant information.

Use the on-bike display for information over interaction while the bike is in motion.

Ease of Use

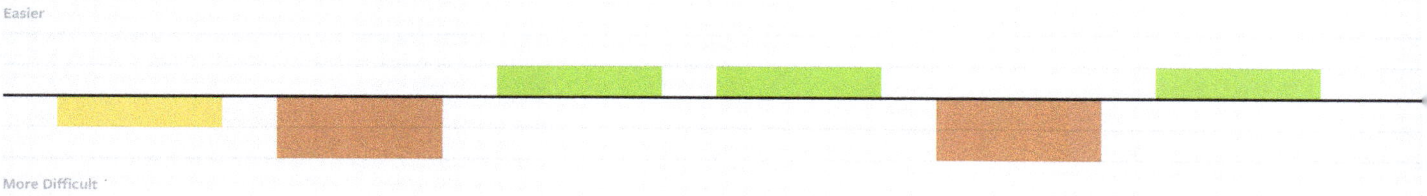

User Actions

First Use I read an introduction to my new bike.	**First Use** I register my bike.	**Preparation** I prepare to ride my bike.	**Preparation** I choose a route.	**Riding** I ring my bell.	**Routing** I follow turn-by-turn directions.
App					
Shows instructions for assembly and use	Requires frame number and personal information; takes up to twenty-four hours	Shows the current status of the bike	Shows three route options to choose between	Rings electronic bell	Shows current step in instructions
On-Bike Display					
Shows a prompt to connect	Shows a prompt to connect	Shows current location	Shows current location	Shows bell animation	Shows current step in instructions
Actions for Improvement					
- Provide a more playful introduction	- Make frame number easier to find - Allow user to use app functions before registration is verified	- Add additional information, like weather, rain predictions, etc.	- Make distinctions between routes (i.e., fastest, scenic, etc.)	- Replace digital interface with a standard bell	- Show current position in overall journey - Show upcoming direction

Keep the user informed of the present while also peeking into the future.

Show the user where they're going and where they've been (even without navigation).

Use statistics to celebrate rather than as competitive fodder.

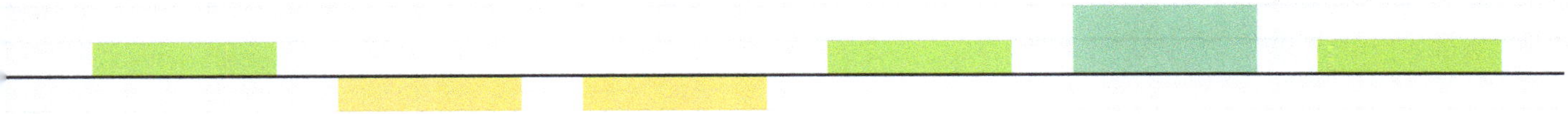

Routing I see remaining time and distance to my destination.	**Routing** I see an updated route when I make a wrong turn.	**Locking** I lock my bike.	**Mapping** I see my current location on the map.	**Maintenance** I see when my bike needs maintenance.	**Statistics** I review all of my rides.
Shows time and distance to destination	Shows rerouting animation, followed by a new route recommendation	Shows instructions for assembly and use	Shows current location on a map	Shows all parts of the bike so I can review wear and tear	Shows ride data for past rides
	Shows rerouting animation, followed by a new route recommendation	Shows the locking sequence	Shows current location on a map		
- Show time and distance to destination on the on-bike display	- Continue showing old route until new route is determined	- Provide a conventional locking mechanism as well	- Add orientation - Add route taken this ride	- Notifications	- Aggregated statistics - Show interesting outlier statistics - Celebrate achievements

Define

The define phase of work takes what was discovered in the previous phase and synthesizes it into artifacts that will affect design decisions. Output from user interviews, business analysis, and immersion might become personas, while expert interviews and competitive analysis could feed directly into concept generation and then into feature definition. By the end of the define phase, observations should be synthesized into artifacts that guide decisions, answering the high-level questions like *What are we designing?* as well as *Why are we designing it?*

The define phase aims to dispel ambiguity and therefore needs to focus not only on the activities around synthesizing information but also on the artifacts that communicate decisions and priority. Despite a heavy focus on synthesis, the define phase is not entirely reductive. For example, activities like concept generation explore the many possible ways that a design team might deliver on the problems uncovered for users in the situations that have been prioritized.

Because the artifacts of the define phase have so much influence over the later design, it's important to create them in formats that are easy to share and impossible to ignore. For this reason, the define phase is not only useful for getting to know your team and their opinions but also for starting to prototype your way of working.

If you start a project after the define phase has already occurred, make sure you understand not only the decisions that were made but also why they were made. It's likely that some conclusions reached in the define phase are stronger than others, and when the design inevitably evolves and challenges those conclusions, you'll need to know which ones are worth redefining.

In This Section:

Personas

Conceptual Model

Concept Generation

Feature Definition

Experience Principles

Offering Map

Experience Journey

Key Scenarios

Strategic Roadmap

Participatory Design

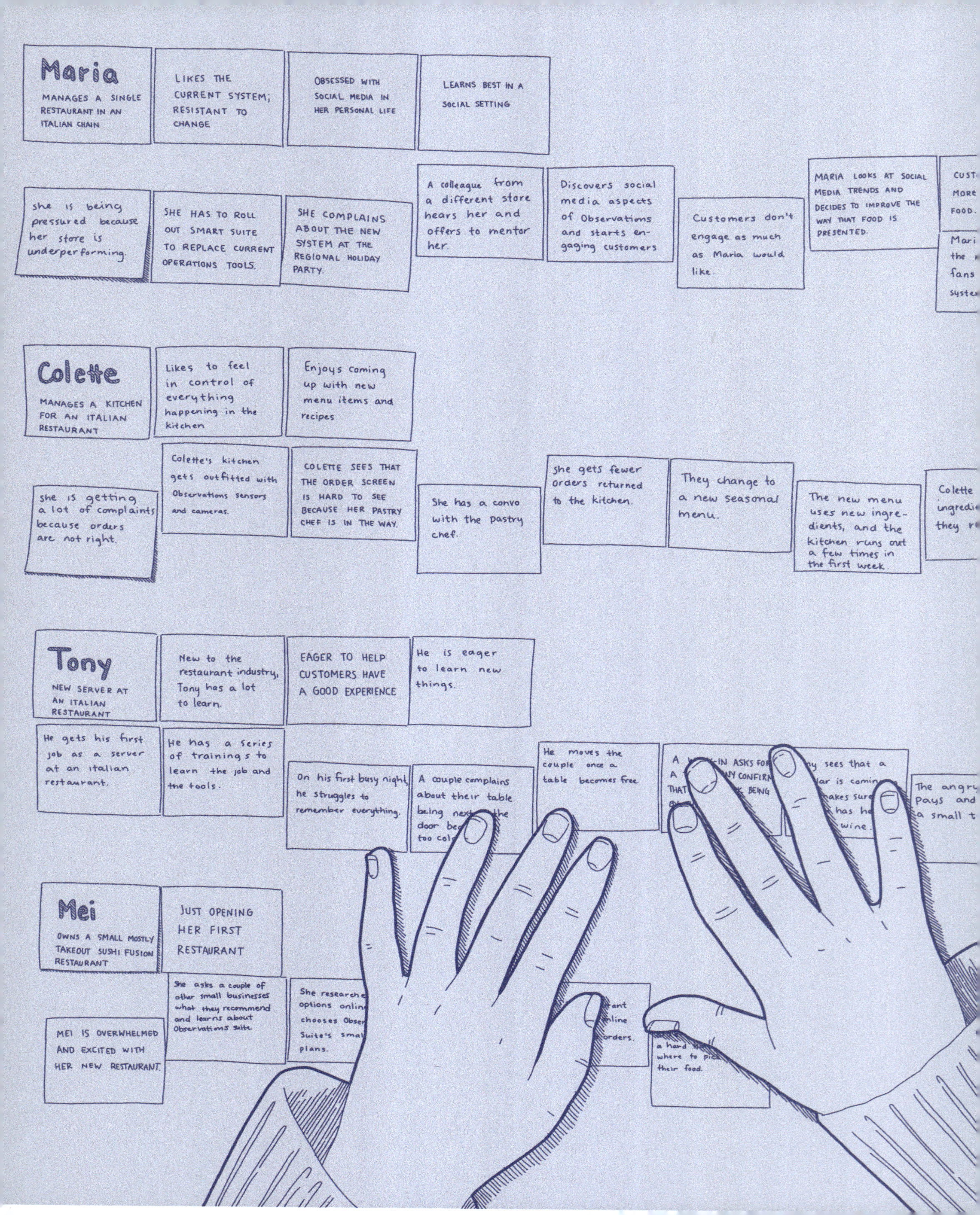
Maria
MANAGES A SINGLE RESTAURANT IN AN ITALIAN CHAIN
LIKES THE CURRENT SYSTEM; RESISTANT TO CHANGE
OBSESSED WITH SOCIAL MEDIA IN HER PERSONAL LIFE
LEARNS BEST IN A SOCIAL SETTING
She is being pressured because her store is underperforming.
SHE HAS TO ROLL OUT SMART SUITE TO REPLACE CURRENT OPERATIONS TOOLS.
SHE COMPLAINS ABOUT THE NEW SYSTEM AT THE REGIONAL HOLIDAY PARTY.
A colleague from a different store hears her and offers to mentor her.
Discovers social media aspects of Observations and starts engaging customers
Customers don't engage as much as Maria would like.
MARIA LOOKS AT SOCIAL MEDIA TRENDS AND DECIDES TO IMPROVE THE WAY THAT FOOD IS PRESENTED.
Colette
MANAGES A KITCHEN FOR AN ITALIAN RESTAURANT
Likes to feel in control of everything happening in the kitchen
Enjoys coming up with new menu items and recipes
She is getting a lot of complaints because orders are not right.
Colette's kitchen gets outfitted with Observations sensors and cameras.
COLETTE SEES THAT THE ORDER SCREEN IS HARD TO SEE BECAUSE HER PASTRY CHEF IS IN THE WAY.
She has a convo with the pastry chef.
She gets fewer orders returned to the kitchen.
They change to a new seasonal menu.
The new menu uses new ingredients, and the kitchen runs out a few times in the first week.
Tony
NEW SERVER AT AN ITALIAN RESTAURANT
New to the restaurant industry, Tony has a lot to learn.
EAGER TO HELP CUSTOMERS HAVE A GOOD EXPERIENCE
He is eager to learn new things.
He gets his first job as a server at an italian restaurant.
He has a series of trainings to learn the job and the tools.
On his first busy night he struggles to remember everything.
He moves the couple once a table becomes free
Mei
OWNS A SMALL MOSTLY TAKEOUT SUSHI FUSION RESTAURANT
JUST OPENING HER FIRST RESTAURANT
She asks a couple of other small businesses what they recommend and learns about Observations Suite.
MEI IS OVERWHELMED AND EXCITED WITH HER NEW RESTAURANT.

Personas

Personas help teams have empathy for users by creating a common understanding around what motivates a user's decisions. Created after discovery-phase activities like user interviews and immersion, personas embody what is known about the target user or users. The design team synthesizes user insights and information into characters that are both more easily referenced and more human.

When creating personas, it's important to understand what's important to users as well as what will resonate with the members of a varied team. A strong persona will help a business-oriented team member understand what factors a user takes into account when purchasing a product, just as it will guide a development-oriented team member to understand what makes the user prefer one feature over others. Most importantly, a persona helps guide design decisions away from a single designer's or stakeholder's opinion and toward user needs.

If you're designing for yourself or tackling a more strategic project that doesn't need to specify end users, you can safely forgo personas. If your project doesn't have time for personas, user-validation feedback and market segments can also provide support when making decisions and rationalizing designs.

Try keeping a diary from a day in the life of the persona.

Role-play scenarios, using personas as characters.

Create a moodboard that captures the persona's preferences and context.

Personas were introduced to the software industry in 1998 by Alan Cooper's book *The Inmates Are Running the Asylum*. He'd been using them long before he wrote about them, though, observing his target audience and then describing and even acting out what he anticipated they might need from the software he was creating.

The Cooper persona took off in the tech industry and beyond, evolving through various applications. Many of these evolutions forgot the original raison d'être of personas, though, focusing instead on demographic-focused character development and stereotypes. As a result, personas have become a polarizing artifact among many UX designers, despite their obvious usefulness.

Activities

To arrive at strong and diverse personas, it's helpful to generate more content than you need and then to reduce it to the strongest personas and the most influential formats.

Start by getting to know your users. If the product is already on the market, gather demographic information to understand the existing user base. Does the existing user base skew more male or female? Is there an age range that prefers your product over the competition? Does the product appeal only to specific income brackets? If your product or service is not on the market, look at competitors' users. These demographics serve as a base for the personas, providing basic information about users; however, personas need to go a step further to capture and communicate motivations.

Once you know who your users or potential users are, seek to understand more about their situations and motivations. User interviews and participatory design can be used to gather this type of input. If it's not possible to reach out to users directly, try to learn more via relevant product reviews, online forums, and friends and family research. It can also be helpful to use competitors' products so that you can better empathize with users; however, make a conscious effort to ensure that personas don't end up reflecting only your experiences.

Whether working with users or with your own experience, try asking these questions:

* What is the user's environment, and how does it make them feel?
* What experiences does the user have with the topic?
* Who influences them (on and off topic)?

From this you can start to imagine what a day in the life of a persona might be like. What's the first thing they do when they wake up? What do they do when they're overwhelmed? Whom do they call when they need advice? What keeps them up at night? As personas start to develop personalities, you can think of them as people you might meet on the street. To get deeper into the mind of your persona, try these activities:

* writing about a day in the life of a persona
* keeping a diary from a persona's perspective
* role-playing scenes where you and your team are the personas
* drawing a personal experience journey for a persona
* creating a moodboard for a persona's home or lifestyle
* capturing the products or apps a persona uses

A product or service often has a wide base of users, and a single persona is rarely enough to capture them all. With such nuanced characters, it may be tempting to create many personas; however, it's important that each persona is unique and memorable. For most experiences, somewhere between three and eight personas is ideal. The more personas you have, the more important it is to prioritize which personas' needs are most important.

Getting full coverage with unique personas can be a challenge. If a market segmentation exists, it's likely that the personas will need to be mapped to the distinct segments to ensure full coverage. Without market segments, it's still easy to ensure coverage by creating a matrix of user types. What are the most important traits that vary between your users? This could be as generic as age, gender, or income or more specific like level of engagement or tech savviness. Once you've chosen criteria, make sure you've represented users of the most important types.

When working on multiple personas, it's important to develop them all at the same time so that none feels more finished or thoughtful than the others. Continuously compare personas to ensure they maintain what makes them unique while also making sure that each persona's execution answers the same questions essential to your design challenge.

While personas can vary as much as actual humans, there are a few types of personas that should be avoided:

* Avoid creating personas after celebrities or famous characters. The baggage of these characters will overwhelm and distract from the aspects that make the persona both unique and relevant.

* Avoid describing personas in terms of their demographics only. Understanding why a user makes decisions requires knowing more than the details on their driver's license.

* Avoid stereotypes like "the know-it-all" or "the fashionista." Aside from being

Market Segmentation

Market segmentation or customer segmentation is often referred to interchangeably with personas. Market segmentations group users into clusters based on similar traits, providing a summary of traits and patterns rather than specific and nuanced motivations. The easiest way to differentiate between a market segment and a persona is to look for a name. Market segments typically refer to users with short descriptions like "early adopters," whereas personas will always have a name, such as "Abdul."

easily dismissed, stereotypes often lead to an overgeneralized understanding of user motivations and needs. Try challenging traditional stereotypes by making personas less predictable. Perhaps the executive is a woman and the personal assistant is a man. To keep things realistic, it's helpful to find motivations that are in conflict with each other to capture a level of nuance that stereotypes overlook.

* Avoid creating personas that you could not find more than one of in the wild. Of course a persona is both unique and specific, but personas should also have motivations that match real people. Realistic personas can even be useful for recruiting when you're ready to test your product.

* Avoid seeing yourself in a persona. It risks that you will overlook details of that persona's motivations in favor of your own motivations.

> *"As I walked, I would engage myself in a dialogue, playacting a project manager, loosely based on Kathy, requesting functions and behavior from my program. I often found myself deep in those dialogues, speaking aloud and gesturing with my arms."*
>
> Alan Cooper

Artifacts

Create a tag cloud of relevant words using size and weight to show importance.

Mock up the persona's home screen or make a moodboard showing the physical products they use.

The best personas are those that get used. A well-designed persona is easy to understand, easy to remember, and easy to reference. To achieve this, personas should be formatted in a concise and scannable way. Printing and hanging personas in a visible place can ensure that they're used and referenced when making decisions throughout the duration of the project.

Get started by giving every persona a name, a photo, and a short and memorable summary. Demographic details can help provide a basic understanding of the persona. Details that are discernible from the photo often do not need to be called out explicitly, while other demographic details, like occupation and income, should be called out only if they're relevant to understanding the persona's disposition.

With the basics covered, most of the remaining content of the persona should focus on the user's motivations. There are many ways to communicate motivation, and presentation is important. Finding the right persona format can go a long way toward ensuring the persona is understandable and memorable. Here are a few methods and formats to try creating:

* a list of hopes and fears
* a tag cloud or relevant words
* a series of goals
* a short anecdote
* a short quote or tweet
* a product or service testimonial
* a screenshot of the persona's home screen
* a moodboard of products the persona uses
* photos of the user's home or office

When choosing how to present motivations, consider both the persona and your audience. While anecdotes might be effective with a design team, your persona's motivations might be more memorable to marketing managers when expressed through quotes and apps the persona uses.

It's likely that your personas will need to live on beyond a single project or product. With each new design challenge, you'll want to adjust your persona a bit to the new context. Throughout their evolution, keep the personas' motivations consistent. You might add depth to motivations, but if you find yourself wanting to shift them entirely, it's probably time to create a new persona.

The four personas for Ambience Mirror represent a broad base of potential users while all being a part of the same family. Because the product exists in a shared space, the four personas will all engage with the same Ambience Mirror at some point in their day.

The personas for Observations Suite are all business oriented, though each has their own role, goals, and experiences. The documentation captures this in text, illustration, and individual experience journeys.

Personas

The Walkers are a family of four living in San Jose, California. They're all generally healthy, and the entire family is tech savvy. They have a small house with two bathrooms and two Ambience Mirrors. They also have Ambience scales, as well as several personal devices.

Kyle

45, Creative Writing Professor

Kyle was recently diagnosed with diabetes and has been much more health conscious as a result. His new healthy lifestyle includes running in the morning and tracking his diet to make sure he doesn't have too many glasses of wine. His recent sabbatical gave him time to finish his third novel and do a small book tour.

Relevant Concerns

- Maintaining his health, especially his glucose levels
- Keeping up with his audience on Twitter
- Checking the weather and air quality before he runs

Devices

- Apple Watch
- iPhone
- Ambience sleep monitor

Allison

49, Medical Informatician

Allison's career is demanding, as she balances research with meetings and guest lectures. She tries to keep the stress of her job in check but doesn't always find the time. Allison often learns about new health tech before it hits the mainstream, and she has experimented and given up on many devices meant to manage her health and stress.

Relevant Concerns

- Managing her stress and general health
- Mentally preparing for the day
- Helping her family stay healthy

Devices

- Apple Watch
- iPhone
- Ambience sleep monitor

Olivia

21, Biology Major at UC Berkeley

Olivia is in her third year of studies at UC Berkeley. She lives at home with her family and enjoys helping her little sister with her science and math homework. She spends a lot of time with her on-again, off-again boyfriend, and on weekends she goes out with her friends.

Relevant Concerns

- Keeping her private life away from her family
- Staying well
- Getting ready to go out

Devices

- iPhone
- Ambience thermometer
- Ambience pedometer

Evie

13, Middle School Student

Evie likes school, especially English, gym, and choir. She recently started caring about fashion and makeup and begs her parents for money so she can go to the mall with her friends. She is on the track team and will go for runs with her dad when she wakes up early enough.

Relevant Concerns

- Keeping up with her friends on social media
- Taking care of her skin
- Remembering when she has tests

Devices

- iPhone

Personas

Persona Types

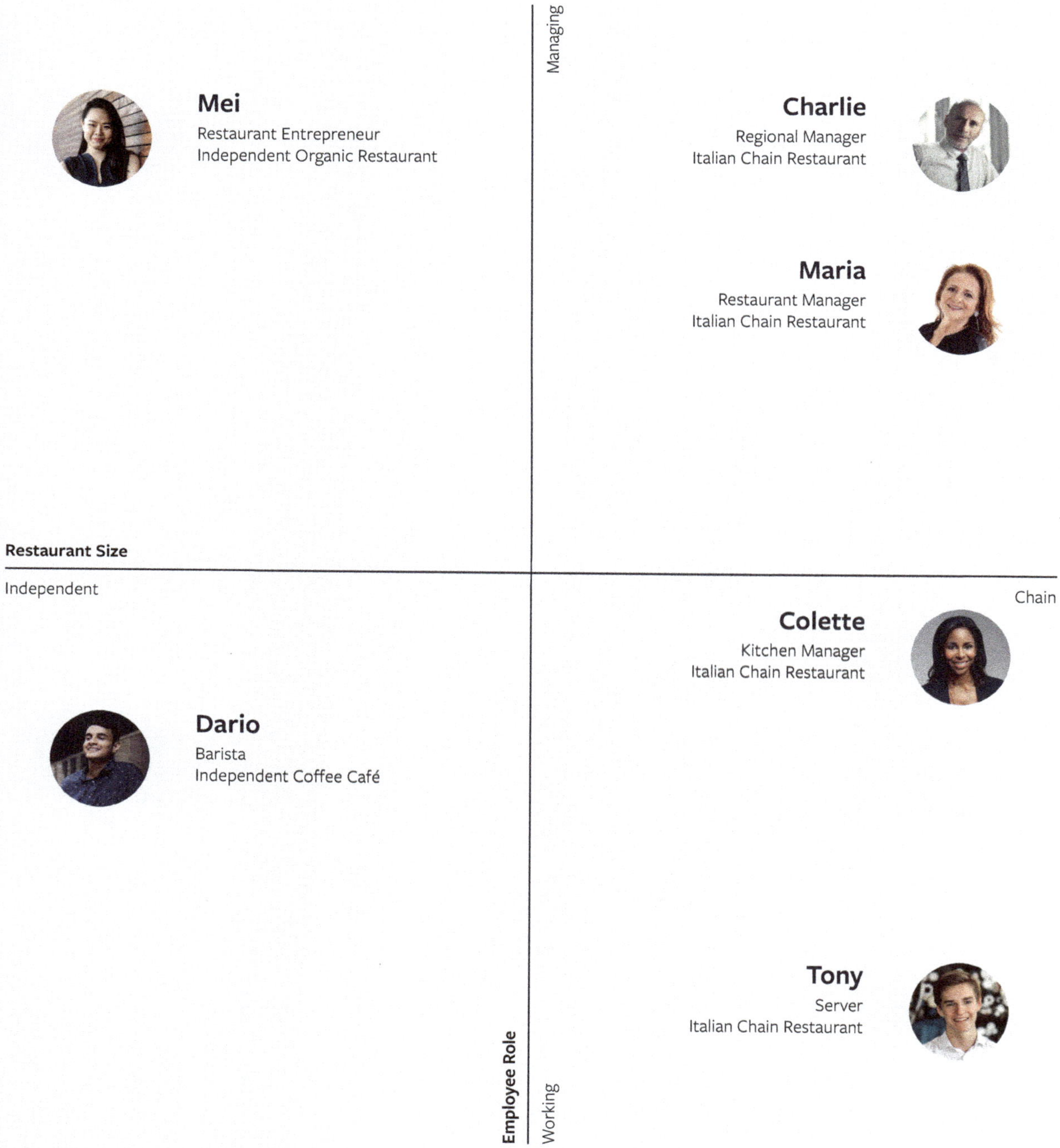

Mei

Restaurant Entrepreneur, Independent Organic Restaurant

> *"I know that a lot of people want food fast and on a budget, but that doesn't mean that it needs to be unhealthy. I provide my customers with great food based on natural ingredients and flavors from the many places I've lived and traveled."*

Motivations

- to provide people with healthy, tasty food that's fast
- to find the simplest business solutions so she can focus on her passion—the food

Journey

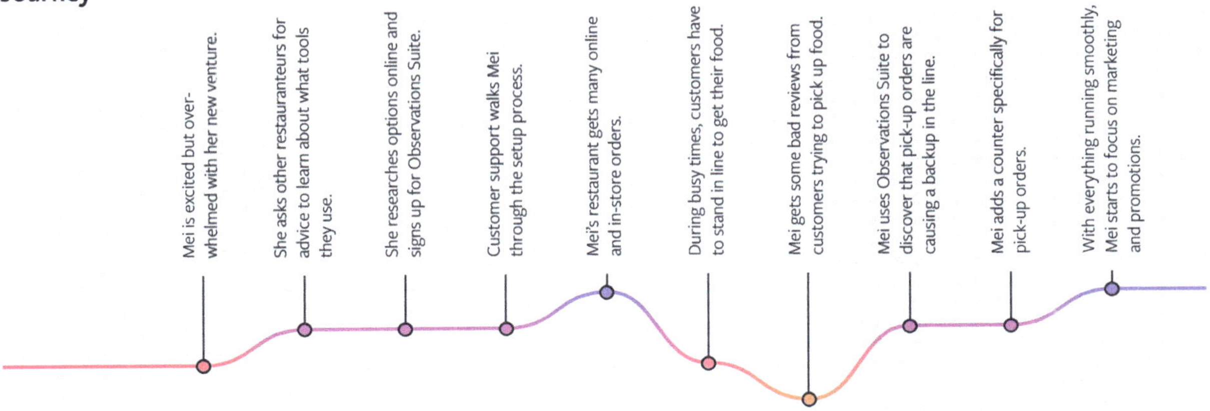

Dario

Barista, Independent Coffee Café

> *"I'm naturally a very social person, so working as a barista is the perfect job for me. It's a personal mission to make everyone I meet laugh, or at least crack a smile. I also sell my ceramics in the café, so it gives me an outlet for my art too."*

Motivations

- to make his customers smile, especially those he meets for the first time
- to find ways to be creative at work—from latte art to selling his ceramics

Journey

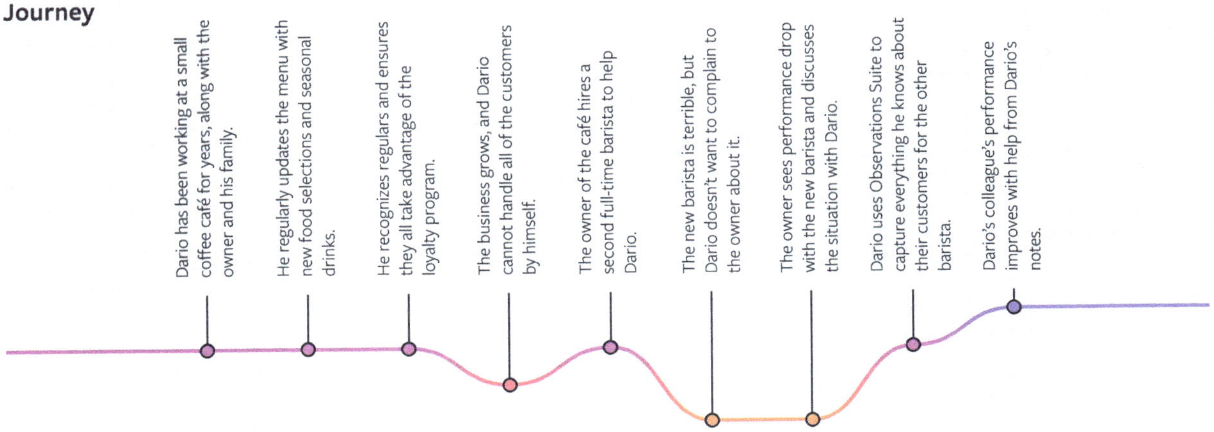

Charlie

Regional Manager, Italian Chain Restaurant

"I've worked very hard to get where I am, and I believe that my ambition will serve the chain well. I am enthusiastic about the role that technology can play in helping us work smarter, not harder."

Motivations

- to impress his boss with better performance numbers
- to be a leader in adopting technology that optimizes the business

Journey

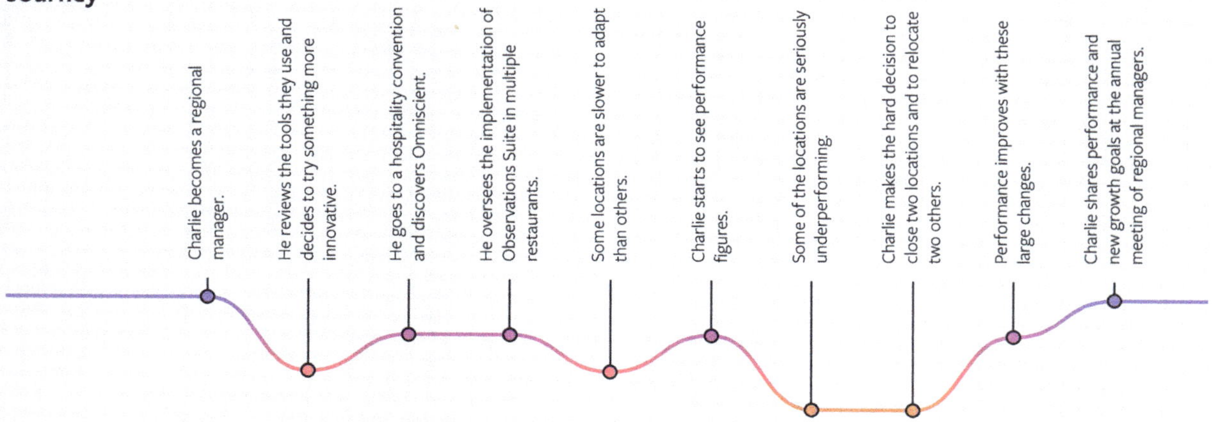

Maria

Restaurant Manager, Italian Chain Restaurant

"I've worked in this restaurant since I was younger; my mother used to be a manager here too. So this restaurant is like my family. I believe that customers are always right and that everything in the restaurant should focus on keeping them happy."

Motivations

- to have a popular restaurant—both in real life and on social media
- to be valued for her experience within her network

Journey

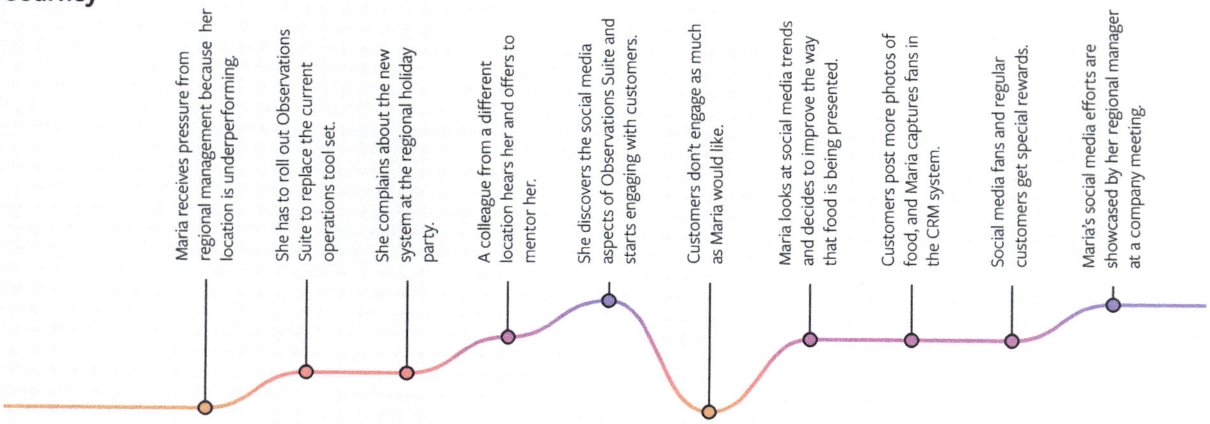

Colette

Kitchen Manager, Italian Chain Restaurant

“Food is my passion. Ever since I was a little kid, I knew I wanted to work in a kitchen. Succeeding hasn’t been easy in a role usually dominated by men. Hard work, discipline, and a tough attitude have been core to achieving my goals.”

Motivations

- to have a handle on everything happening in the kitchen
- to invent new recipes that please both customers and critics

Journey

Tony

Server, Italian Chain Restaurant

“I just started as a server here. I thought it would be pretty easy, but it turns out there’s so much to remember if I want to do my job well. I think I’ll get there eventually, but right now I’m still making a lot of mistakes.”

Motivations

- to learn how to do his job well so he doesn’t embarrass himself
- to make sure customers have a good experience so he gets tips

Journey

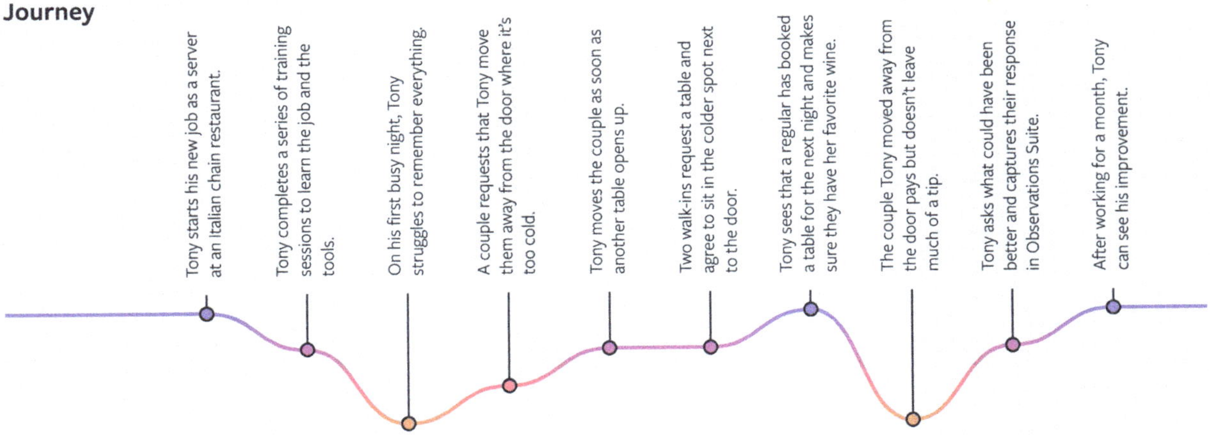

Dashboard
DESCRIPTION
n. customizable aggregation and visualization of available analytics.
SEE
performance
analytics
status
insights
DO
add new chart
add new status
customize
EXISTING CONCEPTS
Insight
DESCRIPTION
n. actionable observations based on data.
SEE
related data
actionable advice
DO
take action
EXISTING CONCEPTS
Performance
DESCRIPTION
n. how something does over time.
SEE
employee
chain
restaurant
campaign
DO
modify date range
filter
EXISTING CONCEPTS
Status
DESCRIPTION
n. how something is doing at the moment.
SEE
employee
chain
restaurant
campaign
DO
hide/show
EXISTING CONCEPTS
Chain
DESCRIPTION
n. multiple restaurants operated by a central entity
SEE
restaurants
performance
analytics
status
DO
add new
remove
edit
manage groups
EXISTING CONCEPTS
Restaurant
DESCRIPTION
n. a place where food is served
SEE
analytics
insights
employees
menu
inventory
DO
EXISTING CONCEPTS
Movement
DESCRIPTION
n. how customers and employees move around a restaurant
SEE
restaurant
employees
customers
status analytics
DO
track
EXISTING CONCEPTS
maps
Goal (restau
DESCRIPTION
n. the objecti
restaurant or ch
SEE
status
perform
details
DO
My Employees
DESCRIPTION
n. a list of my employees
SEE
employees
DO
batch delete/
add/
group
EXISTING CONCEPTS
address book / contacts
Schedule
DESCRIPTION
n. a calendar of events happening and employee shifts
SEE
employees
events
calendar
DO
assign (employee)
add (event)
edit
share
EXISTING CONCEPTS
calendar
Mentor
DESCRIPTION
n. a person that contributes to your growth not necessarily your boss
SEE
employee
performance
goals
DO
assign
EXISTING CONCEPTS
Goal (employee)
DESCRIPTION
n. the objectives of an individual employee
SEE
status
performance
details
DO
update
remove
complete
EXISTING CONCEPTS
reminders
to-do lists
My Recipes
DESCRIPTION
n a database and management tool of recipes
SEE
menu status
ingredients
inventory
alerts
DO
batch activate/
deactivate/
edit / remove
EXISTING CONCEPTS
Recipe
DESCRIPTION
n. an item on the menu to be ordered by customers
SEE
ingredients
instructions
menu status
DO
activate
edit
remove
EXISTING CONCEPTS
cookbook
Inventory
DESCRIPTION
n the amounts of various ingredients a restaurant needs to prepare recipes
SEE
current stock
active (in-use) ingredients
usage analytics
DO
order
adjust / edit
EXISTING CONCEPTS
Ingredient
DESCRIPTION
n. something required to make a recipe, catalogued in the inventory
SEE
status
DO
reorder
EXISTING CONCEPTS
Menu
DESCRIPTION
n the current (food) offering of a restaurant
SEE
recipes
ingredients
inventory
alerts
DO
edit
archive
EXISTING CONCEPTS
physical menu
My Marketing
DESCRIPTION
n. where I review and manage marketing and
Marketing
DESCRIPTION
n. methods used to attract customers
Campaign
DESCRIPTION
n. a marketing method to attract and upsell customers
Acquisition
DESCRIPTION
n. how many customers a restaurant acquires and how

Conceptual Model

The conceptual model of an experience ensures that features are represented in ways that are comprehensible to users. It looks at how users are likely to engage with features as well as what concepts a user already understands based on other experiences and combines these into recommendations for curating, organizing, and naming aspects of the experience.

The conceptual model should be created near the beginning of a project and maintained as the product or service evolves. To get started on a conceptual model, a loose definition of features and user research, such as immersion or user interviews, are helpful inputs. From this, it's possible to begin mapping what the user will already understand of the product or service, and what they will have to learn. Beyond simply capturing how the user understands the experience, the conceptual model is useful for consolidating and strengthening features, providing input for the information architecture and interaction model, and ensuring that the project team has a common language around features.

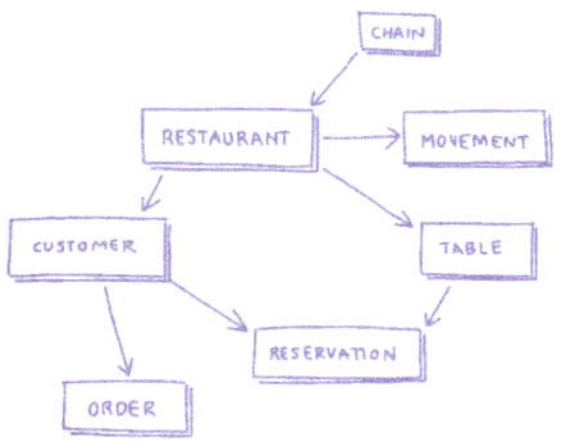

Concept maps show at a high level how different concepts relate to each other.

The conceptual model is derived from the technique of concept mapping developed in the 1970s. Concept mapping is based on the theory that learning is done through relationships and uses a weblike visualization to connect ideas, images, or words. Concept maps are similar to mind maps, but rarely have such a clear center.

> *"The most important single factor influencing learning is what the learner already knows. Ascertain this and teach accordingly."*
>
> **David Ausubel**

Activities

Conceptual-model activities are a great opportunity to pull in business and development team members, both to align language and to encourage more empathy for the user. While broad representation is useful, be selective. Inviting too many voices will hinder progress.

To create a conceptual model, you'll first need to thoroughly understand the product or service you're designing. This understanding could come from the experience journey, experience audit, feature definition, or competitive analysis—anything that defines the basic parts of your user's experience. If your project is still in its beginning phases, defining concepts may be difficult. If it's already well defined, the challenge is looking at concepts with fresh eyes and better understanding the user's perspective.

If a feature is the building block of a product or service, concepts are the building blocks of the user's understanding of that product or service. Rather than thinking about the user's experience in terms of time or a journey, try thinking about how you would describe the experience to the user. What's the elevator pitch? What are the high-level benefits to the user?

Capture concepts on individual pieces of paper. Try to keep concepts simple and high level. For example, "Sharing via social media" would become the simple concept of "Share," followed by a list of sharing options. Distilling concepts can be a challenge, especially for already well-defined experiences. Don't worry about finding the right resolution from the beginning—it will emerge through the process of mapping concepts to each other.

As you document concepts, consider what makes each concept unique and necessary. Capture this in a short description. If you cannot define what makes a concept unique from others, it's likely that you need to cut, combine, or revise concepts. Creating an experience with competing or confusing concepts will only lead to dissatisfied users and unused features.

Add notes when the feature relates to something the user already understands from either the tangible or digital world. For example, if you're building a digital product around wine tastings and you have the concept of "expert recommendations," try correlating this with the wine aficionado's concept of a sommelier. If you're struggling to find things the user already understands, try looking back on the trendscape and competitive analysis. When designing the experience, these references might inform how the features related to that concept are executed. It's likely that you'll even want to rename features to be more in line with the user's existing conceptual model.

Once you've captured the concepts, start to categorize them. For this, you'll want a large space. First, consider whether the concept is a thing (noun), an action (verb), or a modifier (adjective). This will help you categorize and establish relationships between concepts. Next, use the space to group concepts in different ways—by concept type, relationship, frequency of use, complexity, etc. The process of actively arranging and rearranging concepts will help to further define the concepts by their relationships to each other. Capture everything.

Artifacts

A conceptual model has several valuable outputs. The first is the list of concepts that need to exist along with the user's expectations for those concepts. If your team has not yet done feature definition, this can be the foundation. More likely, your team already has features at least loosely defined, and the output from concept generation will be in the form of suggested revisions. In addition to adding to the descriptions and acceptance criteria of features, you may also need to cull features that are conceptually redundant. Consider keeping a graveyard of the features that get eliminated. You may want to revisit these someday.

The conceptual model should also result in a glossary of terms or concepts. This could be as simple as an organized list, or it may have an accompanying diagram showing the relationship of items. For every term in the glossary, make sure to relate technical thinking with what you expect the user to understand. This will help to bridge the gap between how different team members think of concepts. Because this glossary is a foundational communication document, make sure that the artifact is in a place where it's both easily updated and readily accessible to everyone on the team. A shared wiki is perfect for this.

As you move forward, continue consulting the conceptual model. It will provide valuable input for developing an information architecture and an interaction model for the experience. It will help determine priorities for feature definition and the function hierarchy. It will help create stronger copy and iconography for detailed design, and it might even evolve with new discoveries from participatory design and user validation.

Domain vs. Conceptual Model

Development teams use similar models, such as the domain model, to ensure a common language across the team as well as to map relationships. A domain model is different from a conceptual model in that it focuses on the parts that make the system rather than on the concepts that make up the user's understanding.

The conceptual model for Observations Suite captures the different concepts and groups them into themes. Important aspects of each concept are highlighted by what the user can see and do. The conceptual model also captures similar experiences that might be useful to follow or to avoid later in the design process.

Omniscient / **Observations Suite Web App**

Conceptual Model

See · Do · Existing concepts

Data

Dashboard

A customizable visual aggregation of available analytics and performance

performance · analytics · status · insights · add new · customize · Google Analytics

Analytics

An analysis of a restaurant's or chain's performance over time

employee · restaurant · chain · marketing · filter · customize

Performance

How something being measured does over time

employee · restaurant · chain · marketing · campaign · filter · modify · date range

Status

How something is currently performing

employee · restaurant · chain · marketing · campaign · hide/view · filter

Insight

An actionable observation based on analytics

actionable advice · related data · take recommended action

Notification

A way of drawing the user's attention to something important

details · related info · date · dismiss · delete · take action

Report

A summary of performance for a set period of time

details · date · view

Employee Management

Employee

A nonmanagement user employed by the restaurant; performance is tracked over time

basic information · analytics · performance · permissions · edit · remove

Manager

A decision-making employee working for the restaurant, usually has employees

basic information · analytics · performance · employees · add new · edit · remove

Mentor

An employee who helps another to improve at a specific skill, not necessarily a manager

mentees · mentee goals · add mentee · remove mentee

Goal

An objective of an individual employee

status · performance · details · add · edit · remove · complete

My Employees

A directory of employees working at a restaurant or chain

employee · add new · filter · batch edit · batch remove · address books/contacts

Schedule

A calendar of events and shifts at a restaurant

employee · event · calendar · shift · add event · add shift · assign (employee) · share · edit · calendar tools

Shift

A period of time when an employee is scheduled to work

employee · time · edit · share · calendar

Restaurants

Chain

Multiple restaurants by a central entity

restaurant · performance · status · analytics · groups · insights · add · edit · remove · manage

Restaurant

A place where food is prepared and served

performance · status · insights · analytics · employees · movement · manage · edit · remove

Movement

How customers and employees move around a restaurant

restaurant · employee · customer · status · analytics · insight · map

Customer Management

Customer

The end user of a restaurant; engagement with the restaurant is tracked over time

basic information · feedback · loyalty status · engagement data · add new · remove · edit · merge

Reservation

An agreement between the customer and the restaurant for a table at a specific time and date

time · table · location · party size · customer · assign to table · add · edit · remove · decline

Table

A place where a group of customers sit, order food, etc.

location · status · analytics · upcoming reservations · order · edit reservations · pay

Order

A customer's request for food, typically from the menu

price · recipe · customer · special requests · table · add · edit · delete

My Customers

A directory of customers

customer · add new · filter · batch edit · batch remove · address books/contacts

Loyalty

A program that tracks and rewards repeat customers

customer · loyalty status · edit · apply to order · Starbucks

Payment

The amount of money owed for an order

price · order · customer · loyalty · discount · apply discount · accept payment

Feedback

A customer-supplied report about their experience with a restaurant

rating · review · analytics · flag · follow up

Food Management

Recipe

A dish prepared by the restaurant, can be on the menu

menu status · ingredient status · ingredients · instructions · add · edit · remove · add to menu · cookbook

Inventory

The restaurant's stock of ingredients

ingredient · status · analytics · order · edit · adjust

Ingredient

What a restaurant needs to prepare a recipe

status · analytics · order

Menu

The recipes currently offered at a restaurant, often lists ingredients

recipe · ingredient · inventory status · add · edit · archive

How might we balance health, environment, home, and social elements?
How might we make it clear when the mirror is actively watching + listening?
How might we infuse the experience with delight?
GIVE THE VUI A CHARACTER
looking good today!
SETTING LIGHTING MODES
FILTERS
SUMMARIES SCROLL BY
LEARN USER NEEDS
multiple screens
Detailed (customized) dashboard

Concept Generation

Concept generation is helpful for exploring many possible solutions at a rapid pace. Often combined with participatory design and involving team members or users with different backgrounds or perspectives, exercises focus on coming up with new ideas—even bad ones. Activities are mostly generative but may end with reductive exercises to help guide and focus direction.

Depending on when it takes place, concept generation can explore more strategically, coming up with new ideas for products and services, or more tactically, finding different executions of an individual feature. While most projects benefit from concept generation, it can be a distraction when timelines are tight and design work is focused on straightforward execution rather than exploration.

HOW MIGHT WE keep the user informed of the past while also peeking into the future?
EXPERIENCE-AUDIT OPPORTUNITY

HOW MIGHT WE provide the rider with what they need to know to be prepared for the journey ahead?
IMMERSION OPPORTUNITY

TECHNOLOGY
HOW MIGHT WE USE ubiquitous sensing TO promote environmental responsibility?
TREND

Writing good provocations is difficult and often takes multiple iterations.

The idea of concept generation, more commonly referred to as *brainstorming*, is decades old and was outlined and popularized by advertising executive Alex F. Osborn. In the late 1930s, Osborn greatly increased both the quality and quantity of ideas from his team by employing these collaborative ideation sessions. For these sessions, he had two rules:

1. Defer judgment
2. Reach for quantity

Over the years, the art of brainstorming has been continually refined and redefined based on project scope and scale, solution-space context, and team size and composition. Many organizations have their own corporate methodology, and many practitioners have their own techniques. While practices may vary, at the heart of all concept-generation techniques are Osborn's two rules.

Activities

Sometimes concept generation is simply about having and collecting a broad array of ideas. Other times, concept generation can be approached with ulterior motives. For example, concept-generation workshops might be used to better understand the motivations, hang-ups, and pet ideas of stakeholders. Or a concept-generation session may be used to co-create with users to capture more authentic ideas and perspectives from your target audience. Before you decide on a concept-generation approach, it's important to outline your goals and then to select appropriate provocations and participants.

The quantity and quality of ideas that come out of a concept-generation session are dependent on the quality of the provocations, prompts that help your audience generate ideas. Usually provocations are born of opportunities uncovered through the discover phase of work. If you're working to refine an existing experience, use opportunities uncovered through the experience audit, and if you're starting a new experience, look at the outcomes of business analysis and immersion. If you completed a technology analysis or trendscape, these might also have opportunities (or threats) that can inspire provocations.

Now rephrase those opportunities into provocations. They can be as specific as seeking solutions for individual features or as general as finding ways to evoke an emotion from the user. The phrasing of a provocation should cover the opportunity as well as the benefit to the user. While some concept-generation exercises focus on a single provocation, most exercises seek to brainstorm around multiple provocations, usually more than six but less than twenty.

When selecting participants, ask yourself whose input will be the most valuable in steering the project. Whose perspectives will be most insightful to understanding the user's needs? Whose attitude will help the team stay positive and generative throughout the workshop?

Depending on the size and composition of your group, you may be able to do a single concept-generation workshop with everyone in the room working from a single set of provocations, or you may need to break up the room into smaller, more focused groups, each with their own set of provocations. If you're co-creating with users, it's likely that you'll want to hold multiple workshops with smaller groups so that you can more effectively facilitate the collaboration of strangers.

> *"Create a judgment-free environment and you'll unleash a torrent of creativity."*
>
> Alex F. Osborn

However you divide your groups, keep in mind that diversity is the friend of concept generation, so avoid grouping like minds and similar provocations together. For example, while it's likely that a technical group of stakeholders will come up with entirely practical solutions for a set of technical provocations, it's unlikely that you'll find the type of creative and disruptive ideas that concept generation is meant to stir up.

Once you've settled on provocations and selected participants, start planning the workshop. To get the most out of this exercise, you'll want activities to be focused, rapid paced, collaborative, and well documented. To achieve these goals, time and space are both important. Make sure you have enough time that the workshop doesn't feel rushed and enough space that people can draw and easily share ideas. Concept-generation workshops with small teams might run two hours in length, while with larger teams they might take an entire afternoon. Give yourself ample time to introduce the exercise, to deal with likely interruptions, and to synthesize concepts postgeneration. To minimize the risk of distraction, ask participants to leave behind the things that might distract them, like computers and phones.

Concepts consist of rough sketches and descriptions. Additional notes can be helpful for synthesis and follow-up exercises. Keep things light—if a concept takes more than one or two minutes to document, it's likely too detailed. If you suspect your participants will be uncomfortable with the drawing part of the workshop, reassure them that stick figures representing people and rectangles for screens and devices are OK.

To facilitate collaboration, state concepts aloud as you draw and describe them on paper. Once an idea is captured, place it in the middle of the group where everyone can see. Here are a few tips to keep concept generation around each provocation productive:

Aim for Imperfect

Concept generation is intimidating, especially to nondesigners. It's not uncommon for participants to hold back out of fear that their ideas aren't perfect. As the facilitator, you may want to start by sharing a

Capture the Process

Take photos of the process. Whether it's for an executive summary or a case study, photos of team collaboration are likely to be useful later.

few imperfect concepts of your own to help other participants feel less intimidated by the exercise.

Embrace Bad Ideas

Some concepts will be terrible. Avoid judgment during the concept-generation exercise, as this can discourage participants from sharing. Consider that a bad idea might inspire a good idea or might even become a good idea with enough polishing!

Iterate on Good Ideas

Concepts belong to the team, not to individuals. Don't be afraid to iterate on someone else's idea to create a new concept. This type of piggybacking can lead to new ideas and can turn bad ideas into good ones . . . not that anyone is judging.

Ask for Clarification

If a concept isn't clear, ask. Understanding what team members are thinking will help reduce repeat concepts and will likely inspire new ideas. In a concept-generation session, questions must be asked carefully, as they can easily come across as judgment.

To keep things moving, use a timer—usually set somewhere between seven and fifteen minutes depending on the size and energy of the team. After reading a provocation, start the timer and start sketching. While you don't need to stick to the time limit for every session, it can help keep the team from going too deep on a single interesting provocation or from moving on too quickly from a challenging one.

After each timed provocation, hang all of the ideas on a wall so that they're easily seen by everyone. Take a couple of minutes to take them all in, and then move on to the next provocation. If your room doesn't have enough wall space to hang all of the provocations, foam boards will work as makeshift walls.

After several hours of brainstorming ideas and covering the walls with sketches, it's time to be reductive. The process of synthesizing concepts is not an easy one, especially with a room full of stakeholders and/or users. While it is important to understand which stakeholders hold what opinions, it's also important in a collaborative workshop to reduce the effects of hierarchy on the conversation. To do this, start by voting. Rather than each participant voting for their favorite idea for each provocation, try voting based on a number of different criteria across all provocations. Here are some you might use:

Your Favorite Concept

What seems like the easiest choice is often the most difficult. Having participants choose a single idea across all provocations can help you understand not only the preferences of individual stakeholders but also what aspects of the design are priorities.

Your Least Favorite Concept

After several hours of reserving judgment, this is usually the easiest vote to cast. Make sure to capture the rationale behind this vote, as it might affect later decisions.

The Easiest Concept to Implement

Implementation could be technical or organizational. Understanding which concepts are easy wins can be helpful in later design and prioritization processes.

The Concept That Will Be Most Loved By Users

Take yourself out of the equation. Which of the ideas are users most likely to rave about to their friends?

The Concept That Will Make the Most Money

Most products and services need to make money to survive. While this isn't the most glamorous question, it can ensure that monetization is incorporated into the experience rather than tacked on at the end.

The Concept That's Most On-Brand

For brands with strong personalities, this is an important vote. Making sure a product or service feels authentic to a brand from the beginning of the design phase can save a lot of work (and rounds of feedback) later.

Give each person in the room stickers or Post-its with which to cast their votes. Stickers don't need to have individuals' names on them, but everyone should keep track of where they cast their votes. After votes are made, facilitate a conversation.

Move linearly through concepts, stopping at each vote to collect explanations.

It's not unusual for many people to cast the same vote for the same concept. It's also not unusual for participants to cast conflicting votes. The goal of synthesis here is not to reconcile disagreements or to come to a common understanding but to understand where the team is aligned and misaligned to inform the design exercises that will follow.

Artifacts

If concept generation is done with a complete set of stakeholders, the artifact around the activity can be fairly light. Themes and insights from concept generation might be summarized into a single slide in a presentation or in an email to the team. Concepts might be curated or synthesized to make them less overwhelming for consumption, while the original sketches might be scanned and labeled for later reference.

If concept generation is done with a subset of the team or with users, the artifact will need to be more robust. Stakeholders unfamiliar with concept generation may need some additional framing to understand that the activity is generative, meant to create a large quantity of ideas, rather than reductive, meant to reduce and refine ideas. A brief description and photos can support an understanding of the process, and an appendix of all ideas can help nonparticipants see the extent of the exercise without overwhelming them with every single concept.

When formatting concepts for your presentation, consider what input you need from stakeholders. Do you want to get commitment to good ideas and weed out bad ideas? Try collecting rough sketches with the best options highlighted to provide both breadth and focus. You might also organize concepts as the user would encounter them in an experience journey, walking through recommendations for each moment in time. If you are aiming to set a specific direction, you might instead organize sketches by theme, in groupings that will form the foundation for future design explorations.

The Future of Boats used input from expert interviews, technology analysis, and trendscape activities to seed the provocations for brainstorming. The presented concepts are curated based on feasibility and relevance.

Concepts for Ambience Mirror were generated to a series of nine provocations. Participants voted on ideas before the design team synthesized them into five potential design directions for presentation.

Observations Suite broke the concept-generation workshop into three groups with relevant stakeholders to generate ideas around marketing, product, and design. Each group ended the session by curating and presenting their best ideas.

Concept Generation

Health & Safety

Humans designate boats for pickup, and autonomously driving tugs take them away for repair or recycling.

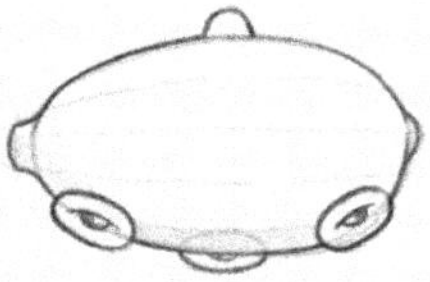

Government drones scan the bottoms of canals for waste and any other items of interest.

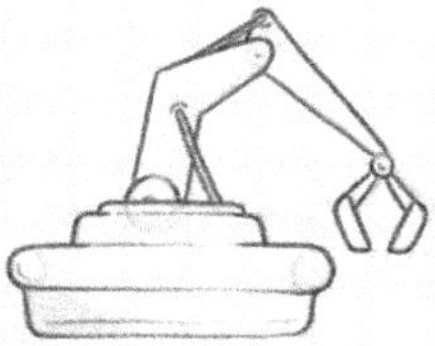

The bottom-feeding boat works with government drones to clean up the bottoms of the city's waterways.

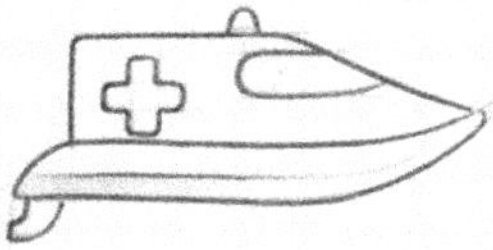

Water ambulances bypass road traffic, ensuring fast and efficient responses to medical emergencies.

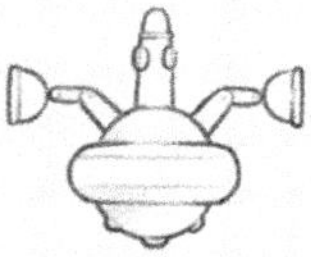

The snitch boat detects dangerous boat behavior and pulls over the perpetrator.

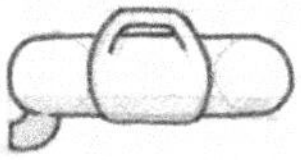

Small lifeboats detect and autonomously respond to unusual events in the water, helping to prevent drowning deaths.

Water-filtration robots travel through the canals, purifying the water.

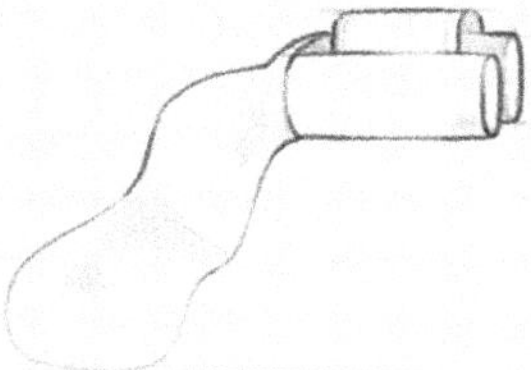

Small floating trash robots comb the canals for floating waste, collecting it in a bag for easy disposal.

Floating clinics provide medical services at a greater number of locations.

Transportation

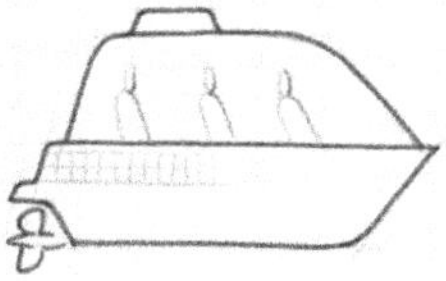

Self-driving water taxis transport riders throughout the city.

Smart ferries observe passenger loads and adjust frequency and routes accordingly.

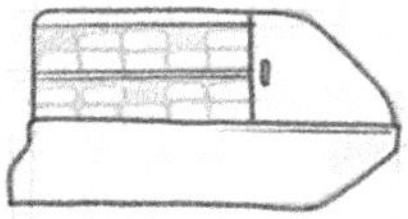

Food-delivery boats move both personal and business deliveries to the canals.

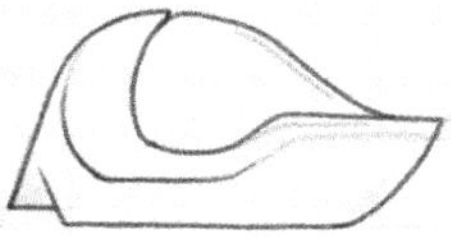

Personal yachts provide secluded transportation for the wealthy.

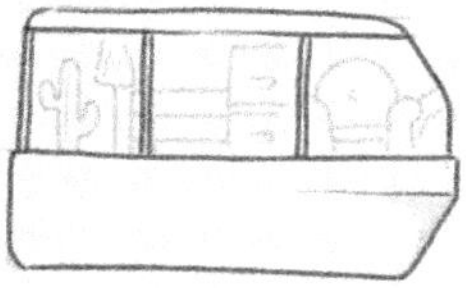

Moving boats help residents move within the city.

Scheduled autonomous boatpools take commuters to work.

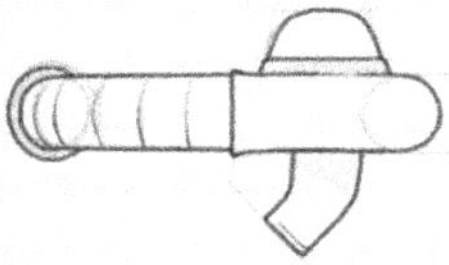

Autonomous valet tugs park boats in large out-of-the-way garages.

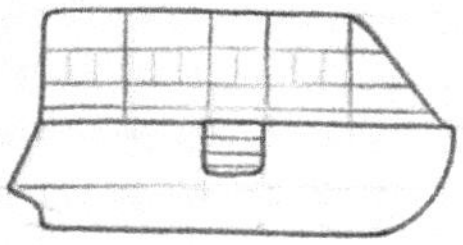

Boat lockers deliver packages without human help.

Infrastructure

Boat sensors feed into a single open-data platform.

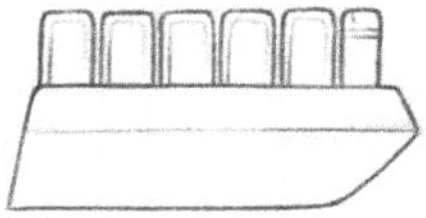

Boats with batteries replace generators with clean, quiet energy within the city.

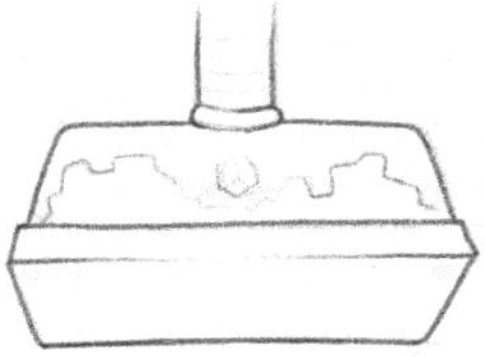

Boat dumpsters allow for construction sites to dispose of waste without blocking the street and sidewalk.

Barrier boats barricade areas and improve traffic flow.

Big transport boats provide neighborhoods a clear place and time to dispose of large waste.

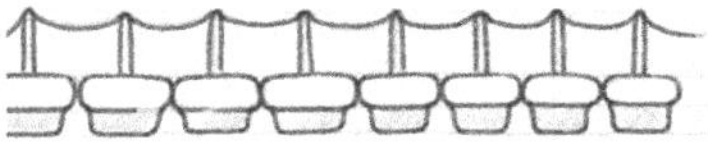

Path swarm boats create ad hoc pedestrian bridges that can easily restructure for boats to pass.

Bike-parking boats provide additional parking infrastructure and can move where needed for big events.

Recreation

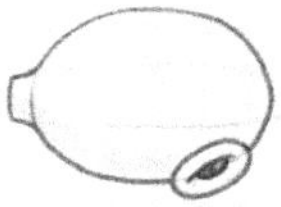

Recreational drones enable hobbiests to see underwater happenings.

Swimmer boats measure water for cleanliness and mark areas where it's safe to swim.

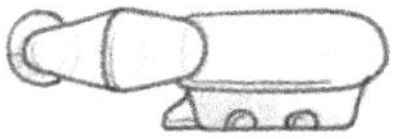

Designated-driver boats turn old boats into autonomous vehicles.

Detachable parks provide a place for recreation during the day and move into the canal at night to avoid unwanted gatherings.

Garden boats grow hydroponic gardens, moving about to optimize sun exposure.

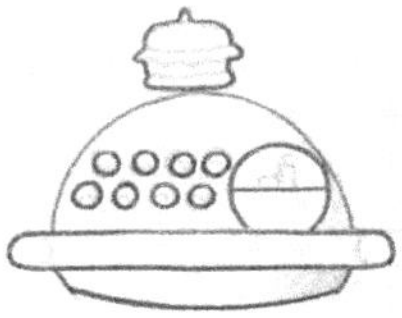

Fast-food boats are the food trucks of the canals.

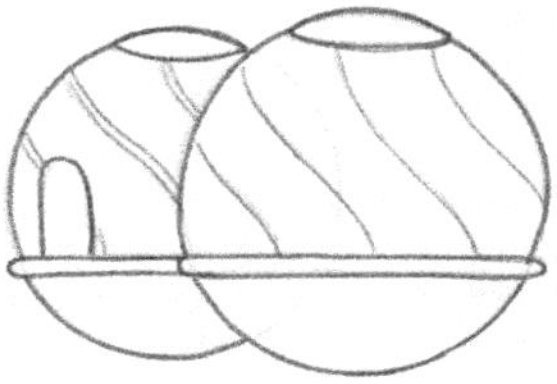

Pop-up boats provide small spaces for restaurants and shops to reach customers across neighborhoods.

Event swarm boats create platforms for large-scale events.

Concept Generation

Process & Session Goals

We generated and voted on over fifty concepts for the user's interaction with the Ambience Mirror. We then synthesized concepts into five possible thematic directions. Today we will choose a theme and favorite concepts to move forward with.

Relationship of Themes

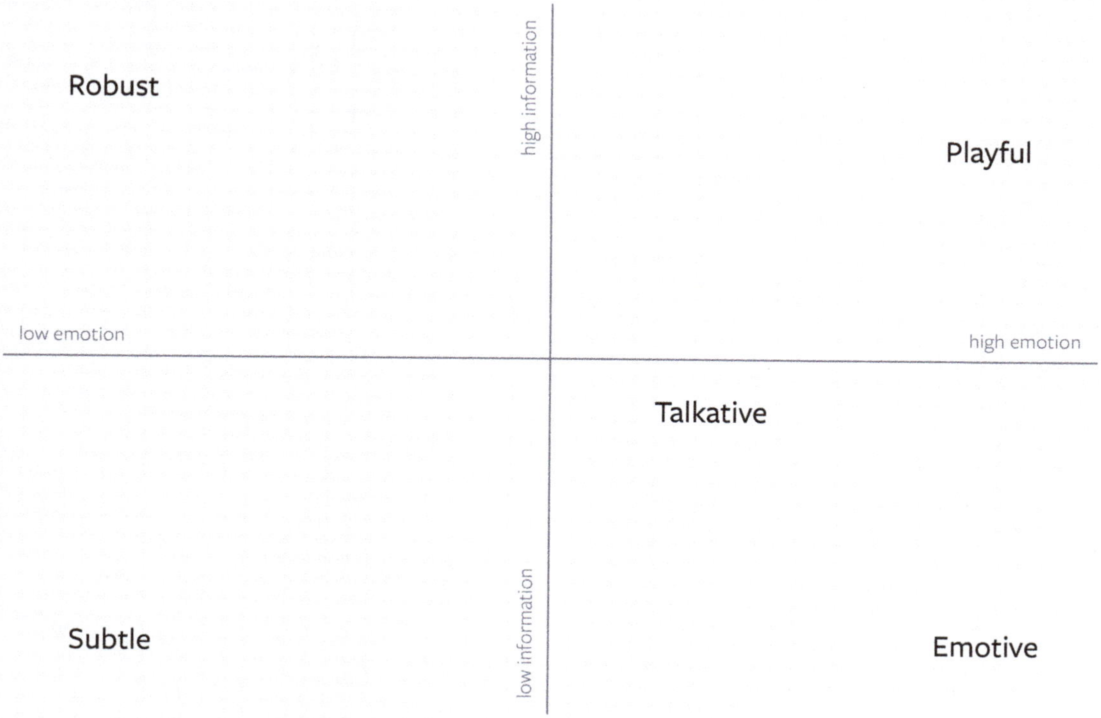

Voting Categories

Robust

Providing rich at-a-glance information, categorizing engagement into themes, allowing deep dives into the details

organize content into different themes (home, health, my day)

use data to make predictions that transcend scenes

provide the user with previews of information

allow the user to select less overt visualizations

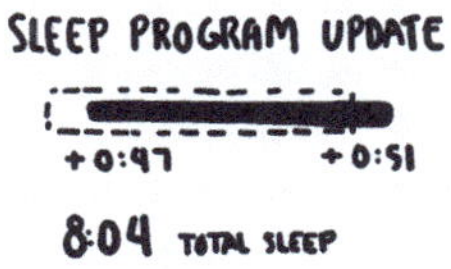

provide helpful visualizations of program data

allow the user to dig deeper into historical visualizations

show certainty with predictions

modify content by "flicking" modules from the phone

Emotive

Creating an experience full of emotion, providing understanding through feeling

detect the user's position and move content around them

show weather conditions

allow users to leave messages to each other

show camera and microphone engagement with light

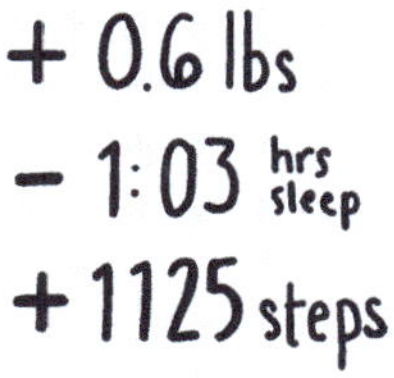

present data in relative terms

show the user what they'll need rather than just data

use metaphors to present potentially sensitive information

celebrate special days

Playful

Engaging the user through play, creating an experience that focuses on joy over all else, providing small activities every day to provide a sense of achievement

use ambient scenes with nonpersonal data as screensavers

show data within scenes

measure compliance in streaks

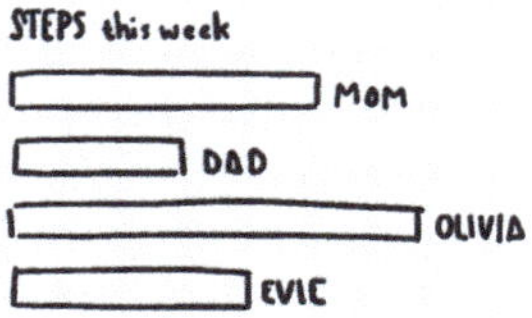

capture nonsensitive data in competitive formats

engage users with interactive exercises

use creative names and scenes for lighting

provide users with daily health challenges

allow users to try on different face filters

Subtle

Engaging only when engaged by the user, using light to draw attention, forcing prioritization of information

don't show anything until engaged by the user

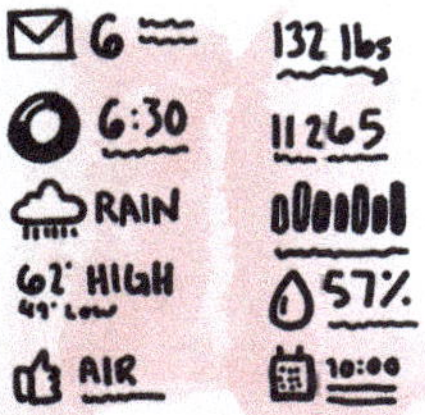

allow the user to pick the top 10 things

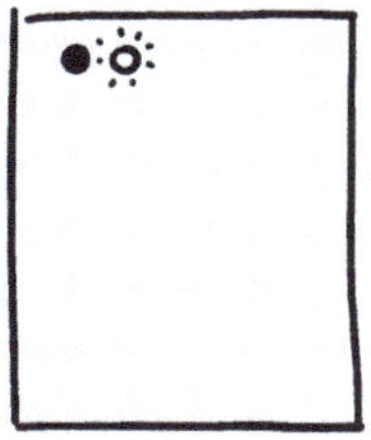

use simple cues like lights to show recording

use an app to select info for the mirror

keep information short and simple

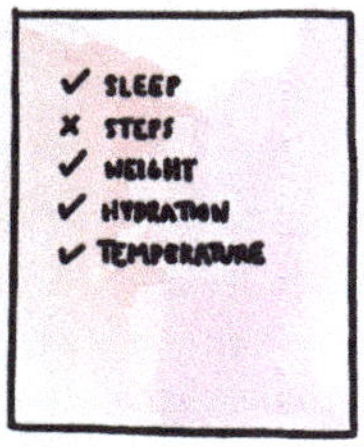

reduce information to simple pass-or-fail summaries

default to showing no email or social media

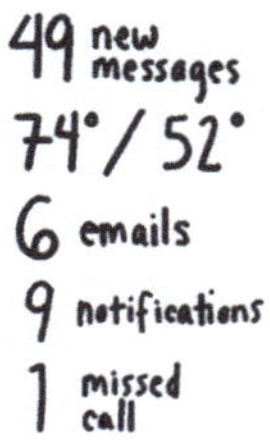

show all data types together in one dashboard

Talkative

Engaging the user through humanlike conversation, presenting data and recommendations in human ways, giving the Ambience Mirror a personality

use a reductive process to create the ideal display

allow the user to add new modules to their interface

ask questions

give the mirror an avatar and a personality

give the mirror a face and voice for engaging the user

remove all information when the mirror is listening

provide insights as a part of the conversation

Omniscient / **Observations Suite Vision**

Concept Generation

Marketing

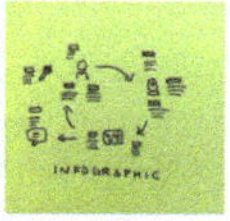

Provide users with a simple, cross-touchpoint infographic showing the different parts of the suite and how they interact with each other.

Provide a service to support the user in switching from their old system to Omniscient's Observations Suite.

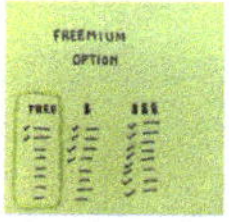

Provide a free demo or freemium version of Observations Suite that the user can experience before investing.

Establish Omniscient as industry experts by speaking at conferences. Capitalize on that expertise with a booth at the same conference.

Product

Positively reinforce good behavior by calling it out across functions in the Observations Suite.

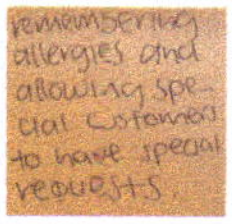

Prioritize customers' needs by remembering allergies, special needs, and birthdays.

Keep track of customers' favorite eats and drinks to make sure everything is in stock and readily offered when they visit.

Remember customers' feedback so that it can be addressed on the following visit.

Design

Create a single design language across both professional and consumer tools, allowing for minimal customization, primarily through content.

Always show data sources for visualizations and insights.

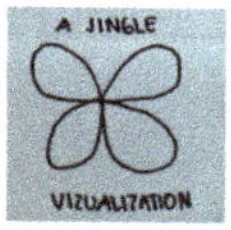

Provide a single simple visualization to express the overall health of the company, allowing the customer to drill into the details.

Lead with text insights, allowing the user to drill down into supporting data and visualizations.

Publish ads in places where potential users are looking for insights and answers.

Create a video channel of informative tutorials for potential and existing customers.

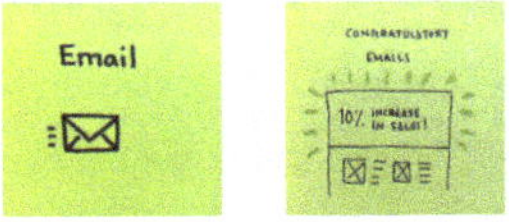

Keep in touch with customers by sending progress reports at regular intervals and celebratory emails at major milestones.

Make the most of engaged users by involving them in the development process by regularly asking for feedback and including users in beta programs.

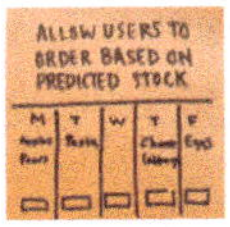

Provide users with easy-to-parse visualizations of predicted stock amounts and outages to make ordering easy.

Empower employees with personalized weekly reports with actionable advice.

Provide an interface for setting goals as individuals and as teams.

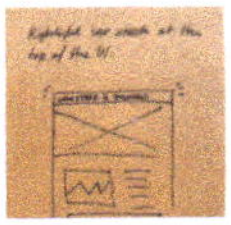

Use notifications to call attention to inventory problems that will cause problems within the day/night.

Limit the UI to the most likely paths of use, creating more buttons or long-press interactions for less common interactions.

Call out qualitative and quantitative success stories that highlight the value of Observations Suite.

Lead with what's happening now to ensure that pressing matters don't get lost in visualizations of long-term data.

Send the most important notifications via push notifications and text messages to ensure they don't get lost.

TITLE	STORIES	ACTIONS	DEPENDENCIES	PRIORIT
Automatic locking and unlocking	When I leave my bike, it automatically locks, so I don't have to hassle with a manual lock. When I approach my bike, it automatically unlocks, so I can immediately start riding.	• Disable/enable auto-unlock/lock • Adjust distance to auto-unlock/lock • Use UI button to unlock/lock • Hear/see confirmation	• Bluetooth • Proximity awareness • Self-locking/unlocking mechanism	1
Manual locking and unlocking	When my phone is dead, I manually lock my bike, so it won't get stolen. When I don't have my phone, I manually unlock my bike, so that I can ride it.	• Use a key to lock/unlock my bike	• Traditional key mechanism	1
E Ink display with backlight	When riding at night, I use the display's backlight, so I can see the directions. When traveling somewhere new, I see directions on my on-bike display, so I don't have to use my phone.	• Manage screen settings • View directions • View alerts	• light sensor • Bluetoo	
Bike location	When I forget where I parked my bike, I use the app to see its location, so I can easily find it. When my bike has been stolen, I view its location, so I know where to find it.	• See location of my bike • See my current location • See last known location (if current location is unknown)		

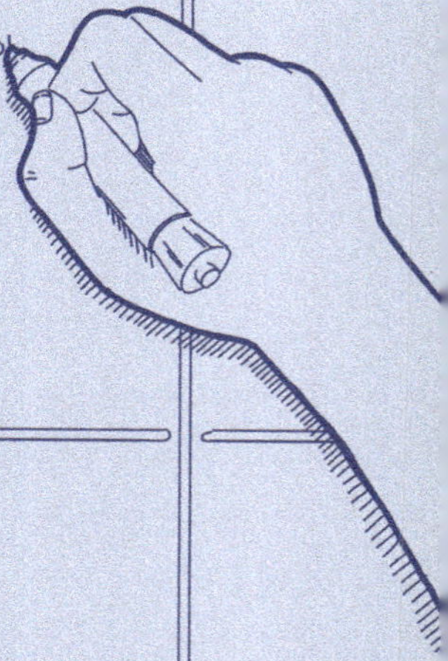

Feature Definition

Products and services vary in scale and complexity, and finding a near-universal way to describe and compare them is a challenge. By breaking an experience into smaller pieces like features, it becomes easier to talk about how it will be designed, built, and ultimately used.

Feature-definition exercises help to align teams on how a product or service will deliver on the value promised to the user. Features should be consistent with the value proposition, with the most important features even being mentioned within it. Feature definition creates clarity by establishing requirements for often-ambiguous business needs and by helping teams prioritize aspects of an experience's functionality.

Because features are the building blocks of your product or service, most activities you've done up to this point will feed into them. Most activities completed after will be to refine and add detail to features; therefore, it's important to revisit features as a team regularly throughout the course of a project.

Capture features that aren't in scope in some sort of backlog.

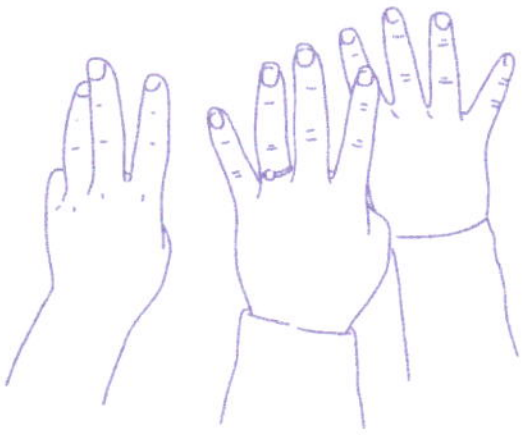

Get input from the team about how much effort is involved.

Activities

Features are the building blocks of products and services, yet the definition of what makes a feature varies depending on methodology, company, and team. So start by understanding your team's approach to features and product definition. Are they using a methodology, and if yes, how rigorously? What language does your team use around features? Who is responsible for features? If there's already a process in place, then how can the design team participate in and influence that process?

Through team conversations or stakeholder interviews, you should also uncover if any product or feature definition has already been done. If you find existing features that the team has committed to, use what already exists as a starting point and review for opportunities to add more user-centered details.

If your team hasn't started defining features yet, start by looking for features dreamed up during concept-generation activities and uncovered through your competitive analysis. The output from expert, user, and stakeholder interviews might also lead to insights for potential features.

It's likely that features will be too numerous and ambiguous at first. While curation and prioritization can help to reduce an overwhelming list, it's important to approach this with some structure. If you're working on an existing product or service, the experience audit can provide this structure. If not, start by organizing raw materials in the order of the user's experience, beginning with discovery and ending with expert use.

As you organize, group ideas that feel similar, combine ideas that feel the same, and add any necessary ideas into the gaps between. Aim for all features to be of a similar resolution. While designers might think of features in more broad terms of what the user experiences, developers often prefer features with smaller, more precise definitions. While the two are compatible, the team should work together to align on a single way of documenting features.

While some features might feel out of place for the product or service, heavy-handed curation can be dangerous in a design vacuum. Consider using participatory-design exercises with users and stakeholders to understand which features are most important and which the experience can live without. Make sure to keep discarded features documented somewhere, possibly in a design backlog, capturing any relevant details in case the team decides to revisit them later.

After curating features to a strong set, work to prioritize them for development and release. This requires input from the team. Business and design might use a number scale to assess the value to the user, while the development team might vote by holding up fingers to signify how much effort is required to bring each feature to life. Prioritization should be derived from these two assessments. While it's easy to prioritize features that are easy to implement and provide significant value to the user, teams often struggle to prioritize high-benefit, high-effort items.

Artifacts

Once you've collected and synthesized a rough feature list, you'll need to refine and reformat items into well-phrased and defined features. While methodologies argue over the best way to do this, most follow similar patterns: each feature should have a short title, a thorough description, clear acceptance criteria, prioritization, and a definition of success. For larger projects with multiple tracks of work, categories of features can also be useful. These might be based on broad clusters of functionality, or they might be based on which team will be working on them.

In a user-oriented process, features are focused on fulfilling the needs of users, with emphasis on what's being done over the specifics of how. Feature titles and descriptions should aim to reflect this. For example, *sharing photos with friends* is a simple user-oriented title that avoids the specifics of how; whereas *sharesheet integration* describes a specific technology without any obvious user benefit. When creating titles, aim for short and easy to remember.

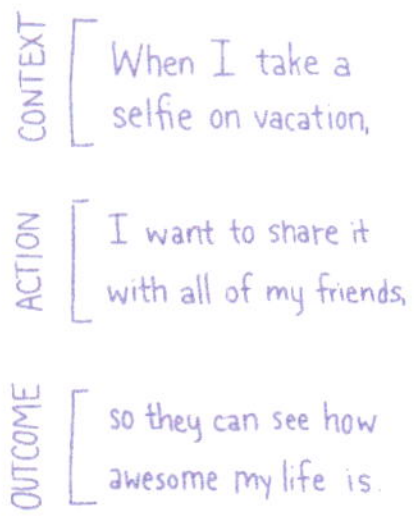

Phrase feature descriptions consistently, capturing context, action, and desired outcome.

Feature descriptions are longer and might describe multiple benefits. There are multiple methodologies to writing these descriptions, so before committing to a specific format, consult with your team to make sure there are no strong preferences. If not, try using a format that captures the user's context, the action, and the desired outcome. Once you've picked a format, stick with it to ensure consistency.

Next you'll need to add details or acceptance criteria. These include functional criteria, such as how a feature should be implemented and how that implementation should be tested, as well as emotional criteria around how the experience should look and feel. These should be written in a clear way so that members of the development team can use them to build and test without a lot of guesswork.

After your feature is clearly defined, add prioritization information. For this step, you might also need to consider enablers. What technologies need to be used, what partnerships need to exist, or what innovations need to come to market in order to deliver a feature? Some enablers might render a particular feature impossible in the near term. If the impossible feature is core to the benefit of your product or service, your team likely needs to meet to reevaluate the path forward. If not, the feature might belong on a roadmap, to be integrated when time and technology allow.

Finally, define what success looks like for each feature. Consider success from the perspectives of business, design, and development. For each notion of success, consider if success can be measured and, if so, how. Defining goals and then measuring if you're meeting them will help future iterations of your product or service.

The final output of feature definition is a shareable list of features, along with

Getting Input

While feature definition is a focused activity, getting input from stakeholders is essential to ensuring that priorities and constraints are correct. Make sure to stay connected with your team throughout the process, getting input wherever there is uncertainty and avoiding assumptions that could later damage the experience you're designing.

their acceptance criteria, prioritization, and definitions of success. The list of features will evolve with input from users, feedback from engineers and manufacturers, and shifts in the market. Feature descriptions will grow as you create mock-ups and design documentation that, in turn, create new acceptance criteria specifying how each feature's implementation should work and feel. For these reasons, it's important to keep the list in a format that's easy to edit and to access. For larger teams, consider a tool that tracks changes. If your team is already using a specific tool, find a way to integrate feature definition with that process; otherwise, a shared spreadsheet or wiki is ideal.

> *"Even the best designers produce successful products only if their designs solve the right problems. A wonderful interface to the wrong features will fail."*
>
> Jakob Nielsen

The design team helped make CityBike's features more user oriented by adding user actions and contexts to existing stories.

The features for Ambience Mirror are documented in a wiki system that has an overview table linking to details and mock-ups for each individual feature.

Observations Suite's first-draft features are documented in a spreadsheet with descriptions and acceptance criteria, as well as prioritization derived from value and effort ratings.

CityBike / **Connected Bicycle**

Feature Definition

Feature	Relevant Stories
Automatic locking and unlocking	When I approach my bike, it automatically unlocks, so I can immediately start riding. When I leave my bike, it automatically locks, so I don't have to hassle with a manual lock.
Manual locking and unlocking	When my phone is dead, I manually unlock my bike, so I can ride it. When I don't have my phone, I manually lock my bike, so it won't get stolen.
On-bike E Ink display with backlight	When traveling somewhere new, I see directions on my on-bike display, so I don't have to use my phone. When riding at night, I use the display's backlight, so I can see directions.
Current bike location	When I forget where I parked my bike, I use the app to see its location, so I can easily find it. When my bike has been stolen, I view its location, so I know where to find it. When riding an unfamiliar route, I see my current location, so I don't get lost.
Navigation	When I'm preparing to go somewhere unfamiliar, I use the app to get directions, so I don't get lost. While I'm cycling, I get turn-by-turn directions, so I can easily navigate to my destination. When I'm riding my bike, I want to see my progress toward my destination, so I know if I'll arrive on time.
Bell	When a tourist steps into the bike path, I ring my bell at them, so they'll be aware of me. After purchasing the bike, I customize the bell sounds, so it feels like it's mine. When I can't find my bike, I ring the bell using the app, so I know where it is.
Account	When I purchase my bike, I create a new account, so I can connect to my CityBike. When I get a new CityBike, I connect it to my account, so I can retrieve it if it gets lost or stolen. When I get a new phone, I log into my account, so I can access all of my CityBike information. When I sell my CityBike, I disassociate it from my account, so the new rider can be the primary owner.
Weather integration	When preparing to ride, I review the upcoming weather, so I can be prepared.
FAQs	When I encounter a problem, I read the FAQs, so I can find a solution. After purchasing my CityBike, I read the instructions, so I can assemble it.
In-app customer-support chat	When I can't fix a problem myself, I chat with customer support, so I can fix the problem.

Required User Actions	Dependencies	Priority
• Adjust distance to unlock • Disable/enable auto-unlock • See visual and hear audio confirmation • Use UI button to unlock	• Proximity awareness • Bluetooth • Self-locking/unlocking mechanism	1
• Use a key to unlock my CityBike	• Traditional key mechanism	1
• Manage screen settings • View directions • View alerts and other important information	• Light sensor • Bluetooth	1
• See location of CityBike • See my current location • See last known location of CityBike if current location is unknown	• GPS • Location tracking • Maps	1
• Input destination and starting point (default to current location) • Choose between multiple routes • Receive step-by-step guidance via the on-bike display	• GPS • Bluetooth • Maps	1
• Customize bell sound • Customize bell volume • Ring bell using on-bike button • Ring bell using the app	• On-bike speaker • Bluetooth	1
• Create an account • Log into an existing account • Associate a new bike with my account (primary account holder) • Disassociate an old bike from my account	• Bluetooth	1
• See daily weather forecast • See immediate forecast	• Weather integration	2
• Read CityBike manual • Read FAQs		1
• Chat with customer support	• Customer-support chat module	2

Feature Definition

Priority ▾	Feature	Description
1	**See today's weather and outdoor air quality**	As Kyle, I want to see the upcoming and current weather condition, temperature, and outdoor air quality, so I can prepare for my run.
1	**View upcoming events**	As Allison, I want to see upcoming events, so I can prepare for my day.
1	**Adjust lighting scenes**	As Olivia, I want to adjust the mirror's lighting, so I can see how my makeup will look when I go out.
1	**See temperature, humidity, and indoor air quality**	As Allison, I want to be sure that my home's conditions are optimal, so that my family stays healthy.
1	**Customize my experience**	As Olivia, I want to customize my experience, so my mom doesn't see something embarrassing.
1	**Voice control my Ambience Mirror**	As a member of the Walker family, I want to control my Ambience Mirror without touching it, so I can have a more robust experience.
1	**Understand my heart rate**	As Kyle, I want to see how my heart rate changes with exercise, so I can better understand my performance.
1	**Understand my cycle**	As Olivia, I want to know when I'm ovulating, so I know to use protection with my boyfriend.
1	**Know when I'm getting sick**	As a member of the Walker family, I want to know when I'm getting sick, so I can take extra good care of myself.
1	**Understand my sleep patterns**	As Allison, I want to know when my sleep has been restless, so I can spend more time meditating that day.
1	**Add multiple users**	As a member of the Walker family, I want my own experience with the mirror.
1	**Set and see reminders**	As a member of the Walker family, I want to set reminders for myself, so I don't forget important things.
2	**See my previous day**	As Kyle, I want to see a summary of the previous day, so I feel accomplished.
2	**See social media notifications**	As Evie, I want to see when I have updates from friends, so I know to check Facebook.
2	**See my email**	As Allison, I want to see a preview of my inbox, so I can plan my day.

Ambience Mirror / AM-001

See today's weather and outdoor air quality

Priority: 1

Description

As Kyle, I want to see the upcoming and current weather condition, temperature, and outdoor air quality, so I can prepare for my run.

Enablers

Location information >

Integration with AccuWeather >

Acceptance Criteria

- I can see the current weather condition.
- I can see the current air quality.
- I can see the current temperature.
- I can see the predicted weather conditions for today.
- I can see the predicted air quality for today.
- I can see predicted temperature for today.

Attachments

Ambience Mirror / AM-003

Adjust lighting scenes

Priority: 1

Description

As Olivia, I want to adjust the mirror's lighting, so I can see how my makeup will look when I go out.

Enablers

Multicolor LED lighting border ›

VUI via Amazon Alexa integration ›

Acceptance Criteria

- I can switch between multiple lighting scenes.
- I can use voice to dictate which lighting scene I want.
- I can set a preferred lighting scene.
- The mirror recognizes me and defaults to my preferred lighting scene.

Attachments

Ambience Mirror / AM-005

Customize my experience

Priority: 1

Description
As Olivia, I want to customize my experience, so my mom doesn't see something embarrassing.

Enablers
Accounts ›
Integration with the Ambience mobile app ›
User recognition ›

Acceptance Criteria
- The mirror recognizes me by a combination of my infrared image and my voice.
- If a user who is not me uses the mirror, they cannot access my personal content.
- I can use the Ambience app to customize what appears for me on the Ambience Mirror.
- I can use the Ambience app to customize the layout of information on the Ambience Mirror.
- I can use the Ambience app to customize metaphors for information on the Ambience Mirror.

Attachments

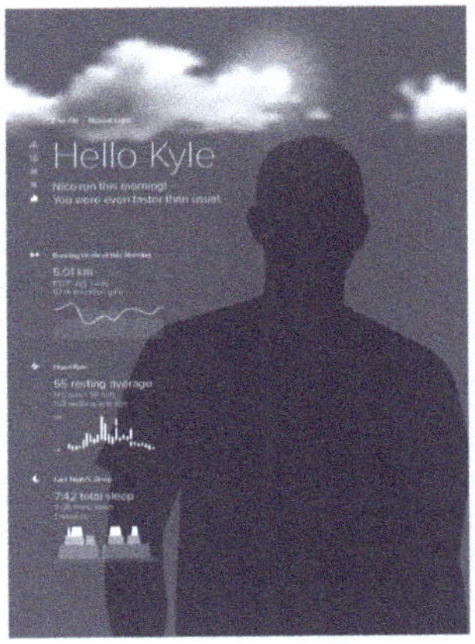

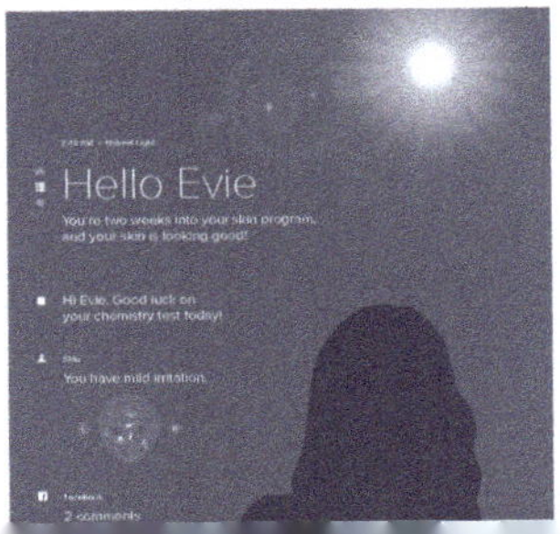

Omniscient / **Observations Suite Web App**

Feature Definition

Category	Title	Relevant Stories
CRM	Gather Basic Customer Info	When a user interacts with my restaurant, I want to capture basic info, like name, gender, and age, so that I can better market to them.
CRM	Gather Basic Customer Data	As customers engage with my restaurant over time, I want to capture the details of their interactions, so that I can provide a more customized experience.
CRM	Manage Customers	When I have multiple entries for a single customer, I want to combine them, so that my CRM tool is clean and organized. When I recognize a customer who doesn't use digital tools, I want to manually enter them into the CRM, so that my database is complete.
CRM	Edit Customer Information	When I learn something new about a customer, I want to add information to their entry in my CRM, so that I have the most complete information.
Movement Tracking	See Movement in an Area	When my kitchen is being inefficient, I want to review the movement map to see where cooks are getting congested. After I rearrange my restaurant, I want to review the movement map, so I can see which areas have the most congestion.
Movement Tracking	See Table Dwell Time	When learning about customer behavior, I want to review how long customers are sitting at tables, so that I can optimize my restaurant.
Movement Tracking	See Server Interactions	When observing my restaurant, I want to see how long it's been since a table's last interaction with a server, so that I know when it's been too long. When reviewing average spend per table, I want to view data about how often servers interact, so that I can optimize my restaurant.
Booking Analytics	Review Bookings	When reviewing my dashboard, I want to see how many bookings I have, so that I can predict my restaurant's revenue. After a busy weekend, I want to review bookings, so that I can quantify how busy my restaurant was.
Booking Analytics	Compare Bookings	When a holiday weekend approaches, I want to review current bookings versus the previous year's bookings, so I can compare how my restaurant is doing.
Progress Reports	Review a Month's Progress	At the end of the month, I want to see a summary of my performance, so that I understand how my restaurant is doing.
Progress Reports	Compare Reports from Multiple Months	When I've been using Observations Suite for a few months, I want to compare monthly summaries, so that I can see how well my restaurant is doing relative to other months. When I miss a summary, I want to review past months, so that I never miss important information.
Progress Reports	Customize Progress Reports	When I'm curious about a specific metric, I want to add it to my monthly progress report, so that it's easier to track. When I dislike something in my monthly report, I want to remove it, so that the information stays relevant to me.
Progress Reports	Receive Reports via Email	At the end of the month, I want to receive a summary of my restaurant's performance via email, so that I can dig deeper into the numbers that interest me.
Free Demo	See a Fake Company	When I want to better understand Observations Suite, I want to use a demo with a fake company, so that I can see how it works.

Acceptance Criteria	Value	Effort	Priority
• Store customer information in a single database • Pull in relevant information from integrated tools	5	3	1
• Collect data about reservations (when, how many people) • Collect data about orders (what) • Collect data about payment (average spend, method)	5	4	1
• Combine multiple user entries • Add new users manually	5	3	1
• Add, edit, and remove details about a customer	5	3	1
• Capture motion data for a given room or area within a restaurant • See visualized data in a heat map	5	3	1
• Capture motion data for a given room or area within a restaurant • See dwell time per table and per customer • Compare dwell time to average spend	5	4	1
• See visualizations of time since last interaction • Compare server interactions to average spend	5	4	1
• See upcoming bookings • Review past bookings	5	3	1
• Compare bookings over multiple time spans	5	3	1
• See an end-of-the-month summary of my restaurant's performance • Start with a curated list of the most relevant metrics	4	3	1
• Review previous months' summaries	4	3	1
• Add items to my monthly progress report • Remove items from my monthly progress report	3	4	1
• Optionally receive an end-of-the-month summary via email • Access my progress report on the web via links in the email	4	3	2
• Create a fake company account with data, visible to all users • Require users to sign up for an account to see the demo company	3	2	2

MAKE THE USER SMILE.

Create elements of joy throughout the experience.

Do not provide a serious health-only experience.

STAY FOCUSED ON THE DAY AHEAD.

Provide insights when confident.

Show past data with the intention of informing future behavior.

Never make predictions about the far future.

BE BRIEF.

Prioritize the glance over the focused gaze.

Avoid obscuring the user's face behind interface elements.

Don't overwhelm the user with social media updates.

Don't overwhelm the user with data.

Summarize data so meaning is obvious.

Keep statements short and simple.

CONSIDER BOTH USER + CONTEXT.

Consider time of day and day of week when showing info.

Avoid showing sensitive info in a public way.

Do not give priority to static information.

Ensure that each user has a unique and appropriate experience.

DON'T REPLACE THE USER'S PHONE.

Use nontouch interactions.

Prioritize showing information from rather than giving control to devices.

Do not replace the app with the Ambience Mirror.

Do not use the mirror as a smart-home control dashboard.

Do not encourage interactions that will result in smudges and fingerprints.

PUT THE USER IN CONTROL.

Always let the user know when they're being recorded (sound, IR video).

Don't coach unless the user has explicitly asked for it.

Start with sensible defaults, but let the user decide.

Allow the user to set his/her own privacy limitations.

Provide the user with options for heavy customization.

Do not provide a generic dashboard for all users.

Experience Principles

Creating a product or service takes time, and more complexity requires more time. Over the life of a project, as teams shift, new trends emerge, and technologies evolve, it can be a challenge to determine which changes should affect the course of your project. With discovery-phase inputs like trendscapes, user interviews, and business and competitive analyses, experience principles provide guidance and ensure that the most important aspects of the vision survive from conception through execution.

When creating experience principles, it's important to consider their entire life span and their many audiences. Experience principles need to be as relevant to a business stakeholder making decisions around marketing as they are to engineering stakeholders making decisions around feature prioritization. A solid set of experience principles will not only keep the product or service focused, it will also ensure that the project team stays aligned.

Historically, designers have used principles in a variety of ways. There are principles that focus generally on what makes good design, such as Mies van der Rohe's "Less is more," as well as principles focused on what makes a good design process, such as IBM's "Always keep your target users in mind as the product is designed." These, along with the principles used to guide the design of a specific product or service, are often all referred to as design principles.

While these principles might all provide value in aligning and guiding teams, they are also too broadly applicable. Though they may help define one designer's or company's work, they do not help distinguish one experience from another. In contrast, experience principles focus on guiding not only what the experience of the product or service should be for the user but also how it stands apart from other products or services.

In addition to targeting a specific experience, experience principles are also oriented around the user. They are more general than principles that describe executional details, like the orientation of windows on a building or the placement of buttons on the screen, and more specific than principles that describe how a design team should function.

Good experience principles are focused on how we want the user to think and feel; they are specific and uniquely applicable to the experience we are designing; and they are phrased in a way that is helpful in guiding business, design, and development decisions.

Activities

If you're well into a project, it's likely that some principles have already emerged, and there may even be already-existing artifacts that resemble experience principles. Start by looking for and collecting anything that expresses a point of view about the experience. For example, a well-crafted value proposition might outline the high-level value the product provides to users along with some details around how it provides it, and a competitive analysis might highlight how the product will be differentiated in the market. An experience audit might have a point of view around what priorities will make the product or service stronger, and stakeholder interviews might reveal already-existing strong positions within the team. If you have these inputs, gather them for synthesis into experience principles.

If you're starting with a blank slate, consider decisions that have been made but not yet documented. If nothing here represents an obviously unique point of view, consider the following prompts to get started in writing experience principles:

* Is the experience front and center or only in the periphery?
* Is the experience playful or serious?
* Do you prefer your user to have deep experiences or frequent experiences?
* Is use more about interaction or consumption?
* Is it a social or a personal experience?
* Is it more of a feeling experience or a thinking experience?
* Will you use data and statistics or human advice to motivate your user?
* Does the experience focus on the present, past, or future?
* Is your experience highly customized and/or personalized, or does it look and feel the same for all users?

With experience principles, it's good to start with more than you need and then to synthesize and curate down to the strongest. You might hold a workshop with the team to help with this process. Show draft principles phrased as statements with examples of decisions that would and would not be in line with their meaning. If you have conflicting input from stakeholders,

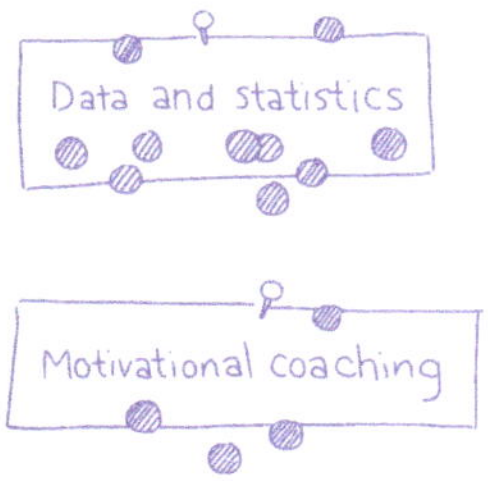

Highlight conflicts and drive toward alignment.

Curate and synthesize to somewhere between five and nine principles.

Make sure every principle has a viable opposite or alternative.

highlight those conflicts in opposing principles. See how stakeholders react, and drive toward alignment.

At the end of the curation and synthesis process, aim to have somewhere between five and nine experience principles. Any more than that will be difficult to remember.

Test your experience principles to make sure that they express a distinct point of view. For each principle, write down the opposite or alternative. If that alternative is not something that a competing product might use, you may need to rewrite your experience principle to be more specific. If you completed a competitive analysis, it can be helpful to compare the experiences of your competitors against your principles. In this way, experience principles can purposefully align and differentiate your product or service.

When writing experience principles, avoid confusing unique intentions with basic expectations. Many companies adopt principles like, "The product is easy to use," because the existing competition has failed to deliver on this promise. While ease of use may set one product apart from the competition, from a user's perspective, it is also assumed. It would be unusual for a company to try to make an experience hard to use.

Once you have a body of experience principles, read through and compare them to each other. If there are repetitive principles, consolidate. If you feel that any key aspects of the experience are missing, add new principles. If a principle seems too small in its scope, consider how it could be extended to apply to the overall experience.

Aiming for a limited number of experience principles might make it tempting to combine principles with different meanings. Avoid doing this. An experience principle with multiple parts encourages picking and choosing the parts that are convenient. If you keep your principles short and focused, you can ensure that team members are more likely to understand them as you intended.

Artifacts

Because experience principles are used from their inception through to the end of a project, it's important to have them in a format that everyone has access to and that no one can forget about. Try printing experience principles on posters and hanging them throughout project rooms so that, despite different roles and deadlines, everyone keeps the same goals top of mind.

Experience principles should also live as a part of the product or service documentation. Consider placing the experience principles in a prominent place on the team's wiki or within the design guidelines for easy reference. Keep track of where the experience principles live so that old versions don't continue informing decisions.

As a product or service increases in fidelity, it's likely that a more specific series of principles will emerge to describe how the user engages with different channels and touchpoints. Consider tying these more specific principles to your original experience principles, providing more detail as well as examples of what to do or not to do. These examples can help to make the abstract more concrete and can ensure original intent remains in the details and across future iterations and extensions of the experience.

CityBike's experience principles describe how screens should be used to support the user's experience with the Connected Bicycle, rather than dominating it. Principles are supported with examples of both good and bad decisions.

Experience principles for Ambience Mirror describe a product differentiated from others in the market. Each principle describes what should be done, what should be avoided, and examples of adherent decisions.

Experience Principles

Keep riding at the center of the experience.

✓

Do put the most important information at a glance on the on-bike display.

Do keep functionality requiring heavy interaction on the phone.

✗

Do not encourage the user to interact with the app while riding.

Do not put detailed information on the on-bike display.

Prioritize frequent light use over deep exploration.

✓

Do present summaries and quick actions for easy navigation.

Do use notifications to bring important information to the user's attention.

✗

Do not lead with browsable histories and content.

Do not present the user with data that's not immediately relevant.

Balance the big picture with the details.

✓

Do provide multiple layers of resolution for exploration.

Do lead with the most relevant level of information.

✗

Do not limit the user's understanding by providing too little context.

Do not treat all levels of information as equal.

Focus on what's happening now and next.

✓

- Do present the user with the current status.
- Do prioritize immediately upcoming actions.

✗

- Do not prioritize past rides or instructions.
- Do not present the user with information too far in the future.

Interrupt the user's focus only when crucial information needs to be communicated.

✓

- Do notify the user when their bicycle needs maintenance.
- Do notify the user when their bike has been stolen.

✗

- Do not present navigation information in an alarming way.
- Do not use notifications for marketing.

Be transparent about what's known versus guessed.

✓

- Do present the user with data that you know to be correct.
- Do visualize uncertainty differently than certainty.

✗

- Do not present guesses about the user's behavior or product state as reality.

Experience Principles

Stay focused on the day ahead.

Do not focus on the past and the far future.

Show past data with the intention of informing future data.

Make predictions about the future when confident.

Provide actionable insights when confident.

Avoid showing all data from the previous day.

Avoid making predictions for the entire week.

Consider both the user and their context.

Do not create an experience that's always the same.

Consider the time of day and day of the week when showing information.

Ensure that each user has a unique and appropriate experience.

Avoid showing information that doesn't change.

Don't replace the user's phone.

Do not create an experience with functionality that rivals the phone.

Avoid interactions that might result in smudges and fingerprints.

Avoid replacing the app with the Ambience Mirror.

Use the Ambience Mirror to show information rather than to control other devices.

Do not mimic the app's functionality.

Put the user in control.

Do not provide a one-size-fits-all experience.

Provide the user with options for heavy customization.

Allow the user to set their own privacy limitations.

Always let the user know when they're being watched or recorded.

Avoid making assumptions about what a user wants to keep private.

Provide coaching only when users ask for it.

Make the user smile.

Do not take a clinical approach.

Create elements of joy throughout the experience.

Find fun ways to visualize information.

Don't avoid emotion.

Avoid providing a clinical experience.

Be brief.

Do not show the user everything out of fear of missing something.

Prioritize the glance over the focused gaze.

Avoid obscuring the user's face behind interface elements.

Avoid overwhelming the user with social media updates.

Do not show the user lots of charts and graphs.

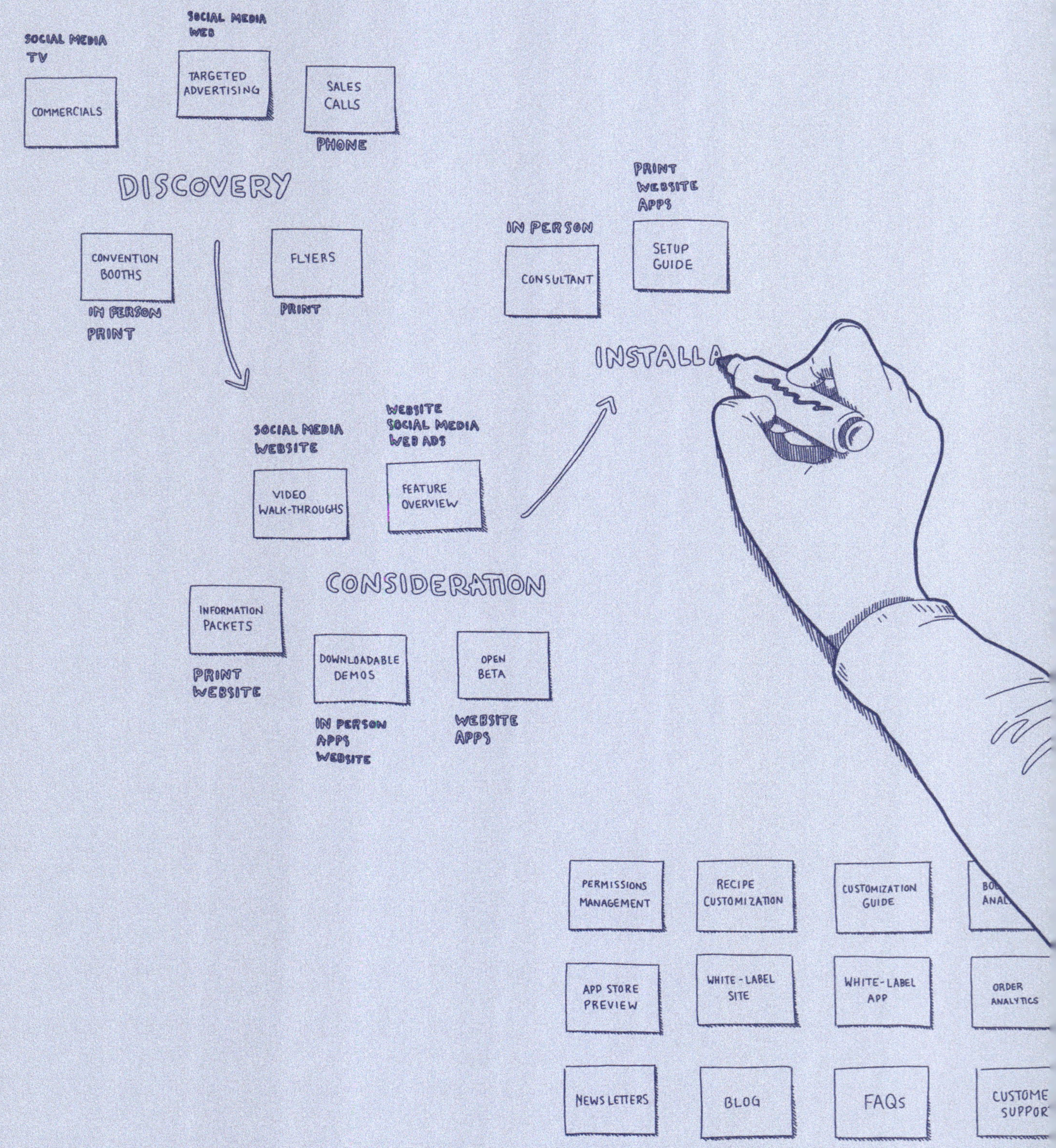
SOCIAL MEDIA
TV
COMMERCIALS
SOCIAL MEDIA
WEB
TARGETED ADVERTISING
SALES CALLS
PHONE
DISCOVERY
CONVENTION BOOTHS
IN PERSON
PRINT
FLYERS
PRINT
SOCIAL MEDIA
WEBSITE
VIDEO WALK-THROUGHS
WEBSITE
SOCIAL MEDIA
WEB ADS
FEATURE OVERVIEW
CONSIDERATION
INFORMATION PACKETS
PRINT
WEBSITE
DOWNLOADABLE DEMOS
IN PERSON
APPS
WEBSITE
OPEN BETA
WEBSITE
APPS
IN PERSON
CONSULTANT
PRINT
WEBSITE
APPS
SETUP GUIDE
INSTALLA
PERMISSIONS MANAGEMENT
RECIPE CUSTOMIZATION
CUSTOMIZATION GUIDE
APP STORE PREVIEW
WHITE-LABEL SITE
WHITE-LABEL APP
ORDER ANALYTICS
NEWS LETTERS
BLOG
FAQs

Offering Map

While a project might focus on the design of a single product or service, the user's experience often extends beyond this. From discovery to retention, the user's engagement involves many interactions across touchpoints. In many organizations, this requires coordination between multiple teams and departments. The offering map supports this coordination by mapping the many different aspects of the user's experience into a single visualization. For a design team or a design agency, it can serve as a tool for planning future projects with stakeholders or clients.

Concept generation and feature definition are valuable inputs for understanding offerings, while the strategic roadmap can highlight when offerings will be available to users. Personas can be helpful to show not only where users engage with what but also how different users have unique experiences. While the offering map is similar to the experience journey in the information it presents, its focus is on the company or organization rather than on the user's experience. If your project is simple and has relatively few stakeholders, you might not need an offering map.

Activities

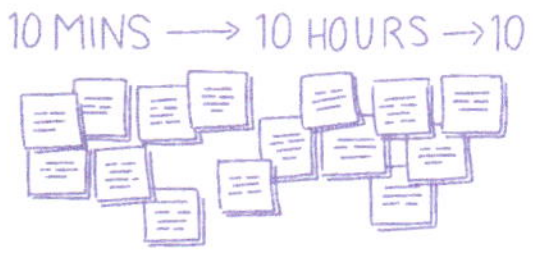

Break the experience down into the first ten minutes, hours, days, and months.

Consider how offerings reach different users or personas.

Map offerings across different touchpoints and channels.

Designing an effective offering map starts with understanding the scope of what it is that you're designing. If you're mapping a user's engagement surrounding a single product or service, you'll want to break your offering map into clusters of similar features, whereas if you're choreographing multiple products and services, you'll likely want each of them to be their own item on the offering map. Once you've settled on a scope and level of detail, lay out the individual offerings of your experience, starting with those that will be experienced first on the left and last on the right.

If you need to expand on a core set of offerings, consider how your company will provide for the user throughout their journey. How will you market and sell the product or service? How will you introduce the user to the experience? What offerings will your user engage with every day? And what will your company do to keep your customer engaged? A simpler framing might be, What do we offer the user in their first ten minutes, ten hours, ten days, and ten months? If you want to turn this into a collaborative activity with the team, you could ask everyone to brainstorm around these categories.

Make sure to consider these questions for multiple types of users or personas. Do they have different roles with different needs? Are their experiences unique?

With a complete set of offerings, begin to map engagements across channels and touchpoints. Consider where each offering will be available. This is the foundation of your offering map.

Next you'll need to decide what additional layers of information to add to your map. You might highlight what features will launch when, mapping out future iterations of the product or service and showing how the user's experience will evolve over time. You could also layer on information about your organization's structure, assigning responsibility for different parts of the user's experience.

If feasibility and/or priority are important to show in your offering map, consider bringing in stakeholders or users to help define what's easiest or what's most important. You might try participatory-design exercises, like card sorts, to help capture priorities or to better understand which aspects are difficult to implement and why. While multiple inputs add complexity to an already-complex process, they will guarantee that the offering map is more aligned to stakeholder expectations and more defensible to those who might challenge it.

Map offerings by what's easiest and/or most important.

Artifacts

Once you've decided on a scope and level of detail, captured the aspects of your experience, and decided which layers of information are most important to expose, you're ready to lay out your offering map. An offering map might be as simple as a spreadsheet, or it might be printed at a large scale to provide a visual talking point that drives alignment. A large-scale poster often uses illustrations and other graphics to draw stakeholders' attention and guide their eyes to what's most important.

If you're designing for multiple roles or personas, divide the offering map vertically to show what roles encounter which aspects of the experience over time. If roles are less delineated, user color coding or annotations to show their unique paths through the experience.

For communicating multiple touchpoints, you might use multiple swim lanes to show where the user encounters each aspect of the experience. Alternatively, you could use illustrations to help highlight whether a feature occurs in print, in person, on the computer, etc.

If you want to highlight feasibility or priority, try putting the most important aspects or the core of your experience at the base of the map, with less important/feasible features farther away from the horizon. If your idea of priority or feasibility is less nuanced, consider highlighting easily accomplished or high-priority offerings of the experience using color or scale.

These many layers of information can be overwhelming, so use a grid and consistent layout to bring order to your offering map. If possible, break the timeline into activity-based categories, highlighting the different types of engagements or goals in the user's experience. Make sure that every offering has a title and a short description of the value it provides users.

When presenting the offering map to stakeholders, consider the conversation you want to have. The offering map can be the main attraction of a meeting intended to inspire stakeholders to see the big picture around a product or service, or it can be supporting material for conversation about priority and responsibility assignment. With decisions made, the map can visualize all of this information for everyone on the team to easily reference.

> *"However tight things are, you still need to have the big picture at the forefront of your mind."*
>
> Richard Branson

The offering map for Observations Suite seeks to drive conversations around prioritization for the first release of the product. It shows which feature clusters will be used by different roles over time, with channels clearly marked so that stakeholders can easily choose what's most important and where users should interact with it.

Omniscient / **Observations Suite Vision**

Offering Map

Channels

Marketing

- TV Television
- SM Social Media
- P Print
- PP In Person
- T Telephone
- C Messaging / Chat Platforms
- W Website
- E Email
- O Other Sites

Observations Suite Apps

- D Desktop App
- M Mobile App
- T Tablet App
- W Web App

Observations Suite Apps

- W Restaurant Website
- A Restaurant App

Managing

Professional Offerings

Working

Discovery

TV SM

Commercials provide an introduction to the product.

SM O

Targeted advertising shows potential customers a glimpse of our product.

T

Through **sales calls** we proactively reach out to potential customers.

P

Print ads in industry magazines provide an introduction to new customers.

PP

Convention booths spread awareness to those in the industry.

Consideration

SM W

Video walk-throughs show new and existing users how the product works.

P W

An **information packet** provides information to users who want information.

PP D M T W

In-person demos show users how it's done by an expert.

D M T

Downloadable demos allow the user to explore the product on their own.

SM W O

Easy-to-parse **feature descriptions** set expectations at a high level.

Installation + Setup

Consumer Offerings

Customization

Booking + Orders

Fulfillment

PP D M T W

On-site consultation and setup ensure that Observations Suite is perfectly configured.

D M T W

Recipe customization captures items for the menu and inventory management.

D M T W

Booking analytics show who's booking when, busy times, and more.

D M T W

Inventory analytics show the patterns in inventory stock and ordering.

P W D M T W

The **setup guide** walks users through setup and customization.

D M T W

A **white-label site** provides restaurants with an integrated off-the-shelf solution.

D M T W

Order analytics provide insights into who orders and when.

D M T W

Inventory ordering enables restocking from preferred vendors.

D M T W

Employee permissions ensure everyone has the right level of access.

D M T W

A **white-label app** provides restaurants an app for their customers.

D M T W

Inventory status shows an overview of current and predicted stock.

D M T W

A **customization guide** ensures that the user has created a fully branded experience.

D M T

The **reservations interface** puts servers in control of table management.

D M T

The **seating-management interface** enables users to manage table availability.

D M T

The **incoming orders** interface shows what's been ordered when.

D M T

The **order-fulfillment interface** provides an interface for managing incoming orders.

O

The **app store preview** tells the user all they need to know before downloading.

W A

The **reservations interface** allows users to book tables before they visit the restaurant.

W A

The **ordering interface** connects users to their favorite restaurants to place orders.

Payments

D M T W

Store-performance analytics visualize a store's revenue over time.

D M T

The **point-of-sale system** allows restaurants to process payments.

P E W A

The **receipt** provides the user with a record of the transaction.

Marketing

D M T W

The **campaign-creation tool** enables restaurants to create promotions.

D M T W

Campaign analytics show restaurants how their campaigns are performing.

D M T W

Online-acquisition tracking shows how online advertising is performing.

D M T

The **campaign-fulfillment interface** integrates campaigns with the PoS.

E W A

Marketing communications inform users of new campaigns and offers.

Customer Engagement

D M T W

The **CRM database** enables restaurants to track their customers.

D M T W

Customer analytics show customers' engagement over time.

D M T W

Customer-feedback analytics show what customers are saying about the restaurant.

D M T

Loyalty-program fulfillment keeps staff apprised of customers' loyalty status.

W A

Feedback forms allow users to provide feedback on food and service.

E W A

Loyalty programs reward users for their patronage.

Store Management

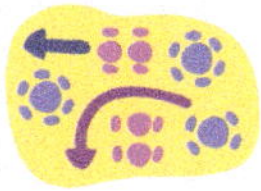

D M T W

Aggregated analytics provide a visual overview in a single place.

D M T W

Movement analytics show how customers and employees are using the space.

D M T W

Insights provide actionable recommendations to improve performance.

Employee Management

D M T W

Employee-scheduling interface enables managers to schedule workers' time.

D M T W

Individual-growth interface helps managers manage the growth of employees.

D M T W

Employee analytics show managers their employees' performance over time.

D M T W

Professional-growth tools help employees track their goals and progress.

D M T W

A **mentorship program** connects employees with mentors to help them grow.

Customer Support

SM P C E
D M T W

24-hour professional support helps Observations Suite users around the clock.

P W

FAQs help new and existing users find the answers they need.

Ongoing Engagement

E

Newsletters keep users apprised of industry news and announcements.

E D M T W

Periodical progress reports celebrate success and highlight opportunities.

PP

Speakers at industry events show how to improve performance with Observations Suite.

D M T W

Feature updates show users when new functionality has been added to Observations Suite.

O W

An industry blog establishes credibility and shares insights with followers.

SM P C E W A

24-hour customer support helps customers of restaurants around the clock.

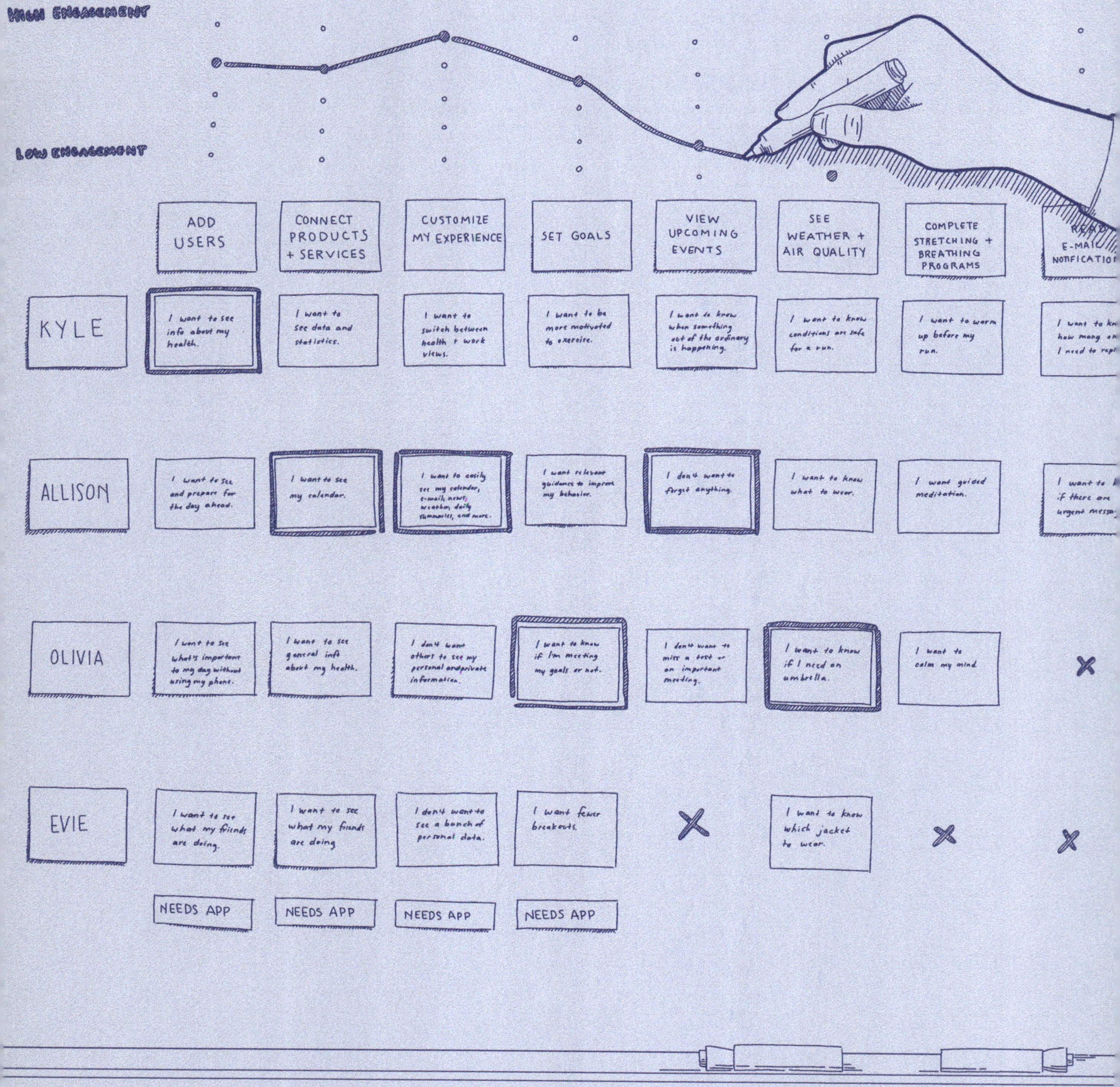
HIGH ENGAGEMENT
LOW ENGAGEMENT
ADD USERS
CONNECT PRODUCTS + SERVICES
CUSTOMIZE MY EXPERIENCE
SET GOALS
VIEW UPCOMING EVENTS
SEE WEATHER + AIR QUALITY
COMPLETE STRETCHING + BREATHING PROGRAMS
E-MAIL NOTIFICATIO
KYLE
I want to see info about my health.
I want to see data and statistics.
I want to switch between health + work views.
I want to be more motivated to exercise.
I want to know when something out of the ordinary is happening.
I want to know conditions are safe for a run.
I want to warm up before my run.
ALLISON
I want to see and prepare for the day ahead.
I want to see my calendar.
I want to easily see my calendar, e-mail, news, weather, daily summaries, and more.
I want relevant guidance to improve my behavior.
I don't want to forget anything.
I want to know what to wear.
I want guided meditation.
OLIVIA
I want to see what's important to my day without using my phone.
I want to see general info about my health.
I don't want others to see my personal and private information.
I want to know if I'm meeting my goals or not.
I don't want to miss a test or an important meeting.
I want to know if I need an umbrella.
I want to calm my mind.
EVIE
I want to see what my friends are doing.
I want to see what my friends are doing
I don't want to see a bunch of personal data.
I want fewer breakouts.
I want to know which jacket to wear.
NEEDS APP
NEEDS APP
NEEDS APP
NEEDS APP

Experience Journey

Experiences have many facets. They vary depending on the user as well as the touchpoint. The first use is rarely representative of ongoing use, while best- and worst-case scenarios might barely resemble each other. The experience journey aims to look beyond all of this to capture and distill an experience into a single path representative of most users' engagements or desired engagements over time.

In addition to the moments that best summarize an experience, experience journeys show additional layers of information, such as emotion, affect, level of engagement, and so on. If you have multiple personas, you might highlight their unique contexts and goals throughout the journey. The format and layers of information that you choose to visualize should be determined by the complexity of the experience you're seeking to represent and the audience to whom you'll be presenting.

Activities

Get stakeholder input around what they consider core to the experience.

Prioritize concepts or features for the journey as a group.

Work with users to build their own journeys out of concept cards.

Like many artifacts, it's dangerous to choose a form for an experience journey before understanding the content within. Because experience journeys are made of moments of engagement, this is the most reliable place to start. Reflect on earlier activities, such as stakeholder interviews, competitive analysis, user interviews, and immersion. If you're working on an already-existing or well-defined product or service, you may look to features as a starting point. Synthesize what you have into moments, with each moment representing a user's action within a specific context as well as the user's goal or desired outcome.

Organize the moments, weaving them into a single narrative organized by time. Consider how the user first encounters the experience, their first use and ongoing use, and what happens when they are finished with the product or service.

If you want to use the experience journey to collaborate beyond the design team, try pulling in stakeholders and users to help you understand which moments are most important and to capture any you might have missed. Here are some exercises you might use:

Card Ranking

Create moment cards. Ask stakeholders or users to sort the moment cards from most important to least important. If you have more than thirty moment cards, consider having users simply sort them into essential and nonessential categories.

Group Prioritization

With a group of stakeholders, ask everyone to vote by placing stickers on the moments that they find most important. You can give each stakeholder a set number of stickers to force hard choices or provide unlimited stickers, allowing everyone to vote as many times as they'd like—even multiple times for the same idea. Discuss the votes afterward as a group.

Storytelling

Create a series of moment cards, and ask users to build their own stories from these cards. Have them tell their stories with details about what frustrates and delights them most. This exercise can be helpful for the experience journey as well as for key scenarios.

Whether you're working alone or with others to collect and organize moments, collect annotations. If you're working with users, consider how they feel about each moment. What are they thinking about? Do they feel positive or negative about the experience? How engaged or focused are they?

If you're working with stakeholders, capture layers of strategic information. Where does the technology or brand of your company provide an advantage over others? Where does the competition miss an opportunity? When does the competition set a standard that your experience will need to meet? What features are most important to the first launch or MVP, and which can wait until later releases?

Experiences vs. Offerings

While prioritizing which information is most important for your experience journey, you might find competing needs. While design and research teams might want more user-centered information, development teams might want to see a representation of the effort required to complete each feature. If you find yourself trying to make the experience journey work for the latter set of priorities, consider creating an offering map instead of or in addition to a more user-centered experience journey.

Additional Applications

The experience-journey format can be useful for capturing notes during user interviews, immersion, and user validation. These individuals' experience journeys are valuable input in the creation and maintenance of the overall experience journey.

Artifacts

Experience journeys are often printed and hung on walls for regular reference by different teams and stakeholders throughout a project. They tend to be long and also fairly large. It's common for experience journeys to have text, illustrations, iconography, and data visualization, all carefully interwoven into an easy-to-read timeline.

With an experience journey, design starts with writing. Once you feel confident that you've covered all key aspects of the experience via the moments, you'll want to rewrite each so that they all have the same structure. Along with making sure that each moment captures at least the user's action and optionally context and goal, also try to write each moment in the same voice, first or third person, and using the same verb tense, usually present. See *Formatting Moments* for some possible approaches.

With your moments more carefully crafted, you'll need to decide whether you have too much, too little, or just the right amount of detail. An easily comprehended experience journey should generally lay

Formatting Moments

There are many best practices for how to capture moments, and it's easy to confuse them. In Agile development, teams often employ user stories, which have a role-feature-benefit structure:

As a user, I want to see data about my runs, so I know how fast I ran.

Product managers might prefer a situation-motivation-outcome approach:

After going for a run, I want to see if I was faster or slower than usual, so I can understand my improvement over time.

If your organization uses one of these methods, you may want to also for familiarity. On the other hand, you may not want to get caught up in the politics of stories that another team is responsible for, so choosing a unique format may be preferable.

out somewhere between eighteen and thirty-six moments in time. If you have fewer than this, consider adding nuance to your moments. You may find that a single moment actually needs to be two or three when looking more closely at the details.

It's more likely that you have too many moments, in which case you'll need to begin the difficult task of synthesizing them into fewer cards. Start by grouping moments that have the same context or that happen at the same time in the experience. Focus on the action or what the user is doing. For example, a user might look at a visualization of workout data to understand if their workout performance is better or worse than their average, to see the calories burned, or to simply understand time and distance. Looking at the visualization of workout data is the action, while everything else is the desired outcome. Capture these various contexts and desired outcomes in the notes of the moment, and synthesize them into one simpler moment: *See my workout.*

Next you'll need to define the structure that organizes the moments. The first decision you'll need to make is whether you want to represent a single experience or whether you'd like to show multiple experiences woven together over time. While a single experience is most common, you might want to map multiple experiences if you're focusing on different personas with vastly different paths through the product or service. It can be helpful to compare and highlight those differences within a single map. For example, you might want to show different engagement levels for a zealous user versus a sporadic one, or you might want to show how different personas have different needs while engaging with the same series of moments over time.

You might also want to visualize an experience across multiple roles. While a single experience journey can follow which personas perform what actions when, this might require that the different personas alternate on the journey or that personas come into and out of focus as the activeness of their roles changes.

Multiple journeys overlaid on each other can also be used to compare a user's current experience without the product to the user's desired experience with the product. These sorts of comparisons can help highlight the opportunities generated by new technology while also capturing the expectations that have been set by the current standard experience.

Once you've decided on whether to visualize a single experience or multiple experiences, finalize the order of moments and the organization of details. Refine as you go—synthesizing where necessary and filling in any gaps highlighted by the new structure.

Next, decide what the most important secondary information is. Usually this will be emotion, affect, or engagement. Emotion is multidimensional and can range from afraid to joyful to lonely to hopeful. Affect is simply the positivity or negativity that a user feels at a point in time. While affect can be mapped easily on the vertical axis, emotions are better captured in more nuanced ways. Try using icons, emoji, or colors to show how a user is feeling at a given point in time. If you're struggling, the most common of these choices is to show affect on the vertical axis.

Once you have the most important aspects of your experience journey mapped out, it's likely that you'll want to continue adding more layers of information to it. Choose layers that are most likely to guide and influence stakeholders toward decisions that benefit the user. Make sure to maintain an obvious hierarchy within this information. Here are some tricks for guiding your audience's attention:

* Use illustration to highlight and humanize the most important moments in the experience journey.
* Use color to highlight moments of great opportunity or friction.
* Use type weight and size to draw attention to important annotations. Make sure that the most important details are viewable from a distance.
* Use location to prioritize content. If you're presenting to a culture that reads left-to-right and top-to-bottom, make sure the least important information is at the bottom and/or right.

The experience journey will likely live on to inform the rest of your project. It might provide provocations for concept generation, or it might create a structure for exploring and presenting design directions. If you used the experience journey to prioritize moments (or features), it might serve as a guide to help maintain focus on the MVP experience. And if you choreographed an experience across multiple channels, it could help ensure a consistent experience across multiple teams.

The experience journey for Ambience Mirror looks at how the four personas engage with the same product over time. Across all personas, it seeks to capture general actions and levels of engagement, highlighting a single specific engagement within each illustration. Color highlights which moments the team has decided to prioritize across the experience.

Personal Intelligence / **Ambience Mirror**

Experience Journey

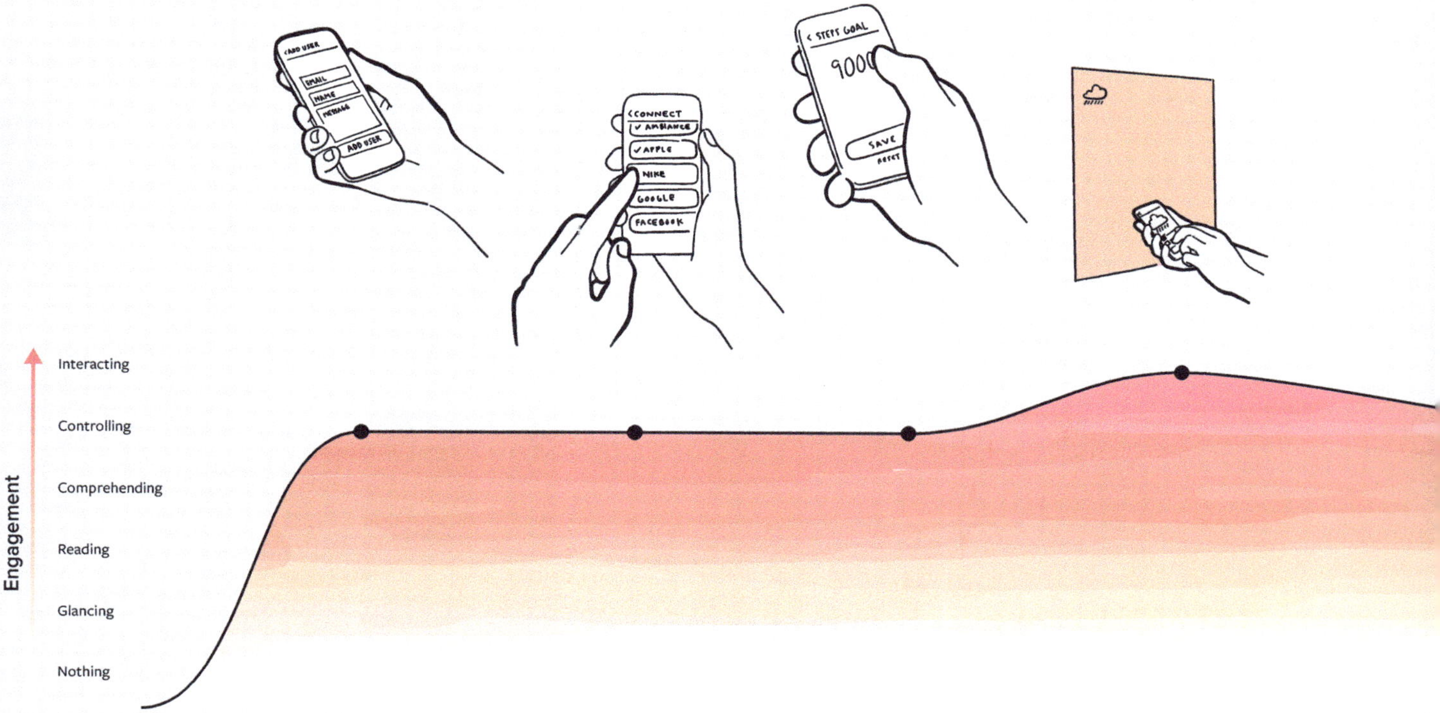

Generic Actions	Add multiple users	Connect products and services to the Ambience ecosystem	Set my goals	Customize my experience
Kyle A father who enjoys running, keeping up with his (book) fans on Twitter, and working at his job, which is not too demanding.	Before using it, I add myself as a user to the Ambience Mirror, so I can see my health information.	After creating an account, I connect my fitness products and services to the Ambience ecosystem, so I can see my stats on the mirror.	After setting up my devices, I set fitness goals, so that I have extra motivation to exercise in the morning.	Once I've set up my mirror, I customize a handful of scenes, so that I can easily switch between health and work views.
Allison A tech-savvy mother with a demanding career who enjoys meditation and anything that helps her stay organized.	After hanging the mirror, I add myself as a user, so I can integrate it with my calendar and email.	After creating my account, I connect my email and calendar to the Ambience ecosystem, so I can get previews of my day on the mirror.	After connecting to my account, I confirm my goals from the ecosystem, so it can provide me with relevant coaching.	Once I've connected everything important, I customize my experience so that I can easily see my calendar, email, news, weather, daily summaries, and insights.
Olivia A college student living at home who likes going out, staying healthy, and keeping her private life away from her parents.	Before using it, I add myself as a user to the Ambience Mirror, so I can see what's important to me without getting distracted by my phone.	After using the mirror for a few days, I connect to the Apple Health app, so I can see additional information about my health.	After connecting to my account, I enter my step goal, so I can see whether or not I'm meeting it.	After the first time I use the mirror, I create scenes and select less obvious visualizations for sensitive personal data, so others don't see my private information.
Evie A young teenager who balances school, friends, and sports and who struggles with her teenage skin.	Before using it, I add myself as a user to the Ambience Mirror, so I can keep up with my friends.	After creating my account, I connect to Facebook, so I can better keep up with my friends.	When setting up my account, I add healthy-skin goals, so that I have fewer breakouts.	When I'm setting up the mirror, I customize my experience, so I don't have to look at things like sleep that I'm not interested in.

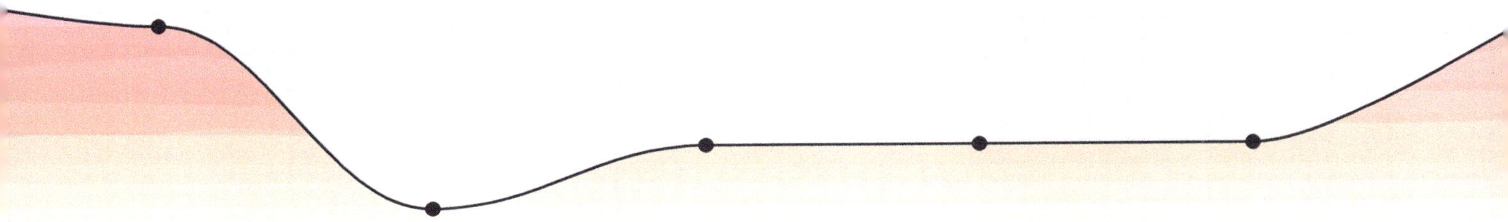

Voice control my Ambience Mirror

When I enter the bathroom, I greet the mirror, so I can see information about the previous night's sleep.

When I want to see upcoming events, I request my "today" scene, so that I can mentally prepare.

When I enter the bathroom, I say hello to the Ambience Mirror, so it wakes up and displays what's important to me.

When I enter the bathrrom, I say hello to the Ambience Mirror, so I can see if I have any Facebook notifications.

See today's weather and outdoor air quality

Before going for a run, I check the air quality, so I know it's safe.

Before getting dressed, I look at the temperature and weather conditions, so that I'm sure to be warm enough.

Before heading to class, I see today's weather, so I know if I need to bring an umbrella.

Before grabbing a jacket, I look at the outdoor temperature and weather conditions, so I know which one to wear.

View upcoming events

Before starting my day, I view upcoming events, so I know if there's anything out of the ordinary.

When I'm uncertain about my schedule, I view upcoming events, so that I don't forget anything.

Every morning, I view upcoming events, so I don't miss a test or an important meeting.

See my email

Before going to work, I see my email, so I know if there's anything pressing I should reply to.

Before going to work, I see my email, so I know if there are any urgent matters.

Receive news alerts

When something newsworthy occurs, I receive news alerts, so I'm up to date with the latest news.

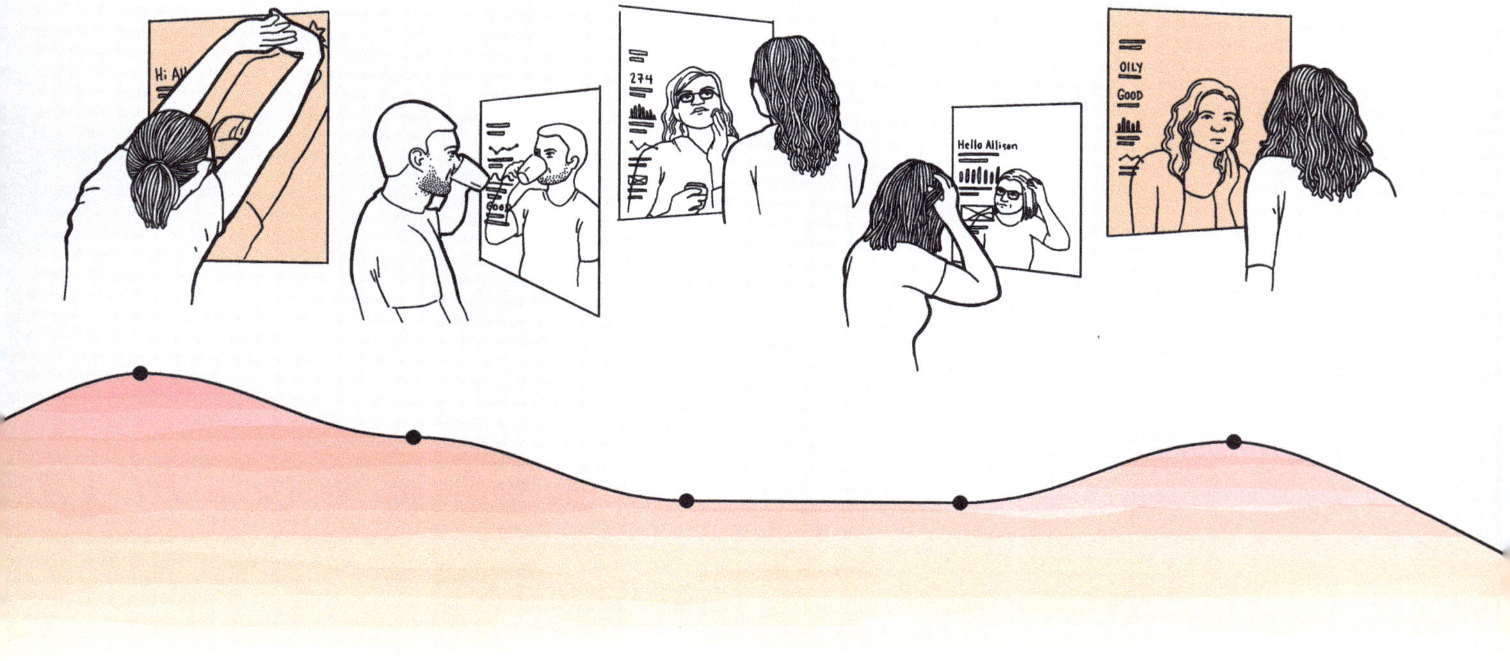

Complete stretching and breathing programs

Before going for a run, I complete a stretching and breathing program, so that my body wakes up.

After waking up, I complete a stretching and breathing program to help me meditate.

After showering, I complete a stretching and breathing program to help me stay calm and focused on the day ahead.

Understand my heart rate

After going for a run, I review my heart rate and cooldown, so I can better understand my fitness.

See my workout

After going for a run, I review my workout, so I know if I was better or worse than normal.

After going to the gym with my friends, I see my workout, so I know how many calories I burned.

After a run with my dad, I'll look at my workout, so I can see how fast and how far we went.

Check my hydration

Every morning, I check my hydration, so I'm sure I'm getting enough water.

Especially in the winter, I check my hydration, so I know if I need to be drinking more fluids.

After a night out with friends, I check my hydration, so that I can avoid hangovers.

Check skin-irritation levels

After a long day in the sun, I check my skin-irritation levels, so I know if I need to do anything special for my face.

When I'm feeling stressed, I check my skin-irritation levels, so I don't get a terrible breakout.

Every morning and evening I check my skin-irritation levels, so I know if I need to do something to prevent a breakout.

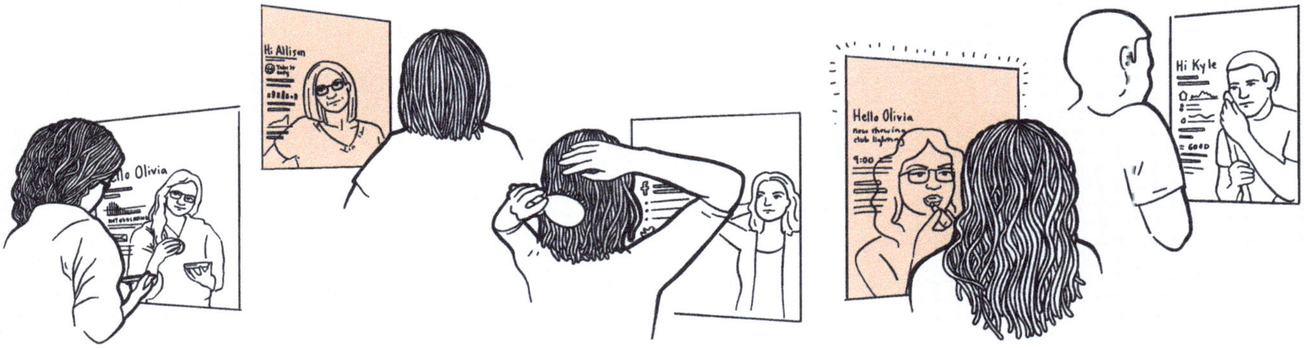

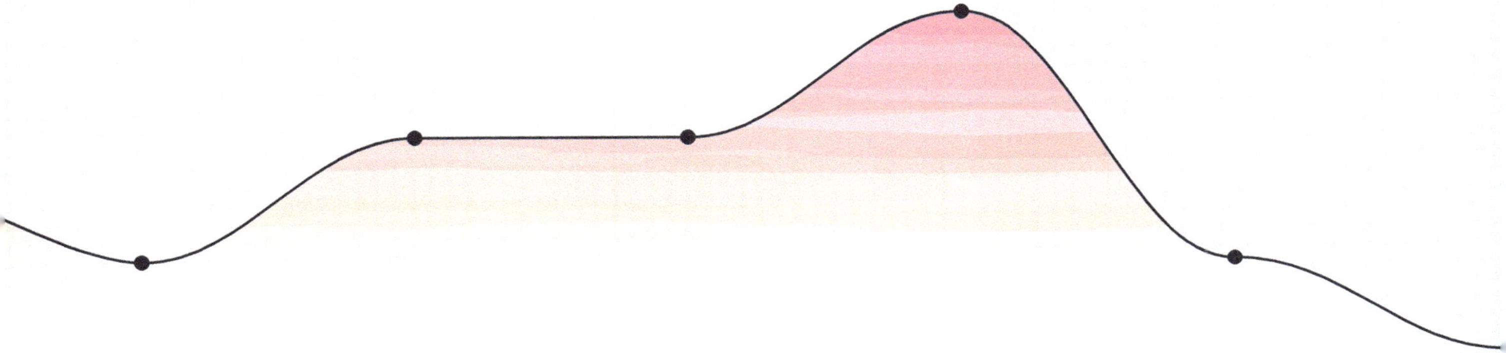

Understand my cycle

At the beginning of the month, I'm notified when I'm about to start my period, so that I can take medicine for cramps and headaches.

When meeting my boyfriend, I check where I am in my cycle, so I know if I need protection.

Know when I'm getting sick

Before I notice the symptoms, I receive a notification that I'm likely getting sick, so I can drink more water and get extra sleep.

Before I feel sick, I receive a notification that I'm showing symptoms, so I can take better care of myself.

When I feel a bit off, I receive a notification that I'm likely getting sick, so I don't plan to go out as much.

When I'm feeling unwell, I check with my Ambience Mirror, so I know if I should ask to stay home from school.

See social media notifications

Before going to work, I see how many direct messages I have on Twitter, so I know whether I'll have a busy day ahead of me.

When friends message me on Facebook, I see notifications, so I know to check the app.

When friends post new things on Facebook, I see notifications, so I know when I need to check the app.

Adjust lighting scenes

When I have a headache, I adjust the lighting scene, so it's less harsh.

Before going out on date night, I check my makeup with the restaurant lighting scene, so I'll look my best.

Before going out dancing with friends, I do my makeup using the club lighting scene, so I know I'll look good.

When I'm bored, I do my makeup with different lighting scenes, so I can see what it looks like.

See temperature, humidity, and indoor air quality

When the seasons change, I check the temperature, humidity, and indoor air quality to make sure everything is functioning properly.

Every day, I see household measurements, so I know that our home is healthy.

USER Laura
CONTEXT Receives CityBike as a gift
NEEDS Transportation in a city (New York)
FEATURE Install the app
DESCRIPTION Laura downloads the app from the app store
DOWNLOAD
FEATURE Account
DESCRIPTION Laura connects her new bike to the app
FEATURE E-bike display with backlight
DESCRIPTION Gets directions to a friend's birthday celebrat
FEATURE
DESCRIPTION
USER tim
CONTEXT visiting his daughter in a foreign city
NEEDS navigation so he doesn't get lost.
FEATURE account
DESCRIPTION tim downloads the app and creates an account and connects to his daughter's bike.
FEATURE multiple users per citybike
DESCRIPTION tim's daughter authorizes him to use her bike.
FEATURE faqs
DESCRIPTION tim reads to lear more about how to use his daughter's bike.
FEATURE navigation
DESCRIPTION tim
navigation
muse

Key Scenarios

Products and services often start with lists of features. While effective for aligning teams and measuring progress, feature-only approaches can lead to experiences that treat all features as equal, giving the unlikely worst-case scenario and the joyful moments of everyday use the same amount of attention and care. Design teams can help prevent this misstep by choreographing features into key scenarios that represent the most common or important paths the user takes through the experience.

Most traditional projects will use either key scenarios or an experience journey to highlight how users will move through an experience. Depending on the phase of the project, key scenarios can provide focus at the start, structure through execution, or a framework for testing once the product or service is built. Key scenarios are also useful for highlighting how a user will interact with new features or offerings when iterating on an experience.

While key scenarios are relatively specific to UX design, their roots lie in traditional storytelling techniques. Before detailing out the individual frames of an animation or shooting scenes in a movie, directors will use a detailed script or storyboards to understand the characters, the context, the actions, and the emotions of a scene. Key scenarios seek to deliver the same details, though only for the most important moments in an experience.

Neither Cases Nor Stories

If you're approaching key scenarios in a development-driven organization, they might seem similar to use cases or user stories. While there may be some overlap, these development techniques are often too feature-focused and rigid to adequately capture a user's experience and emotions.

Activities

Key scenarios should arise from an understanding of the product's business goals combined with the user's needs and behaviors. Ideally key scenarios are approached early in a project's life and then referred back to as the product or service is refined and built. To get started, gather existing artifacts like personas along with any feature definition that's already been done. Business analysis, competitive analysis, trendscapes, and user interviews are also useful for grounding the key scenarios in reality.

Because key scenarios are the synthesis of so many processes that came before, they also serve as a great point for aligning your team. If you're in the define phase, consider hosting team members and stakeholders for a midprocess readout of relevant work followed by a workshop to generate key scenarios.

For the workshop, give participants access to personas and features. These could be printed on cards or on sheets of paper. You may need multiple sets depending on the size of your team and the scale of your product or service. If you're working with more than six participants, consider breaking into smaller teams with one persona per team and a full set of features per team. If you have a smaller group, you can work through all of the personas and features together.

For each persona, choose the three to five features that would be most desirable, most used, or most specific for that user. Discuss why these features are key to the persona and how they intertwine with other selected or nonselected features. Then build the story or stories around those features.

Consider what the user thinks and feels throughout the story, both while they're using and in the time surrounding their use of features. When do they engage the experience? When are they most fulfilled or most frustrated? What questions do they have? Capture these aspects of the persona's experience alongside features to form the basic structure of your key scenario.

Documentation of key scenarios can come in many forms. They might be in written form, with descriptions of the user's interactions and emotions; they might be more visual, like a storyboard or a graphic novel; or they might be even be acted out and recorded. Acting is a great tool, especially when collaborating, to get inside the user's head. Playing out a scene can be especially helpful when working with multiple characters, with contexts where the user's attention might not be solely on your product or experience, and with products and experiences that have multiple touchpoints. For example, in a key scenario for the Connected Bicycle, the user might wonder, "Should I be looking at the product or at my screen?"

If your team is camera shy, but you'd still like to use acting as a part of your workshop, consider making a paper-puppet kit of personas and other actors, products and props, and contexts. Your team can then stage different interactions and take photos.

Later in the refine and build phases, prioritizing design around key scenarios ensures that the most important to the user experiences are completed first, creating the structural skeleton for everything else. Designing around key scenarios can also

Choose the features that best fit with each user or persona.

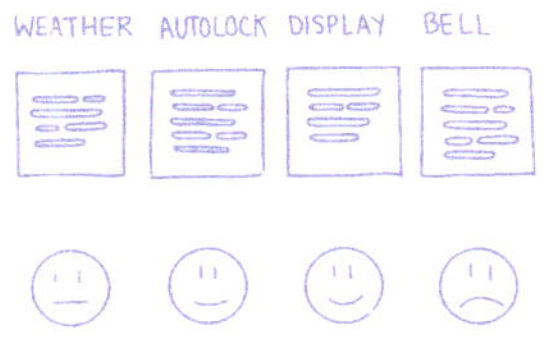

Consider the user's emotion or affect as they move through the scenario.

Illustrated storyboards can communicate key scenarios early in the process.

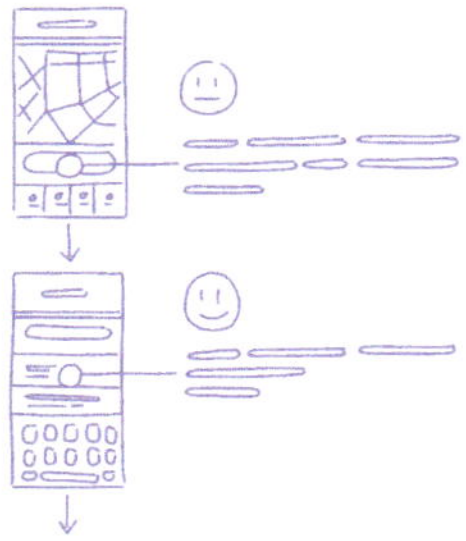

If you already have mock-ups, use these to show what the user interacts with.

ensure that design details are optimized for those most important moments, rather than allowing edge cases and worst-case scenarios to burden the most common experiences.

If you're starting key scenarios in the refine or build phases, mock-ups, detailed design, and flow diagrams are helpful inputs along with feature definition and personas. Here, key scenarios are less of an opportunity to collaborate but can still serve as valuable tools for alignment. Rather than overwhelming stakeholders with all possible screens, states, flows, etc., use key scenarios to walk through the most likely stories and to provide context for what's being reviewed. This focus can be especially useful in service projects when designing scripts for humans or bots.

In the final phase of bringing a product or experience to life, key scenarios can be useful for quality assurance and user testing. For quality assurance, the team might look back on key scenarios to measure the experience in a qualitative way against what was intended. For user testing, key scenarios provide a starting point for what to run through with users for feedback.

Artifacts

It's likely that your team will often refer back to key scenarios, especially if they are developed early in the project. For this reason, it's important that key scenarios are not only accessible and shareable but also that they can be updated, revised, and enhanced as your product or service is refined, built, and revised.

If you are early in the design process and have the resources, consider creating storyboards capturing not only the user's story with but also surrounding your product or service. Use line weight, scale, and contrast to draw attention to what's most important. You might use color to capture the user's mood or affect as they move between positive, negative, and neutral experiences, or you might use it to highlight the user's engagement on different touchpoints.

For experiences that don't yet have mock-ups, avoid showing the product or service in its final form. This will prevent stakeholders from getting attached to a placeholder design language or making important decisions based on unfinished work. As the product or service increases in fidelity, update the key scenarios to match. This could mean refining the storyboards to have greater detail or adding additional scenes to provide more depth to the story.

When starting key scenarios in the refine and build phases, you might skip the storyboard-style illustrations altogether. Try capturing the scenario in text alongside illustrations or using mock-ups to show how the user moves through the experience. Highlight what the user interacts with along with the specific feedback they receive from the product or service.

If your project schedule and budget are tight, use less fidelity in your key scenarios. In the define phase, rough sketches or photographed scenes can quickly capture characters, props, and contexts. In later phases, having the stories written down alongside mock-ups in detailed design and documentation artifacts can be sufficient. These shortcuts provide the benefits of thinking in key scenarios, even if they're less effective for communication.

Key scenarios for CityBike follow three personas through their experiences with the product. Backgrounds change to capture when things are going as expected and when things go wrong.

Observations Suite's key scenarios show the needs and challenges of five personas as they discover and use the product. In each scenario, engagements with various touchpoints are highlighted with yellow.

Key Scenarios

Laura Loses Her Bike

Laura received her CityBike as a present last year, and she's been using it to get around ever since.

Right after Laura received her CityBike, she downloaded the app to get the most out of it.

At first she used the navigation features, but now that she knows the city by bike, she rarely actively uses the app.

> Account
> Navigation

One night, Laura takes her bike to meet some friends for drinks. She's unfamiliar with the bar but knows the general location, so she doesn't use navigation.

> On-bike E Ink display with backlight
> Current bike location

Laura walks away from her bike, forgetting that she's turned off autolocking.

> Automatic locking and unlocking

After the last call, Laura leaves the bar and searches for her bike. She tries to ring the bell using the CityBike's widget, but hears nothing.

> Bell

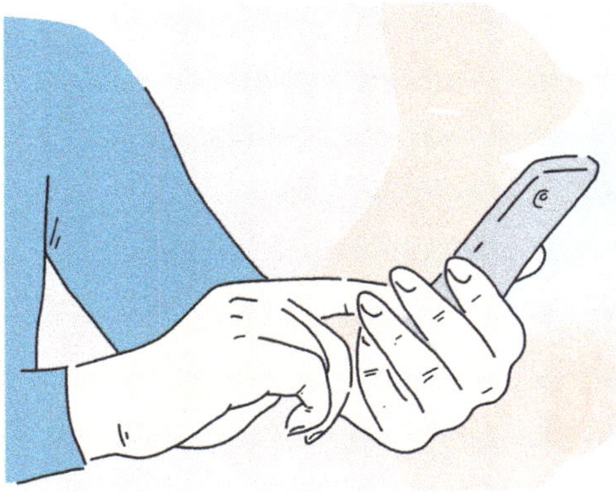

Laura uses the app to locate her bike and sees that it's nowhere near the bar.

She marks her bike as stolen so that it will lock the next time the thief stops. Hopefully they'll leave her bike behind as soon as they realize they can't ride it.

> Current bike location
> Remote locking

Tim Goes Sightseeing

Tim regularly visits his daughter Julia in Copenhagen. This trip, he borrows her CityBike to get around, relying on the navigation to not get lost in unfamiliar surroundings.

When Tim arrives, Julia encourages him to download the app and create an account so that he can use her CityBike's navigation features.

> Account
> Navigation

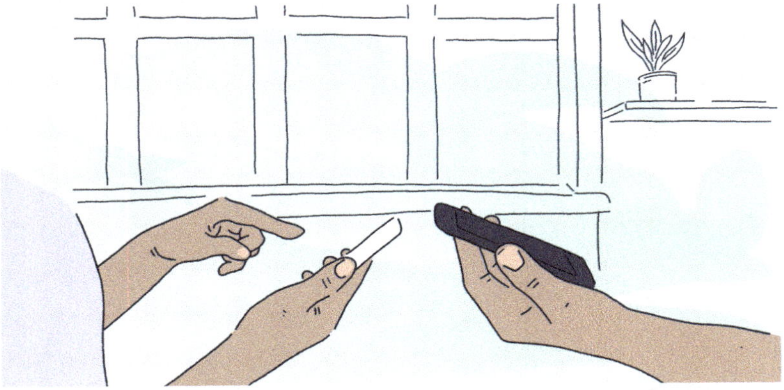

After Julia authorizes him to use her bike, Tim explores the CityBike's app to see what he can do with it.

> Multiple users per CityBike
> FAQs

The next morning while Julia is at work, Tim decides to do some sightseeing. He enters the museum as his destination and selects the scenic route.

> Navigation

Tim follows the instructions on the bike's screen and makes it to the museum without any drama.

Tim parks his bike outside the museum. He hears it automatically lock as he walks away.

> On-bike E Ink display with backlight
> Navigation
> Automatic locking and unlocking

After all of his sightseeing, Tim returns to Julia's house. His phone runs out of battery as he arrives, so he uses the key to lock her bike.

> Manual locking and unlocking

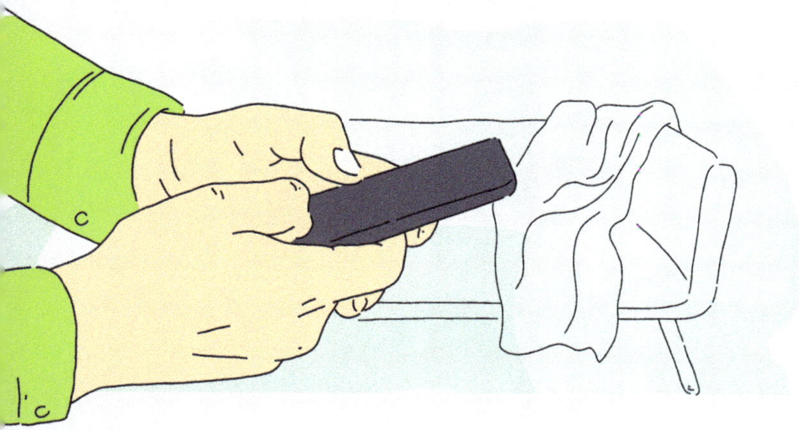

Mo Optimizes His Route

Mo recently moved to Amsterdam. Before buying a bike, he did a lot of research to make sure he got the right one.

Mo rides his bike to work every morning. Before heading out, he launches the CityBike's app and checks the weather to make sure he won't get rained on.

> Weather integration

Mo reviews past rides. He's surprised to find that a route he doesn't usually take is shorter than his usual route.

> Historical statistics

Mo's bike unlocks as he approaches it. He hops on and sets off on his commute. He knows the city by heart, so he doesn't use navigation.

> Automatic locking and unlocking
> Current location

Aside from a few incidents with tourists in the bike path, Mo's commute goes smoothly.

> Bell

When he arrives at work, Mo glances at his bike's display to see the distance of his new commute. It was nearly half a kilometer shorter than usual.

> On-bike E Ink display with backlight
> Current ride statistics

When he has more time, Mo reviews the data from his morning ride. In addition to being slightly shorter, his new route was also faster than normal. He decides that he'll use this way to get to work from now on.

> Current statistics
> Historical statistics

Key Scenarios

Mei Discovers Observations Suite

Mei is opening a new restaurant and is looking for the best tools to simplify all of the complexity of her venture. While reading an industry magazine on an airplane, she comes across an ad for Observations Suite and marks it so she can research the product later. Once at home, Mei visits the website and reads feature descriptions to better understand what the product suite offers and how payment works. She digs deeper into the FAQs to see what the most common issues are. With many of her questions answered, Mei decides to create an account and try out Observations Suite. After playing with the various features for an hour, she decides that the tool is worth the investment, and she pays for the membership. After a week, her installation package arrives, complete with a setup guide so that Mei can take care of everything she needs to in time for her grand opening.

Mei Optimizes Customer Flow

After a month in business and a handful of write-ups by local media, Mei has a lot more customers, and the busy times at the restaurant are overwhelming. Queues run out the door, and her customers are growing frustrated and leaving negative reviews. Mei turns to Observations Suite to see what she can do to improve efficiency. She looks at her aggregated analytics dashboard, which highlights a correlation between long wait times and online orders for pickup. She reviews the restaurant-layout analytics and discovers that customers are waiting in the normal line even when they're just picking up. The next morning, she experiments with signage to create a clear and separate place for pickup orders. The experiment works, resulting in lower queue times and better customer reviews.

Tony Works His First Busy Night

Tony starts a new job as a server and has a good deal of training to get ready for his first Friday night rush. He spends his first day watching video walk-throughs and learning his way around the Observations Suite tools that he'll use. He shadows another employee for a few days before he's ready to try things on his own. On his first busy night, Tony starts by looking through the incoming reservations and assigning guests to tables, making sure that guests with seating preferences get the tables they prefer. As guests begin to trickle in, he takes their orders, making sure to accommodate special needs and allergies. He even greets a regular guest with her favorite drink to celebrate her birthday. As guests wrap up their meals, Tony collects payment and receives many gracious tips for a job well done.

Additional Scenarios

Colette Customizes Recipes

It's autumn and time for Colette to release the restaurant's fall menu. The restaurant owner has asked for more local and sustainable dishes to keep up with trends in the market, so Colette puts together a handful of new and experimental dishes that she believes their customers will love. During the first week on the new menu, the ordering of new dishes is irregular, and the kitchen often runs out of key ingredients. Colette is able to order more easily using the Observations Suite interface, but the deliveries can't come fast enough. Colette grows increasingly frustrated with her inability to predict when ingredients will run out of stock. After three weeks of struggling with the new menu, Colette receives insights from Observations Suite about when she should order what to meet the fluctuating demands of the restaurant's customers. She takes the system's advice and no longer has issues with stocking.

Colette Solves a Kitchen Mystery

Colette has been managing the kitchen in a small chain restaurant for over a year when the company she works for decides to install the new Observations Suite system. At about the same time, Colette notices an uptick in the number of dishes being sent back to the kitchen due to being prepared incorrectly. Because there have been so many changes—from employees to the menu itself—Colette doesn't know what's to blame. One night after the restaurant closes, Colette looks into the analytics to see what the problem is. She reads some customers' reviews to confirm that special requests are often being forgotten and reviews her employees' scheduling. There is no correlation. In a final effort to understand the problem, she reviews her kitchen layout. In this visualization she discovers that the pastry chef is often working in front of the incoming-orders display and preventing other kitchen staff from seeing the details of customers' orders.

Maria Markets Her Restaurant

Maria enjoys running a restaurant, especially the marketing side of things. She uses Observations Suite to maintain her store's website, to track analytics from her social media efforts, and to create, share, and track campaigns and special promotions. With Valentine's Day approaching, she decides to create a special promotion for a prix fixe including a special red-velvet heart cake dessert for two. She creates the campaign and then sends it out in an email, publishes it on the site, and uses social media to promote it. Over the next two weeks, as her restaurant gets many reservations for Valentine's Day, she watches her campaign's performance. At the end of the quarter, she receives an email where she can see that the campaign performed better than others, and so she decides to create similar offers for other holidays.

Dario Makes Customers Feel Special

Dario has been a barista at a small coffee café for years. This morning, a regular customer comes in, and Dario greets her with a smile. She wants her usual drink, and because it's her tenth, she gets one for free. Dario makes her coffee.

As the café grows, he's received coaching from his boss to do a better job of capturing everything he knows about their customers in Observations Suite's CRM system, so whenever a new customer comes in, Dario asks if they'd like to be a part of the loyalty program. If they say yes, he enters them into the CRM system so that the company can better serve its customers.

Charlie Discovers Observations Suite

Charlie visits a big industry conference with other regional managers of his chain. While at the conference, he sees a representative from Omniscient speaking, and he's inspired to check out the Observations Suite booth afterward. At the booth, he meets with a representative who shows him what the Observations Suite can do for the restaurants in his region. Not wanting to make a rash decision, Charlie takes an information packet. A month later, Charlie decides to switch over to the Observations Suite and has the company come out to do complete installation and customization for each of his twenty-seven stores.

Charlie Manages Stores in His Region

With Observations Suite tracking performance in all of his restaurants, Charlie feels able to experiment more. Each week, he optimizes store layouts and employee shifts based on data and insights, keeping an eye on how each change affects both his customer feedback and his stores' performance. By the end of two months, the entire region is outperforming all others.

As the quarterly meeting approaches, Charlie uses Observations Suite's visualizations to highlight the improvements he's made, creating a presentation to the board. With such quantifiable success, the board decides to roll out Observations Suite to other regions as well.

Now

Construction-Waste Boat
- Reduce blockages in the streets caused by large waste dumpsters.

Battery Boat
- Replaces noisy and polluting generators in the city.
- Needs a swap-out system—also by boat.

Farm Boat
- Floating gardens / small farms move throughout the canals, following the sun.

Barrier Boats
- Small swarms of boats create barriers to control traffic in canals
- Controlled by humans at ... later versions could be ...nated.

Valet Tug
- Parks boats for drivers, optimizing canal-side parking.

Boatpool
- A carpool, but for boats
- Sponsored by local companies and schools.

Small Lifeboats
- Small boats detect and auto-deploy when someone falls into the water.

Swim Boats
- Boats detect levels of toxins in the water and mark safe areas to swim.
- Could pair with water ... boats.

Delivery-Locker Boat
- Reduces traffic caused by delivery trucks.
- Moves to multiple pickup locations throughout the day.

Water Filtr...
- Clean wat...
- Sensors de... levels to k... need filtrat... reported b...

Moving Services
- Use boats instead of trucks when people move along the water.

Floating-Bridge Boats
- Can create temporary bridges for bikes and pedestrians for events or construction projects.

Designated-Driver Tug
- Tugs a boat so that the occupants can drink freely
- On demand, can be ... to a location.

Water Taxis
- Autonomous taxis transport people from one part of the city to another

Autonomous Driving

Sensor Technology

Electric-Charging Infrastructure

Swarm Connectivity

Filtration Technology

Strategic Roadmap

Products and services take time to develop, and being competitive often means releasing only a fraction of the overall vision at a time. While focusing on the details of the present, it's easy to forget the big picture. This is where the strategic roadmap plays an important role, helping the team keep the end goal in mind while executing on a specific release.

Using inputs such as technology analysis and feature definition, a strategic roadmap is useful for laying out how an experience will change over time. Before a specific product or service is defined, a roadmap might be more inspirational, looking ahead to anticipate what experiences could fulfill emerging technologies and user needs. With an experience in mind, more realistic roadmaps might focus on showing the future of an individual product or service or of a company's portfolio of products and services.

Aside from simply capturing goals over time, you might collaborate with business stakeholders, technology experts, and development or manufacturing partners to show the relationships between features and offerings and to highlight external dependences.

Activities

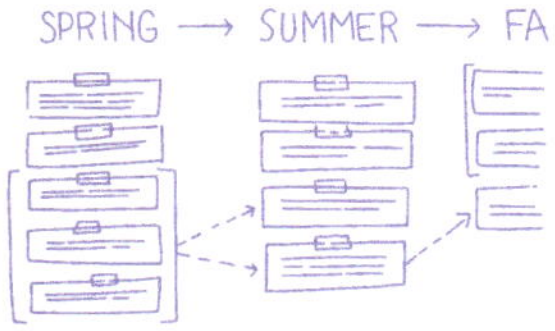

Facilitate a conversation with the team around what features should be launched when.

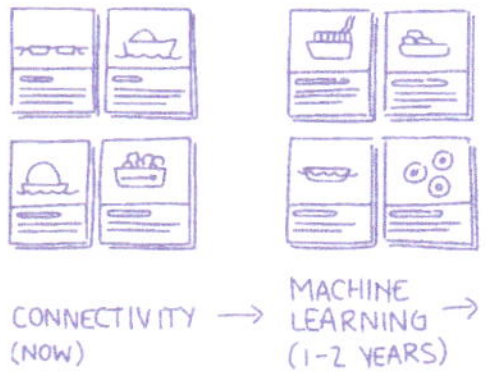

Hold a concept-generation workshop around technology opportunities.

The strategic roadmap begins with a thorough understanding of scale and goals. If you're exploring the features for a single product or service, the elements mapped will be features, and if you're mapping a user's engagement with a company, products and services will be the elements mapped. If you're creating a more inspirational roadmap at the scale of an industry, map out concepts for products and services.

Now consider the goals of the roadmap. Are you seeking to provide guidance about what can be delivered when, or are you looking to inspire and provoke? Realistic roadmaps focus more on what's known, providing a clear picture of the future that might even be used to measure progress. Inspirational roadmaps provide a less certain look into the future, instead focusing on what technologies and behaviors will inspire and enable innovation.

For either roadmap, the predictions are made believable through an understanding of the technology that constrains and enables those predictions. If you don't have the output of stakeholder interviews, expert interviews, and a technology analysis to work with, consider doing lightweight versions of these activities now. User interviews, competitive analysis, and trendscape activities can also provide useful inputs for prioritizing and ordering the events of a strategic roadmap around the needs and behaviors of users.

A realistic roadmap usually represents only the most tangible features and priorities collected through the early parts of the definition phase, though it could also look beyond what is certain or likely and make less substantiated predictions. There is generally decreasing certainty the further you look into the future, and for this reason realistic roadmaps tend to be less long term.

Because realistic roadmaps are used to set goals and measure progress, it can be useful to collaborate as a team to establish milestones. Consider working together to organize cards with features or products and services in order of priority. When putting the cards in order, think about what's important to the user as well as what's easy to implement. Also capture dependencies and important deadlines. This can serve as the rough draft of the realistic strategic roadmap.

The more imaginative inspirational roadmap requires less rigor around planning and more creative thinking about what's to come. Rather than working with the team to establish milestones using features that have already been defined, consider holding a concept-generation workshop to brainstorm possible design fictions worth mapping. Keep concepts rooted in reality, using findings from expert interviews, stakeholder interviews, and technology analysis both to develop workshop prompts and to curate and rank concepts.

Like the realistic roadmap, the inspirational roadmap needs to consider existing timelines and dependencies to make predictions about what's to come. Collaborating with stakeholders and experts to understand when new technologies will be mature enough to use can ensure that an inspirational roadmap is believable.

> *"Science has not yet mastered prophecy. We predict too much for the next year and yet far too little for the next ten."*
>
> Neil Armstrong

Artifacts

Strategic roadmaps can be simple data visualizations with little more than position, size, and color differentiating between events, or they can be large-scale posters with illustrations, mock-ups, and annotations. The type of roadmap you create depends on whom you're sharing it with and how often you plan to update it.

A realistic roadmap is more likely to need regular updates, so it should be in a format that works digitally as well as physically. Realistic product roadmaps represent events like new features, products, and services clearly on a timeline. Map dependencies, making it obvious which events depend on others. You might add additional layers to the roadmap, such as a summary of benefits to the user or goals that the company hopes to achieve with each milestone.

While realistic roadmaps can be beautiful, using iconography or illustration to provide a more glanceable visualization than just text, this isn't essential. Because so many different stakeholders might use this roadmap, it might look more like a project-management artifact than a design artifact.

An inspirational roadmap takes events and lays them out over time based on the order they might occur in and worrying less about specific dates. These roadmaps might look far into the future, getting less exact with timing as they do so. Instead of using dates, map out specific technologies that enable, or user behaviors that demand, innovation. Inspirational roadmaps often feel more designed, using illustration and mock-ups alongside data visualization to communicate.

The inspirational strategic roadmap for the Future of Boats seeks to uncover potential and likely developments in waterway usage so that European Waterworks can better invest in and prepare for the future.

Observations Suite uses a more realistic roadmap to plan an aggressive approach to designing, testing, and developing future iterations of their product. This roadmap has deadlines that the company hopes to meet and will need updating if and when plans change.

European Waterworks / **Future of Boats**

Strategic Roadmap

Waterways in cities are often underutilized spaces. They're difficult to keep clean, and they provide little value aside from beauty and tourism. But what if we were to reconsider a city's waterways as a more integrated part of the city?

This speculative series of boat concepts provides a glimpse into how future technologies and creative thinking might transform our waterways.

Dependencies

- M Machine learning
- S Sensors
- I Infrastructure
- C Connectivity
- N Autonomous navigation
- L Laws and regulations
- F Filtering technology

Benefits

- Safety
- Transportation
- Public health
- Government
- Commerce
- Recreation
- Waste management
- Traffic reduction
- Food
- Energy

Government Drone

Amsterdam canal bottoms collect a lot of heavy trash—from bicycles and boats to even an occasional car. To determine where to clean or to search for something in particular, Waternet uses partially submerged drones to look beneath the water's surface. The drone allows the professional to explore the floor of the canals using multiple cameras and a virtual-reality interface.

Dependencies

C L

Benefits

Roomboat

A lack of sufficient waste infrastructure in the city center leads to trash floating in the canals. The roomboat, an autonomous cleaning boat, collects trash floating near the water's surface in scheduled parts of the city to help keep the canals clean. The boat is monitored, and when its container is full, it returns to its dock to unload before returning to work.

Dependencies

S N

Benefits

Canal Traffic Camera

Amsterdam's 100 km of canals pose both public- safety and nuisance concerns beyond what the police can keep up with. Small police-boat bots equipped with cameras document and report illicit behavior on the water. In busy intersections, cameras run continuously, collecting data and reporting problems.

Canal traffic cameras work with barrier boats to entrap offenders until the police arrive.

Dependencies

M S C

Benefits

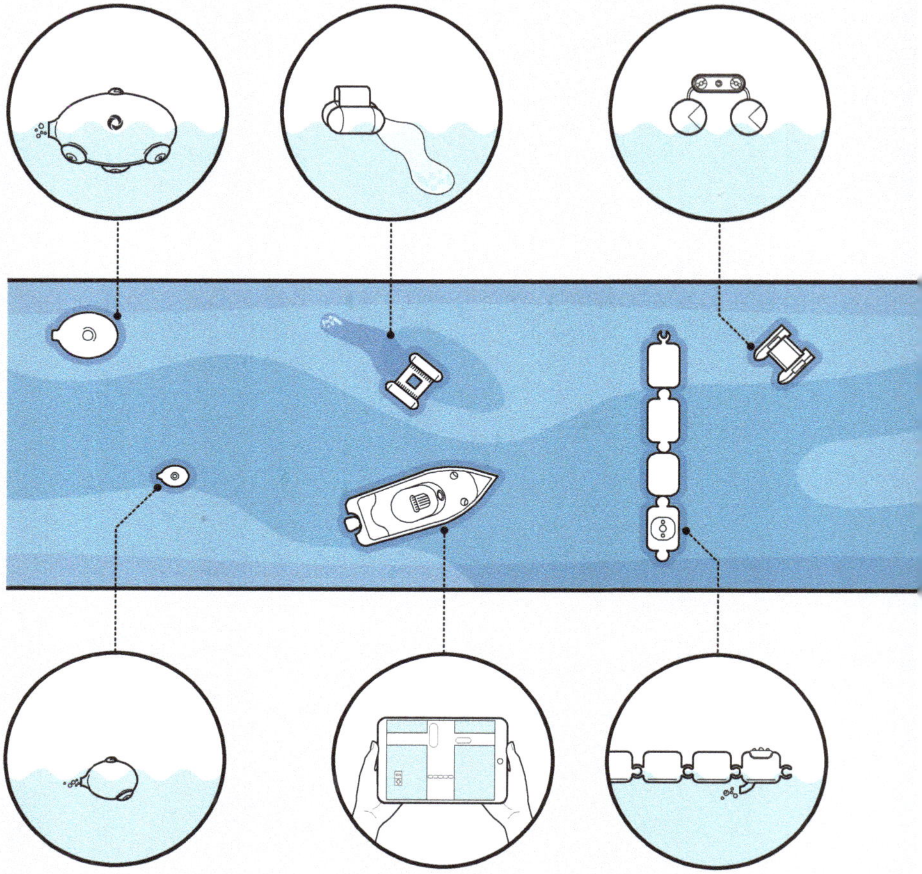

Personal Drone

With the heavy regulation of drones in the Netherlands making it virtually impossible to fly drones in Amsterdam, hobbyists turn to underwater drones. With the proliferation of DIY consumer-grade drone kits, everyone can explore the underwater world of treasures that lives in the canals. This boat drone allows users to discover what's under the water's surface using a camera and virtual reality.

Dependencies

L

Benefits

Canal Traffic Map

Especially on sunny days, Amsterdam's canals are overwhelmed with boats. To keep traffic moving smoothly, both private and commercial boats are individually equipped with GPS, enabling the city to track and produce an anonymized map of boat traffic in the canals. The map is accessible to all drivers via an app and a website.

Data collected is used by the city to help control traffic where necessary and eventually informs self-driving boat algorithms for optimized efficiency.

Dependencies

C L

Benefits

Barrier Boats V1

The laissez-faire attitude around traffic management in the Amsterdam canals has failed to scale to the increased tourist traffic. Swarming barrier boats manage traffic to keep flow steady without decreasing rentals or commercial boat lines. In their first iteration, barrier boats take instruction from the police to block off areas, especially during events.

Dependencies

C N

Benefits

Fire Boat

Old canal houses are very vulnerable to fire; therefore acting fast and preventing the spread of flames is crucial. While Amsterdam's crowded streets, often clogged with delivery vehicles, can make responding to an emergency challenging, a fire boat can get to the site with ease. Thanks to being on the canal, it can pump the water directly to put out the fire, and it's ready to work almost immediately after arriving.

Dependencies

S N

Benefits

Bottom Feeder

Approximately 15,000 bikes are salvaged annually from Amsterdam's canals. Cleaning canals and picking up sunken bikes, apart from being quite a spectacle, are necessary to maintain waterways' safety and accessibility. The bottom feeder is a boat that detects unwanted objects on the canal bottom and automatically removes them.

Dependencies

M S

Benefits

Floating Battery

Loud power generators placed in the tight canal streets during construction work create congestion and air pollution. Construction and other companies can rent a boat with batteries to provide power for construction sites. Battery boats are monitored and hot swapped out as needed. Charging of batteries occurs outside the city using solar and wind power. This solution reduces noise and air pollution and saves space in the narrow Amsterdam canal streets.

Dependencies

N L

Benefits

Large Waste Barge

Bulk waste collection is unsightly for the city and often inconvenient for citizens. The large waste boat carries containers to different parts of the city throughout the month in order to collect waste before taking it to a sorting facility to determine what's usable, what's recyclable, and what should be incinerated.

Dependencies

S N

Benefits

Detachable Parks

Park docks provide much-needed green space in the city, but become problematic late at night when nuisance tourists crowd them. The new iteration of park docks attaches to the side of the canal during the day and detaches during night hours, moving into the center of the canal to keep away trespassers.

Dependencies

I N

Benefits

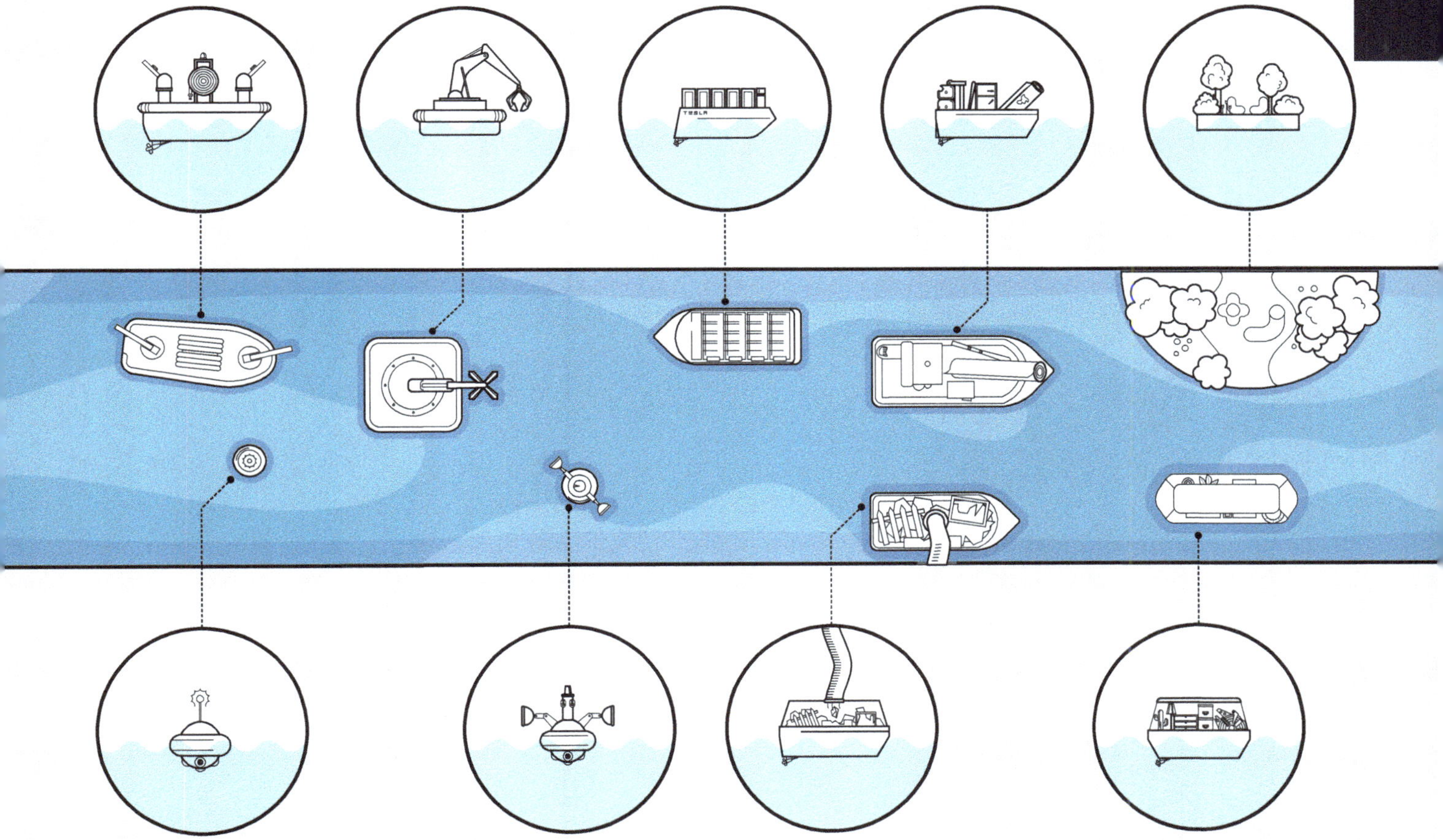

Swimmers V1

While tempting, swimming in Amsterdam's canals is often unsafe due to chemicals and other toxins in the water. Small boats use sensors to detect levels of toxins in the water, and, when a stretch of the canal is clean and the area safe, boats provide visual indication to humans that the area is safe for swimming.

In case of accidents, swim boats come with floatation devices and first aid kits.

Dependencies

S

Benefits

Snitch

Leaking boats and loud, drunken boaters are just two threats to safety on the canals. Small, resilient sensor boats live in set locations throughout the canals, sensing irregularities in craft behavior and pollution. When an irregularity is detected, the snitch boat attaches itself to the offending vehicle and alerts officials using light and sound as well as specific notifications. Alerting behavior might also attract the attention of passersby, who may want to avoid the situation.

Dependencies

M S C

Benefits

Construction-Refuse Boat

Construction-waste containers create congestion for car, bicycle, and pedestrian traffic. Rather than take up space on the land, construction-waste containers are moved from the streets to the canals, allowing normal traffic to resume. For construction projects, the waste-boat service can be ordered ahead of time and scheduled for the duration of the project. When full, an empty boat arrives, while the full boat returns to its dock to recharge and dump its waste in a designated place.

Dependencies

S N

Benefits

Moving Services

To help reduce congestion, the city of Amsterdam mandates that large delivery and moving trucks be replaced with boats in the canal belt. Delivery and moving boats become common for residences and businesses on canals. Boats can be scheduled with or without crew to help with loading and unloading.

Dependencies

N

Benefits

Driverless Water Taxi

With tourist crowds in the city center, taxis become less and less effective as a means of transportation. Autonomous water taxis avoid getting stuck in the road traffic and take passengers anywhere as long as it's on a canal. Ordering a taxi is done via an app. Surge pricing may apply.

Dependencies

N

Benefits

Grocery Delivery

With too much congestion on the streets of Amsterdam, Albert Heijn replaces many of their trucks with boats for its grocery-delivery service. Refrigerated boats carry significantly more groceries than trucks, reducing the amount of time spent restocking. Humans complete the delivery, bringing grocery boxes from boat to door.

Dependencies

M N

Benefits

$

Water Filtration

Amsterdam's canals are cleaner than they have been in 400 years, but the water often remains unsanitary for activities like swimming. Amsterdam's Waternet aims to purify it even more. Both to reduce pollution in the canals and to help beautify the city, Amsterdam launches a fleet of filtration vessels that float on the canals. These small, autonomous boats filter toxic and dangerous chemicals from the water. They detect areas with more pollution and work where they are needed most.

Boats also report data back to the city for use with Amsterdam's City Data program.

Dependencies

S C N F

Benefits

Mini Lifeboats

Police and Public Health Service reports indicate that 7–15 people drown in Amsterdam's canals every year, a number that's on the rise with immigration. Small boats use pump-jet engines to move quickly through canals, enabling them to rapidly approach a drowning person, help them remain afloat, and get them to land. When not in use, lifeboats attach to dedicated charging docks on canal walls and are ready to go when they are summoned by a scream. Boats find a person in need by detecting sound, movement, and heat.

Dependencies

S I N

Benefits

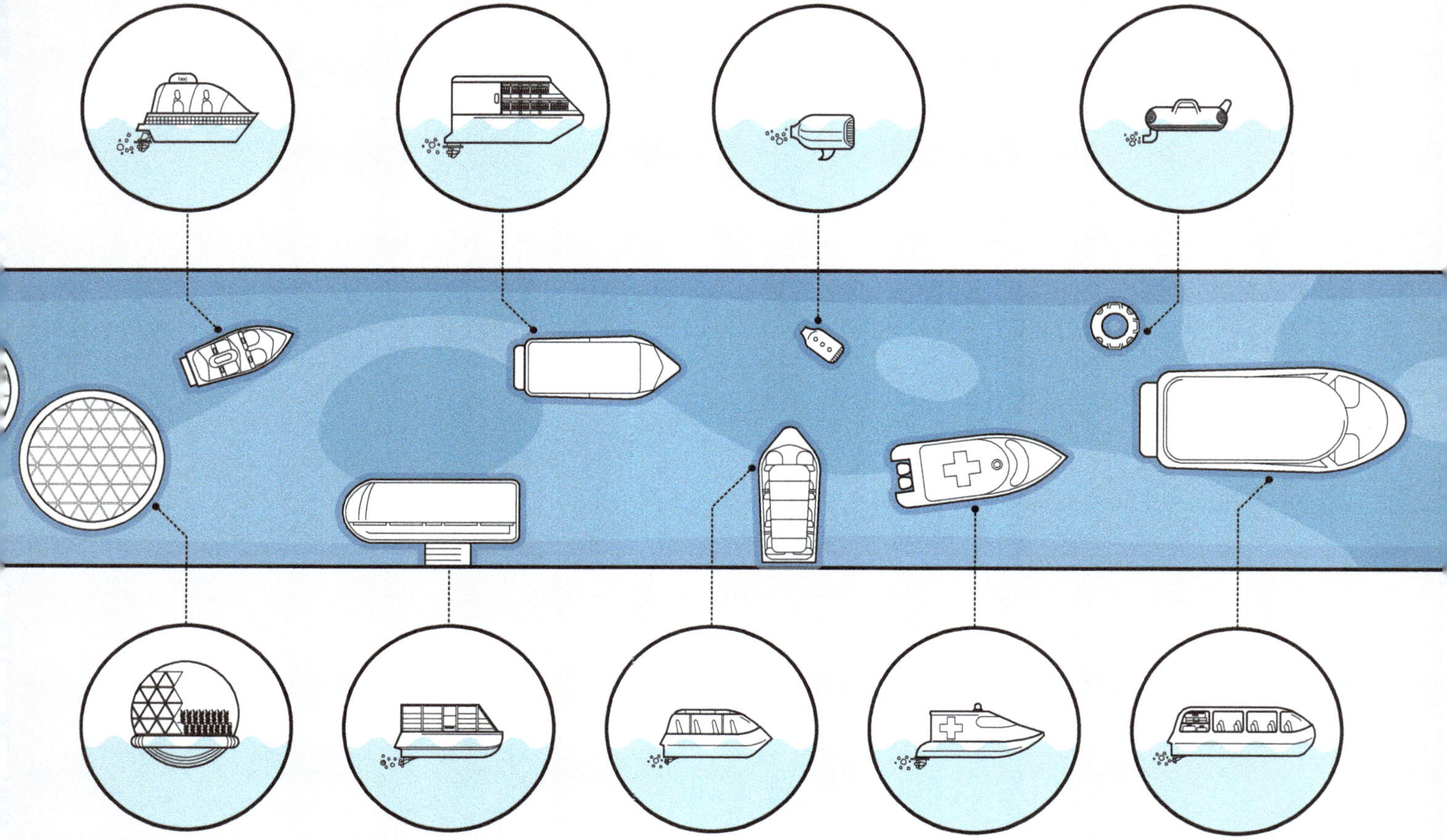

Vertical Water Farm

Both limited space and access to sunlight make sustenance gardening in Amsterdam a challenge. Farm boats provide local hobbyists and origin-conscious restauranteurs space to effectively grow ingredients locally. Following the sun, farm boats use mobility and sensors to get optimal amounts of light and fresh water for crops to grow.

Dependencies

M S N

Benefits

Delivery Locker

Delivery trucks often clog city streets, trying to deliver packages for residents who aren't at home. To reduce traffic problems, autonomous delivery boats meet recipients when and where it's convenient for them to pick up their parcels. Users open their lockers using NFC.

Dependencies

M N

Benefits

$

Boatpool

As the city center becomes less and less hospitable to private vehicles, boats become the new way to commute. Sharing a journey with passengers who regularly travel the same route reduces both street and canal traffic. Boatpooling can be arranged on a website as well as via a dedicated app.

Dependencies

N

Benefits

Water Ambulance

With more than 800,000 citizens and over 5 million tourists visiting every year, Amsterdam rescuers struggle to help everyone in need. Conventional ambulances can easily get stuck in clogged canal streets, losing precious time. Rescuers use ambulance boats to move through the city traffic fast to help take care of the injured, maintain life functions, and transport people to a hospital for further care.

Dependencies

N

Benefits

Smart Ferries

Plane, train, and other transportation schedules change unexpectedly, leading to travelers getting stuck or being late. Smart ferries make themselves available in case of transportation delays and cancellations or bad weather conditions to help travelers and commuters keep up with their schedule and to take them where they need to be.

Dependencies

M N

Benefits

Urban Yacht

With the city's government growing more aggressively anticar, Amsterdam's elite need to find a new way to move through the city. These individually sized private boats transport those who can afford it through Amsterdam's canals. Each boat is piloted by an AI chauffeur who integrates with users' digital personal assistants, knowing when to appear and where to go without needing any input from the user.

Dependencies

M N

Benefits

Barrier Boats V2

When all boats are equipped with GPS, barrier boats predict upcoming difficulties on waterways and assist to redirect the traffic. In this later iteration, the swarming barrier boats use access to boat location data and machine learning to manipulate flow, optimizing traffic through the canals. While they are still able to view and manually adjust barrier behavior, police take a less active role in directly manipulating barrier boats.

Dependencies

M C N

Benefits

Pop-Up Boat

Development in inner Amsterdam has made affordable real estate unavailable to unestablished brands, so the city searches for new ways to facilitate the growth of small businesses. Valet tugs make new space available on many canals, and open docks enable boats to have more robust functionalities and make pop-ups available to multiple neighborhoods. Mobile retail and kitchen boats provide locations for emerging talent through a series of mobile pop-up restaurants and shops.

Dependencies

I N L

Benefits

$

Floating Bridge

Amsterdam's infrastructure can be flexible and adjust to ensure accessibility. When a bridge is closed for renovation or when an additional bridge is needed to provide easy access to an event, a temporary solution is placed on water, assembled from a swarm of boats. When necessary, boat bridges can restructure, allowing other boats to pass.

Dependencies

M S C

Benefits

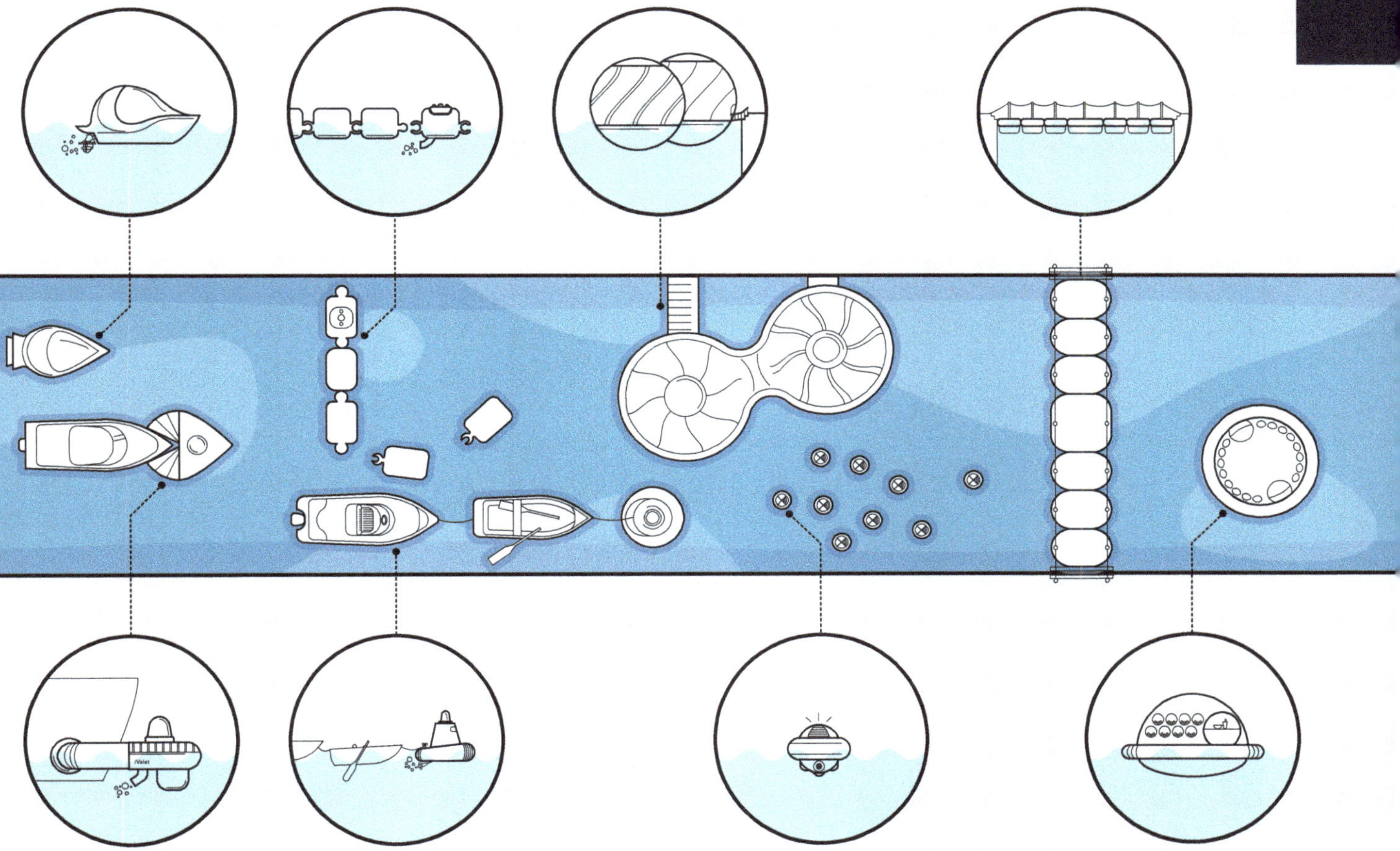

Valet Tug

To cope with overwhelmed parking along Amsterdam's canals, the city creates a parking program where tugs collect boats from docks where they let off passengers, and parks them in out-of-the-way structures safe from thieves and weather. Boat owners use an app to request their boat from parking and for pickup.

Dependencies

N L

Benefits

Tug Tows

Half-sunken, forgotten boats take up coveted space while making Amsterdam less beautiful. To free up available parking space and to prevent abandoned boats from sinking, the city creates a program similar to its bike program, where boats are towed when they show signs of being abandoned. A human walks along the shore to detach boats while the towboat collects the boats and moves them to a garage where they can be either picked up or purchased if unclaimed.

Dependencies

S N

Benefits

Swimmers V2

While the first iteration of swim boats helped people find safe places to swim, the second iteration is far more proactive. Swarms of small filter boats use sensors to detect levels of toxins in the water. When a stretch of the canal has filterable toxins, the flock of boats begins filtering and moves to physically indicate a safe zone for swimming.

Dependencies

C N F

Benefits

Fast-Food Boats

To help subsidize their pop-up program, the city government recruits food chains like FEBO to take advantage of the city's open-docking program. This provides established companies with the infrastructure to have locations where they otherwise might not—at festivals, concerts, and tourist events.

Solar panels on boats feed energy back into the grid.

Dependencies

I N L

Benefits

$

Omniscient / **Observations Suite Vision**

Strategic Roadmap

Timeline	2019 March	June	September
Marketing Plan	**Establish a Presence** FAQs Feature Descriptions Industry Blog Information Packet Convention Booths Sales Calls Feature Descriptions	**Support the Soft Launch** Setup Guide In-Person Demos Video Walk-Throughs 24-Hour Business Support Weekly Newsletter	**Initial Promotion** Targeted Advertising Conference Booth
Observations Suite **Features** Features will be released simultaneously across all existing platforms		**Seating Management, CRM & Analytics Tools** CRM Tool Seating Management Aggregated Analytics Customer Analytics Movement Analytics Booking Analytics Periodical Progress Reports Setup Guide Demo Mode Employee Permissions	**Location Management & Employee-Scheduling Tools** Store-Performance Analytics Employee Analytics Employee-Scheduling Interface Feature Updates Insights
Platforms Web iOS Android Windows MacOS			
Consumer Tools **Touchpoints** Web Mobile			
Goals	• 5,000 subscribers to news about Observations Suite • 500 sign-ups to participate in Observations Suite beta program	• 10 installs with subscriptions	• 50% subscription upgrades to include new tools • 50 new installs with subscriptions • 100 app downloads • 4+ star rating in app store

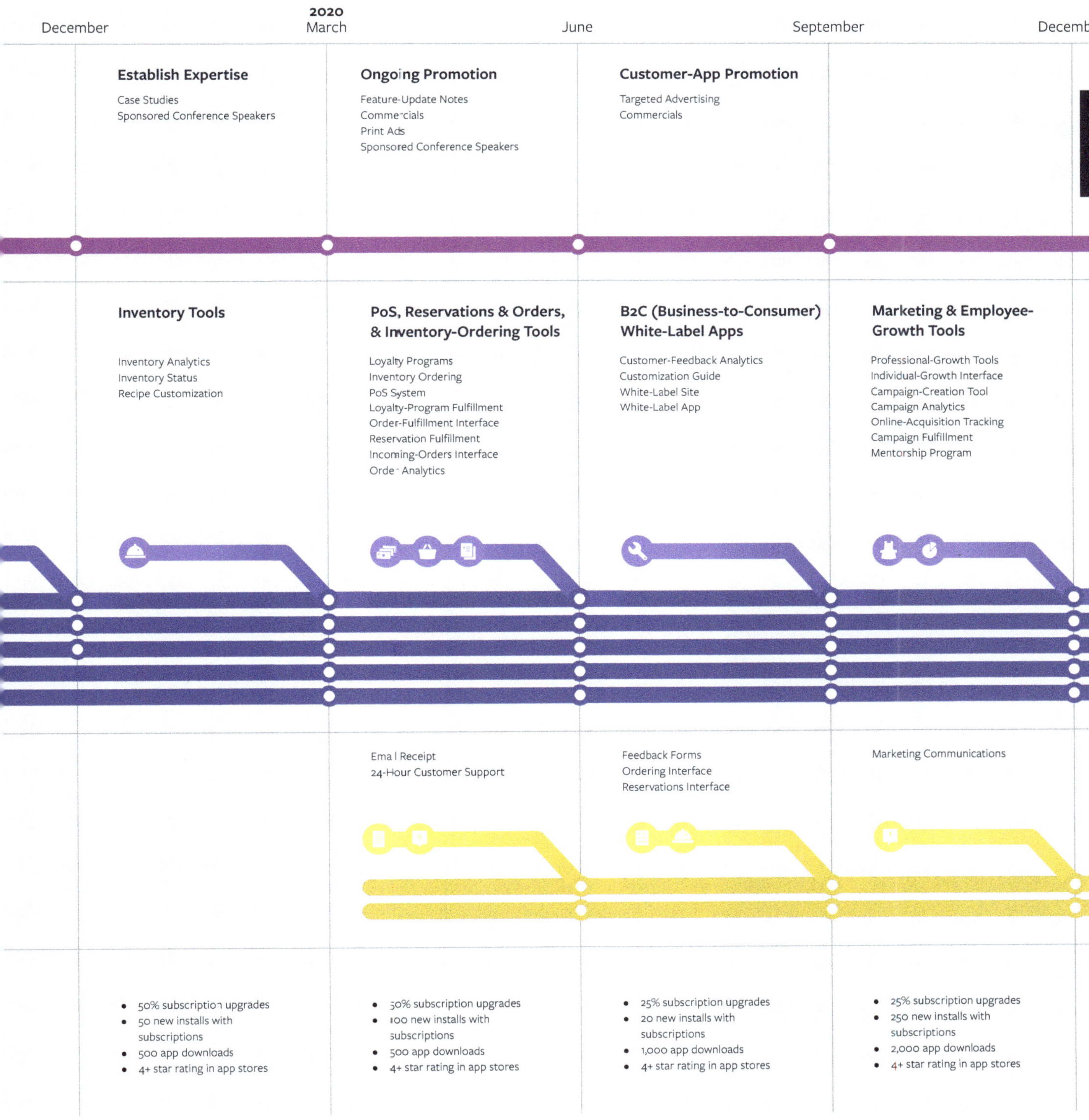
2020
December
March
June
September
December
Establish Expertise
Case Studies
Sponsored Conference Speakers
Ongoing Promotion
Feature-Update Notes
Commercials
Print Ads
Sponsored Conference Speakers
Customer-App Promotion
Targeted Advertising
Commercials
Inventory Tools
Inventory Analytics
Inventory Status
Recipe Customization
PoS, Reservations & Orders, & Inventory-Ordering Tools
Loyalty Programs
Inventory Ordering
PoS System
Loyalty-Program Fulfillment
Order-Fulfillment Interface
Reservation Fulfillment
Incoming-Orders Interface
Order Analytics
B2C (Business-to-Consumer) White-Label Apps
Customer-Feedback Analytics
Customization Guide
White-Label Site
White-Label App
Marketing & Employee-Growth Tools
Professional-Growth Tools
Individual-Growth Interface
Campaign-Creation Tool
Campaign Analytics
Online-Acquisition Tracking
Campaign Fulfillment
Mentorship Program
Email Receipt
24-Hour Customer Support
Feedback Forms
Ordering Interface
Reservations Interface
Marketing Communications
• 50% subscription upgrades
• 50 new installs with subscriptions
• 500 app downloads
• 4+ star rating in app stores
• 50% subscription upgrades
• 100 new installs with subscriptions
• 500 app downloads
• 4+ star rating in app stores
• 25% subscription upgrades
• 20 new installs with subscriptions
• 1,000 app downloads
• 4+ star rating in app stores
• 25% subscription upgrades
• 250 new installs with subscriptions
• 2,000 app downloads
• 4+ star rating in app stores

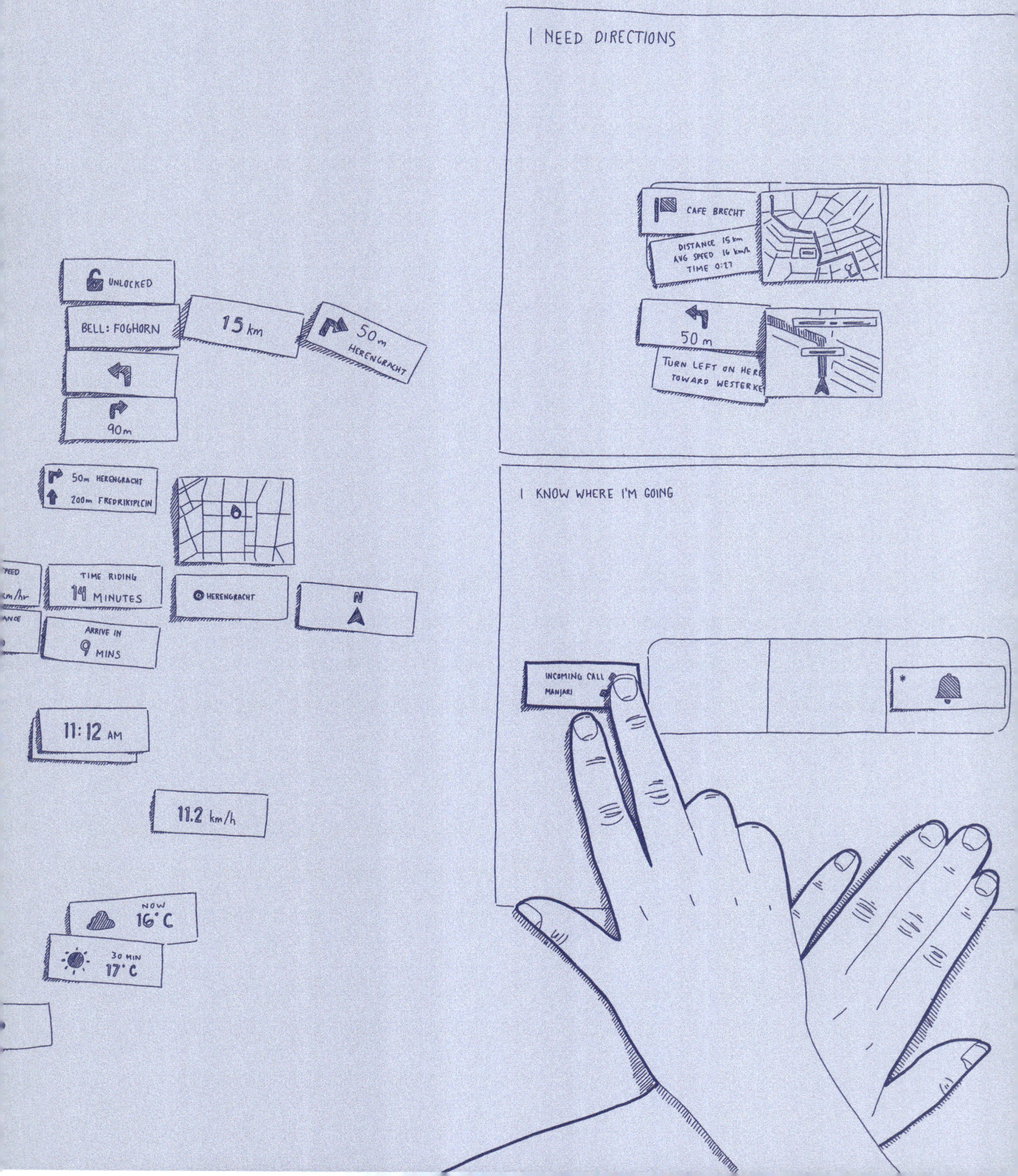

I NEED DIRECTIONS
CAFE BRECHT
DISTANCE 15 km
AVG SPEED 16 km/h
TIME 0:27
50 m
TURN LEFT ON HERE
TOWARD WESTERKE
I KNOW WHERE I'M GOING
INCOMING CALL
MANJARI
UNLOCKED
BELL: FOGHORN
15 km
50 m
HERENGRACHT
90 m
50m HERENGRACHT
200m FREDRIKPLEIN
TIME RIDING
14 MINUTES
ARRIVE IN
9 MINS
HERENGRACHT
N
11:12 AM
11.2 km/h
NOW
16°C
30 MIN
17°C

Participatory Design

Creating a design means making a lot of assumptions about what users are thinking and feeling. Creating a great design means validating those assumptions with actual users. In the discover phase, this can be done through immersion and user interviews. In later phases, the process of participatory design can be used not only to confirm or disprove assumptions but also to discover aspects of users' experiences you may not yet have considered.

Participatory design or co-design brings users into the design process with the intention of better understanding their needs and priorities. This input helps to build confidence in a design and to make better-informed decisions. While participatory design is most commonly done with existing or potential users, it could also be used to get into the minds of experts and stakeholders.

The collaborative activities of participatory design can be used to achieve many goals. In early phases, you might work with users to use their experience to generate new ideas, while in later phases you might enlist users to help refine a feature set or even to design their ideal product.

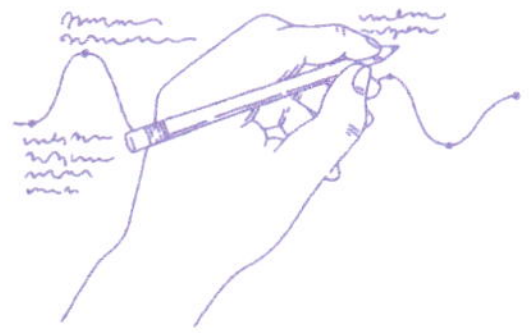

Work with users to sketch the journey of their experience.

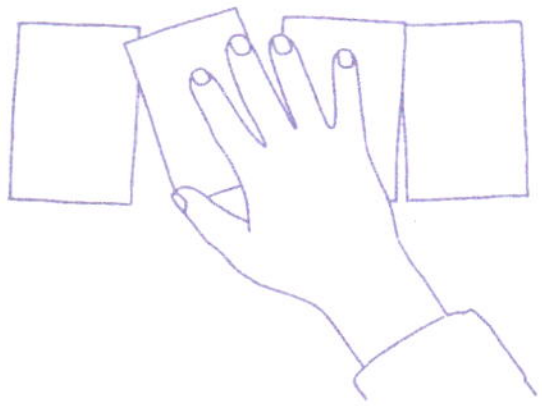

Ask users to prioritize the features most important to them.

Participatory design arose out of a need to involve users in the decisions being made for or about them. The theoretical origins of participatory design are most often traced back to 1960s Scandinavia, where work with trade unions resulted in a series of approaches where everyone in the organization is involved in understanding, proposing, and making decisions about technology solutions. These theories evolved into a number of practices more closely involving the observation and inclusion of users.

Similarly, 1970s tech companies such as IBM were struggling to create solutions that satisfied end users. To improve both the quality of the product and the efficiency of the process, the joint-application-design methodology was created, involving users at specific points throughout the already-established development process. Users' input would range from overarching goals and concerns to detailed objectives depending on the stage of the process in which they were participating.

The definitions and methodologies associated with participatory design have evolved over time, and organizations have created their own proprietary approaches to involving users in product or service design. This book uses a simple definition: participatory design is a collection of techniques for actively involving users or stakeholders in the design process. Participatory design goes beyond observing or gathering feedback from users. Instead it seeks to create experiences by uncovering opportunities, capturing priorities, generating concepts, or collaboratively mocking up the product or service with users.

Activities

Because participatory design can be used throughout the different phases of a project—from prioritizing features to establishing interaction models to refining the details of an individual feature—the methods of creating the setup can vary widely.

Before you get started, establish your goals. What are you seeking to achieve, and how will user input be valuable? Are you hoping to infuse your team's thinking with new ideas? Do you want stakeholder input on prioritizing features? Do you want to brainstorm with customers about how the actual product might look, feel, and function? Design activities that support your goals. Here are a few ideas to get you started:

Uncovering Opportunities

Work with users to understand how their experience could be better by collaboratively creating an experience journey or key scenarios. You might provide users with a series of illustrated key frames with which to build their own storyboards, or you might pair an illustrator with users to create their own storyboards from scratch. Encourage users to analyze and improve routine experiences as well as their most positive and negative experiences. The facilitator should seek to highlight opportunities and to capture any initial ideas users have for improving their experiences.

Capturing Priorities

Create games out of feature cards to discover participants' priorities. Talk through selections to better understand the user's needs.

Provide users with a set of feature cards, and have them prioritize them from least to most important. If you have an overwhelming number of features, try instead asking users to place feature cards into three buckets—must have, nice to have, and don't need. For users who struggle to make decisions, put a limit on how many cards can be in each bucket. If time is limited, ask users to pick their top three to five features and to explain why each of those is important.

Hold a concept-generation workshop with users.

Provide users with a tool kit to build their own ideal experience.

Generating Concepts

Plan a concept-generation workshop with users. Provide specific prompts to understand how they might solve different problems. Have users write, draw, or sculpt solutions.

For a less intimidating format, break users into small groups of two to three people each and provide each group with a prompt. Groups should ideate, curate, and refine solutions before presenting to the larger group.

Mocking Up the Product or Service

Collaborate with users or groups of users to design their ideal interactions.

Provide participants with a starting point and any constraints, and ask them to sketch, sculpt, or act out their ideal interaction. For more structure, provide the users with feature or element cards and ask them to arrange these within a template.

With your goals and activities in mind, start recruiting participants. If you're looking to design with users, consider which users' input will be most valuable. Recruit from your target audience to avoid cluttering your data with outlying opinions. If your goal is to learn from stakeholders, decide what you want to learn and then pull in the stakeholders most relevant to your discovery. If you have limited time and budget, but still want to gather outside opinions, recruit volunteers from friends and family of the team.

Keep in mind that because participatory design aims to harness the insights, understandings, and emotions of participants, it's important to create a safe environment for collaboration. Social customers might feel more comfortable sharing if they're with peers or friends, while more vulnerable participants might need to be alone in a session. Always consider how the other people in the room might affect a participant's contribution.

Participatory-design sessions should start with an introduction to the other people in the room, to the project's context, and to the session's activities. If you're conducting group sessions, have participants introduce themselves to each other. It can be helpful to include a project-related prompt to make introductions more colorful. Introducing the project's context can be done through presentation or through more immersive techniques. If you're asking users about shopping experiences, consider holding the participatory-design session in a store, or if you're asking users to design their ideal on-bike interface, have them sit on an actual bike. Before diving into activities, explain any materials and what's expected of participants.

When conducting activities, there should be a dedicated facilitator. This person's purpose is to guide the user through the process. A second team member might participate by capturing the process through notes and photos. If you have a large group that wants to observe sessions, consider live streaming the session or observing from behind one-way glass. Always choose methods that make each participant feel as uninhibited as possible.

Before starting sessions, it can be helpful to hold a test run to make sure that materials are comprehensive, instructions are clear, and everyone is comfortable with their roles. Practice the exercises with team members who aren't already familiar with them. Fine-tune your activities so that when users or stakeholders participate, you can make the best of their time.

> *"People ignore designs that ignore people."*
>
> Frank Chimero

Artifacts

It's important to aggregate, summarize, and synthesize your findings from participatory-design sessions to influence stakeholders and to inform future decisions. The format of the summary depends on which exercises you performed. If you captured priorities or documented personal experience, look to capture patterns and anomalies; if you generated concepts, pull out the most common or provocative ideas; and if you worked with users to design the product or service, capture common themes and highlight any interesting anecdotes.

Lead with the summary and follow up with supporting details. If you did participatory design with a larger group of participants, use pie or doughnut charts and percentages to show where they aligned. For smaller groups, share quotes and session photos to show how users engaged or what they designed.

Unused notes, photographs, concepts, and designs belong in an appendix. Depending on the extent of your participatory design and the thoroughness of your project, you may want to go so far as to catalog statements with reference numbers for easy access later in the project.

CityBike worked with users to design their ideal bike display based on a series of features. Users could also add their own features. To warm users up, each session began with a ten-minute session of city bicycling.

Ambience Mirror asked users to sort a series of feature cards by which were important and which weren't. Each user was allowed to choose up to ten features for the important bucket. Users described their choices throughout the process.

CityBike / **Connected Bicycle**

Participatory Design

Approach

We recruited twelve cyclists from the bike paths of Amsterdam and worked with them one on one to design their ideal on-bike display. We used a premade selection of both in- and out-of-scope features to understand users' priorities in addition to ideal layout.

User Recommendations

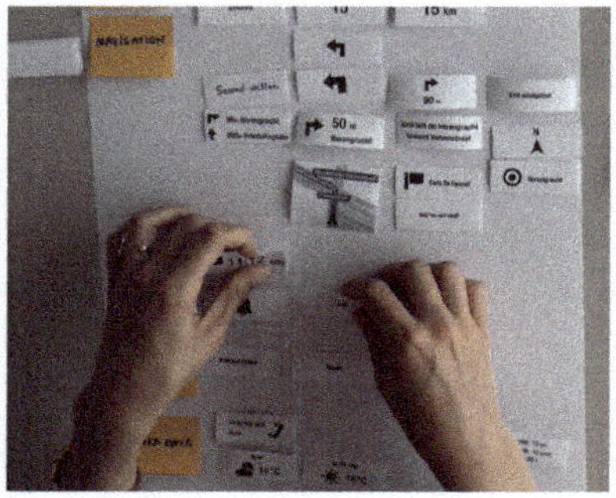

Commit to a consistent layout with limited information.

"It's really hard to read and bike, so the screen can't be changing with new messages all the time."

"There won't always be notifications, but putting other stuff in their place might make me think I'm missing something."

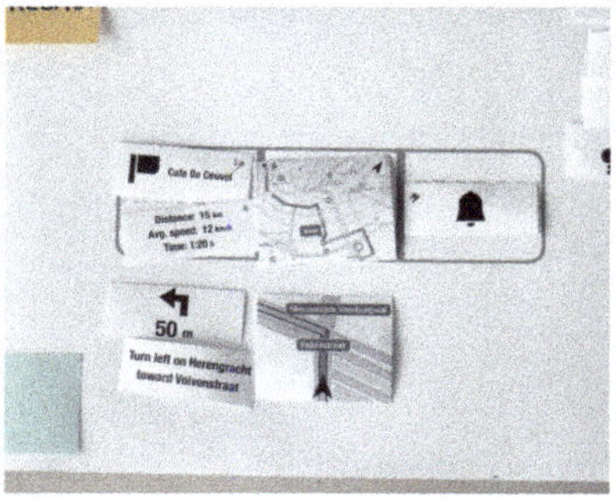

Regardless of mode, keep the map in the center.

"The map is the most important thing to me."

"I want the most important stuff in the center, and since the map is the only thing I'll probably be looking at while I'm riding—it goes in the center."

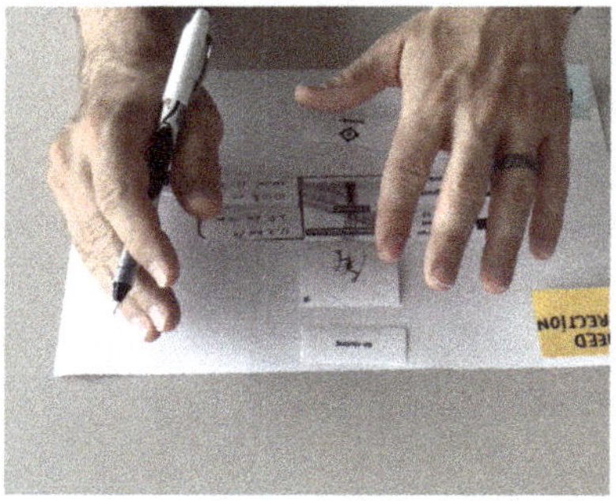

Show the user more of their journey on the map.

"I want to be able to zoom out on this view."

"Biking is so different than driving; it makes sense to have different navigation for a bike as well."

"I want to see my current location and my destination all in one screen."

User Statistics

7 users
disliked the bell
as a button

9 users
wanted to see
the current time

11 users
placed the map
in the middle

5 users
wanted more detail
in the map

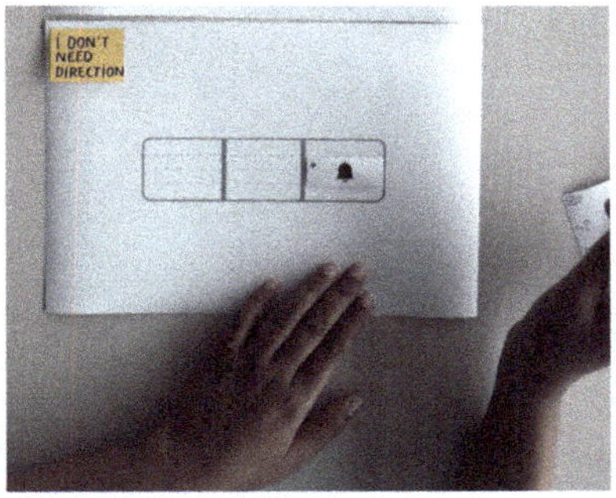

Make the entire screen area the bell.

"I don't want to cause an accident because I was looking for my bell."

"When I need to ring the bell, I usually don't have the time to search for it."

"The bell should be intuitive. I shouldn't have to look for it."

"Having a bell that just works is the most important thing after having a bike that just works."

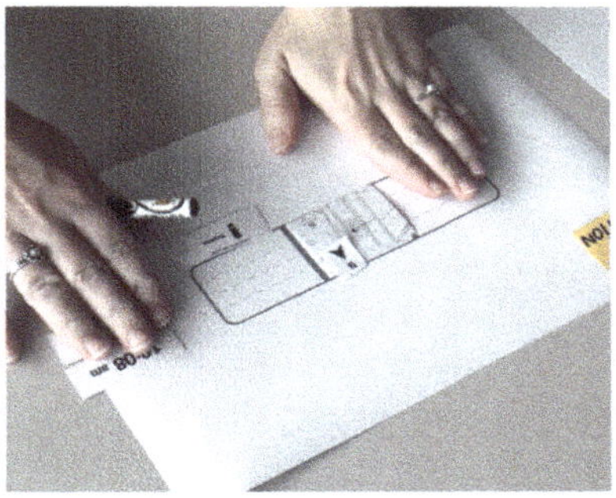

Keep the user apprised of status, even if there's nothing alarming.

"Sometimes the best notification is having no notifications at all."

"Especially here, I think it's always nice to know whether or not I'm going to get rained on."

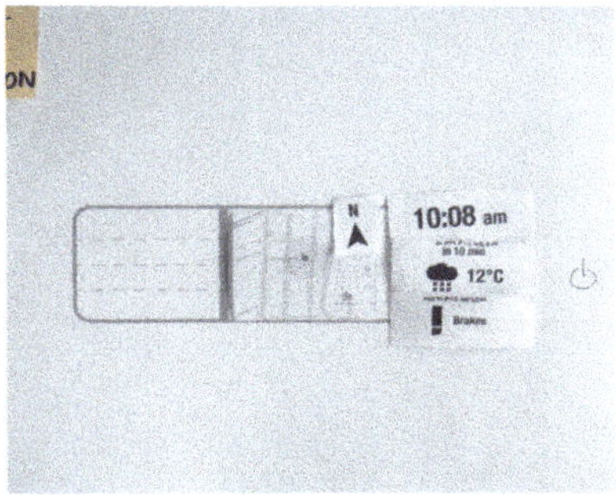

Allow the user to turn off the on-bike display if they don't want to use it.

"Especially at night, I can imagine the screen being a distraction. Maybe I just want to turn it off."

"I don't think I'd use the screen all that often, to be honest."

Participatory Design

Overview

We conducted thirty-nine participatory-design sessions with men and women of many ages to determine the Ambience Mirror's most desirable feature set.

Participant Breakdown

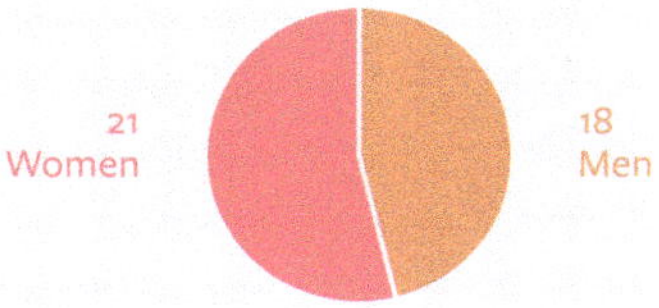

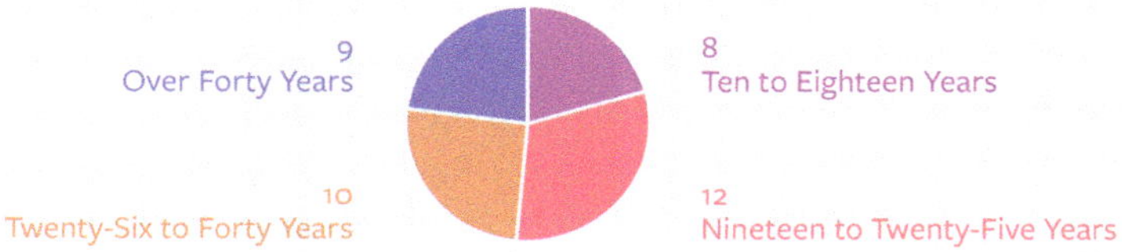

Twelve Favorite Features

100% want to see the day's weather

97% want to set reminders for themselves

90% want to see a view of the day ahead

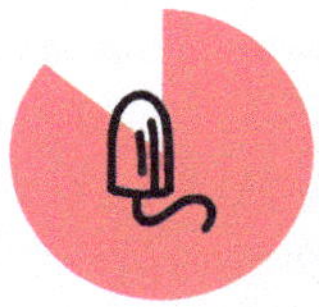

86% of women want alerts about their cycles

79% want to adjust lighting modes

77% want to see notifications

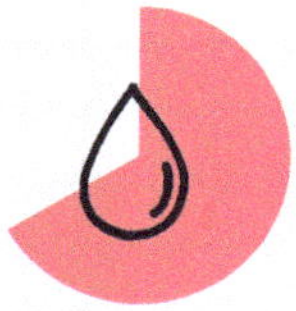

67% want to better understand their hydration

54% want reminders to take medication or vitamins

54% want help brushing their teeth for a full 2 minutes

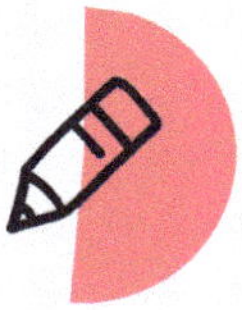

51% want to leave notes for others

51% want to see their step counts

46% want to understand their sleep

Worth Considering

"I'd like to confirm that my alarm is set and see a preview of when it's set for."

– **Natalia, 28**

"I want to see my nicotine consumption per day and when I have the most with data from my connected vape."

– **Tim, 36**

"Stretching and meditation would be nice, but all of the other stuff would distract me."

– **Denise, 41**

"Digital notes would be so nice—especially if you could do them in your own handwriting! It would be like writing messages in the fog on the mirror."

– **Amelia, 14**

"I would really love to replace the Sonos in my bathroom with something like this!"

– **Joris, 33**

"I would really love for it to recognize outfits and then to tell me the last time I wore something."

– **Theresa, 21**

"I know I drink too much caffeine. Maybe seeing just how much would help me drink less."

– **Logan, 24**

Refine

The refine phase of work uses what was uncovered in the discover phase and the decisions that were made in the define phase and applies these to the actual design of the product or service. Any project seeking to bring a new experience to market or iterate on an existing one will use the refine phase to ensure the design fulfills the needs and goals from previous phases. Only projects focusing exclusively on strategy will not need this phase.

At the end of the refine phase of work, the design should deliver on defined priorities and should have a clear structure and aesthetic direction. This is achieved through both generative and reductive activities, exploring multiple executions and then focusing on a single option, often using input from stakeholders or users. Because so much of the refine phase is about establishing the design itself, the focus shifts to artifacts, and the activities are largely a means to those ends. Each artifact in this phase aims to imbue the design with more detail and certainty, starting with structural artifacts like the information architecture and interaction model and ending with documentation like the component library and design guidelines.

The refine phase can change dramatically with scale. A single designer can design a brochure and a small team of designers and developers an app, but experiences that combine digital and physical products and services require large, multidisciplinary teams to bring them to life. To be most effective, the designer needs to understand the scope of the design and then to collaborate with other disciplines to ensure consistency across the experience.

The artifacts that come out of the refine phase are often useful beyond an individual project, informing future iterations of the product or service. For this reason, it's important to capture not only the design but also the rationale for design decisions. This documentation is especially useful in ensuring continuity when agencies deliver to in-house teams or when team members change.

In This Section:

NOTIFICATIONS

- UNUSUAL ACTIVITY
- MAINTENANCE (TIRES, BRAKES)

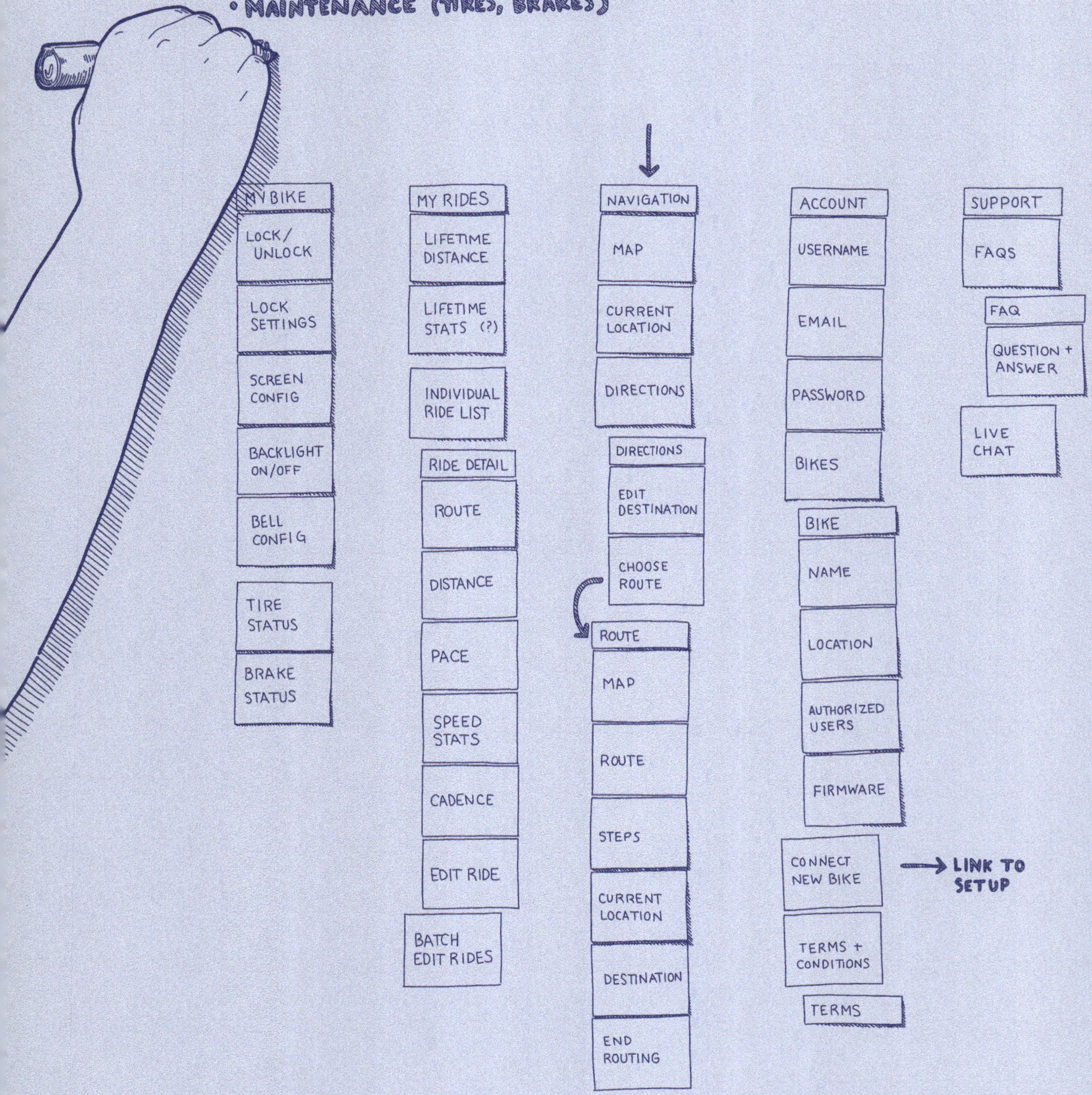

Information Architecture

For rich experiences with multiple interactive parts, an information architecture captures how the different features will be organized and accessed. Most project work that's already been done is relevant to this process. Take into account the features that need to exist as well as the user's needs from key scenarios. Consider the user's intuition captured by the conceptual model, and look at how others have organized features through competitive analysis and trendscape activities. Use experience principles for guidance when making decisions about what to prioritize and what to deprioritize.

The information architecture will help business stakeholders see how users will engage with the experience, will give developers an initial idea of how they'll be implementing features, and will provide a draft navigation structure to the design team. It is the foundation for many activities that follow, so it's important to give yourself enough time to work through the details and to get stakeholder commitment before charging ahead.

Explore different ways of grouping and organizing features.

Information architecture as a practice was established by Richard Saul Wurman. Once established, this practice was applied to many different fields, and thus there are many differing opinions on what makes a good information architecture—ranging from the naming, labeling, and organization of a structure to the choreography of context, information, and available functionality of an experience. While both are important, this is a book about experience design, so it will focus on the latter.

> *"I mean architect as used in the words* architect of foreign policy. *I mean architect as in the creating of systemic, structural, and orderly principles to make something work—the thoughtful making of either artifact, or idea, or policy that informs because it is clear."*
>
> **Richard Saul Wurman**

Activities

To create an information architecture, you'll need to synthesize what was learned from previous activities and artifacts. There are a number of activities you might approach lightly now if you didn't before. A competitive analysis might highlight patterns in how other companies organize similar experiences, while a roadmap might provide some foresight into how the experience will need to grow to accommodate new features. Feature definition provides an outline of your information architecture's contents, and the conceptual model can ensure that the concepts that are top of mind for users are easily accessible and that related concepts remain related in the structure of the experience.

How challenging it is to settle on a single intuitive information architecture depends heavily on the complexity of the product or service you're designing. If you're designing a simple and focused experience, your information architecture is likely to be straightforward. Perhaps the user has a single destination like a gallery or a feed. Here, the user might switch between overview and detail views of a single or multiple content types. Or perhaps the user has a primary flow through an experience, like taking, editing, adding commentary to, and publishing a photo or video. Because of their focused nature, both of these experiences have a limited number of executions, even when considering supporting features like account, settings, about, etc.

Rich experiences that provide users with many features and multiple paths across various channels and touchpoints provide a greater number of possibilities, and it can be difficult to arrive at a single information architecture. Consider an experience that includes a physical product, a conversation with a person (or bot), an app, a website, and email. Each touchpoint has a strength, and it's likely some features will exist only in some places. Features might also become more or less robust depending on a touchpoint's unique capabilities. For such experiences, you might approach the architecture at multiple levels. You may want to work at a high level to establish which aspects of the experience are available to the user on what touchpoints and then to explore in more detail the specific architecture of the experience on each individual touchpoint.

It's easy to overcomplicate an experience's architecture or to settle too quickly on the most obvious solution. To avoid these mistakes, start by trying a variety of solutions. Capture the different features or aspects of features in your experience on individual cards. Consider which features are noun oriented, like *gallery*, *photo*, or *map*, and which are verb oriented, like *share* or *duplicate*. For this exercise, try to avoid getting too deep into the details. For example, unless your experience is focused on sharing, you probably don't need to highlight the difference between sharing via email and sharing via social network.

Now experiment with possible organizations. If you're designing an experience that's similar to something that already exists, organize the cards to reflect a similar architecture. If you're designing an experience that has multiple leading features, try architectures that present these features side by side as well as architectures that prioritize a single feature over the rest. Work through the obvious solutions, embrace less obvious ways of doing things, and iterate on your successes. Document the different organizations with photos.

Participatory-Design Opportunity

It's possible to engage users to iterate quickly on possible architectures. Using the feature cards, allow users to prioritize what's most important to them and then to lay out their ideal navigation. This method works best for single-touchpoint experiences that users already have some familiarity with.

Artifacts

When presenting the information architecture, aim to minimally represent the user's experience in a way that can be communicated with decision-making and execution-oriented team members. Keep text short and to the point, lead with terms that everyone is familiar with, and use a structure that puts the most important elements at the top and less important elements at the bottom. The user's entry point is usually positioned at the top left. You might use color to differentiate between touchpoints, organizational silos, or versions of an experience. Typography could be used to show hierarchy or to differentiate between the nouns and verbs of an experience. Boxes could be used to highlight relationships while lines might connect features.

Keeping things minimal can be difficult, especially for complex experiences. If you're creating a deep and complicated information architecture, consider using multiple diagrams to communicate to stakeholders. Start with the big picture and then zoom into the details. Try to avoid more than three levels of hierarchy on any given diagram, and avoid long titles and descriptive text.

For some teams, the information architecture is an important milestone. If this is the case, consider printing the artifact out at a large scale to share and encourage interaction. For other teams, the information architecture is merely a stepping-stone in the process of design. If you're seeking to get buy-in without much conversation, consider presenting the information architecture as a lead-in to other artifacts like the interaction model, gestural design, or mock-ups. If you're presenting multiple options, consider presenting the information architecture with the interaction model so that the two can provide a more complete understanding to stakeholders.

The information architecture for CityBike is simple and straightforward, drawing inspiration from mapping and fitness apps. The shallowness of the structure makes for a better experience, even while riding a bike.

Observations Suite has a more complex structure where every overview has details and interactions that the user can dig into. The information architecture focuses on the web app and offerings, along with how features will expand over time.

Information Architecture

Notifications

- Unusual activity
- Maintenance alert
- Firmware update

Widgets

- Locked status
- Ring bell

Bike

- Lock/unlock
- Lock settings
- Screen configuration
- Screen backlight setting
- Bell sound setting
- Bell volume setting
- Tire status
- Brakes status

Ride statistics

- Lifetime distance
- Aggregated map data
- Individual ride list
- Route (map)
- Total distance
- Average pace
- Fastest speed
- Average cadence
- Edit Ride
- Batch ride edit

Navigation

- Map
- Current location
- Find directions
- Edit destination
- Choose route

↓

Route

- Map
- Route
- Steps
- Current location
- Destination
- End routing

Account

- Username
- Email
- Password
- Associated-bike list
- Bike name
- Bike location
- Associated users
- Firmware
- Connect new bike
- Terms & conditions link
- Terms & conditions detail

Support

- FAQs list
- FAQ detail
- Live chat

Omniscient / **Observations Suite Web App**

Information Architecture

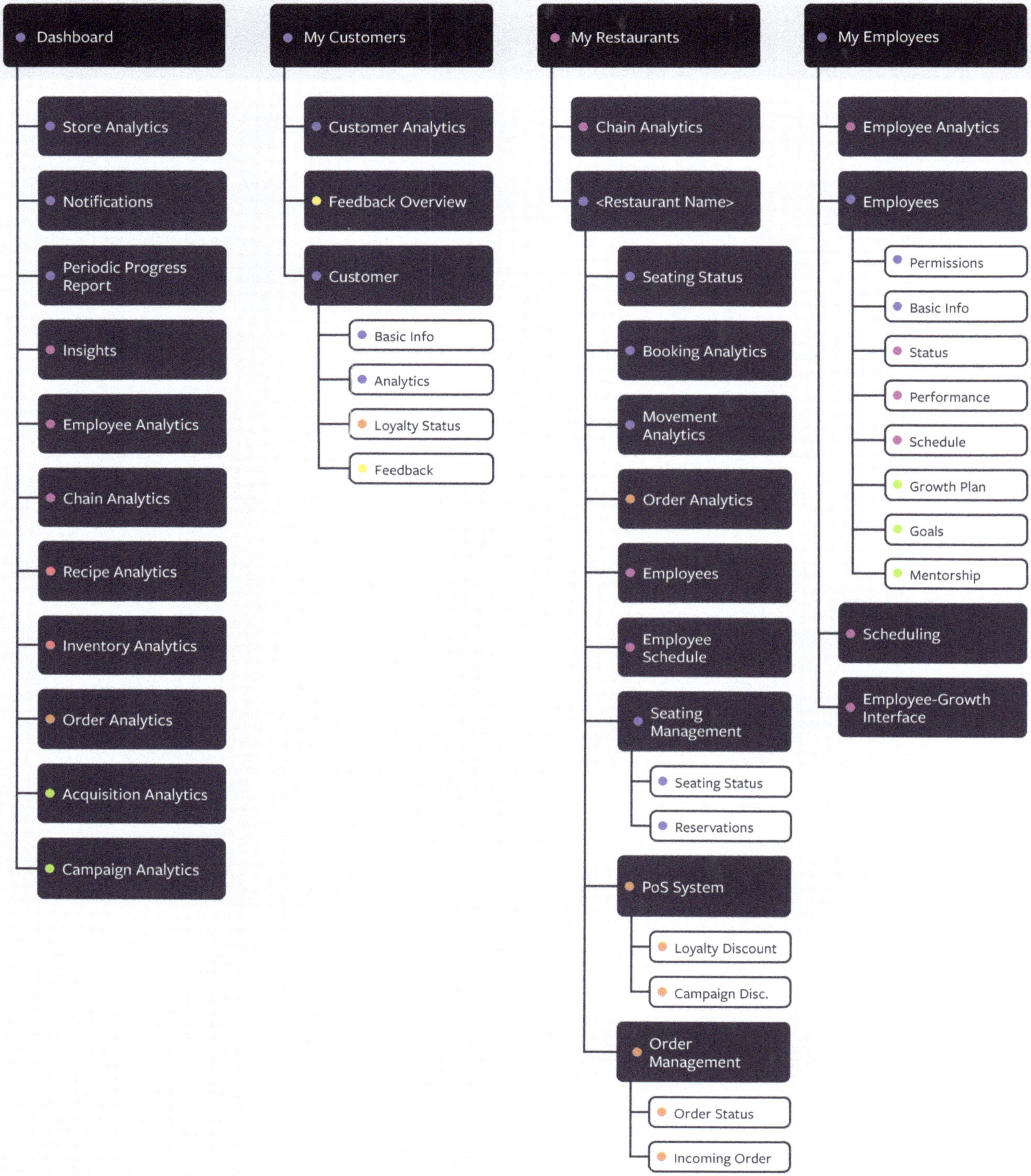

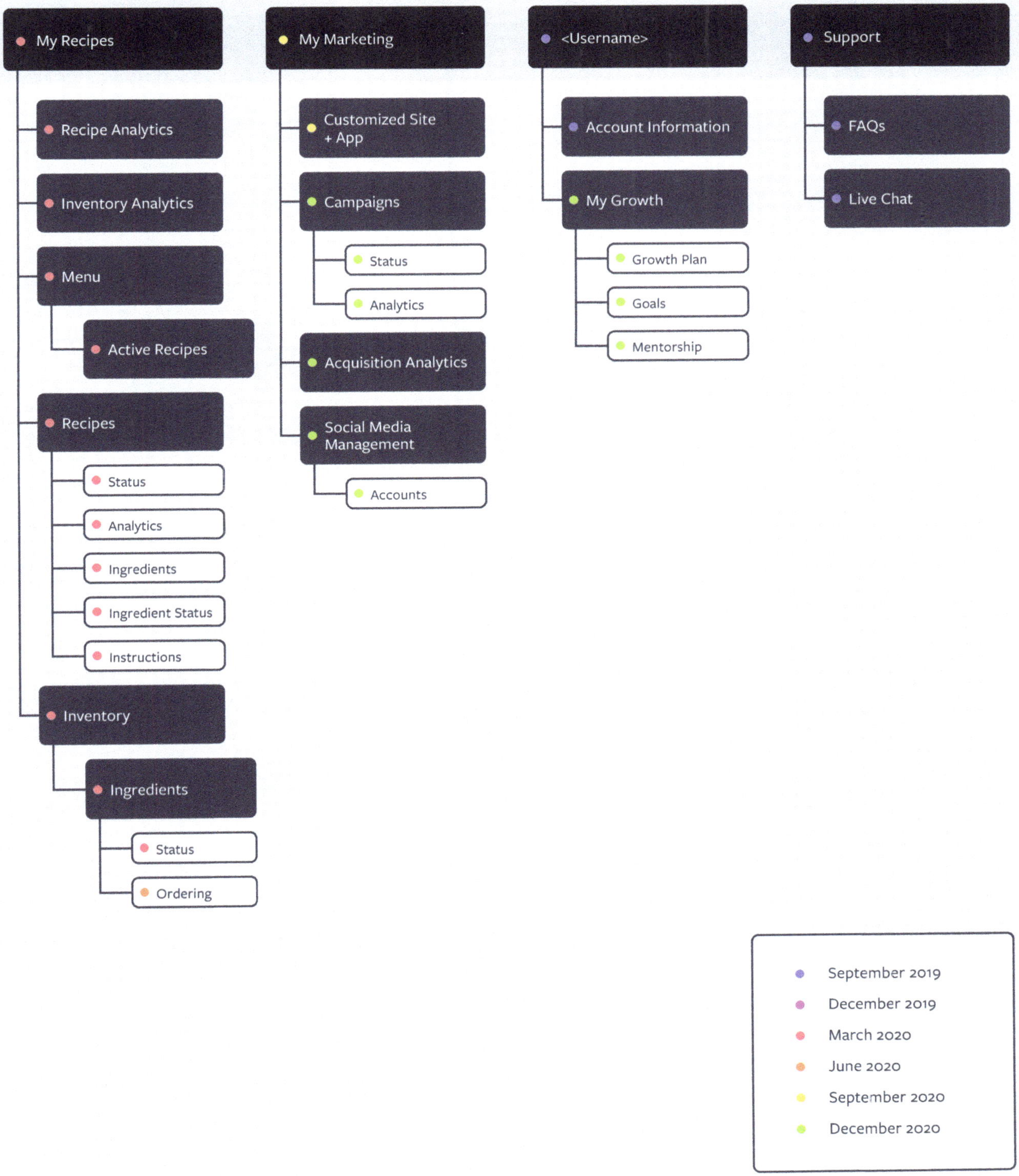
My Recipes
Recipe Analytics
Inventory Analytics
Menu
Active Recipes
Recipes
Status
Analytics
Ingredients
Ingredient Status
Instructions
Inventory
Ingredients
Status
Ordering
My Marketing
Customized Site + App
Campaigns
Status
Analytics
Acquisition Analytics
Social Media Management
Accounts
<Username>
Account Information
My Growth
Growth Plan
Goals
Mentorship
Support
FAQs
Live Chat
September 2019
December 2019
March 2020
June 2020
September 2020
December 2020

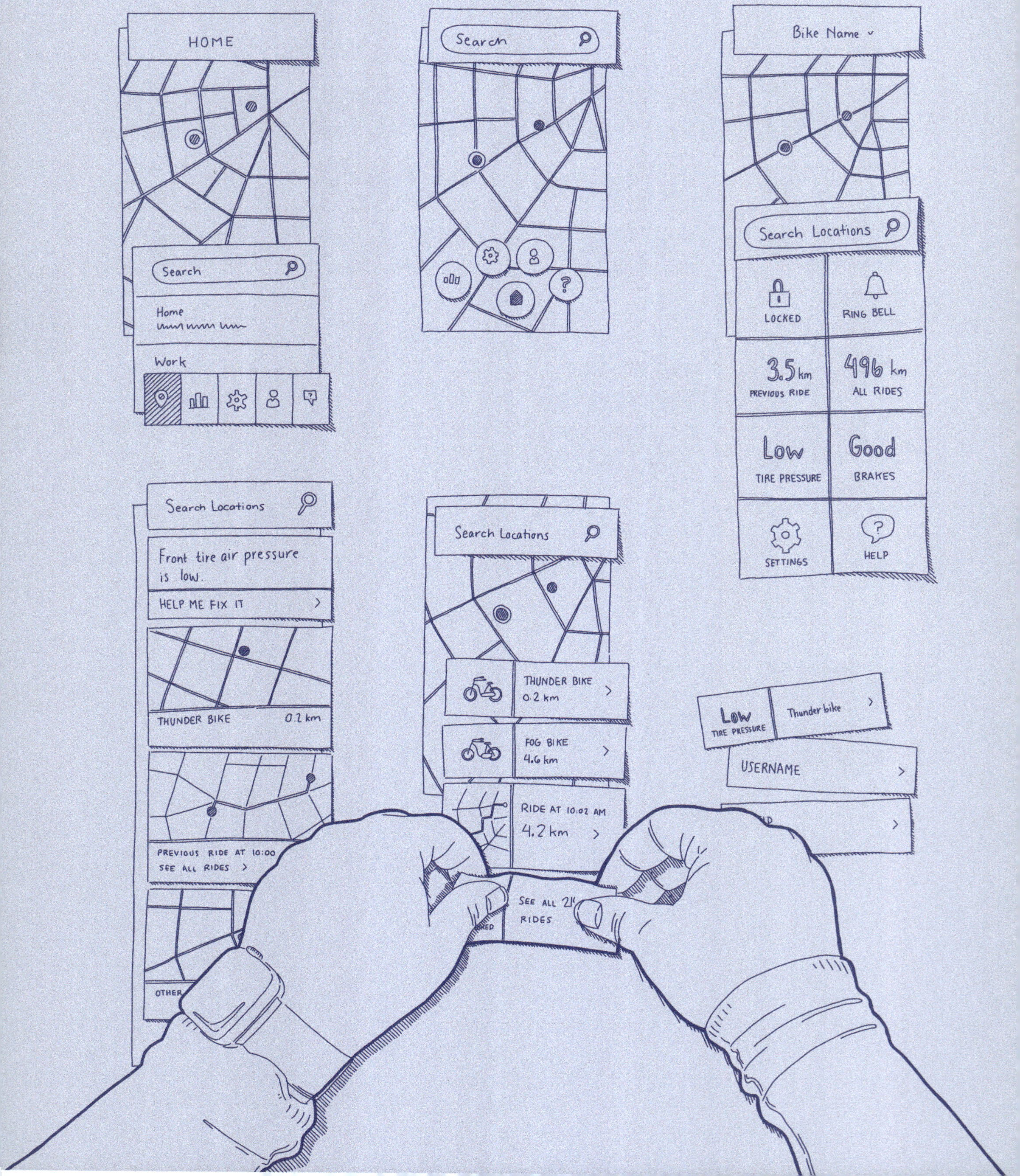

HOME
Search
Home
Work
Search
Bike Name
Search Locations
LOCKED
RING BELL
3.5 km
PREVIOUS RIDE
496 km
ALL RIDES
Low
TIRE PRESSURE
Good
BRAKES
SETTINGS
HELP
Search Locations
Front tire air pressure is low.
HELP ME FIX IT
THUNDER BIKE
0.2 km
PREVIOUS RIDE AT 10:00
SEE ALL RIDES
OTHER
Search Locations
THUNDER BIKE
0.2 km
FOG BIKE
4.6 km
RIDE AT 10:02 AM
4.2 km
SEE ALL 21 RIDES
Low
TIRE PRESSURE
Thunder bike
USERNAME

Interaction Model

Interaction models seek to combine what the user already knows and understands from similar experiences and real-world metaphors with the features of a product or service to create a high-level overview of how the user engages the experience over time. Interaction models are useful for any experience that reacts to a user's interactions. Depending on the goals of an experience, you might optimize your model to reduce friction, to encourage interaction, or to elicit joy or some other emotional response from the user.

Interaction models can be applied at both large and small scales. For example, an interaction model might get into the details of how a user adjusts the settings on a single product, or it might show how the user navigates multiple apps to access various services. Regardless of scale, they seek to create a consistent structure for features to exist within. Early in a project, interaction models might explore multiple options for mapping the information architecture to physical or digital space, while later they might communicate decisions within the design guidelines. Not only is the interaction model a useful foundation for later design work, approaching this before diving into other refine activities helps designers to think more systemically about future design decisions.

Activities

Synthesize related concepts into unique themes or approaches.

Explore your feature set with models from similar experiences.

Experiment by applying models from dissimilar experiences.

When designing a new experience, it's imperative to balance invention with familiarity. Following the patterns of existing experiences can ensure that you create something the user can easily comprehend, and learning from best-in-class products and services can ensure more widespread adoption. Ease of use cannot, however, stand alone. Products and services need to be differentiated either through benefit or through design, and sometimes a well-integrated and executed bit of novelty can elevate a standard experience to something that's desirable beyond the competition.

The strongest interaction models come from a process of generation, iteration, and reduction. To start creating an experience model, select a scale. Are you designing for an experience across many channels or for interaction on a single touchpoint? Next, prioritize the most important aspects of the experience for the interaction model. Use the outputs from feature-definition, conceptual-model, and information-architecture activities to determine the core of the user's experience. When playing with multiple interaction models, these provide the skeleton around which all explorations are built.

Once you've established the scope of your model, start gathering materials for inspiration. Outputs from concept generation, competitive analysis, and trendscape activities will all be useful for exploring potential interaction models. The following exercises outline how:

Synthesize Related Concepts

If you had a concept-generation workshop focused on the design of the experience, you probably already have a number of options to choose from. Search through the ideas to find the strongest and most varied themes, and then gather similar ideas together. Next, interpret these to be appropriate to the scale of your interaction model. For example, if you're designing an interactive mirror, themes might be conversational, playful, and emotive. Each of these will express itself in an interaction model that optimizes for that theme. While some themes are obviously stronger than others, it's important to stay generative at first, seeking to strengthen weak ideas rather than cull them altogether.

Appropriate from Similar Experiences

Whether you're designing a feature or a multitouchpoint experience, chances are there's something similar that already exists. Consider how others have approached what you're doing. If you're designing a banking service, look to other banking services; if you're designing a music app, look to other music apps; and if you're designing a set of tools for filtering content, look to other experiences around filtering content. Copy what already exists within the context of the features and constraints of your product.

Reinterpret Dissimilar Experiences

Look to the trendscape to discover patterns that are familiar to users yet new to your industry. There is both opportunity and peril in finding new ways to disrupt the way things have always been done. For example, if you're designing for professionals, you might consider looking to consumer tools for inspiration. Educational tools might infuse learnings from social networks, home-automation services might integrate conversational interfaces, and fitness products for adults might be inspired by kids.

With these exercises behind you, it's likely that you have too many possible interaction models. Synthesize and reduce. Some directions will be obviously stronger or more unique than others. Both are important to consider when curating. As you throw away interaction models, make sure to capture their strengths for potential integration into the remaining model or models.

If you're presenting multiple options to stakeholders, reduce and iterate until you have curated down to the smallest possible number of directions that are distinct enough to be memorable, usually three or four. If you're presenting a single direction, be prepared to highlight why it's best.

Artifacts

When engaging stakeholders with interaction models, the goal is either to explain the structure of a product or service or to choose a single direction for a series of options. For the former, you might show the interaction model within the context of other deliverables, like mock-ups or design guidelines. For the latter, you might combine multiple interaction models with gestural-design directions, describing what makes each unique.

Regardless of whether you're explaining one model or many, the challenge of communicating the interaction model is often greater than coming up with the model in the first place. Consider your audience as you decide on the fidelity, format, and level of description to use to support your interaction model.

Interaction models can be shown in many different fidelities—from representative gray boxes (wireframes) to full-fledged visual design. While mature stakeholders might be able to imagine how things work based on low-fidelity sketches, most

> *"Any intelligent fool can make things bigger, more complex, and more violent. It takes a touch of genius—and a lot of courage to move in the opposite direction."*
>
> Ernst F. Schumacher

audiences need more detail to make an informed decision.

Interaction models can be communicated in different ways. If your scope is multitouchpoint, you might need to show how each touchpoint relates to the others to ensure stakeholders of consistency. If you're designing a shallow experience, you could use a flat diagram to visualize how the user navigates through the experience; whereas, if you're designing a deep experience, a three-dimensional diagram might be better to show spatial relationships.

You might want to describe how each interaction model works by comparing them to analogous experiences, such as *This interaction model leads with search like Google*, or *This interaction model features an inbox like email apps*. For stakeholders who might find it difficult to compare and contrast the benefits of multiple interaction models, providing a series of pros and cons for each can facilitate decisions.

The interaction-model artifact for CityBike shows three options for how the user might navigate through the app. Each option has a map showing how the user gets to the top-level parts of the information architecture, as well as a 3-D diagram to show the structure of the different elements on a screen.

Observations Suite's interaction model shows how the web app scales between large desktop and small mobile displays. It calls out key elements across both touchpoints to help stakeholders understand the similarities in structure, despite differences in appearance.

CityBike / **Connected Bicycle**

Interaction Model

Option 1: Tabs

The app uses a shallow interaction to access the main functions, all of which have their own top-level screens. The home screen is the first of the five functions—the map and directions. The user switches between multiple bikes from the accounts screen.

Option 2: Dashboard

The app uses a two-level interaction model with a dashboard on the home screen to provide users with glanceable content and quick access to primary and secondary functionality. For bike-specific functionality, the user can switch between multiple bikes from the navigation bar.

Option 3: Cards

The app's home screen presents the user with a list of cards containing summaries of individual app functions. The user accesses secondary functions without data summaries via buttons at the bottom of the scrolling list. The user has access to all of their bikes via these cards.

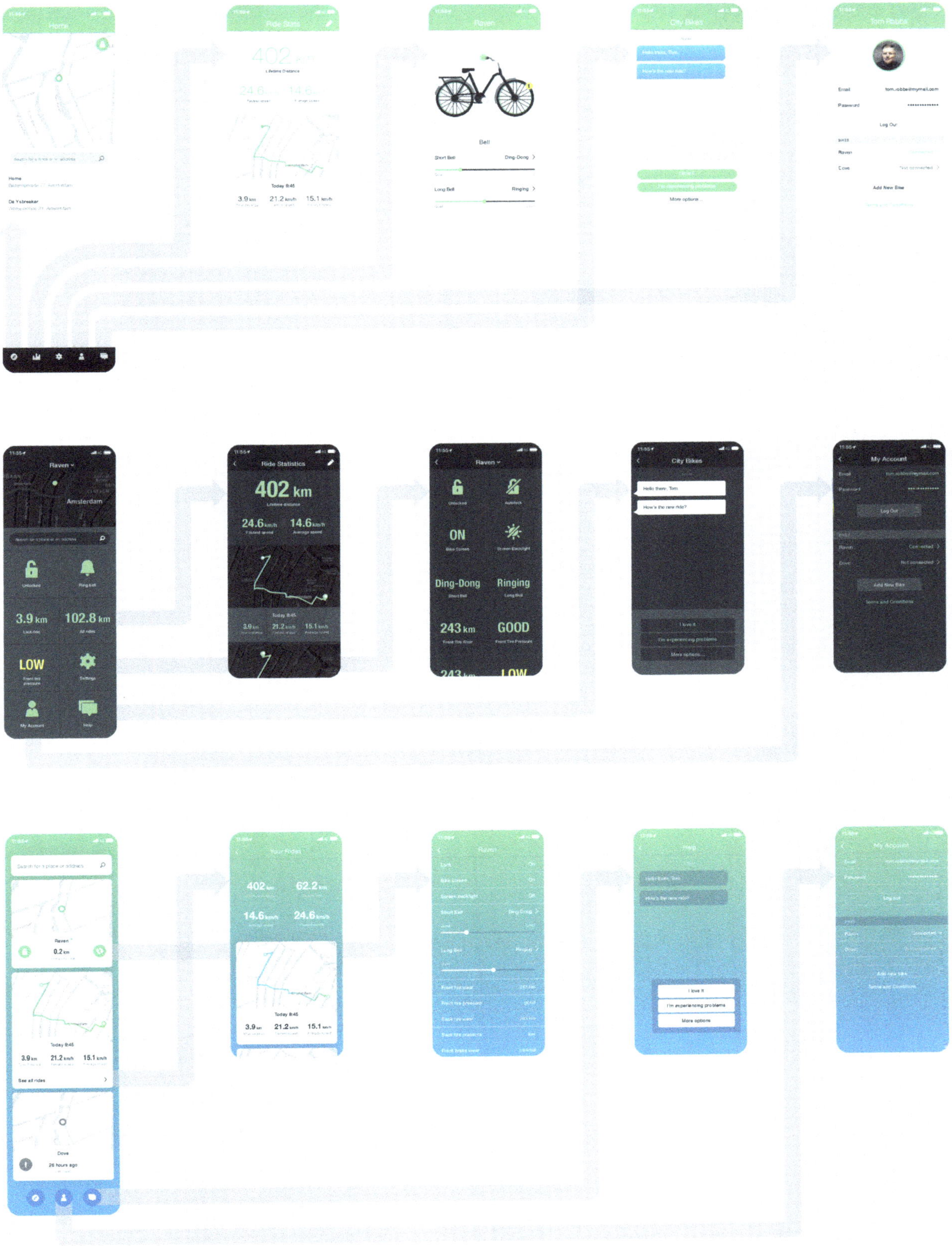
Home
Ride Stats
Raven
City Bikes
Tom Robbe
Bell
Short Bell
Ding-Dong
Long Bell
Ringing
Email
Password
Log Out
Add New Bike
Raven
Amsterdam
Unlocked
Ring bell
3.9 km
102.8 km
LOW
Settings
My Account
Help
Ride Statistics
402 km
Lifetime distance
24.6 km/h
14.6 km/h
Today 8:45
3.9 km
21.2 km/h
15.1 km/h
Unlocked
Autolock
ON
Ding-Dong
Ringing
243 km
GOOD
City Bikes
Hello there, Tom
How's the new ride?
I love it
I'm experiencing problems
More options
My Account
Log Out
Add New Bike
Terms and Conditions
Your Rides
402 km
62.2 km
14.6 km/h
24.6 km/h
Raven
0.2 km
Today 8:45
3.9 km
21.2 km/h
15.1 km/h
See all rides
Dove
26 hours ago
Help
I love it
I'm experiencing problems
More options
My Account

Omniscient / **Observations Suite Web App**

Interaction Model

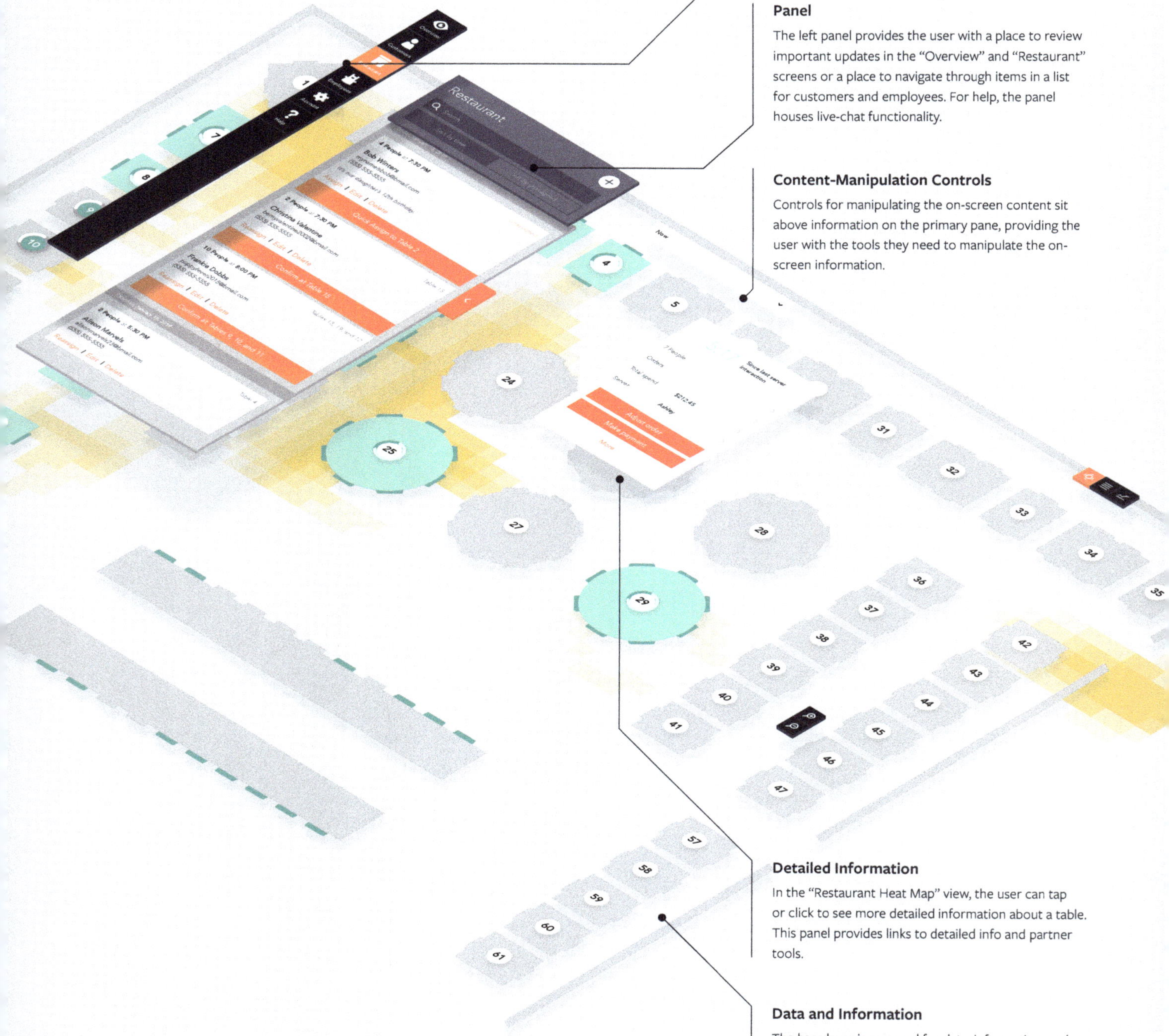

Desktop

Navigation

The web app's primary navigation sits above all other content, highlighting the user's current location.

Panel

The left panel provides the user with a place to review important updates in the "Overview" and "Restaurant" screens or a place to navigate through items in a list for customers and employees. For help, the panel houses live-chat functionality.

Content-Manipulation Controls

Controls for manipulating the on-screen content sit above information on the primary pane, providing the user with the tools they need to manipulate the on-screen information.

Detailed Information

In the "Restaurant Heat Map" view, the user can tap or click to see more detailed information about a table. This panel provides links to detailed info and partner tools.

Data and Information

The base layer is reserved for data, information, and other content.

Mobile

Navigation

The web app's primary navigation sits above all other content and can be accessed with a single tap. The visible icon highlights the user's current location.

Panel

The overlay panel provides the user with a place to review important updates, navigate through items in a list for customers and employees, and live-chat in "Help." It is accessible by tapping the open icon next to the page title. A small indicator alerts the user to new notifications.

Content-Manipulation Controls

Controls for manipulating the on-screen content sit above information on the primary pane, providing the user with the tools they need to manipulate the on-screen information.

Detailed Information

In the "Restaurant Heat Map" view, the user can tap or click to see more detailed information about a table. This panel provides links to detailed info and partner tools.

Data and Information

The base layer is reserved for data, information, and other content.

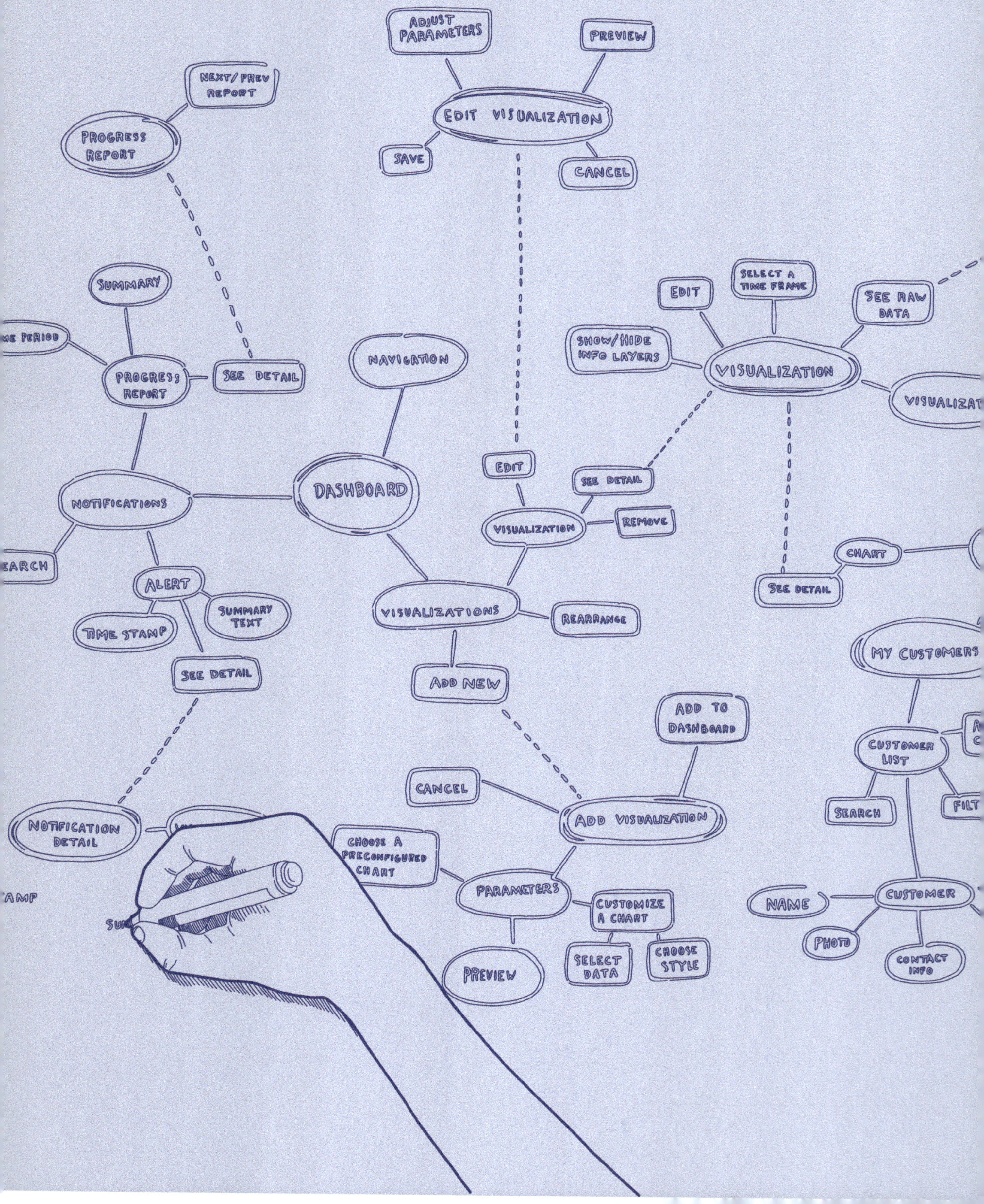

ADJUST PARAMETERS
PREVIEW
EDIT VISUALIZATION
SAVE
CANCEL
NEXT/PREV REPORT
PROGRESS REPORT
SUMMARY
PROGRESS REPORT
SEE DETAIL
NAVIGATION
DASHBOARD
NOTIFICATIONS
ALERT
SUMMARY TEXT
TIME STAMP
SEE DETAIL
NOTIFICATION DETAIL
EDIT
SEE DETAIL
VISUALIZATION
REMOVE
VISUALIZATIONS
REARRANGE
ADD NEW
ADD TO DASHBOARD
CANCEL
ADD VISUALIZATION
CHOOSE A PRECONFIGURED CHART
PARAMETERS
CUSTOMIZE A CHART
SELECT DATA
CHOOSE STYLE
PREVIEW
EDIT
SELECT A TIME FRAME
SEE RAW DATA
SHOW/HIDE INFO LAYERS
VISUALIZATION
CHART
SEE DETAIL
MY CUSTOMERS
CUSTOMER LIST
SEARCH
CUSTOMER
NAME
PHOTO
CONTACT INFO

Function Hierarchy

Somewhere between information architecture and mock-ups, decisions around what's most important in a given moment, what the primary actions are on a screen, or what buttons should be easiest to access on a physical product need to be made and documented. The function hierarchy serves this purpose, collecting what needs to exist and prioritizing what's most important without making recommendations pertaining to layout or visualization.

For simple products and services, an information architecture might be enough, but for more complex experiences, the information architecture and the function hierarchy provide a complete picture of how the experience will be structured. This can be useful for ensuring alignment with stakeholders before moving to a higher fidelity or for making sure that functionality is agreed upon before exploring the more aesthetic aspects through gestural design or mock-ups. If you don't do a function hierarchy, it will emerge through mock-ups and detailed design. Making a physical artifact simply ensures consistency and completeness with less iteration.

Activities

If you're designing for an experience that spans multiple functions, it's helpful to complete an information architecture and possibly to have established an interaction model before starting on the function hierarchy. For more focused experiences, it's possible to dive right into the function hierarchy. Don't be surprised if the experience turns out to be more complex than you originally thought. If this is the case, you may need to zoom out to create an information architecture or to update the one you have with more details.

What about Wireframes?

Wireframes are often used in web and UI design as a means to express function and content separately from form. While they are a useful tool for designers to quickly think through and sketch various low-fidelity solutions, they often also make suggestions about layout and visual design that can be a distraction to stakeholders who have yet to align on functionality.

Start by collecting the high-level functions. A function is the tactical version of a feature. A feature might be *The user sees their restaurant's floor plan,* while its functions would be more specific, for example, *Zoom in and see occupied tables*. For each screen, state, or page, consider what your user needs to be able to accomplish. Maybe they need to lock and unlock their bike, or perhaps they need to assign a reservation. Capture everything you can think of, and then check your list against the features you've defined. If you completed a competitive analysis or trendscape, look at those experiences to ensure you haven't forgotten any important functions.

Now group ideas and add detail. For example, the different types of metadata on a piece of content would be grouped, as would the various actions a user could take on their profile. As you work, consider what the user can see as well as what the user can do. Use the conceptual model to ensure that your groupings of functions are familiar to the user. Revisit your information architecture often and update if necessary.

Once you have your list of functions, start prioritizing. Put the most important things on top and the less important things below. Consider grouping functions into primary, secondary, and tertiary categories. In some cases, you might find a few functions that would be nice to have but are not necessary. Make sure to call this out in your hierarchy.

Artifacts

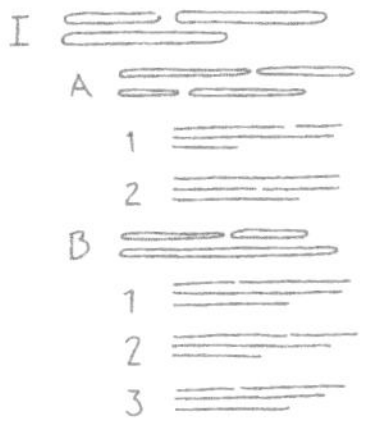

Use traditional outlining techniques to establish a simple, readable hierarchy.

Once you've completed this process for the most important of, if not all, screens, states, or pages, you'll need to document it in a way that's easily referenced and shareable. You can use any text tool that does simple formatting, or you can work in a design tool. If you choose the latter, make sure you stick to text to avoid unintentionally suggesting layout decisions.

Function hierarchies tend to be more detailed and technical than can easily be reviewed with stakeholders. Rather than reviewing everything in detail, focus on high-level decisions in the hierarchy, or those that will have broad consequences if changed. Use the function hierarchy to provoke conversations around areas of known contention, getting stakeholders to align before investing effort in fully visualized or rendered mock-ups.

When laying out the hierarchy of functions, use traditional outlining techniques. For experiences with multiple discrete states, treat each state as a title. Next lay out the different groupings of functionality. Give each section a heading, like *Navigation* or *Visualizations*. Fill in the details. Consider showing what the user can see versus what they can do in different styles or colors. Use indentation to show relationships. For example, if a visualization has associated actions, these should be indented under it.

The function hierarchy is useful when exploring the overarching design system. When paired with gestural design, a single function hierarchy can provide consistency for multiple aesthetic explorations, or multiple hierarchies could be explored to instead show stakeholders a variety of options for structure and priority. For experiences that have limited interactions between screens, states, and pages, you might combine the function hierarchy with a high-level flow diagram to communicate the architecture in more detail. Developers might also use the function hierarchy as input to their processes, generating use cases or user stories based on the functions described. Once the thinking has been carried forward into other artifacts that will live on, the function hierarchy doesn't need to be maintained on its own.

Observations Suite captures the first release's feature set in the function hierarchy, highlighting what the user can do, as well as what they can see.

Omniscient / **Observations Suite Web App**

Function Hierarchy

Dashboard

Primary Navigation

Notification List

- Search
- Notification detail
    - Time stamp
    - Notification text
    - Link to visualization detail
- Periodic progress report notification
    - Summary (including time period)
    - Link to progress report

Visualizations

- Add visualization
- Move visualization
- Visualization
    - Remove visualization
    - Link to visualization detail
    - Edit visualization

Visualization

- Visualization
- Select a time frame
- Adjust related data layers (add/remove)
- Link to original data
- Close visualization

Add Visualization

- Add visualization to dashboard
- Cancel

Parameters

- Select preconfigured visualization
- Select primary data type
    - Select additional parameters
- Select secondary data type
    - Select additional parameters
- Select tertiary data type
    - Select additional parameters
- Select visualization style

Preview

- Visualization preview

Edit Visualization

- Save revised visualization
- Cancel (do not save changes)

Parameters

- Select primary data type
    - Select additional parameters
- Select secondary data type
    - Select additional parameters
- Select tertiary data type
    - Select additional parameters
- Select visualization style

Preview

- Visualization preview

Progress Report

- Jump to other report
- Link to sign up for email
- Close progress report
- Summary (including time period)
- Visualizations
    - Time stamp
    - Notification text
    - Link to detail (visualization)

Original Data

- Raw data in list format
- Close original data
- Export as CSV

My Customers

Primary Navigation

Customer List

- Search
- Filter
- Add customer
- Customer
    - Photo, name, contact info
    - Tags
    - Link to customer detail

Customer Visualizations

- Select a time frame
- Visualization
- Link to visualization detail

Customer

- Photo, name, contact info
- Tags
- Notes
- Visualizations (spend, dwell, visits)
- Edit tags
- Edit notes
- Remove customer

Add Reservation

- Add name, contact info, party size, time, notes
- Assign
- Save
- Cancel

Edit Reservation

- Name, contact info, party size, time, notes
- Edit name, contact info, party size, time, notes
- Status (assigned / unassigned)
- Assignment
- Assign / reassign
- Save
- Cancel

My Restaurant

Primary Navigation

Upcoming Reservations

- Search
- Sort (time, unassigned)
- Add reservation
- Reservation
    - Status (assigned / unassigned)
    - Assignment
    - Name, contact info, party size, time, notes
    - Assign / reassign
    - Contact
    - Edit reservation
    - Delete

Restaurant Visualizations

- Select a time frame
- Visualization
    - Link to visualization detail
- Restaurant map
    - Select room
    - Show / hide information layers
    - Zoom
    - Pan
    - Table
        - Status (spend, dwell, server interaction, etc.)
        - Order (link to partner tool)
        - Pay (link to partner tool)
- Reservations per table
    - Date navigation
    - Table number and availability
    - Reservation details
        - Name, contact info, party size, time, notes
        - Reassign
        - Contact
        - Edit
        - Delete

My Colleagues (nonmanager)

Primary Navigation

Employee Directory List

- Search
- Sort
- Photo, name, role

Employee Detail

- Photo, name, contact info, role

My Employees (manager)

Primary Navigation

Employee Directory List

- Search
- Sort
- Photo, name, role

Employee Detail

- Photo, name, contact info, role
- Permissions
- Adjust permissions
- Edit
- Archive

My Account (nonmanager)

Primary Navigation

- Photo, name, contact info, role
- Permissions
- Edit photo
- Edit contact info
- Reset password

My Account (manager)

Primary Navigation

My Information

- Photo, name, contact info, role
- Edit photo
- Edit contact info
- Reset password

Billing

- Summary of invoices
- Link to invoices
- Pay invoice

Invoice

- Invoice amount and breakdown
- Status (paid / unpaid)
- Pay invoice

Support

Primary Navigation

Live Chat

- New message
- Live-chat history

FAQs

- Search
- FAQs

See (blue) / Do (pink)

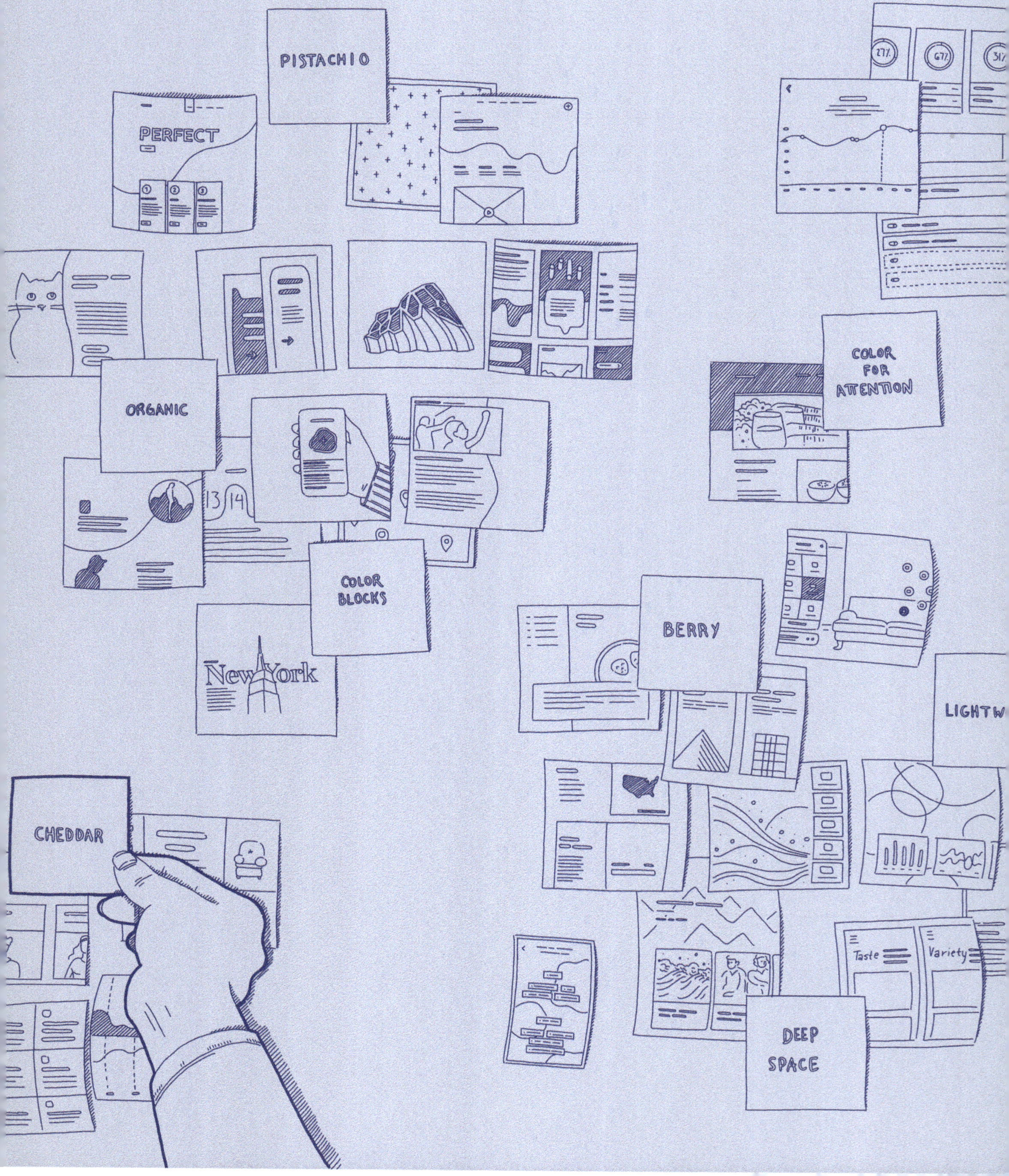
PISTACHIO
PERFECT
ORGANIC
COLOR BLOCKS
COLOR FOR ATTENTION
BERRY
LIGHTW
CHEDDAR
DEEP SPACE
Taste
Variety
New York

Moodboards

When designing experiences that don't exist within an already-defined design language, moodboards can be helpful for communicating different aesthetic directions to stakeholders. The activity of curating imagery provides an opportunity for the design team to align on design directions through the exploration of brand and existing materials, aesthetic trends, and other input.

Typically presented as collages of imagery around a theme, moodboards avoid questions about features and interactions, focusing instead on conversations about elements such as color, typography, and motion. By sharing with stakeholders, a design team can observe initial reactions to how a product or service looks or feels. Later activities, like gestural design and mock-ups, should use moodboards as a guiding light, ensuring that the vision survives execution.

Activities

Moodboards start with a collection of images. These images could come from a variety of inspirational sources and should cover the needs of your project. Search for images that represent the brand of the product or service you're designing for as well as the industry you're working within. Find images that relate to the culture you're designing for and that represent the best-in-class experiences for the personas you've developed. Include imagery from the competitive analysis, the trendscape, and experiences stakeholders have mentioned. Search for images that represent what's standard and what's popular. Don't limit yourself to imagery that's specific to what you're designing. Digital design can be influenced by industrial design, industrial design by architecture, and so on. With moodboards, it's hard to start with too much imagery.

While gathering imagery, look for themes in how different products use space, light, graphic elements, and layout. Move images around to see how they work with each other. Sometimes what's immediately obvious can be a distraction—for example, a direction should be able to survive even if a stakeholder doesn't like the color blue or the Futura family of fonts. In other words, color and typographic style are likely less important to a direction than contrast and typographic hierarchy.

Explore more themes than you need. If you want to end up with three moodboards, usually a good number for decision-making, start with twice that. Curate out what doesn't work and synthesize what does. As you narrow your selection and refine each moodboard, be intentional about what they will have in common and where they will be unique. Consider your brand when making final decisions. For example, if you're designing for a brand with strong opinions on typography, perhaps all of your moodboards will have similar typographic ingredients.

After establishing distinct aesthetic directions, ensure that each board has a well-rounded sample of ingredients. Consider each ingredient on its own as well as how it relates to others.

Color

How is color used throughout the design? What's the color scheme—monochromatic, analogous, complementary, etc? Are hues vibrant or muted? How much contrast does the design have? Does color hold a specific meaning—to guide action, to provide feedback, or to establish the brand?

Shape and Form

Is it round or angular? Does it have soft or sharp corners? Are forms bold or delicate? Is the design made of many small parts or from one monolithic form? Is it trying to feel large or small? Does it stand out or blend in with its surroundings?

Surface and Finish

Is it glossy or matte? Does it have texture or pattern? Does it simulate a deep space or a shallow space? Does it feel synthetic or natural? How variable is the surface? How tangible are the controls?

Typography

How much does the design depend on typography versus other glyphs or icons? How dynamic are the typography's proportions? How heavily does the experience rely on type? What styles and weights of typography are used? How is type used to establish hierarchy?

Iconography

When does the design use iconography? What forms are used to create icons? How tangible are they? How do icons relate to type?

Photography

Does the design use photography? Is the photography created by users or selected by the brand? Is the focus on the details or on the big picture? Do photos have a treatment? How do photos interact with other aesthetic elements?

Illustration

Does the design use illustration? Where and how is illustration used? Is the illustration technical or whimsical? How detailed is it? Does the illustration have a style that evokes a certain time or place?

Traditional moodboards focus on capturing an aesthetic and a feeling with a few images.

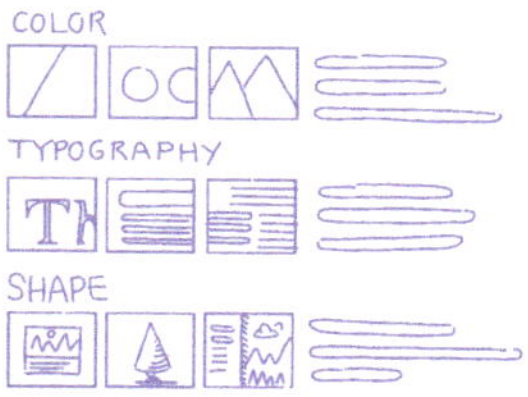

Focusing on individual ingredients can be helpful for less savvy stakeholders.

Transitions

Are transitions subtle or exaggerated? Do they feel natural or playful? What moments do transitions seek to amplify?

Tone of Voice

How do you express your message? Is your message brief or detailed? Are you seeking to direct the user's experience or to support it?

Sound and Haptics

How are sound and haptics used—to provide feedback, to communicate, or to create a mood? Are they subtle or obvious? Are they natural or synthetic?

As you collect and organize images, consider the different words you'd use to describe the groupings. Themes might be described as editorial, ethereal, dynamic, rich, simple, and so on. These words are often useful when describing moodboards to stakeholders.

Artifacts

While moodboards can be presented alone, they rarely are. Typically they play a supporting role in early refine-phase presentations, working alongside gestural design to help stakeholders make decisions about how their product or service is perceived by users. There are different ways you might structure your moodboards depending on the narrative that you're weaving and the audience you're presenting to.

If you have a design-savvy audience, select a handful of images, no more than eight, that best capture and communicate a possible look and feel. Images should feature a variety of ingredients and should work together to tell the story. You might even adjust the layout of your moodboard to fit the mood. A short description can provide a helpful summary. This type of moodboard aims to make an immediate impact on the audience and seeks decisions made based on feelings rather than analysis.

If you have a more technical audience, you might create a moodboard that individually calls out specific ingredients. For each ingredient, choose three or four images that best show the direction, and then use a few words to provide a description. Do this for each ingredient that is relevant to the project. While this way of working prioritizes individual elements over the whole, it also makes conversations about specific design decisions like buttons or typography less reactive.

To facilitate the conversation, it can be helpful to give each moodboard a title. For a more mature audience, this might be derived from the words used to describe the moodboard. For a less mature audience, consider using straightforward labels like *Option 1* or *Direction A* to keep stakeholders from choosing against a direction simply because they don't like the name.

"Design is thinking made visual."

Saul Bass

Moodboards for Observations Suite capture four possible directions for the new product. Each focuses on a variety of ingredients, but all have a point of view about visualizations—one of the central elements of the design. These directions were refined and used to inform gestural design.

Moodboards

Cheddar

A strong grid of squares and rectangles provides the overall structure for both interfaces and marketing materials. Elements use bright colors to guide the user's attention and size and weight to establish typographic hierarchy. Iconography provides a touch of visual interest in familiar areas like navigation.

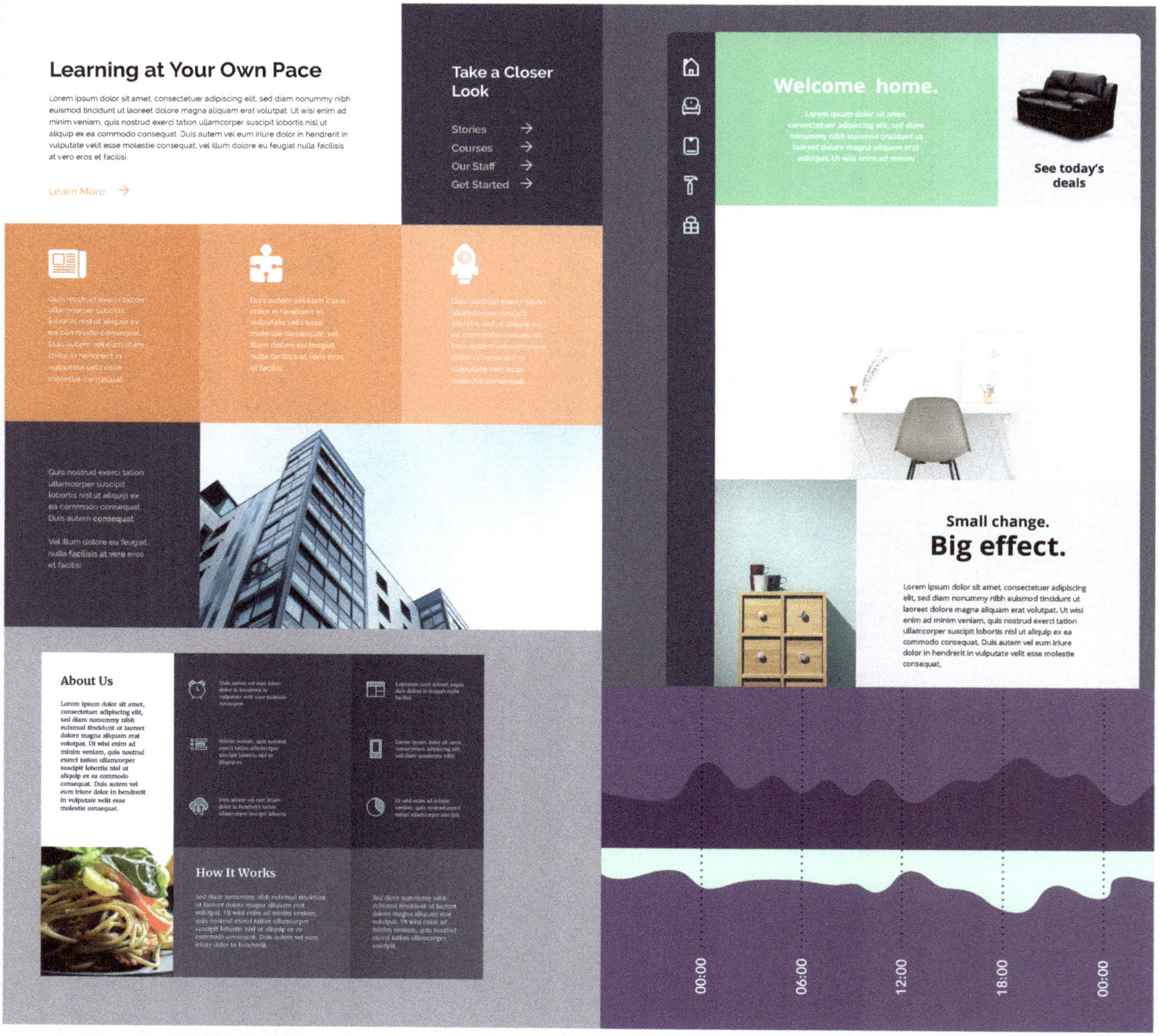

Carrot

Monochromatic gradients and overlays make for a more technical feel, which is more familiar for most dashboards. A slightly offset grid accompanied by shallow depth provides hierarchy for content and visualizations. Lightweight typography uses size to establish hierarchy, while icons are used to draw attention to actions.

Pistachio

Flat blocks of color and organic shapes infuse serious interfaces with a touch of playfulness. Controls and visualizations are bubbly but concise, prioritizing what needs to be communicated most. Multiple fonts are used to create typographic hierarchy, while iconography is used sparingly throughout the design.

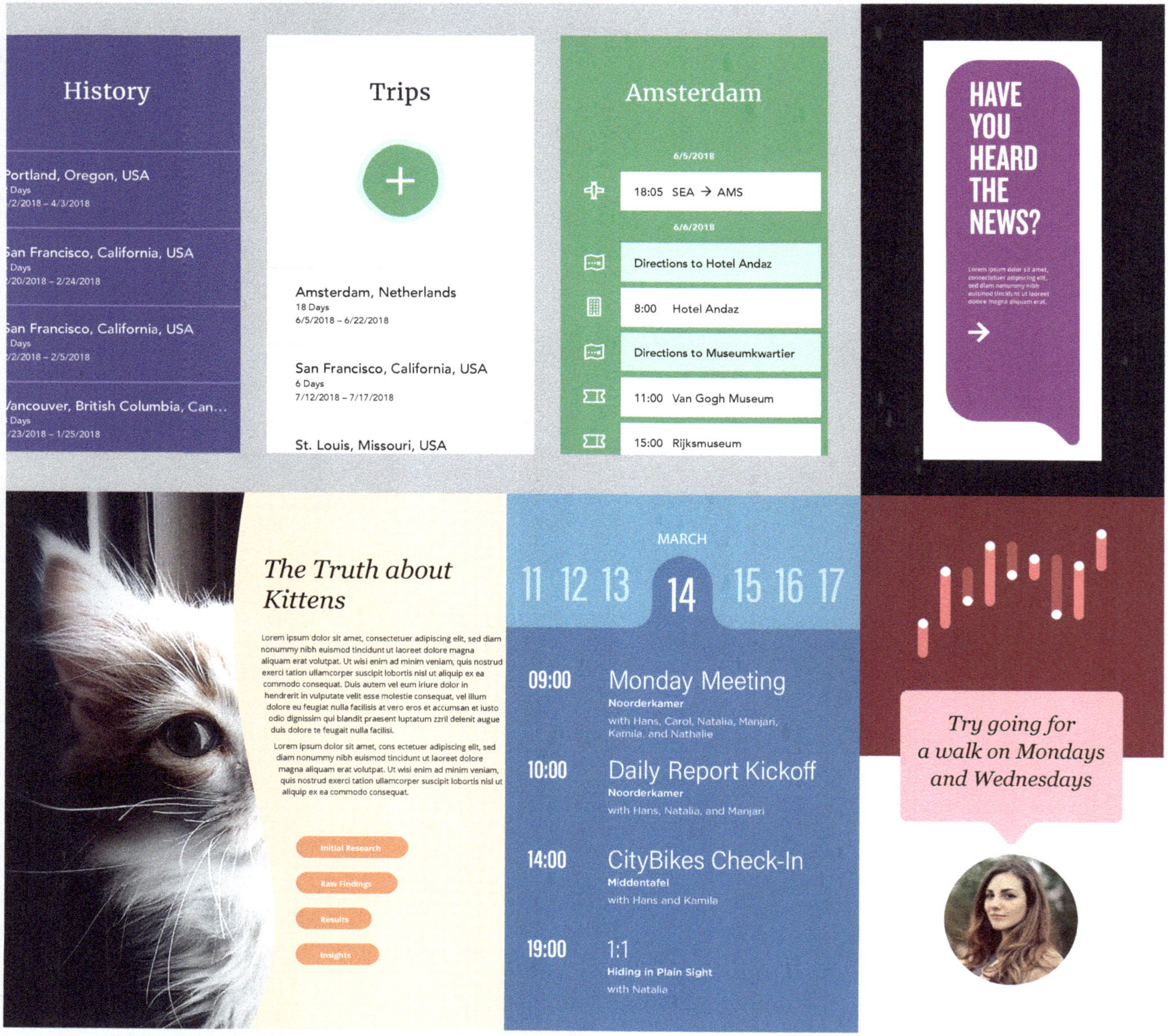

Berry

Berry uses deep spaces with minimal color to keep focus on the content. Blurred photography creates a base for interactive elements and content cards, using lightweight controls, sharp corners, and iconography to add a feeling of precision. Typography is also lightweight, relying on size to establish hierarchy.

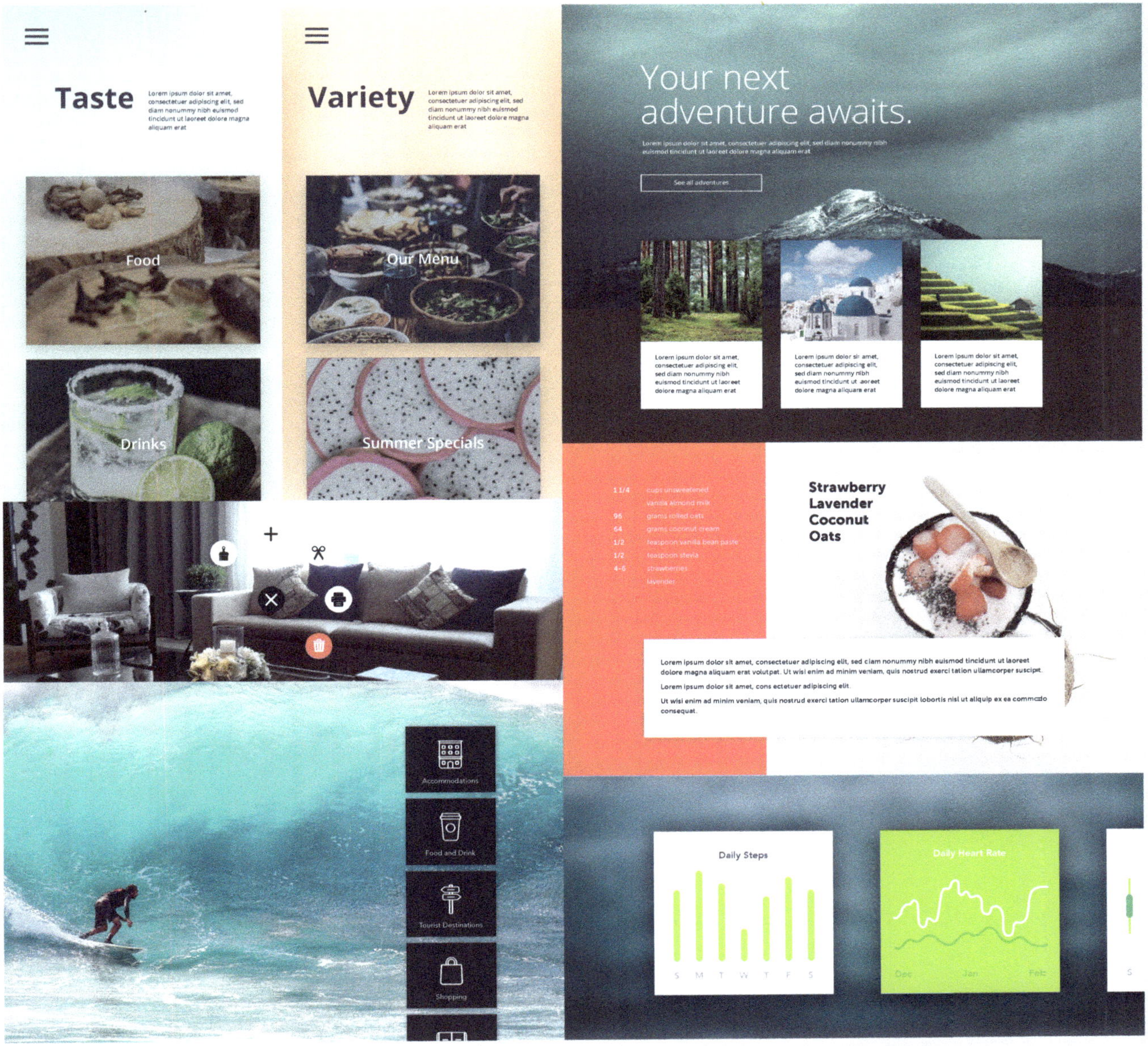

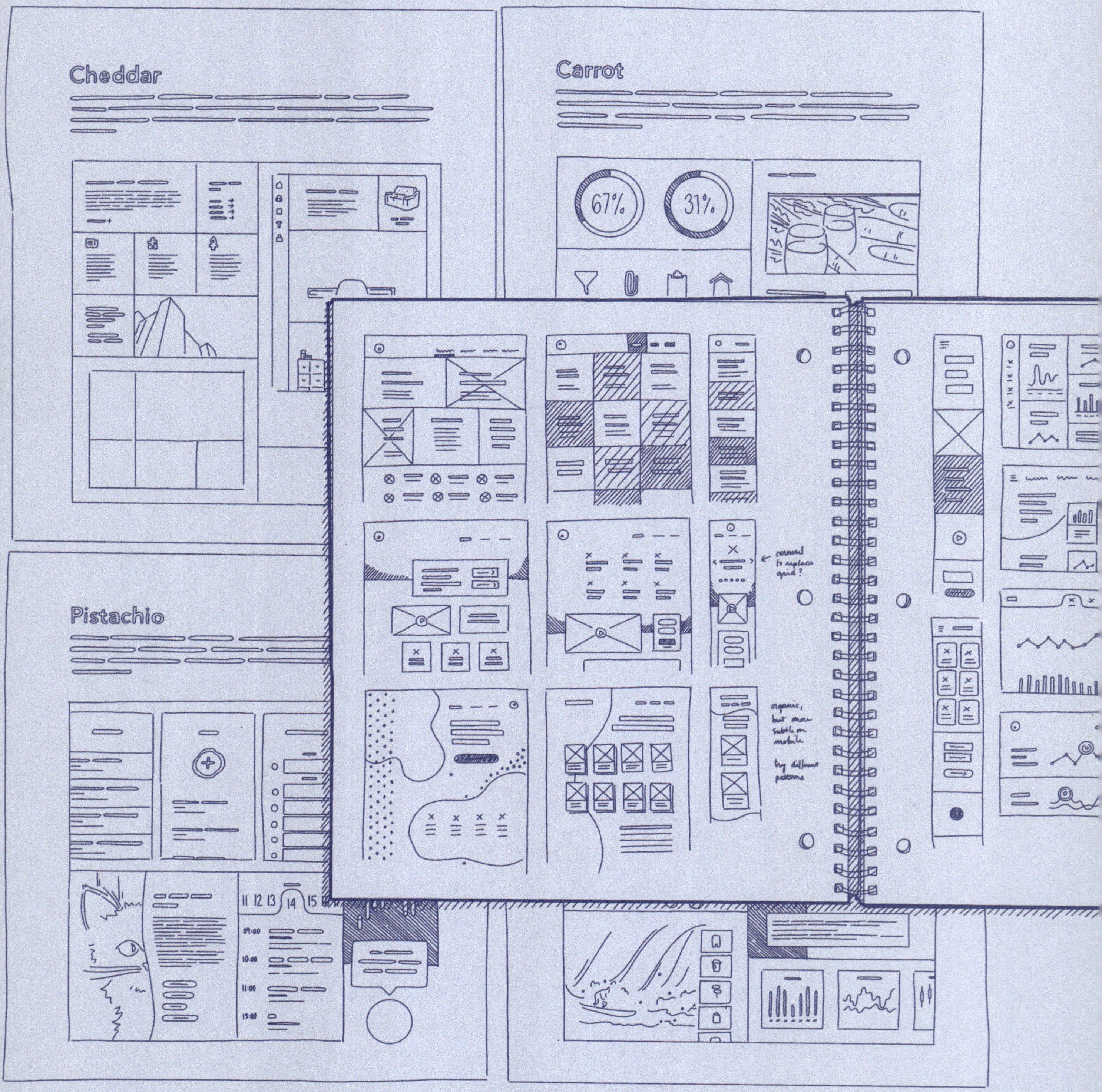
Cheddar
Carrot
67%
31%
Pistachio
11 12 13 14 15

Gestural Design

Gestural design is the quick and explorative design work done after a product or service has been defined but before it has been fully fleshed out. Typically gestural design considers multiple ways of achieving the same goals, focusing on getting just enough of the interactions and aesthetics in place that nondesigners can get an idea of what the final product could be. This early feedback can provide clear direction, supplying confidence when choosing a direction to pursue. While it may seem high fidelity, gestural design is usually done with the intention that much of the work will be used to solicit stakeholder and user input and then will be integrated or thrown away.

Gestural design might explore only aesthetics, showing how visual design can provide many distinct feels to a single information architecture or interaction model, or it may be explored in conjunction with these deliverables to show multiple ways of solving for the same set of features. The approach depends on the complexity of the system you are designing, the maturity of stakeholders, and the amount of time and budget available for exploration. While not every project needs to consider multiple options with gestural design, most benefit from the exploration.

Design options should vary from safe and predictable to innovative and surprising.

Gestural design borrows its name from figure drawing. Gesture drawing is the act of quickly capturing the essentials of the figure with little effort or time. A gesture drawing may take as little as ten seconds, yet results in a sketch that accurately communicates the figure's position and form. Gesture drawings may evolve into more considered works with time but are rarely precious on their own.

Throwing away design work can be difficult, and so it is important to go into gestural-design exercises knowing that the purpose is not to make a final design but rather to explore possibilities, cultivate opinions, and purposefully provoke. It's a time to be experimental and to let ideas and the possibilities of execution run wild.

Activities

Before beginning down the path of gestural design, consider the work that has already been done, decisions that have been made, and what remains to be investigated. If you're working on an experience that already has an established visual-design language, your gestural designs might be more oriented toward exploring different interaction models, while if you're working on designing a product or service with a fairly common and straightforward interaction model, you might focus more on exploration based on different moodboards. If you're working for a brand without an established aesthetic and on a product without established interaction patterns, then you might explore both at the same time.

Gestural design is often stakeholders' first glimpse into what the final product could be, so it needs to be both realistic and aligned with stakeholder expectations. Consider whether you're exploring aesthetics, interaction, or both, and capture what you know in three buckets: decisions that have been made and that should not change, significant decisions that need to be made or reconsidered, and decisions that are insignificant to the design. The middle bucket, significant decisions to be made or reconsidered, should define your directions. If you have three directions, they can often be mapped onto a spectrum from *safe*, as in following all of the rules, to *innovative*, which might challenge decisions that have already been made. After all, if you're going to challenge the status quo, the solution should be notably better, or amazing. Not all gestural-design explorations have to challenge expectations, but each direction should provide distinct advantages over the others.

Aim for at least three discrete directions. With two directions, stakeholders will seek to compare; however, with three options, stakeholders will focus more on each direction's strengths and weaknesses, driving conversations toward stronger (and less reactive) decisions. It's easiest to simply aim for variety. Just as gesture drawing seeks to capture as many poses in as little time as possible, gestural design should

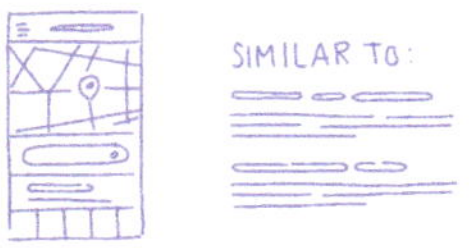

Highlight how a direction is similar to other experiences.

But focus on what makes each direction unique.

seek to explore as many options before the deadline as possible. Always aim for more than enough, and then curate down to the strongest options.

As you work, keep track of what makes each direction unique, and make notes of what makes each option strong or weak compared to the others. Capture where a direction is similar to previously researched products and services or where it aligns to a stakeholder need or something a user or expert said during interviews. All of these annotations will be helpful later when presenting your work.

Give yourself enough time to really explore. Try to avoid getting too caught up in a single direction and having a favorite. When you feel a direction is weaker than the others, give it more attention. If you're struggling, consider bringing in outside designers for a fresh perspective.

When you wrap up, all gestural-design directions should be of a similar fidelity and should feel as if they were done by a single team. It should not be obvious to stakeholders who designed which direction, or which direction is preferred by the designers who worked on it. Also ensure that the only differences between directions are those you're comfortable discussing. For example, if you want to focus on the layout of photos but not the content, show the same photo across all directions.

Artifacts

Gestural design is best presented as a series of options for stakeholders. If you've explored aesthetics only, aim to have at least three options. If you've also explored various architectures, through either information architectures or interaction models, you may want to show more with multiple visual representations per interaction exploration. This will help stakeholders understand that interaction and visual direction aren't entirely tied to each other. More importantly, it will help a good interaction model to live on even if the gestural-design direction's aesthetics aren't preferable.

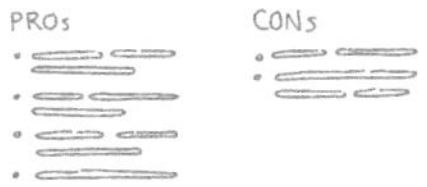

Present the strengths and weaknesses of each direction.

With your gestural-design directions considered and curated, plan your presentation. Gestural design is the culmination of previous activities, so start by reminding stakeholders of the previous decisions that went into creating the directions. Briefly run through any relevant decisions that have been made about the experience, including the features, architecture, and aesthetics. Provide your stakeholders with a brief overview of the same context that guided your decision-making process in creating and refining the gestural-design directions.

Next, present gestural design along with its supporting artifacts. If you didn't previously align on moodboards with the team, consider showing lightweight moodboards to call out specific aesthetic decisions before diving into each direction. You might even create an introductory moodboard highlighting detailed views of individual ingredients from each gestural-design direction. If you explored various information architectures or interaction models, add these to the introduction as well, showing how each works before diving into how they look and feel.

For each direction, provide a summary of what makes it unique as well as specific strengths and weaknesses. Consider business needs, technical constraints, and user expectations, as well as aesthetics when pointing out pros and cons. At the end of your presentation, provide an overview so that stakeholders can compare directions to each other. If you want to go beyond the presentation, 3-D print designs or save screenshots on devices so that stakeholders have a more realistic representation to discuss.

No presentation can capture all of the thinking that goes into the design directions, so prepare yourself for the conversation that will follow. Know which direction you'd recommend, but be prepared to change your mind based on the conversation. Also consider which aspects of each gestural design could be compromised as well as how one direction might be compatible with others. Most importantly, know the limitations of your explorations. It's always preferable to tell a stakeholder that something will need to be explored further than to make a promise you cannot keep.

CityBike uses gestural design to explore different interaction models and aesthetics specifically for the Connected Bicycle's app. Each direction is distinct, despite making use of on-brand typography, iconography, and color palette.

Observations Suite's gestural design presents multiple aesthetics across many touchpoints. Each direction is inspired by, and takes its name from, a moodboard. Descriptions from moodboards are refined to be appropriate for each direction.

CityBike / **Connected Bicycle**

Gestural Design

Fog

Fog uses subtle transparency, soft gradients, and light to create hierarchy among elements. Color highlights navigation and action elements. Typography is clean with an abundance of negative space.

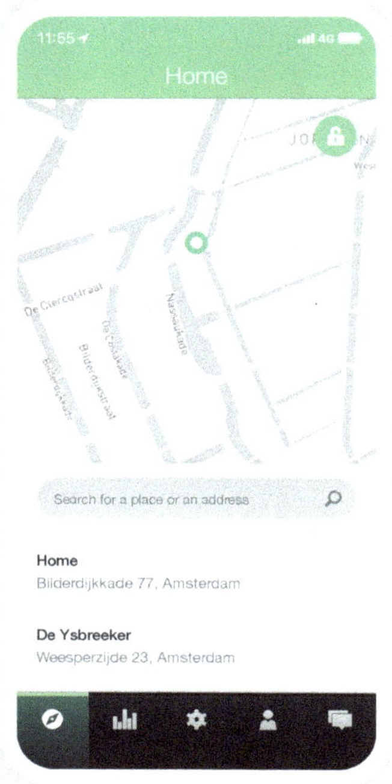

Thunder

Thunder uses a strong grid of tiles to organize both information and action elements. Pops of color guide the eye to action. Bold typography balances with iconography to create a glanceable interface.

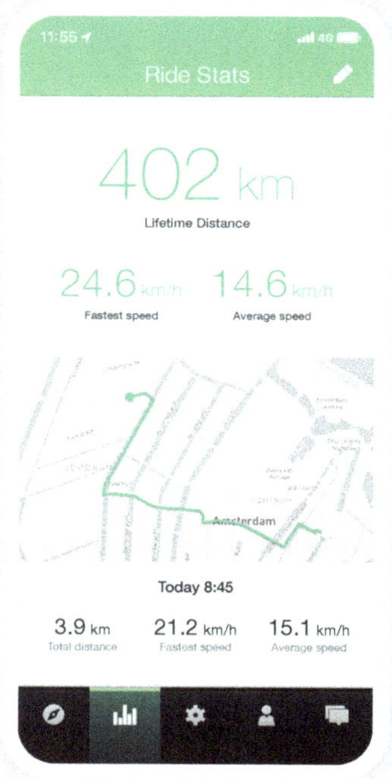

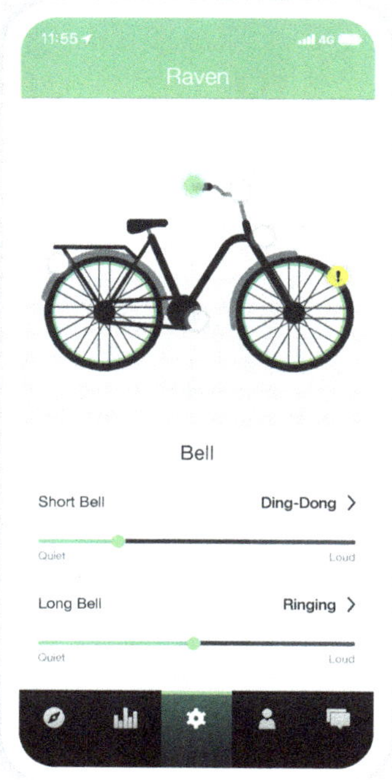

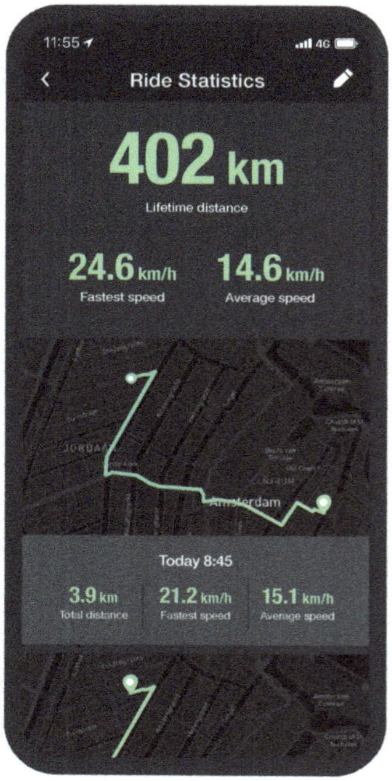

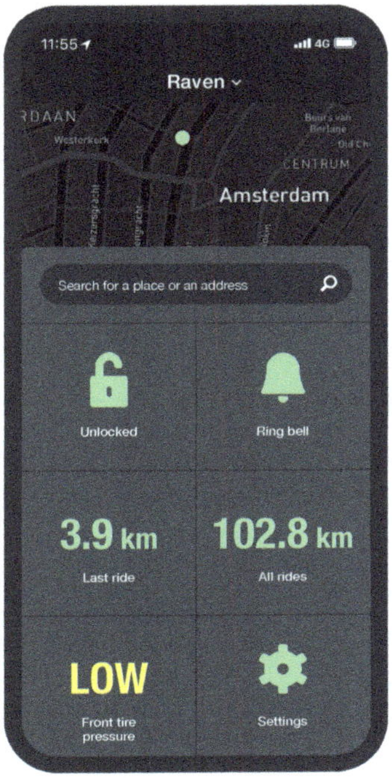

Rain

Discrete containers with curves and rounded corners float atop an ambient gradient. Color ties the foreground to the background. Simple typography puts legibility above style.

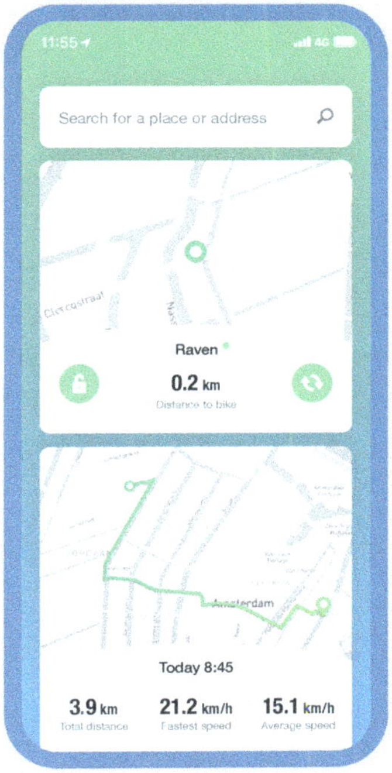

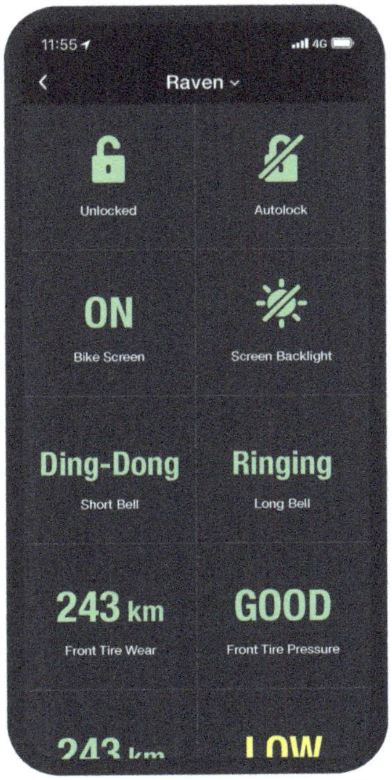

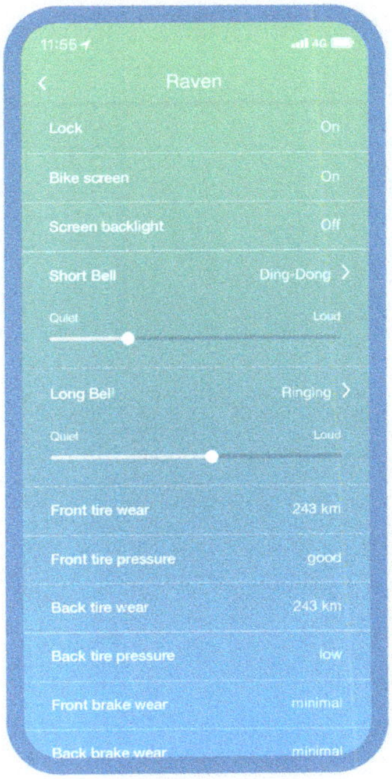

Omniscient / **Observations Suite Web App**

Gestural Design

Cheddar

A strong grid of squares and rectangles provides the overall structure for both interfaces and marketing materials. Elements use bright colors to guide the user's attention and size and weight to establish typographic hierarchy. Iconography provides a touch of visual interest in familiar areas like navigation.

Option one makes use of bright complementary colors to guide the user's attention, while option two uses a softer and more muted palette to provide a more luxurious feel.

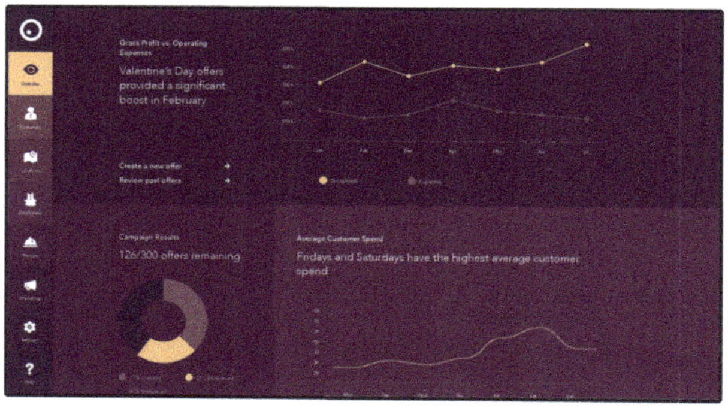

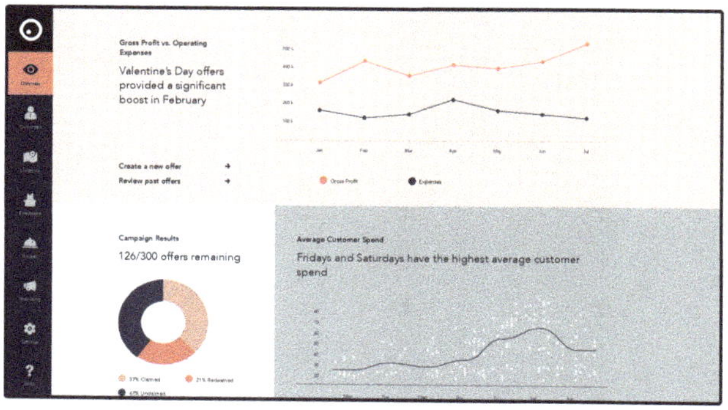

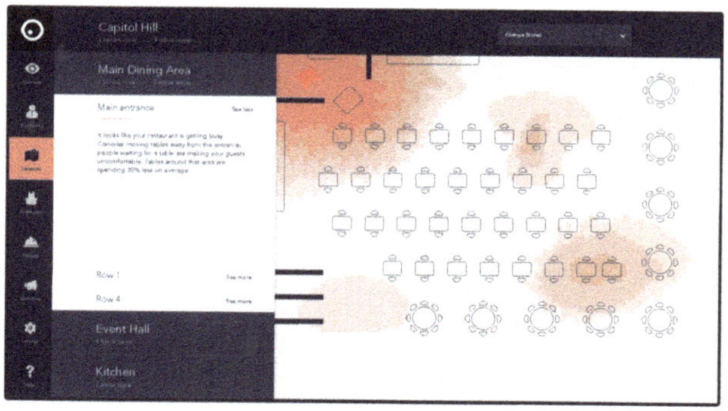

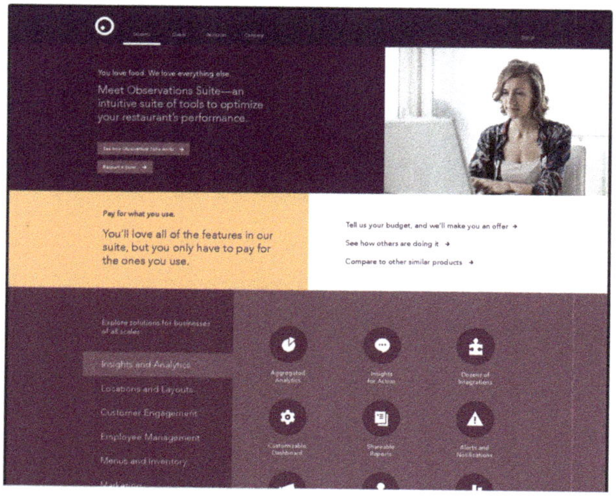

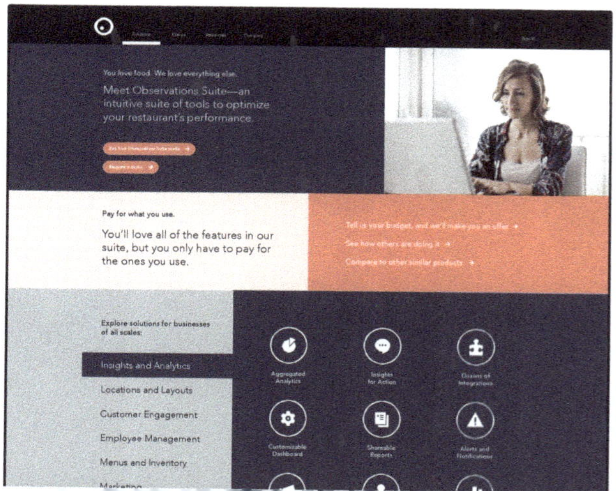

Carrot

Monochromatic gradients and overlays make for a more technical feel, something more familiar for most dashboards. A slightly offset grid accompanied by shallow depth provides hierarchy for content and visualizations. Lightweight typography uses size to establish hierarchy, while icons are used to draw attention to actions.

Option one uses bright gradients as backgrounds for rounded cards, while option two uses white cards with sharp corners.

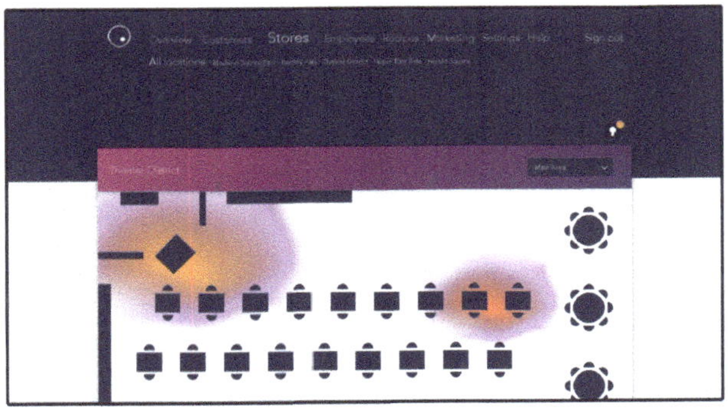

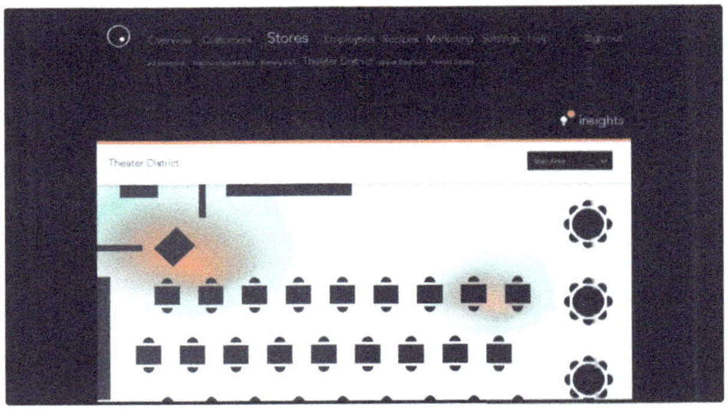

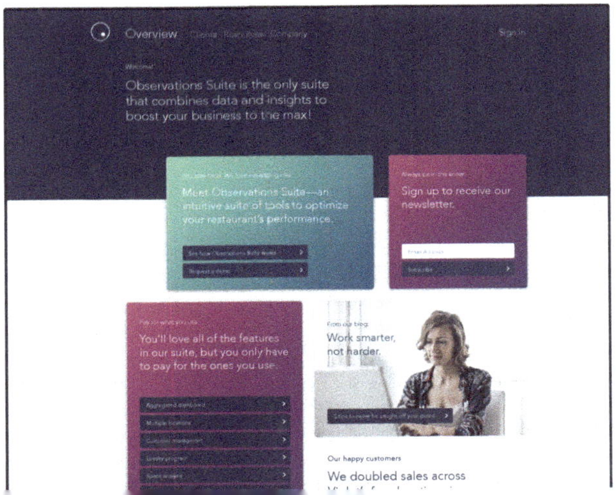

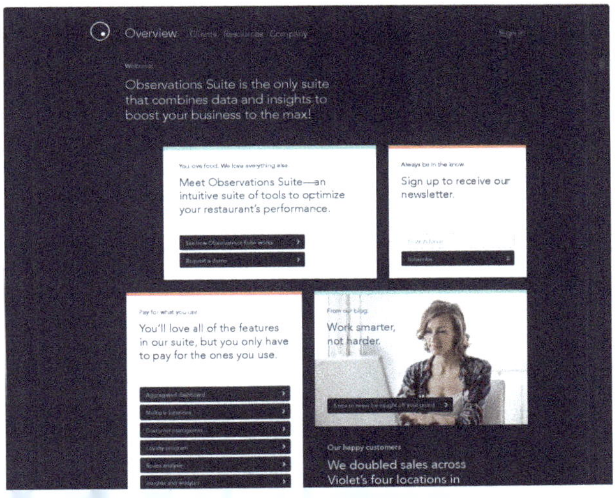

Pistachio

Pistachio uses color to provide context. Two type families provide hierarchy, guiding the user's eye toward the most important information. Fluid and organic shapes provide visual interest, while patterns in the background create a sense of depth in the shallow space.

Th

illustrations.

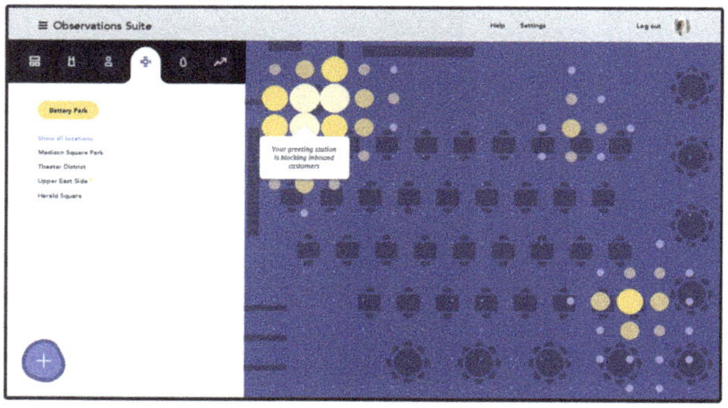

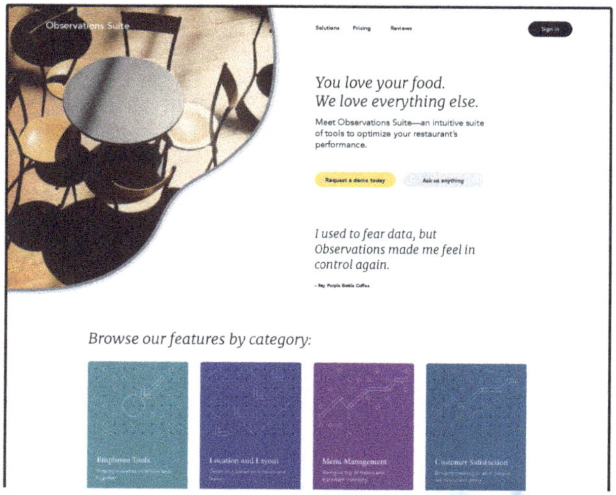

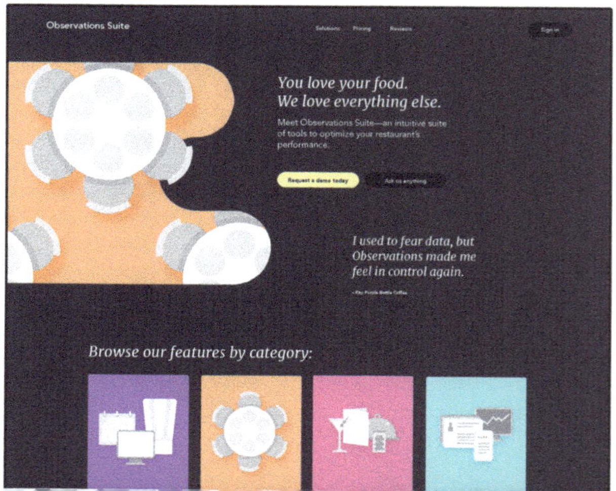

Berry

Photography provides a backdrop to this card-based interface that uses a deep space to establish a hierarchy among elements. Color draws attention to actions or selections. Light typography establishes a hierarchy through size, while lightweight iconography draws attention to action elements.

In the first option, photography provides the color, while a single accent color draws attention. In the second option, a more abstract background is accompanied with a more robust, complementary warm-and-cool color palette.

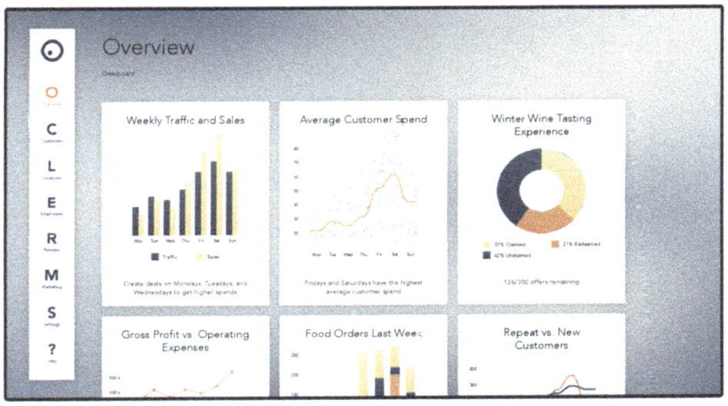

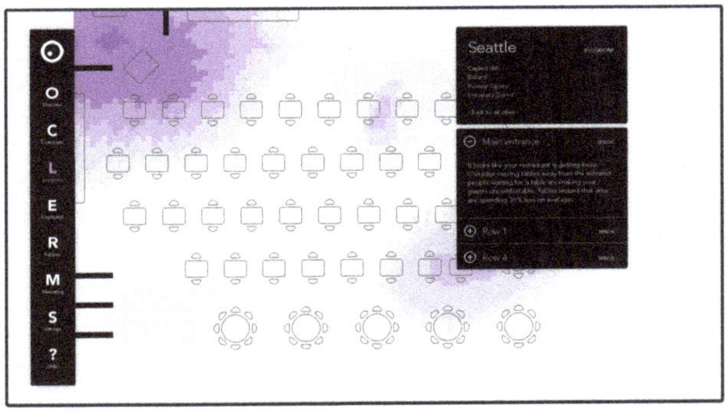

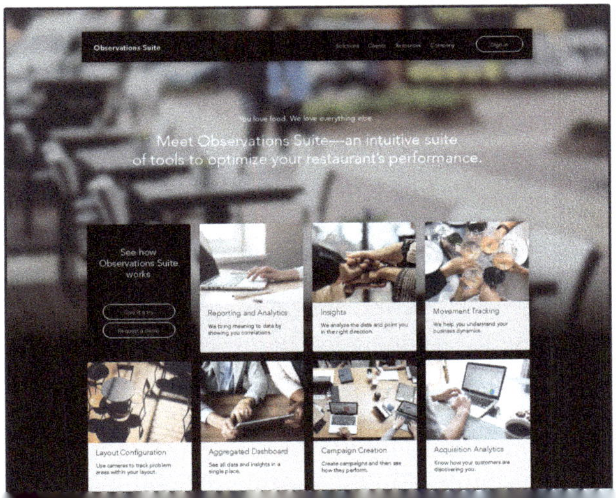

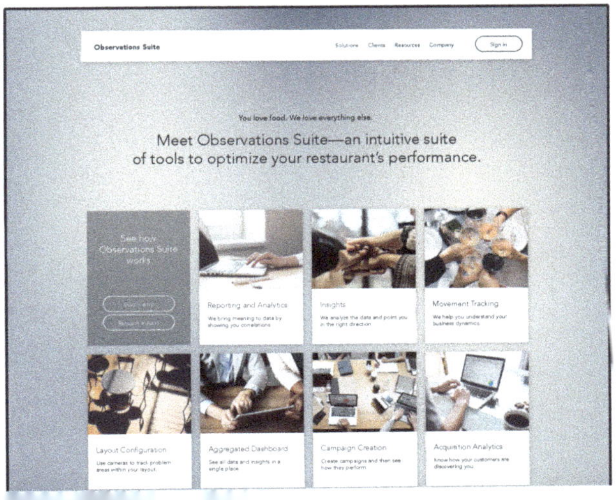

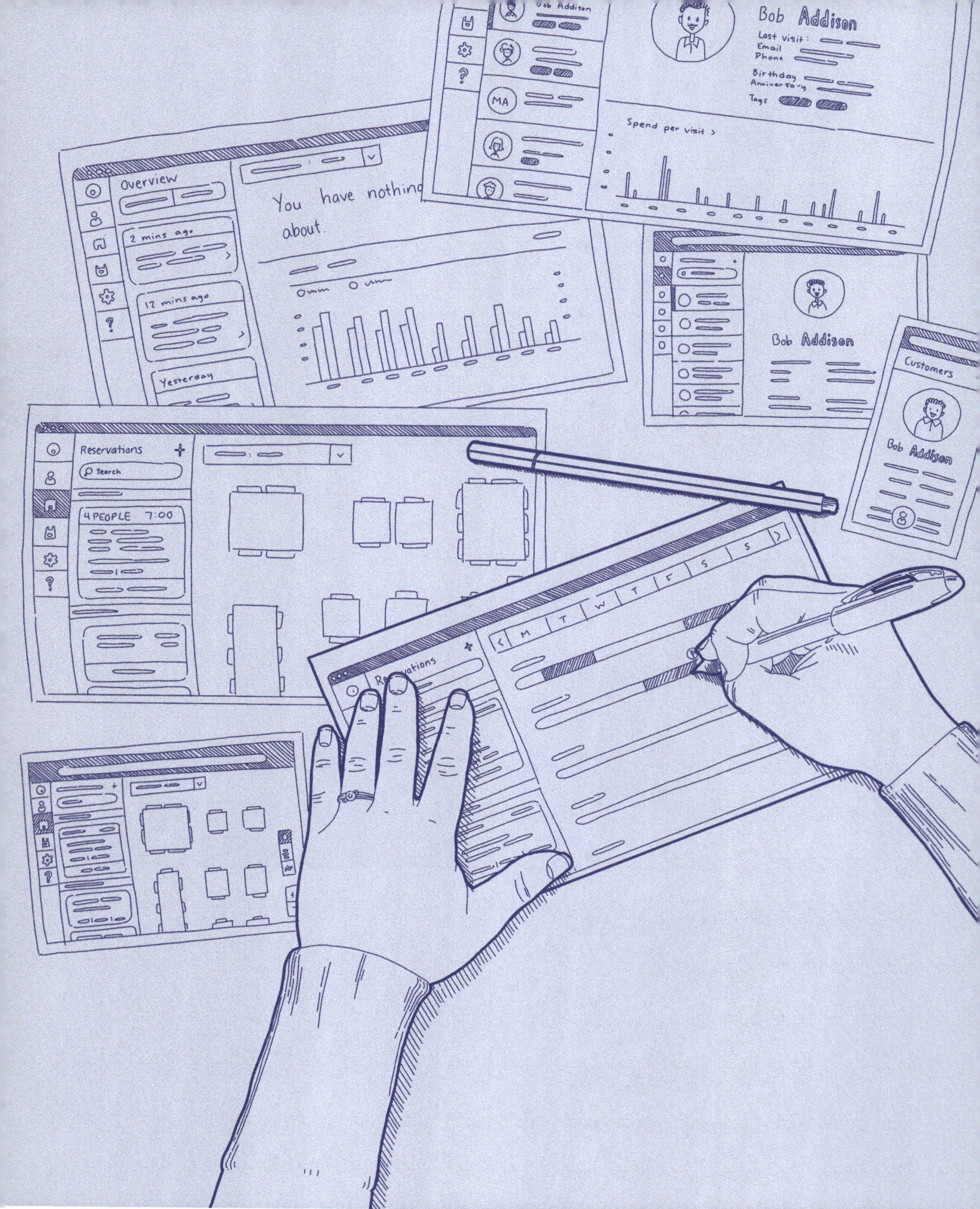

Bob Addison
Last visit:
Email
Phone
Birthday
Anniversary
Tags
MA
Spend per visit >
Overview
2 mins ago
12 mins ago
Yesterday
You have nothing
about.
Bob Addison
Customers
Bob Addison
Reservations
Search
4 PEOPLE 7:00
M T W T F S S
Reservations

Mock-Ups

When people refer to design, and especially the output of design, they're usually referring to mock-ups. Mock-ups provide stakeholders with a realistic idea of what the product or service will look like and how it will behave. If you're designing a physical product or space, the mock-ups are probably renderings, and if you're designing a digital product or service, the mock-ups are probably designs of screens or pages.

Before approaching mock-ups, you should already have a thorough understanding of what the experience encompasses as well as how it looks and feels. Compared with gestural design, mock-ups need to be complete, consistent, and without mistakes. Similar to detailed design, they should consider edge and error cases, though they do not need to show every variation. With mock-ups, stakeholders should be able to understand, provide feedback about, and begin building the product or service.

Activities

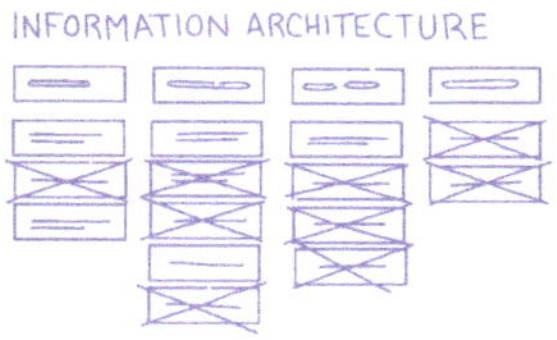

Start by identifying the most important screens or states.

Begin by designing for the touchpoints or channels that will be most used.

Before designing mock-ups, you should already have a thorough understanding of the experience. From feature definition, you should know what it needs to do, and from the information architecture and interaction model, you should know how it is organized. You should know how it is prioritized based on the function hierarchy, and you should understand the look and feel from moodboards and gestural design. If you're unsure of the needs, organization, prioritization, or look and feel of the product or service you're mocking up, you may need to revisit previous activities and artifacts.

Knowing where to start can be a challenge. The outputs of information-architecture and key-scenario activities can help you to focus your efforts. Identify the most important high-level screens or states, and start there. Even if you've already done some high-fidelity work through artifacts like gestural design, it can still be helpful to return to sketch fidelity, drawing out screens to get a better feel for composition and placement. Gain confidence in the system, and then increase fidelity. Starting in high fidelity often results in committing to a design before it's been thought through.

Expand to the moments that are likely to define the experience for a majority of your users. The design of these moments can establish a baseline for the design of the rest of the experience. If you're designing an experience that spans multiple channels or touchpoints, select a small number of formats to target at first. Aim for near perfection before extending to less critical formats.

Seek feedback on your work by holding critiques with other members of the design team. Structure critiques so that the feedback is useful to where you are in the process. Consider where you're least confident in the work and what feedback will be most valuable. If multiple designers are working on mock-ups, these sessions should be held more regularly to ensure alignment.

Through this handful of mock-ups, start to create systems of rules, layouts, and components that can be reused elsewhere. Consider every decision you make a hypothesis that will be tested as you build out the system and possibly when you test the design with users. As you reuse components, consider capturing them in a component library, and when making decisions, document rules for use in the design guidelines.

As you bring your mock-ups to the most realistic fidelity, it's likely that you'll need the contributions of specific specializations. For example, you may need the input of illustrators, microcopywriters, mechanical engineers, data-visualization experts, or 3-D animators. Try not to lose momentum, using placeholders until it's possible to integrate with the necessary expertise. Do aim to engage experts as quickly as possible, as it can be dangerous to test or make decisions based on incomplete mock-ups. It's also a risk that budget and time will run out before experts are engaged and that whatever was placed temporarily will end up in front of users.

As you design your experience, consider not only users and stakeholders but also the other designers you are working with and others who will inherit your work. Keep your files organized and well labeled, and even consider adding notes so that others who work with your files can better understand your intentions.

Thinking Ahead

When creating mock-ups, it's useful to anticipate how users will react to the experience you're designing. Try to predict friction points and to preempt accessibility concerns. Keep notes about which areas of the design you're uncertain about for testing later.

Artifacts

The more realistic the mock-up, the better the feedback will be.

Choosing how to share mock-ups depends on context. Who are you sharing with? What is their experience with the project? What is the desired outcome of sharing?

For initial meetings with team members as well as meetings with stakeholders who haven't been involved in the process, you'll need to provide some background so that they see not only the output of the work but also the effort and rigor that went into making design decisions. You might communicate the design system by showing mock-ups within the interaction model, or you might show more of the user's full experience by placing mock-ups into key scenarios. These more formal presentations can take time away from the design process and so should be used strategically.

With a team that's aligned and meeting regularly, you may be able to share mock-ups without much additional context. When sharing, give mock-ups simple and consistent titles and provide an overview of any important decisions that have been, or that need to be, made. Rather than showing mock-ups in a presentation, try saving them to the device they'll live on or 3-D printing them. This informal method of sharing makes it easy to quickly get mock-ups in front of stakeholders to gather reactions and feedback.

If you're creating mock-ups for developers, it's likely that some additional documentation will be required. Mock-ups can feed into the flow diagram, their components into the component library, and their rules into the design guidelines. By integrating more closely with development teams, designers can ensure the quality of their designs through production. Be prepared to adopt tools and processes to facilitate this communication. Try to streamline this process as much as possible so that you can focus on making good decisions rather than on creating documentation.

If you're creating mock-ups for testing with users, it's important to provide a realistic experience. Produce tangible physical-product mock-ups and show digital products on devices. If you have time, use mock-ups to create lightweight prototypes that users can interact with.

Mock-ups for CityBike's Connected Bicycle are presented in the context of key scenarios, providing stakeholders with a view into how the user will engage with both the on-bike display and the app over time.

The mock-ups for Ambience Mirror highlight how the layout and rule set can be used to provide value to the user across a handful of prioritized features.

Observations Suite mock-ups show how top-level pages reformat to accommodate users on desktop, tablet, and mobile platforms.

CityBike / **Connected Bicycle**

Mock-Ups

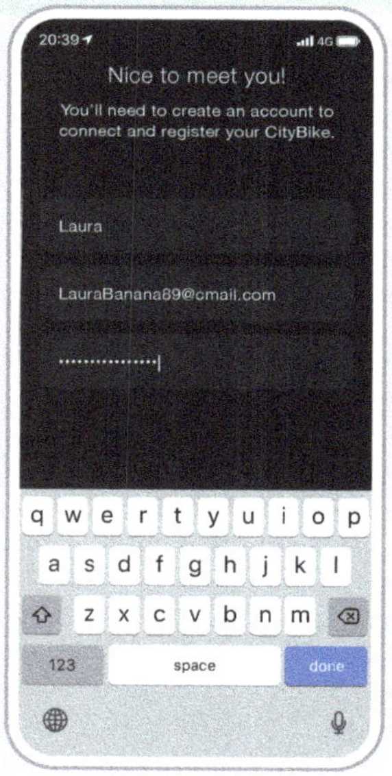

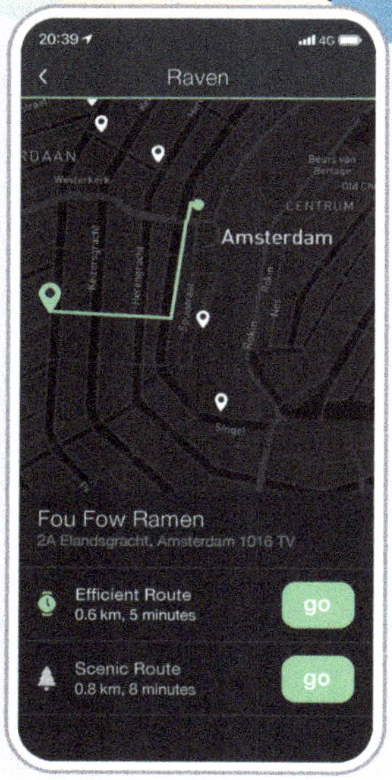

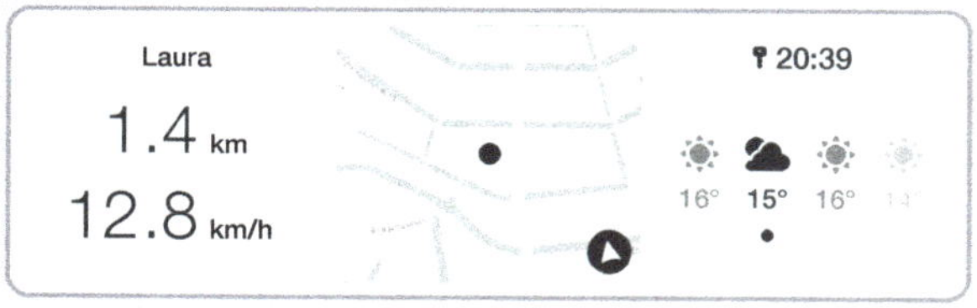

Right after Laura received her CityBike, she downloaded the app to get the most out of it.

At first she used the navigation features, but now that she knows the city by bike, she rarely actively uses the app.

One night, Laura takes her bike to meet some friends for drinks. She's unfamiliar with the bar but knows the general location, so she doesn't use navigation.

Laura forgets that she's turned off autolocking as she walks away from her bike.

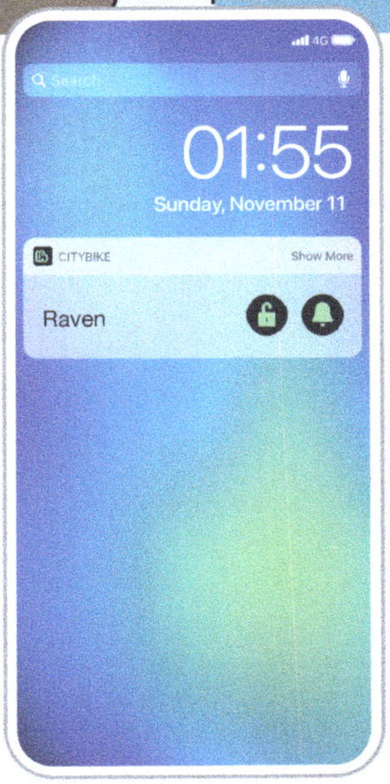

After the last call, Laura leaves the bar and searches for her bike. She tries to ring the bell using the CityBike widget but hears nothing.

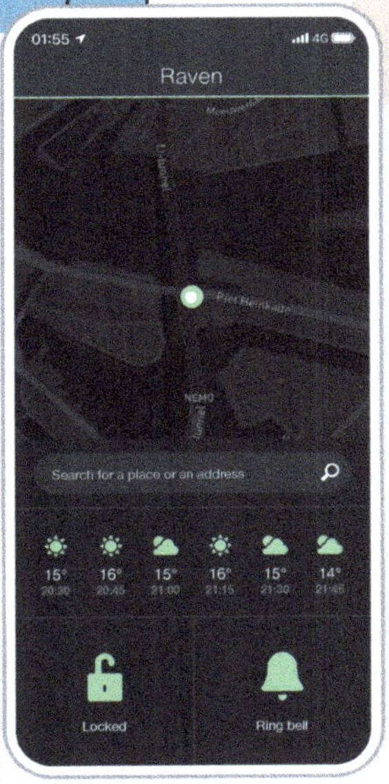

Laura uses the app to locate her bike and sees that it's nowhere near the bar.

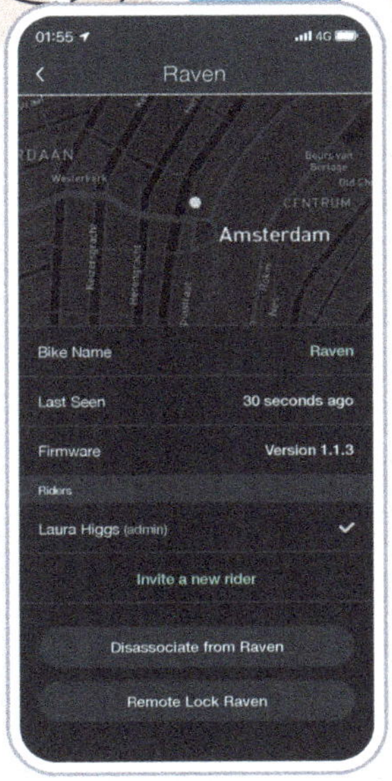

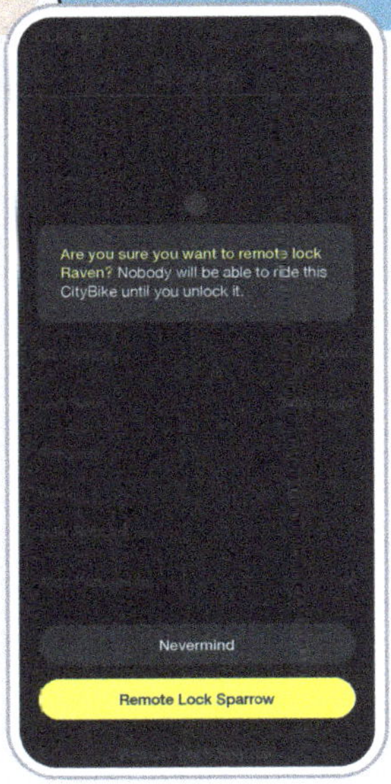

Laura marks her bike as stolen so that it will lock the next time the thief stops. Hopefully they'll leave her bike behind as soon as they realize they can't ride it.

Mock-Ups

Setup

Setup experiences such as creating multiple mirror profiles, connecting to products and services, and customizing the information displayed are all done using the app. The mirror's display supports the user but doesn't attempt to provide the same functionality as the app. The user can make customization requests using the mirror's voice interface.

Custom Scenes

The user can choose up to five unique scenes: weather, summary, calendar, social, and history. Upon unlocking, the Ambience Mirror defaults to weather to avoid showing sensitive information. The user can choose what to show and how for their summary, social, and history scenes. The calendar scene pulls data from the calendars the user has connected.

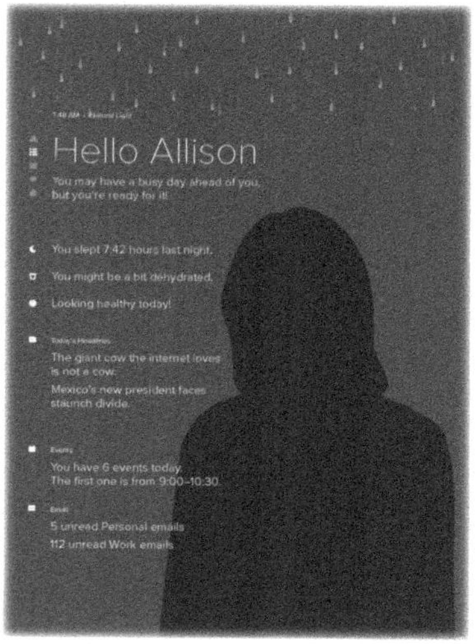

Programs

Ambience Mirror has a handful of built-in programs that can guide the user through an experience, such as stretching or establishing a face-cleansing routine. Initiated by voice, these full-mirror immersive programs use text, imagery, and light to guide the user.

Dynamic Content and Lighting

For each user's preferences, the Ambience Mirror adjusts scenes and lighting to reflect appropriate information and recommendations for the time of day. Specific content and insights are delivered based on the data the mirror collects about users.

Omniscient / **Observations Suite Web App**

Mock-Ups

Overview

The “Overview” screen is split into two parts, providing the Observations Suite user with access to notifications and report summaries to the left in the overlaid list and data summaries in the customizable dashboard.

Screens can be expanded to hide notifications and reports, focusing the user on the contents of the dashboard.

With Notification Panel

Desktop

Tablet

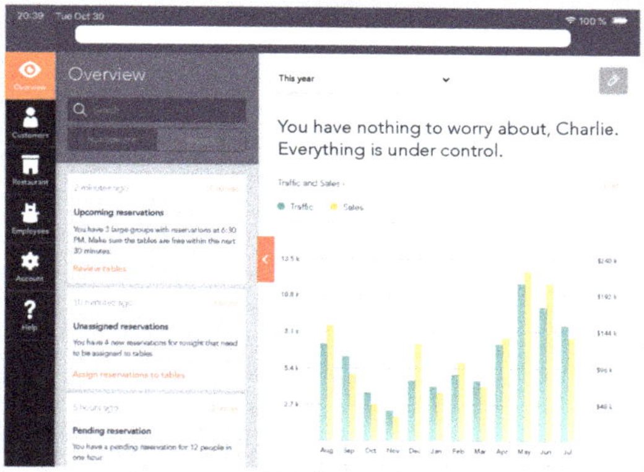

Mobile

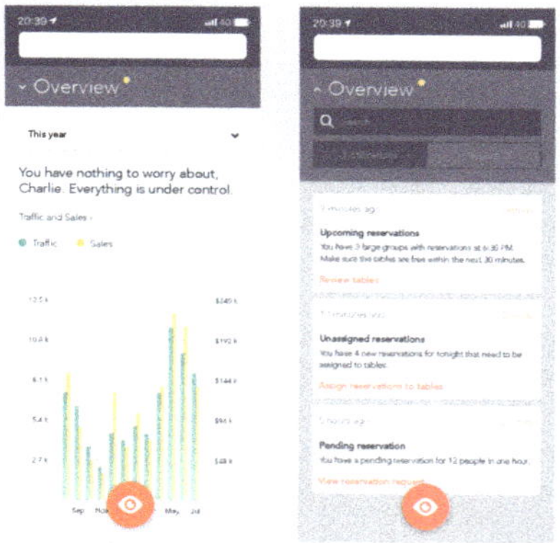

Expanded Dashboard

Desktop

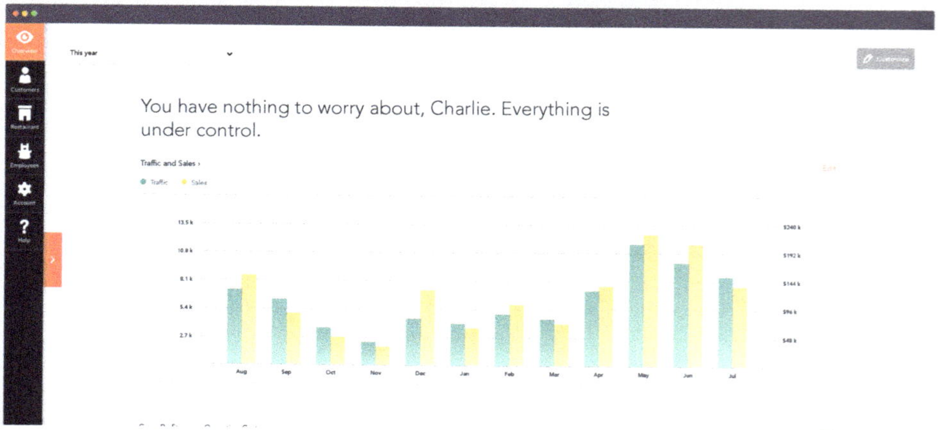

Restaurant

The Heat Map view of the "Restaurant" screen provides the user with a camera-generated heat map of the restaurant, defaulting to the past thirty minutes, or "now." The user can also browse data for historical time periods. In the "Now" view, tapping on a table provides table details.

The "Table Details" view of the "Restaurant" screen shows the user each table's availability for the day. The user can navigate to upcoming days to see future reservations or to previous days to review table usage. The overlaid panel provides a list of reservations, prioritizing those that need action, either assigning or confirming seating assignments.

The "Restaurant Overview" provides the user with a customizable dashboard of restaurant visualizations. This screen is a placeholder for future releases, when the user will be able to browse analytics by location.

Heat Map

Desktop

Tablet

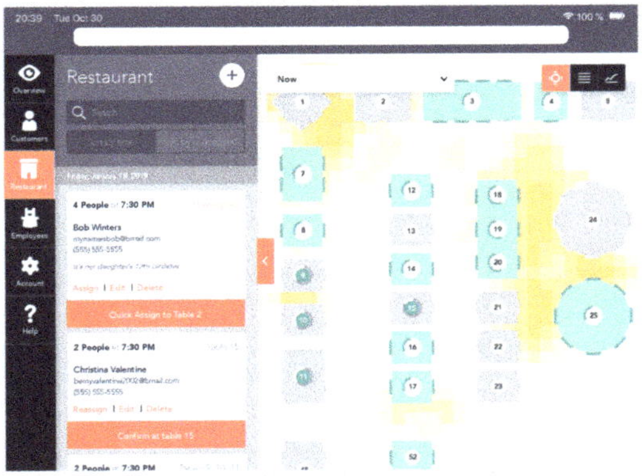

Mobile

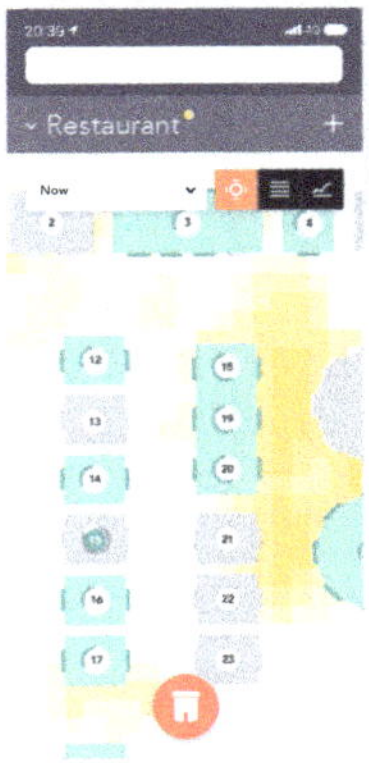

Table Details

Desktop

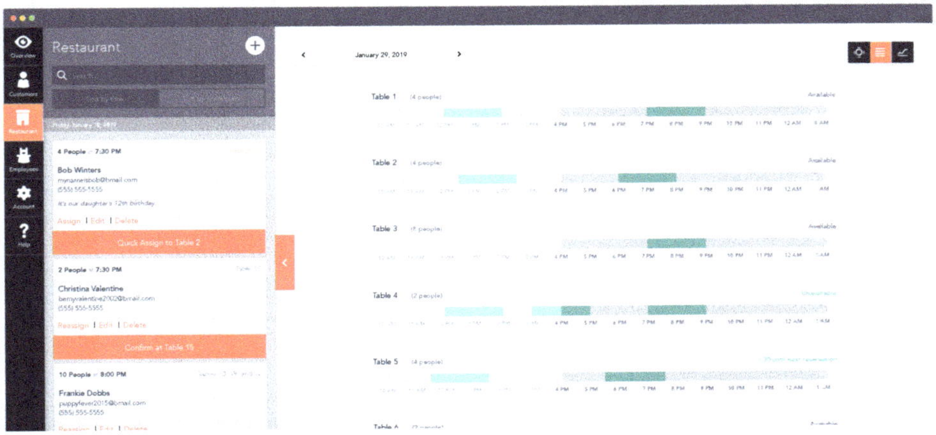

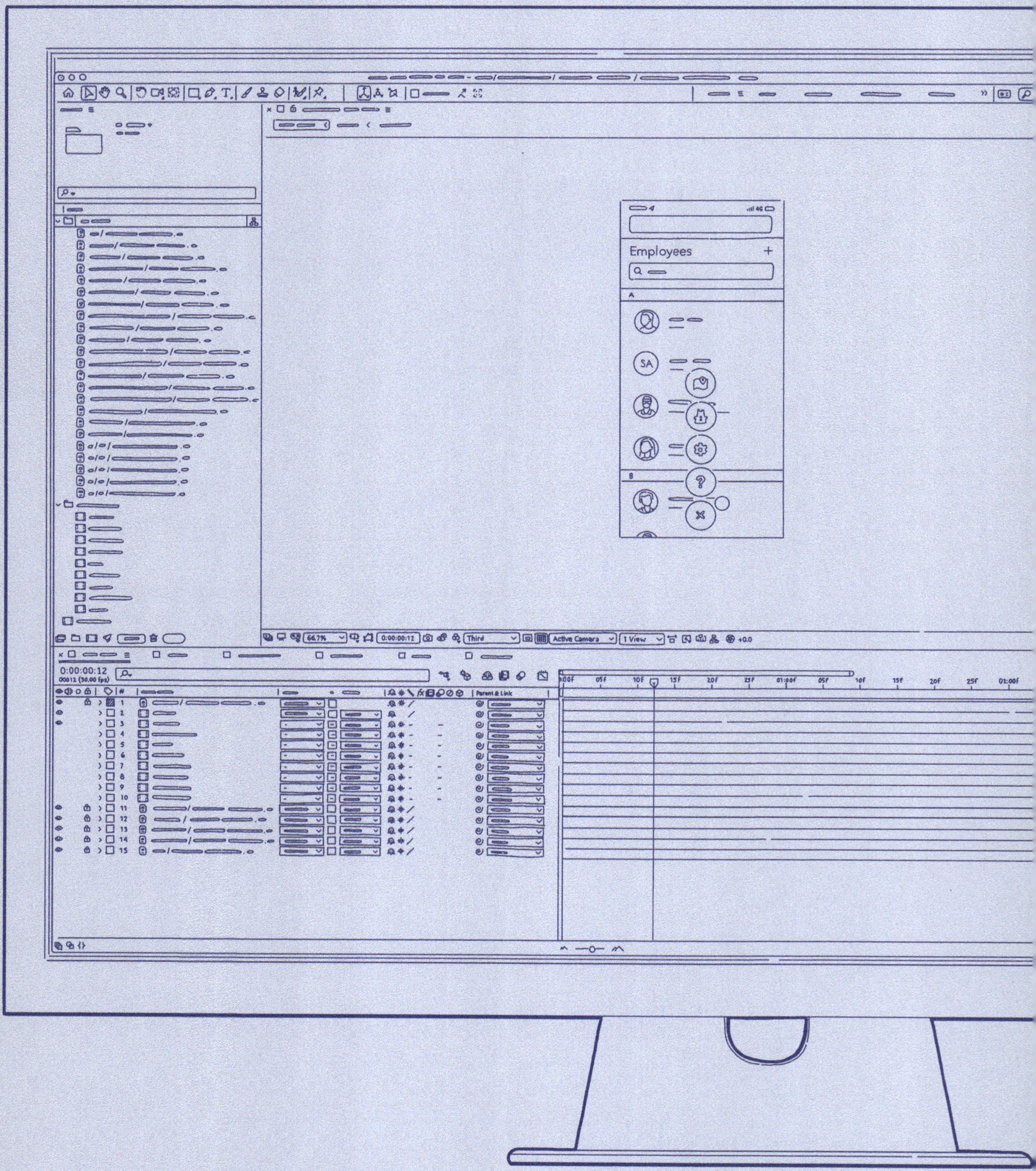
Employees
SA
0:00:00:12
66.7%
Third
Active Camera
1 View
+0.0
Parent & Link

Motion Studies

Motion studies show how components or mock-ups behave over time; they bring static states to life by showing how they behave with interaction; and they help make the relationships between parts of a design more intuitive through transitions.

When shown alongside artifacts like moodboards and gestural design, motion studies are more exploratory. These low-fidelity samples can be used to quickly iterate and to align the team. When done in the build phase, alongside flow diagrams or design guidelines, motion studies communicate specific behaviors to those implementing the design. When integrated with prototypes, motion studies can be tested with users. In all cases, motion studies can be strictly visual, or they can incorporate haptics and sound to capture how something feels over time.

Motion can be one of the most difficult aspects of a design to communicate, so even if your project doesn't have the time or capability to create motion studies, try to convey what is meant by referencing existing examples.

Activities

Understand how the platform deals with transitions before diving into motion design.

Before you start creating motion studies, understand the constraints of the technology you're designing for. From blinking lights on a physical product to transitions on a website, every movement or change needs to be programmed. Understand what is and isn't possible before diving in. Keep in mind that not everything that moves needs a motion study. For example, many transitions for apps are standard, using the platform to create consistency across experiences. Custom transitions should serve a purpose and should feel different enough from standard transitions to stand out to users.

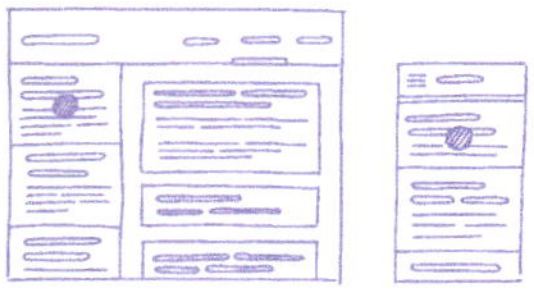

Use click, tap, and gesture indicators that stand apart from the interface.

Next decide on your goals. If you're seeking to explore multiple possibilities before choosing and refining a single direction, you might create a motion study that focuses only on the animation or transition you're investigating, ignoring other details or leaving them in lower fidelity. Iterate quickly, exploring different transition types, durations, easing, and so on. Refer to real-world examples for inspiration. Consult fresh eyes often to refine and curate so that stakeholders see only the best, notably different options.

If you're showing transitions, show the interactions as well. Find a clear yet nondistracting way to show clicks, taps, and other gestures to stakeholders. Make sure to use indicators that have enough visual and stylistic contrast that they're distinct from elements in the interface.

If you're creating motion studies for a long flow, do some planning first. Sketch or act out with gestures the different transitions you want to explore. If you're creating a high-fidelity flow with multiple transitions and animations, create storyboards to show the different states and to capture which transitions happen when.

If you're looking to communicate with developers, you'll want to make sure the details of screens or components are consistent with other documentation to avoid misleading anyone. Motion studies might begin in a motion-design tool, but eventually they should be executed and specified for the technology they're built on. In an ideal flow, this happens within or alongside the design team so that transitions are perfected and possibly even made into individual components before widespread application.

Artifacts

Motion studies are often used to enrich other artifacts. Presentation, fidelity, and duration can all change, depending on the motion study's context.

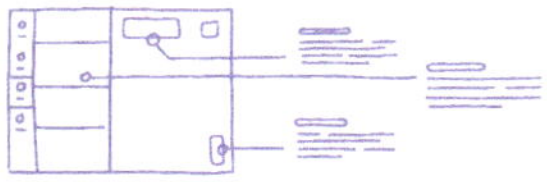

Present motion studies within or alongside gestural design and mock-ups.

Gestural Design and Mock-Ups

Short and focused motion studies presented alongside static mock-ups can help stakeholders envision how a user would move through an experience. These might be embedded into presentations or shared on actual devices. When presented alongside gestural design, motion studies likely show multiple options, while when presented with mock-ups, they would focus on a single direction.

Animate entire key scenarios.

Key Scenarios

Longer sequences of transitions can show an entire key scenario. These might stand on their own or live in a presentation with animated key scenarios. They could also be paired with live-action video to give a higher-fidelity feel of the situations the user is facing throughout their experience.

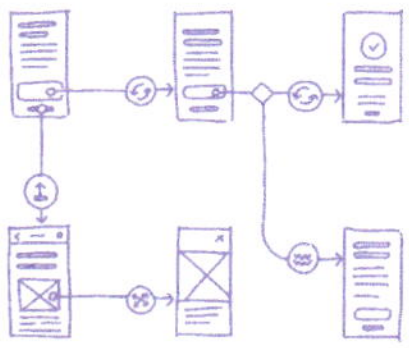

Reference motion studies from documentation like the flow diagram.

Flow Diagram

Motion studies might be used to highlight an entire segment of the flow diagram, similar to a key scenario. If this is the case, make sure to highlight the relevant part of the flow and provide a reference to the motion study. Alternatively, individual transitions in the flow diagram might reference specific motion studies, making it easy for developers to know which to use when.

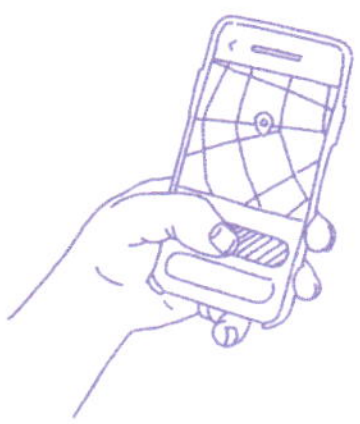

Show motion within prototypes.

Prototypes

Integrate motion-study clips into prototypes to give users or stakeholders a more realistic experience. Make sure to highlight which transitions are designed for the experience, versus those that are native to the platform. Don't let the limitations of the prototyping tool you're using dictate the animations of the experience.

Motion studies for Observations Suite focus on showing novel design elements, such as mobile navigation. Quick explorations were done by design before collaborating closely with web developers to refine the actual implementation.

Omniscient / **Observations Suite Web App**

Motion Studies

Mobile Navigation Expansion

The user taps on the floating Current Nav Button. The button changes to the pressed state.

Upon release, the Current Nav Button returns to the normal state and additional navigation icons slide from behind it, one at a time.

The transition should take no more than 1 second.

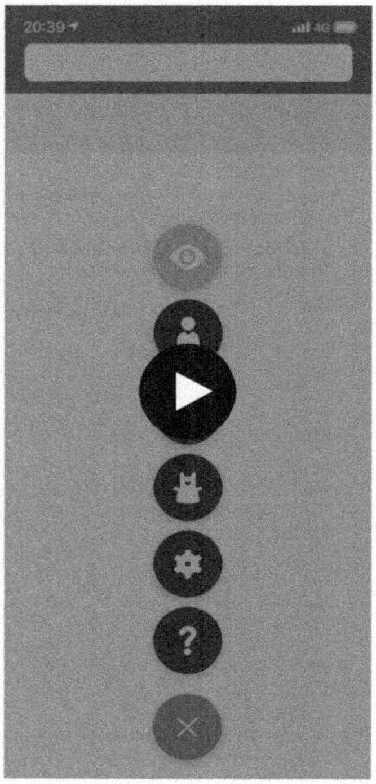

Mobile Navigation Selection

The user taps on an icon in the navigation list. The button changes to the Current Nav Button in the pressed state.

Upon release, the Current Nav Button turns to the normal state and slides down to the floating navigation location.

Icons above the selected icon slide under it, while icons below are covered by the selected navigation icon as it moves to its new position.

The transition should take no more than 1 second.

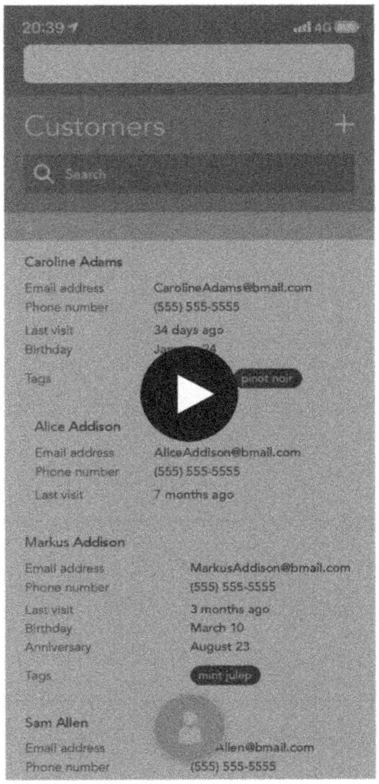

Mobile Customer-Card Selection

The user taps on the customer card. The card changes to the pressed state.

Upon release, the card returns to its normal state.

After content is loaded, the card navigation slides to the left, revealing the customer information below.

The transition should take no more than 0.5 seconds.

Mobile Reveal-Table Information

The user taps on a table to reveal information about that table. When their finger leaves the screen, the information pane slides up from the bottom of the screen. Simultaneously, the map centers the table in the remaining space.

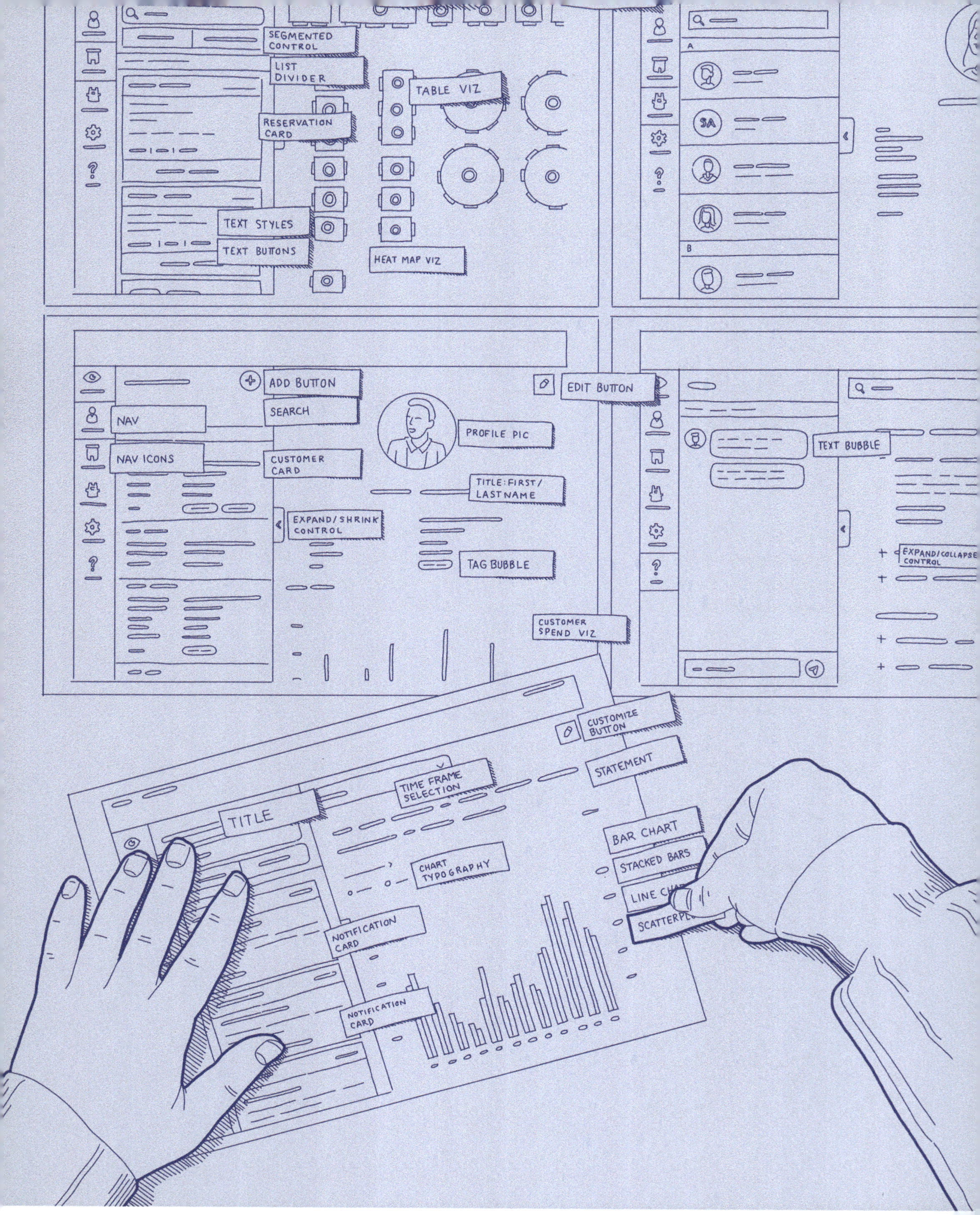
SEGMENTED CONTROL
LIST DIVIDER
TABLE VIZ
RESERVATION CARD
TEXT STYLES
TEXT BUTTONS
HEAT MAP VIZ
SA
ADD BUTTON
EDIT BUTTON
NAV
SEARCH
PROFILE PIC
NAV ICONS
CUSTOMER CARD
TEXT BUBBLE
TITLE: FIRST/ LASTNAME
EXPAND/SHRINK CONTROL
TAG BUBBLE
EXPAND/COLLAPSE CONTROL
CUSTOMER SPEND VIZ
CUSTOMIZE BUTTON
STATEMENT
TIME FRAME SELECTION
TITLE
BAR CHART
STACKED BARS
CHART TYPOGRAPHY
NOTIFICATION CARD
NOTIFICATION CARD

Component Library

The component library ensures that a design is consistent and that a design language is easily extensible by creating a tool kit of reusable base elements. Component libraries can be built at the scale of a single product, to maintain consistency within a family of products, or to set standards across entire brands.

The audience of a component library might be designers, engineers, or developers, and the format of the component library will change depending on whether the components are physical or digital. Industrial designers in a company manufacturing kitchen appliances might share a library of common components to ensure that all of their power switches are the same, while a software company might have a component library to make sure that their error handling is consistent across multiple apps and websites. As all elements are gathered into a single place, component libraries are useful for creating assets, and they can even be translated into coded elements to be used and reused across software-development projects.

Activities

After you've narrowed explorations to a single design direction and refined elements to the point where you find yourself copying and pasting them from one screen or model or page to the next, it's time to create a component library. Before starting a new component library from scratch, do some research to make sure that your organization doesn't already have a library or tool kit that serves this purpose. If it does, determine to what extent your project's component library will need to integrate into or borrow from the existing version before diving in.

In addition to using inputs from gestural design and mock-ups, look across your organization to find other products and services and to see what's been built in the past. Gather materials from brand guidelines, design language systems, and common component libraries. If you're doing digital design, consider the tools and standard components the operating system gives you. From color and shape to sizes, proportions, and grids, all of these influences should be considered as you establish the specific elements of the experience you're designing.

With all of these inputs, it's easy to get overwhelmed. Take the time to categorize your findings into three buckets: elements worth adopting or aligning with, elements that do not work with your design, and things that are irrelevant to your project.

As you select which elements will be added to the component library and which elements will need to be updated for consistency, reduce your selections as much as possible. Any time you uncover an element that is similar to another element, but not the same, aim to consolidate. For

Atomic Design

When designing and developing websites, the atomic-design methodology has a similar breakdown of design elements into atoms, molecules, organisms, templates, and pages. While the component library sticks to smaller-scale elements, when combined with design guidelines, it can also be scaled to capture templates and pages as well.

example, if you have physical power buttons with slightly different icons, these should be aligned. The less complexity a component library has, the easier it will be to use.

Some elements may come with stories. These, too, are important to take note of. For example, a particular navigational UI element might be difficult for users to discover, or a multipurpose physical hardware button might prove too nuanced for users to remember. Collecting such anecdotes to avoid remaking mistakes is useful, even if it's not a direct part of the component library.

As you consolidate and refine components, you'll also need to refine any mock-ups and other materials you're working on. Depending on the tools you're using, you may be able to use symbols or libraries to expedite this process. Because so much work and documentation depend on the component library, it's best to create one earlier in the refine phase.

> *"The only thing that you absolutely have to know is the location of the library."*
>
> Albert Einstein

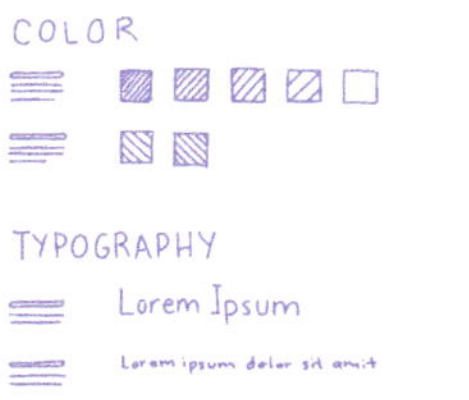

Start by capturing the base ingredients of the design, like color, type, and icons.

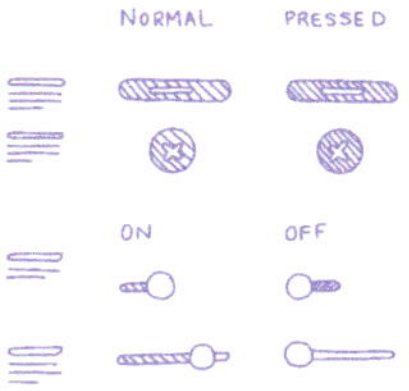

Collect simple controls like buttons, switches, and sliders.

Save multipart components with complex behaviors for last.

Artifacts

Before laying out your component library, consider the scope of your project. Are you creating a library that's applicable to a single app, or are you creating a library that encompasses multiple touchpoints? Are you working on a specific slice of an experience, like illustrations, or are you working on the many different pieces of an experience, from buttons to layouts and icons to animations?

Components should live in whatever tool or tools you use for design. The library might also be organized in this tool, or it might live within one of the many platforms designed specifically for this purpose. Regardless of where it's maintained, the component library should be organized from the start. Establish processes early on for adding new elements, and create a structure that separates common elements in a way that will be easy to discover and maintain even as the library scales.

Use elements' scale to determine a layout. Start with ingredients. These are the basic building blocks of your design, like color and typography. Then move on to controls such as simple buttons and switches. Lastly, capture complex multipart components like charts and profile cards. Controls often are made of ingredients, while components usually have a combination of both ingredients and controls. Think not only in terms of the visual representation of an element but also of the behavior. For example, a search component is simple in appearance but often consists of multiple controls—a field and a button. In addition, that search component also has a complex series of behaviors that distinguish it from simpler text-entry fields, which would be only controls. Gather and group ingredients, controls, and components in whatever tool you're using for the component library.

Keep elements generic. For controls like buttons, which might house multiple icons, consider using placeholders to show how the icon would be positioned within the button. For form fields that could have any number of titles and inputs, use dummy copy (your favorite variation of lorem ispum) so that you have to capture each type of field only once.

Consider and capture different states of individual controls. How does a button behave when pressed? How does the user understand when they need to wait for the product or service to complete an action? What colors and patterns do lights use to indicate that there is a problem? It's likely that the component library will contain elements from mock-ups as well as components representing states that haven't been mocked up. For example, you may not mock up a screen with pressed states, but these should still be captured in the component library.

The component library and design guidelines work together to show components and to describe intention, implementation, and behavior. If you're not planning to do design guidelines for your project, consider adding annotations to your component library to describe when controls should be used, what combinations of elements are appropriate, and any behavior that might not be evident.

Component libraries should be maintained as a product or service evolves and expands. If you're working in software, consider keeping versions of the component library that match major releases. If you're working in a space that has less obvious milestones, you may want to annotate this in the component library. In either case, keep the component library relevant, avoiding the clutter of obsolete or outdated elements.

The component library for CityBike's Connected Bicycle focuses on capturing key elements of the app for building out the design and communicating basic behaviors to the development team. Hardware and on-bike display component libraries are maintained separately.

The sample of elements from Observations Suite's component library show different states as well as scaling to multiple screen formats. The component library feeds into, and evolves alongside, design guidelines and detailed documentation.

CityBike / **Connected Bicycle**

Component Library

Ingredients

Color

Brand Palette

Neutral Palette

Alert Palette

Typography

Helvetica Neue

Light, Regular, Medium

72 pt Light

48 pt Light

40 pt Light

30 pt Regular

24 pt Medium / Light

20 pt Medium

18 pt Medium / Regular

16 pt Medium / Regular

14 pt Medium / Regular

12 pt Medium / Regular

Iconography

Controls

Buttons

Primary Button
normal, pressed

Secondary Button
normal, pressed

Secondary Button
normal, pressed

Text Button
normal, pressed

Small Icon Button
normal, pressed

List Elements

List Divider

Bike List Items
connected, not connected + problem

Editable List Item
reading, editing

Drill-Down List Item
connected, not connected + problem

Noneditable List Item

Ride Multiselection List Item
not selected, selected

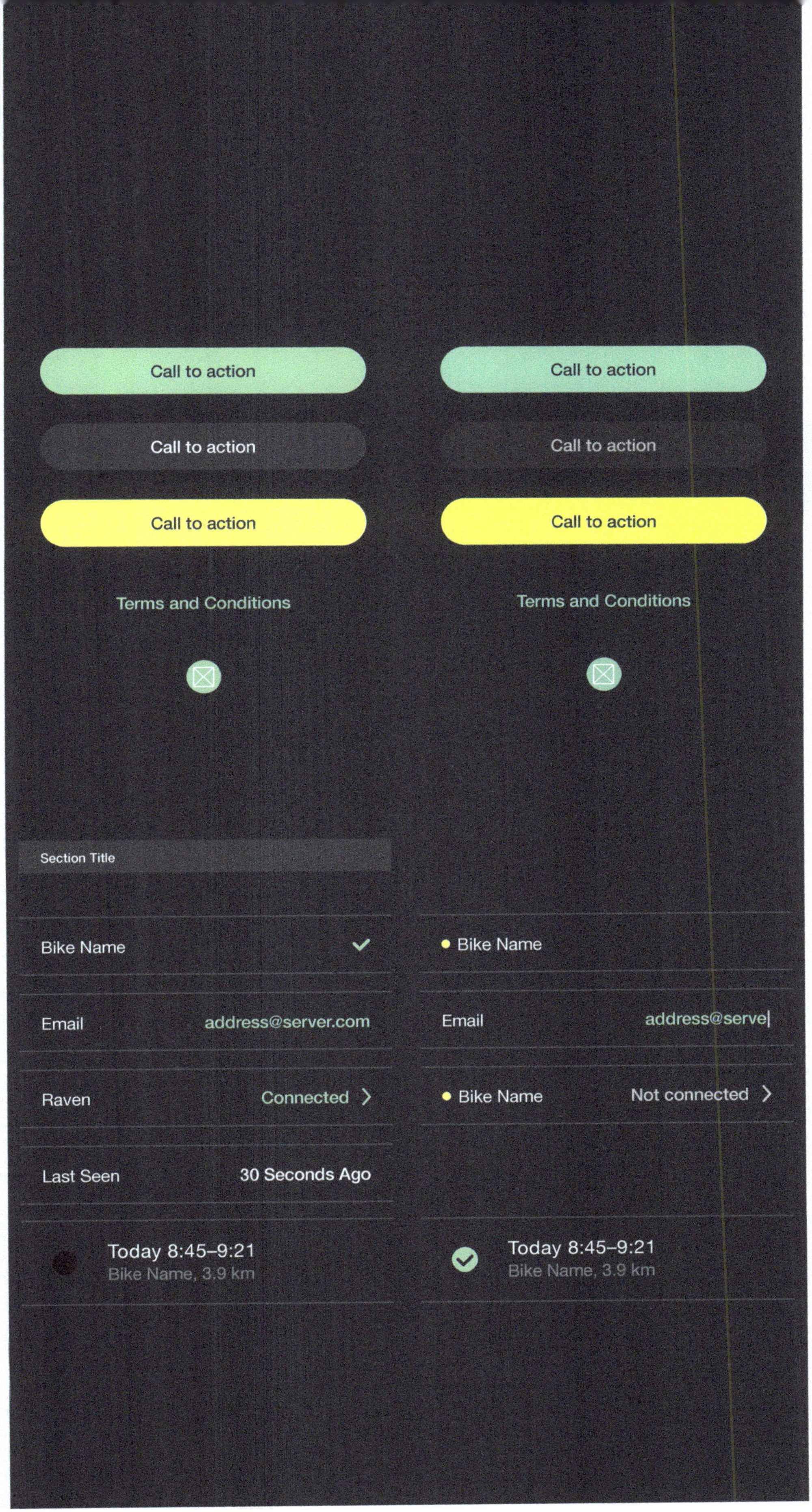

Components

Nav Bars

Single Bike Top Level
no problem, problem

Multiple Bikes Top Level
no problem, problem

Detail Level with Action

Ride Detail Level

Fields

Messaging Component
empty, with text

Search Field
in focus, typing, searched

Etc.

Ride Module

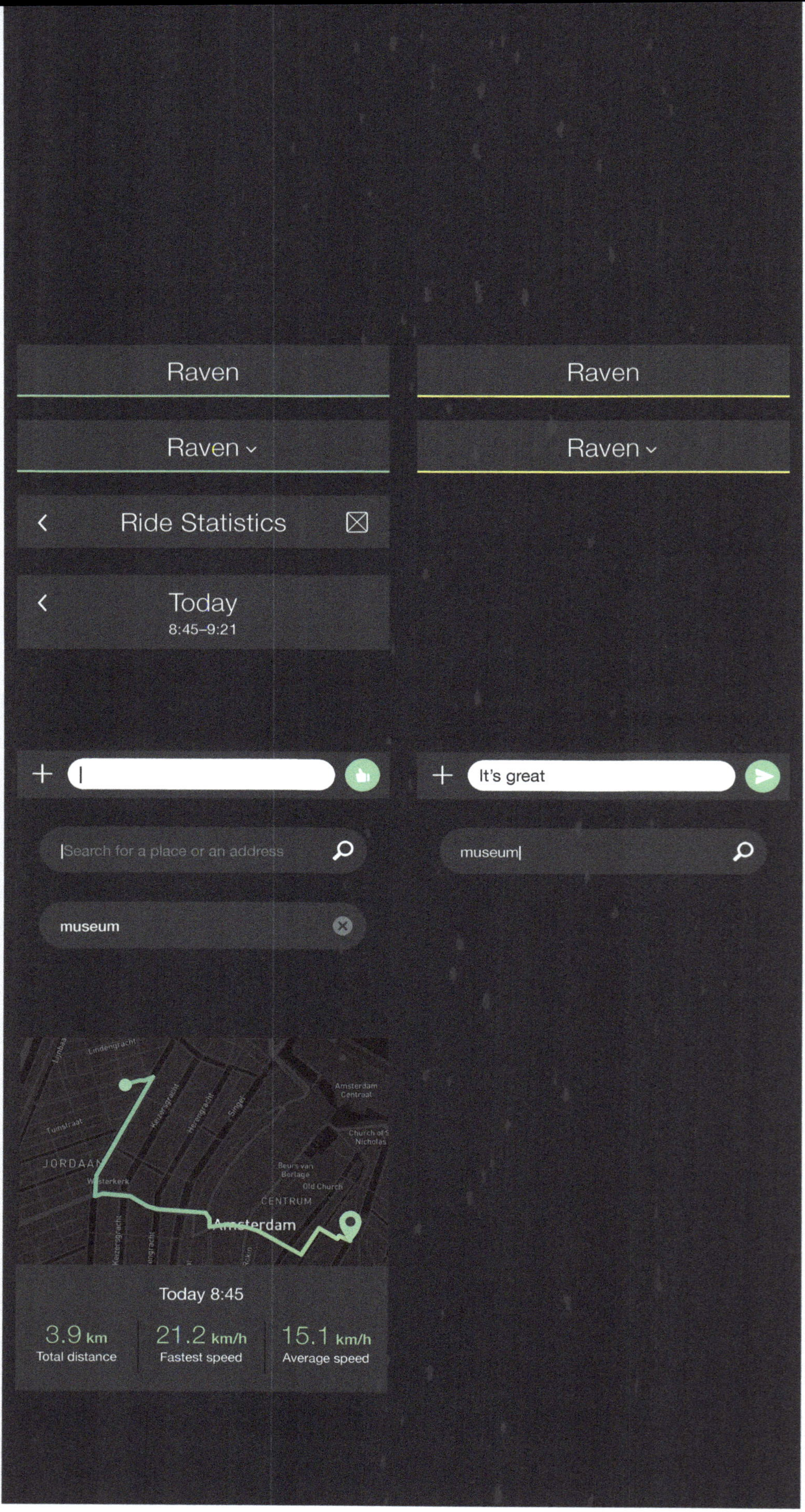

Dashboard Tiles

Notification Tile
normal, pressed

Icon Action Tile
normal, pressed

Short Status Tile
normal, pressed

Quantitative Status Tile
no problem, problem

Qualitative Status Tile
no problem, problem

Navigation Tile
normal, pressed

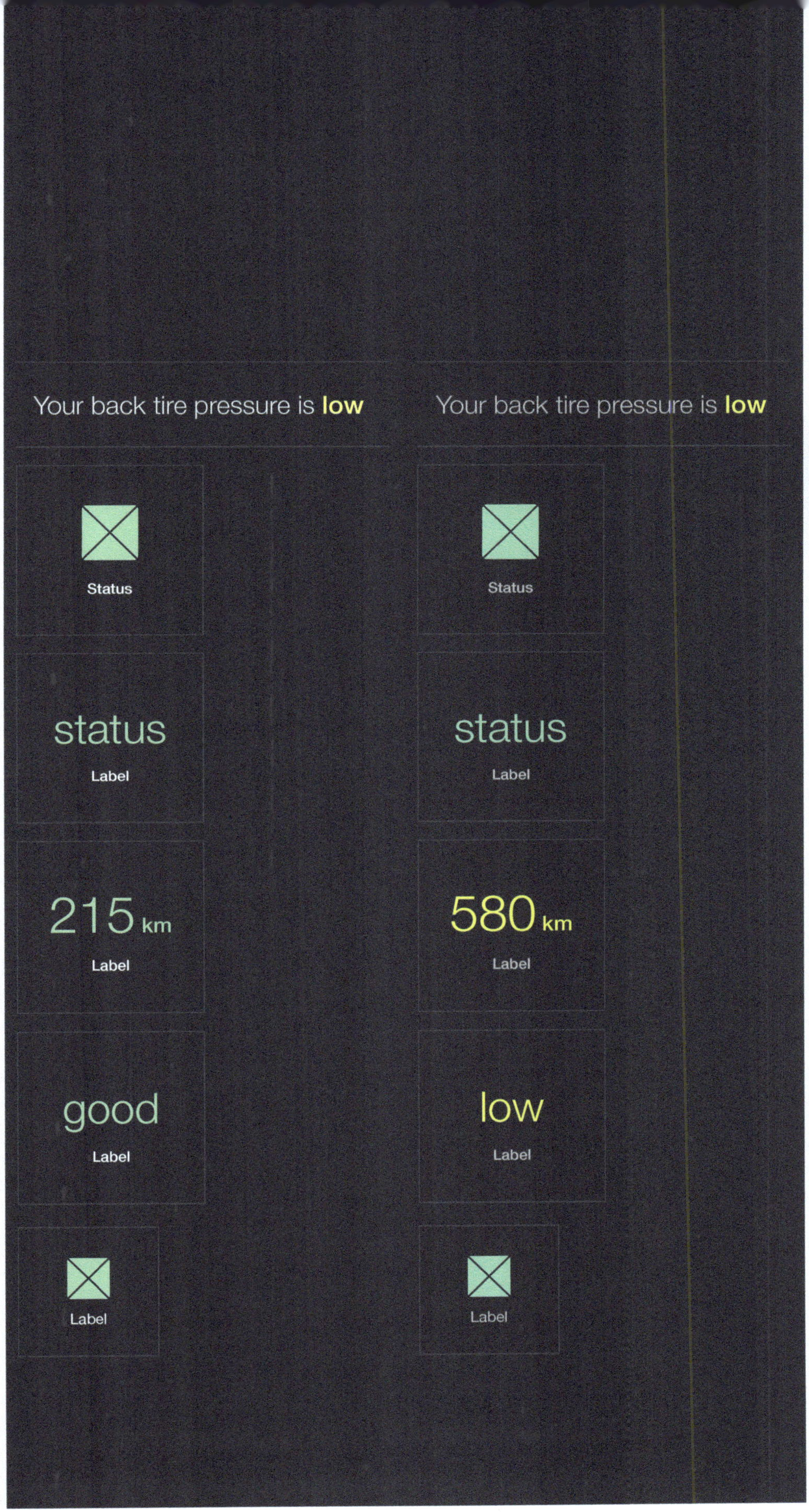

Omniscient / **Observations Suite Web App**

Component Library

Ingredients

Typography

	wide	narrow	mobile
Section Title	Abcdefg	Abcdef	Abcdef
Statement	Abcde	Abcdef	Abcdefg
Subtitle / Last Name	Abcdefghij	Abcdefghij	Abcdefghij
First Name	Abcdefghij	Abcdefghij	Abcdefghij
Information Label / Chart Title	Abcdefghijklmno	Abcdefghijklmn	Abcdefghijklmn
Large Information	Abcdefghijklmno	Abcdefghijklmn	Abcdefghijklmn
Copy / Chart Legend	Abcdefghijklmnopq	Abcdefghijklmno	Abcdefghijklmno
Chart Label	Abcdefghijklmnopqrst	Abcdefghijklmnopq	Abcdefghijklmnopq

Color

action palette

data palette

neutral palette

Iconography

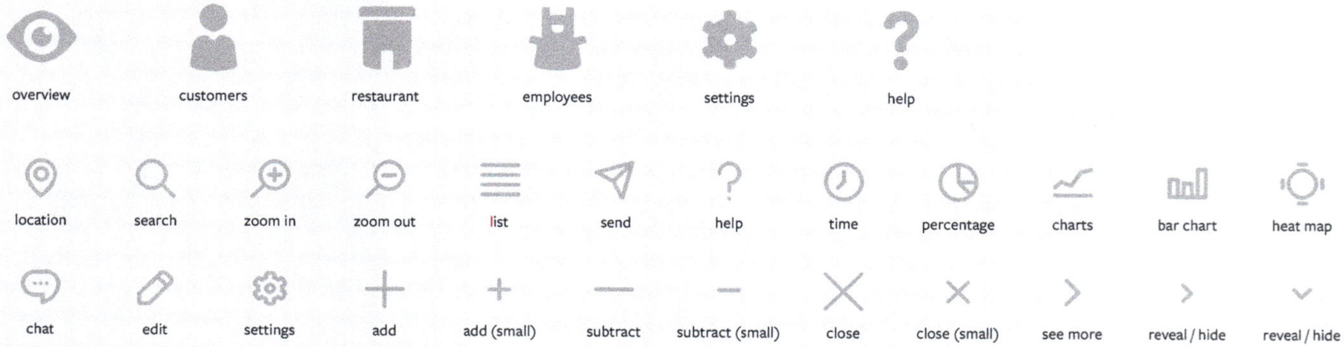

Controls

Buttons

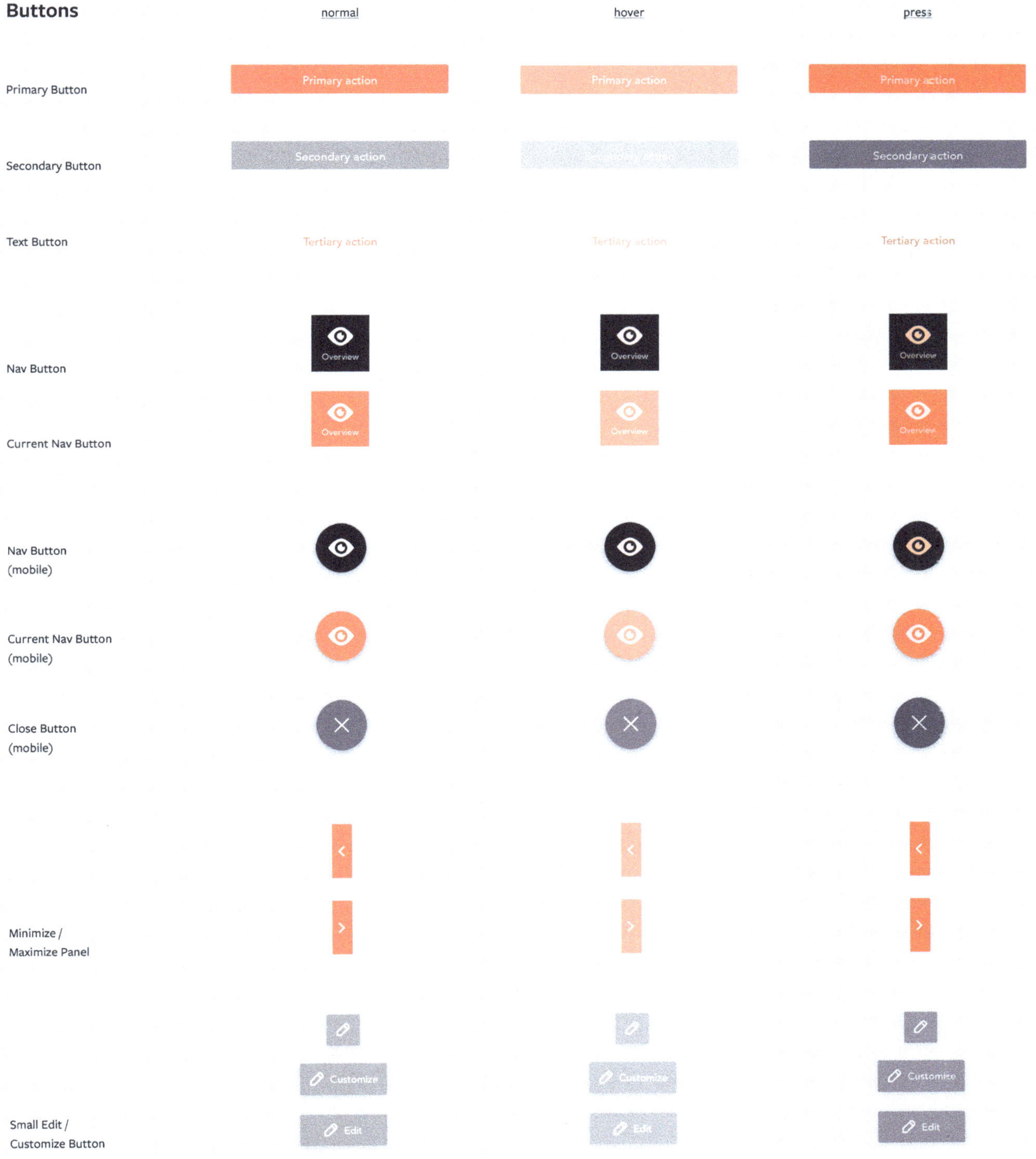

Components

Cards

Notification card

2 minutes ago Dismiss

Upcoming reservations

You have 3 large groups with reservations at 6:30 PM. Make sure the tables are free within the next 30 minutes.

Review tables

Reservation card

unassigned

4 People at **7:30 PM** Unassigned

Firstname Lastname
FirstLastname@bmail.com
(555) 555-5555

Lorem ipsum dolor sit amet.

Assign | Edit | Delete

Quick Assign to Table XX

upcoming, assigned

4 People at **7:30 PM** Tables XX and XX

Firstname Lastname
FirstLastname@bmail.com
(555) 555-5555

Lorem ipsum dolor sit amet.

Reassign | Edit | Delete

Confirm at Tables XX and XX

assigned

4 People at **7:30 PM** Tables XX and XX

Firstname Lastname
FirstLastname@bmail.com
(555) 555-5555

Lorem ipsum dolor sit amet.

Reassign | Edit | Delete

Customer

unselected (2-col. layout)

FirstName LastName

Email address	FirstLastname@bmail.com
Phone number	(555) 555-5555
Last visit	XX months ago
Birthday	January 1
Anniversary	February 14
Tags	first tag second

selected, mobile

FirstName LastName

Email address	FirstLastname@bmail.com
Phone number	(555) 555-5555
Last visit	XX months ago
Birthday	January 1
Anniversary	February 14
Tags	first tag second

Employee

unselected (2-col. layout)

Firstname **Lastname**
Role

selected, mobile

Firstname **Lastname**
Role

no photo available

FL Firstname **Lastname**
Server

Components

Visualizations

wide format

mobile

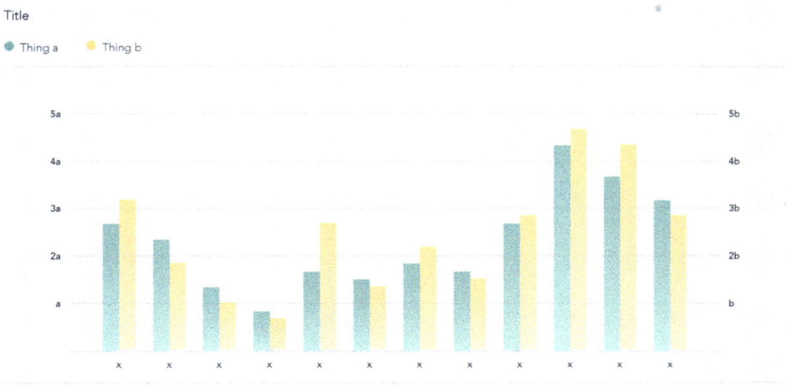

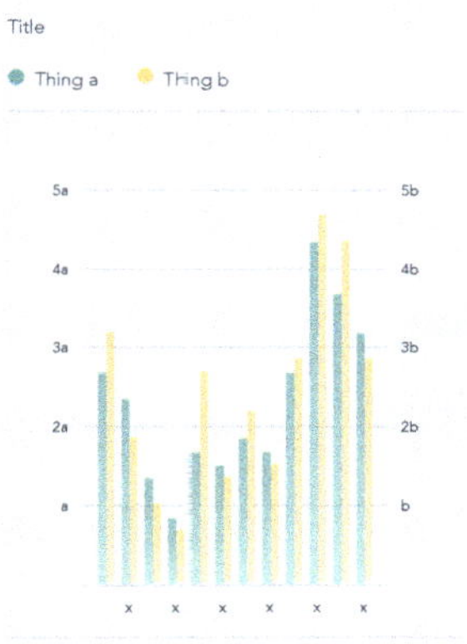

Comparative bar chart

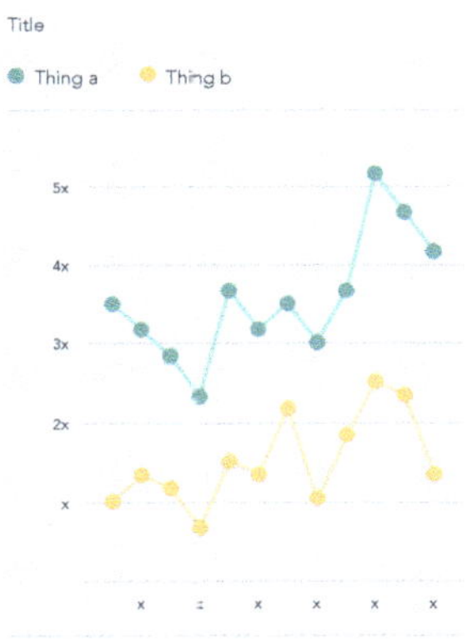

Comparative line chart

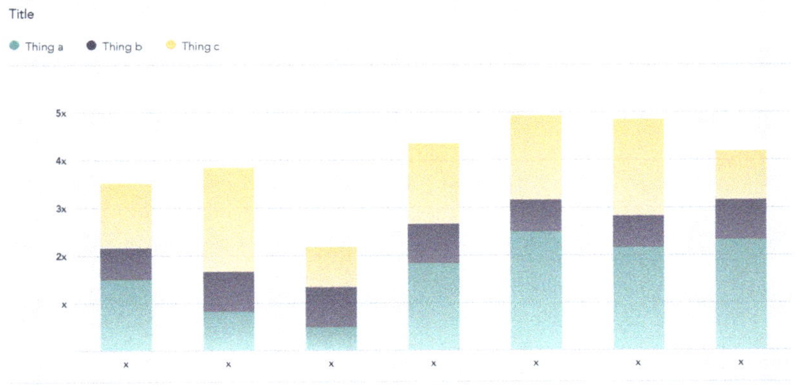

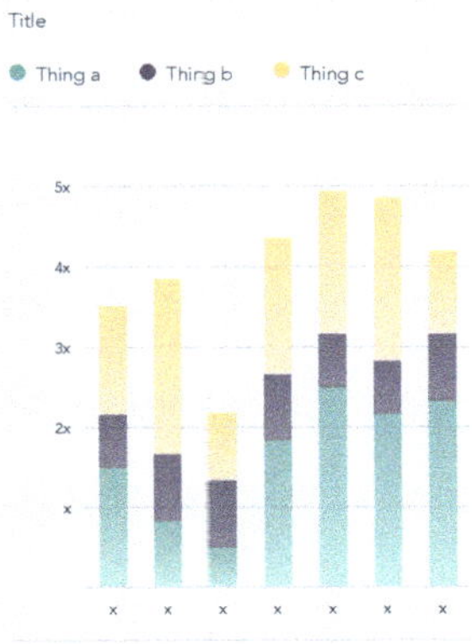

Stacked bar chart

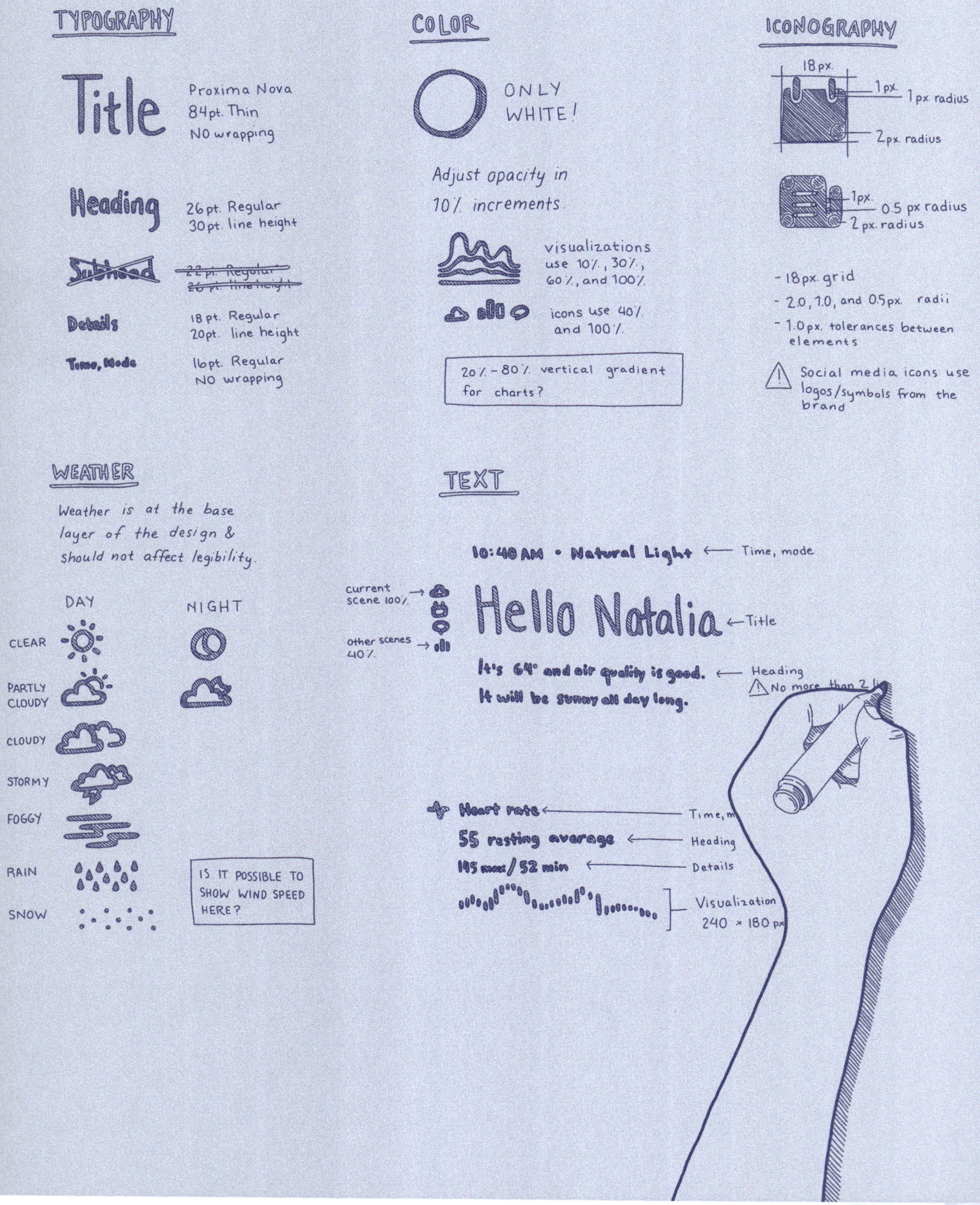
TYPOGRAPHY
Title
Proxima Nova
84pt. Thin
NO wrapping
Heading
26pt. Regular
30pt. line height
Subhead
22pt. Regular
26pt. line height
Details
18pt. Regular
20pt. line height
Time, Mode
16pt. Regular
NO wrapping
COLOR
ONLY WHITE!
Adjust opacity in 10% increments.
visualizations use 10%, 30%, 60%, and 100%
icons use 40% and 100%
20%-80% vertical gradient for charts?
ICONOGRAPHY
18px.
1px
1px radius
2px. radius
1px.
0.5 px radius
2px. radius
- 18px. grid
- 2.0, 1.0, and 0.5px. radii
- 1.0px. tolerances between elements
Social media icons use logos/symbols from the brand
WEATHER
Weather is at the base layer of the design & should not affect legibility.
DAY
NIGHT
CLEAR
PARTLY CLOUDY
CLOUDY
STORMY
FOGGY
RAIN
SNOW
IS IT POSSIBLE TO SHOW WIND SPEED HERE?
TEXT
10:40 AM • Natural Light
Time, mode
current scene 100%
other scenes 40%
Hello Natalia
Title
It's 64° and air quality is good.
It will be sunny all day long.
Heading
No more than 2 li
Heart rate
Time, m
55 resting average
Heading
145 max / 52 min
Details
Visualization
240 × 180 px

Design Guidelines

Design guidelines capture high-level decisions and the thinking behind them. Aimed at maintaining design intention over time, the primary audience of design guidelines is design teams, though design-savvy developers might also find them useful. Design guidelines should not get into executional details and specifications of detailed documentation, but should instead focus on arming designers and product owners with the information they need to make decisions around the product or service.

In a documentation-heavy process, the design guidelines can aggregate other artifacts such as experience principles and conceptual models and can guide readers to other documents such as flow diagrams and detailed documentation. Because of their central role in the creation of a consistent product or service, design guidelines should be diligently maintained throughout the life and various iterations of an experience.

Activities

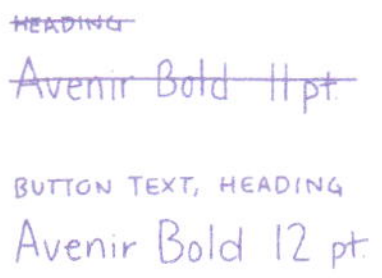

Reduce complexity by combining styles and rules that are similar but not the same.

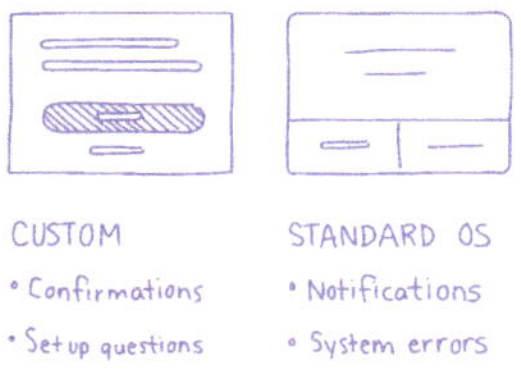

Consider the styles of the platform, and decide where to align and where to diverge.

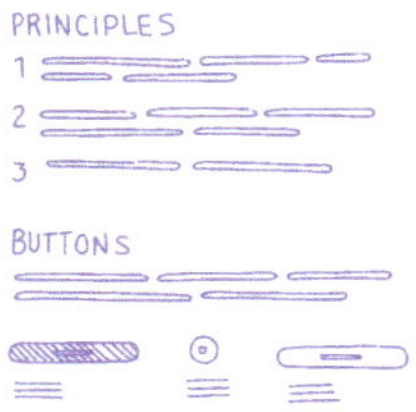

Guidelines should consider high-level principles as well as rules about execution.

As soon as you start making decisions about design, you're ready to begin collecting input for the design guidelines. Decisions might be specific, like, "*We use 24 pt. Sentinel Bold for headlines*," or more general, like, "*We design for glanceability from a distance.*" Any time you notice a pattern in your thinking or execution, it's likely fodder for the design guidelines.

If you've been using your company's design language or guidelines to create mock-ups and components, you should consider how the guidelines for your project interact with those that already exist. Will you feed into them, adding new rules where necessary? Or will you create a new set of guidelines for the project you're working on, referencing prior work and using a compatible format?

If you start your design guidelines in the early stages of design, use a collaborative process within the design team. In this early documentation, aim for visibility over formality. Capture rules on pieces of paper, posting them in a shared space so that the entire design team can see them, add to them, and dispute them when there are inconsistencies or conflicts. If you're working with an existing set of guidelines, capture these as well. Keep track of which rules are new to your project.

If you're beginning design guidelines after the design is well underway, your process will need to focus on reviewing the existing design to find the patterns and rules. As you review, make sure you inventory patterns at both general and detail levels. It's likely that this process will uncover inconsistencies in the design. Try to resolve design issues as you find them, and document the inconsistencies left unresolved.

Whether you start the guidelines early or late in the design process, the set of rules you capture will need curation, iteration, and refinement. Find a way to mark conflicting rules and to capture where rules get more complicated than seems necessary.

Seek Opportunities to Simplify

If two rules are similar but not the same, try combining them. For example, your design probably doesn't need black overlays at both

75 percent and 80 percent opacity. When deciding which rule to move forward with, make sure to test with the most complex applications to be sure.

Consider the Platform

When you're designing an experience like an app that lives within another ecosystem, consider the design language of that ecosystem. For example, when you're designing nonsystem alerts for iOS, you can use the interface elements provided by Apple, or you can create your own language for alerts. If you're not going to use the elements provided, make sure those you design are differentiated so you avoid being similar but not the same.

> *"Understand the implicit patterns of use, layout, and function in your work. Then, make them explicit."*
>
> Michael Gough

Think Big and Small

It's inevitable that future iterations and extensions of your experience will need to stretch beyond the strictest of your design rules. Including higher-level guidelines will ensure that your design's integrity stays intact as it is stretched beyond its original implementation.

Artifacts

When laying out design guidelines, start general and zoom into the basics. While the early sections of the guidelines are likely to be of interest to many stakeholders, later pages might be specifically intended for the design and possibly implementation teams.

Start by establishing why the product exists, along with the decisions that guide its functionality. Describe the purpose or value proposition of the experience, and then share and describe the experience principles. Lay out how the experience principles are made tangible, possibly showing both good and bad examples. If your experience crosses channels or touchpoints, briefly describe them and their relationships. Describe the signature experiences, the moments that most deliver on the value proposition or the moments that you expect to be most meaningful to the user.

Follow up with descriptions and diagrams about how functionality is structured. Show the overall structure via an information-architecture diagram as well as the interaction model. Describe how the same experience translates to different scales, and provide written guidance about when to provide what functionality. If layouts are repeated throughout the experience, define the templates that exist as well as how they should be used.

Finish with executional details about what makes the experience look and feel the way it does. Show organizational elements like grids and hierarchies before moving into ingredients like color, typography, shape and form, transitions, tone of voice, etc. Highlight how ingredients combine to form controls and how controls combine to create components. Written descriptions should focus on when elements are used and how they bring consistency to the system. Avoid getting into the specifics of implementation like height, width, or the distance between objects. These sorts of specifications should live in detailed documentation rather than in design guidelines.

Once you've created design guidelines, you'll need to maintain them so that they continue to be relevant through multiple iterations, releases, and extensions of your experience. With each iteration, make sure to walk stakeholders through the changes. The more team members understand and use design guidelines, the more effective they will be.

This excerpt from Ambience Mirror's design guidelines shows how each scene is constructed via layers of elements and then how those elements are composed of just a handful of simple ingredients.

The Observations Suite design guidelines live in the same document as detailed documentation. These excerpts occur early in the document, highlighting high-level rules and ingredients before diving into the details.

Personal Intelligence / **Ambience Mirror**

Design Guidelines

Structure

The Ambience Mirror presents information to the user in five layers, three being digital. The user uses a VUI to interact, never touching the mirror itself.

Navigation Layer

The navigation layer is always present and provides the user with the time, lighting mode, current user, scene, available scenes, and blurb.

Scene Layer

Customized content based on the user's selections. Available scenes include weather, today, calendar, social, and history.

Weather Layer

The weather layer sits at the top of the mirror, adding ambience through the slow, subtle animation of scenes.

Mirror

The mirror layer reflects the user. Additional layers of information can be turned off for a simpler mirror experience.

Light

Light comes from the edges of the mirror. A chain of individually addressable LEDs allows for carefully controlled lighting scenes.

Elements

The Ambience Mirror combines dynamically generated weather illustrations with simple icons and typography.

Iconography

Icons are designed to be pixel perfect on an 18 px. square grid and use rounded corners with 0.5, 1.0, and 2.0 px. radii. Spacing between elements is 1.0 px.

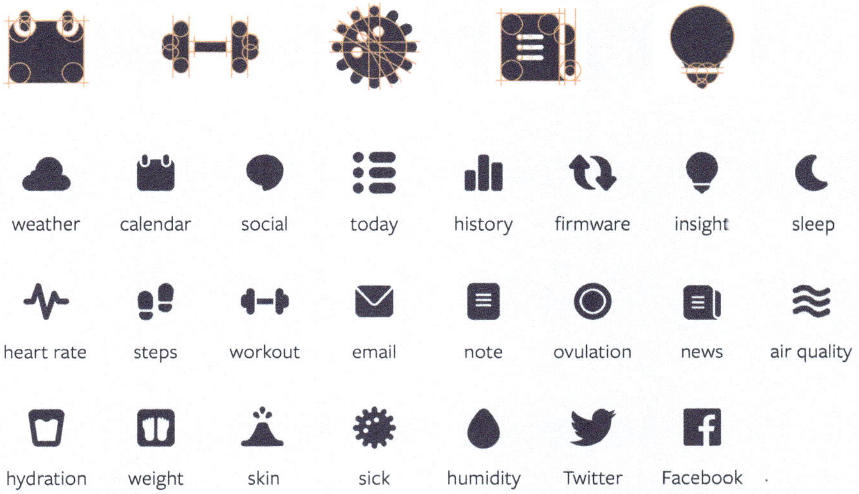

Typography

Ambience Mirror's design balances subtlety with legibility.

The interface uses only Proxima Nova in thin, regular, and medium weights in four distinct styles.

Greeting, Current User
Proxima Nova Thin
84 pt. / no wrapping

Hello

Blurb, Data Summaries
Proxima Nova Regular
26 pt. / 30 pt. line height

You slept well last night.
Time to conquer the day!

Data Details
Proxima Nova Regular
18 pt. / 20 pt. line height

6'03" avg. pace
57 m elevation gain

Time, Lighting Mode, Titles
Proxima Nova Medium
16 pt. / no wrapping

7:48 AM • Natural Light

Weather Layer

The weather layer sits metaphorically behind navigation and scene layers. Weather is generated and animated using actual weather data.

Clear Day / Night

The sun or moon moves through the sky, rising and setting with the day or night.

Partly Cloudy Day / Night

The sun and moon move through the sky accompanied by randomly generated clouds whose movement is based on wind speed and direction.

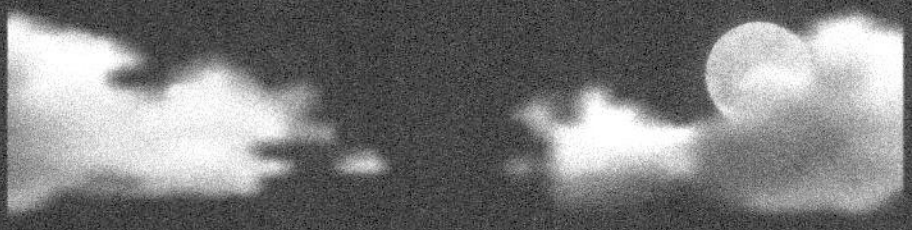

Foggy / Cloudy / Stormy

Fog shifts subtly.

Cloud formations move through the sky based on wind speed and direction. Intensity is increased based on real-world data.

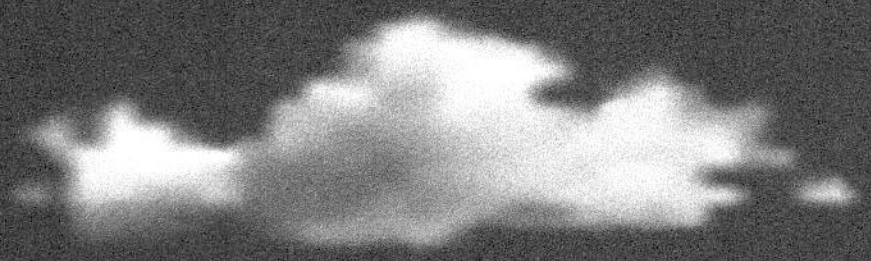

Storms build in intensity with randomly generated lightning and cloud formations.

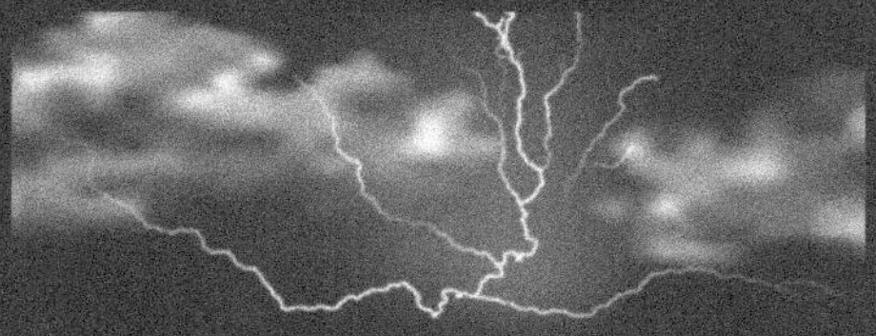

Rainy / Snowy

Both rain and snowfall are randomly generated at a density based on actual weather data.

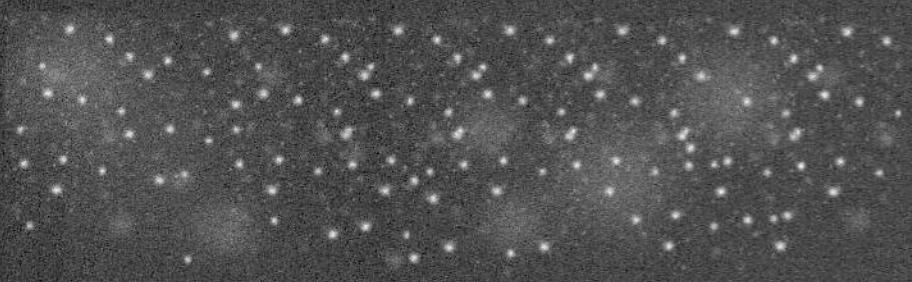

Navigation Layer

The navigation layer provides the user with a sense of place.

Anonymous

When no user has identified themself, the mirror displays generic weather content.

Time and lighting mode are always shown, regardless of log-in state.

Navigation

When a user has identified themself, the mirror prominently displays their name.

A series of icons represents the scenes the user has configured for display using the app.

Weather is always the default scene to avoid revealing any sensitive information.

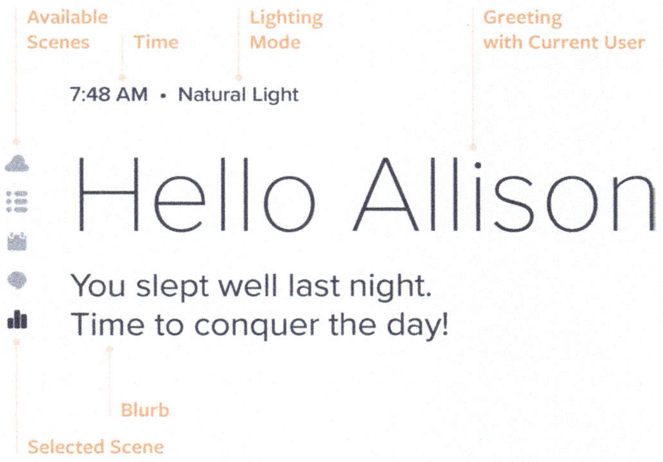

Scenes

The user configures their Ambience Mirror to have up to five scenes. Available scenes include weather, today, calendar, social, and history.

Only weather and today scenes are required.

Today, social, and history scenes are highly customizable.

Omniscient / **Observations Suite Web App**

Design Guidelines

Structure / Signature Moments

Understand Users

Create profiles for users, and supplement them automatically based on orders and behaviors.

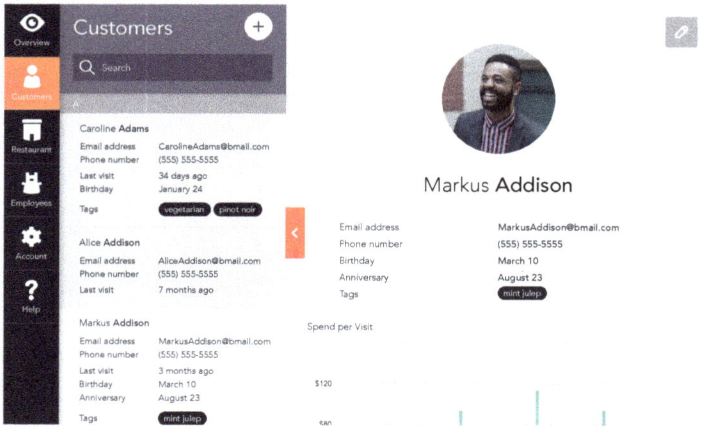

Optimize Engagement

See an overview of flow within the restaurant, and dig into individual customer engagements within a single view.

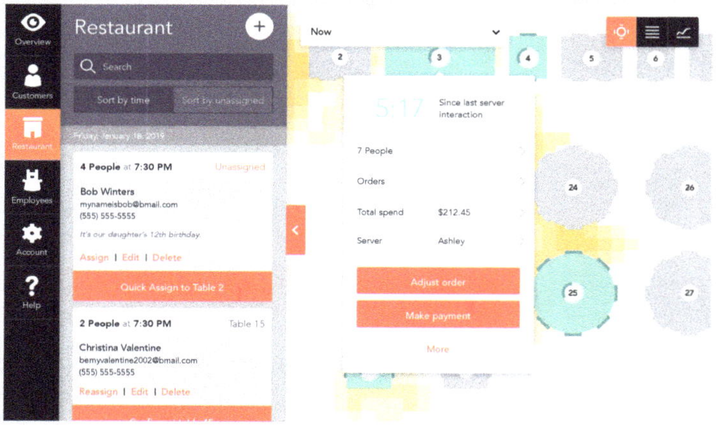

Manage Tables

Review availability for individual tables, navigate between days, and see problems highlighted.

Review and assign incoming requests.

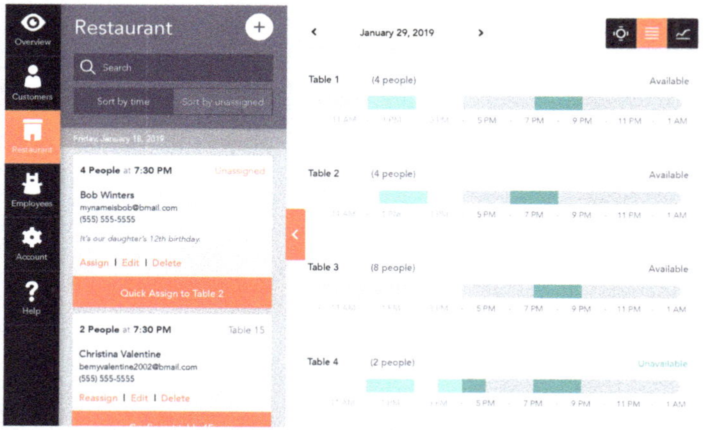

Structure / Interface Rules

Provide a consistent experience across touchpoints.

✓ Provide the same functionality on small screens as on large ones.

✗ Provide a simplified but reduced experience on smaller screens.

Draw the user's attention to action items.

✓ Use a highlight color to draw attention to the user's most likely actions.

✗ Use the same color palette for navigation, buttons, and visualizations.

Enable the user to focus on content.

✓ Create an expandable canvas to house information and visualizations.

✗ Establish no hierarchy between navigation, notifications, and content.

Encourage exploration of data.

✓ Provide users with the controls to manipulate and explore data.

✗ Provide users with a premade selection of charts and parameters.

Take an inbox approach to notifications.

✓ Send notifications whenever the user needs to address something.

✗ Send notifications only when something is wrong.

Design for an expanding feature set.

✓ Design for a consistent experience as future features are added.

✗ Redesign the experience for each additional group of features.

Ingredients / Iconography

Suite Navigation

Suite-navigation icons are designed snapped to a 36 px. grid.

Suite-navigation icons are always filled, differentiating them from secondary navigation and action icons.

Icons are softened with rounded corners, either with a 2 px. radius or a 1 px. radius for narrower elements.

Where possible, icons use a curved element, tying back to the eye of Observations Suite.

Secondary Navigation and Actions

Additional icons are designed to a smaller 24 px. grid.

Icons use 2 px. outlined forms.

Both edges and joints are rounded.

The signature curve element is reserved for suite icons and is never used in other icons.

Ingredients / Colors

Action Palette

Melon is used to show action and to show place in navigation.

Dark Melon # F47D59	**Melon** # F8A68C	**Light Melon** # FCDBD6

Data Palette

Turquoise is the primary color used in data visualizations; turquoise is also used to show occupied tables in the heat-map visualization.

Dark Turquoise # 3AA09D	**Turquoise** # 7FCDC5	**Light Turquoise** # C9E9E6

Daffodil is the secondary color of data visualizations; daffodil is also used to show traffic flow on the heat map.

Dark Daffodil # FFD367	**Daffodil** # FFE5A7	**Light Daffodil** # FFF7E3

Neutral Palette

Neutral colors are used for typography, backgrounds, and as a tertiary color in data visualizations.

Black # 0F1023	**Darkest Gray** # 555263	**Dark Gray** # 736D80
Gray # AFACB7	**Light Gray** # D0CED5	**Lightest Gray** # EBE7EE
White # FFFFFF		

Build

The build phase is the final phase of work. It typically lasts the longest and often requires more work from implementers than designers. Because this phase faces the pressures of execution, integration, and scaling, it can be the most stressful. Here it is the designer's responsibility to support these goals, and so it is important to be patient as well as thorough and organized. At the end of the build phase, the design should be implemented in a way that is true to the original intention.

Artifacts like the flow diagram and detailed documentation seek to capture and communicate the specifics of a design to developers, while activities like user validation aim to test the many assumptions of a product or service with actual users. The ongoing process of design assurance throughout the build phase ensures that everything that's being built or manufactured is seen by a designer's eye before being shipped to users. For all of these activities and artifacts, design teams must integrate with other teams, supporting the execution of the final experience.

The build phase of the project is often less about completing activities in a specific order and more about working through the individual processes iteratively alongside a development team or manufacturer to tackle the details as they're being built. For software projects, the build phase is often broken into feature-focused sprints. Each sprint consists of communicating the design, building the design, and testing the build. Nonsoftware projects may not use the term *sprint*, but they likely use the same steps iteratively to work toward the best possible product.

The ultimate artifact of the build phase is a finished experience—either a product or service or a collection of choreographed products and services in use in the real world. Usually there are many other artifacts that play a supporting role. These artifacts communicate what to build and how to validate it with users. They can also capture feature intentions and plans for future design and development.

In This Section:

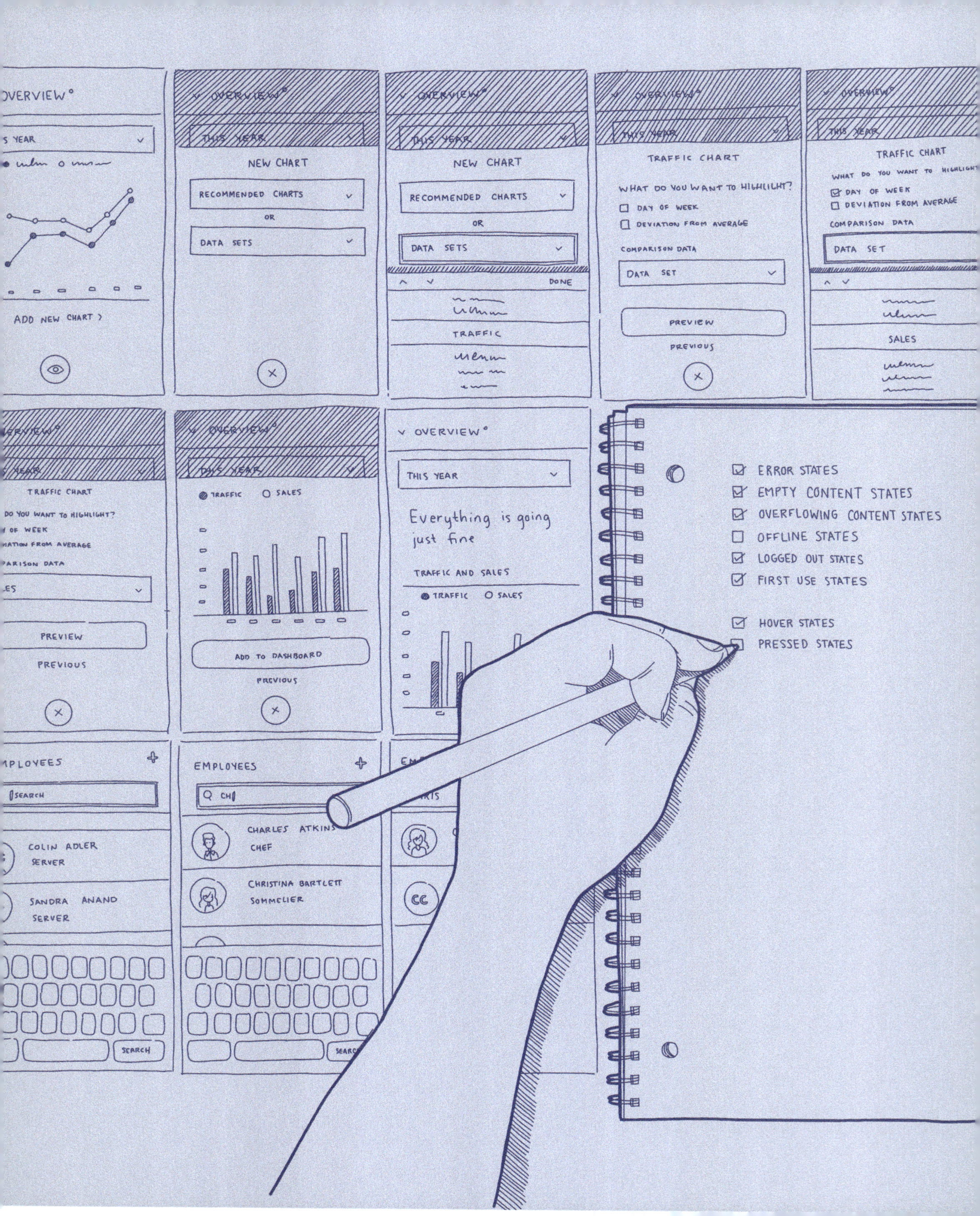

ERROR STATES
EMPTY CONTENT STATES
OVERFLOWING CONTENT STATES
OFFLINE STATES
LOGGED OUT STATES
FIRST USE STATES
HOVER STATES
PRESSED STATES
OVERVIEW
THIS YEAR
NEW CHART
RECOMMENDED CHARTS
OR
DATA SETS
DONE
TRAFFIC
TRAFFIC CHART
WHAT DO YOU WANT TO HIGHLIGHT?
DAY OF WEEK
DEVIATION FROM AVERAGE
COMPARISON DATA
DATA SET
PREVIEW
PREVIOUS
SALES
ADD NEW CHART
ADD TO DASHBOARD
Everything is going just fine
TRAFFIC AND SALES
EMPLOYEES
SEARCH
COLIN ADLER
SERVER
SANDRA ANAND
SERVER
CHARLES ATKINS
CHEF
CHRISTINA BARTLETT
SOMMELIER

Detailed Design

While mock-ups establish the rules and interactions of a product through the design of common states, detailed design defines how the system reacts under pressure by thoroughly exploring errors, edge cases, and transitional states. Detailed design might occur at different points in the process. A design-first or waterfall method might have detailed design occurring right after the design of mock-ups, with all decisions made before development or manufacturing is involved. A more integrated or Agile approach is likely to include detailed design feeding into the implementation schedule.

Not all projects need detailed design. If you're working alongside a design-savvy developer or the product you're building is super simple, mock-ups and close communication may suffice. The level of detail required depends on the needs of stakeholders and implementers. At first you may do detailed design as a result of noticing something wrong in the implementation or to answer a stakeholder's questions. With iteration, the process will get less reactive, and you'll develop better intuition for predicting what others need before they need it.

Activities

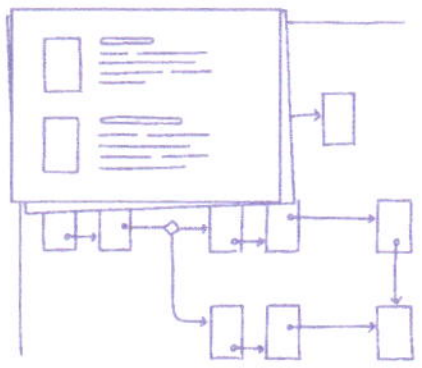

Start by collecting existing documentation.

Before starting detailed design, you'll need to have done mock-ups. Look through the mock-ups, considering how time and interaction will affect them. If you've done a flow diagram, use it as well. Create a list of relevant concerns that need to be considered, and then assess every mock-up to make sure all concerns are addressed. When creating your list, consider the following:

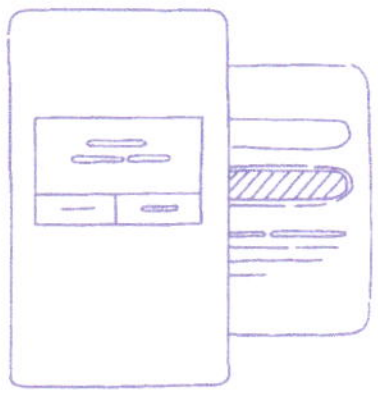

For every screen, consider the many states of interaction.

* Are there places where screens will have different appearances for different users?
* Are there error states or edge cases that need to be accommodated?
* What happens if a user's name is too long, or if they post something with too much text?
* Are there visualizations that will significantly change based on unusual data or outliers?
* Are there mock-ups that change depending on if it's the user's first time through the experience or their tenth?
* Consider how the design reacts to every button press and gesture. Are there states that are missing?

Separate items into components and states. For example, a title that contains a user's name with too many characters probably needs to be shown at the component level, while a reactive search interaction requires multiple screen states. Not all interactions need to be mocked up in detail. Those that use native controls provided by the development platform may be specified simply as using the default behavior.

In some places, detailed design will need to explore multiple options, while in others it will simply require executing on common patterns. Whatever workflow you used to create, gain approval for, and organize approved mock-ups should provide a good starting point for detailed design; however, you may need to adjust as stakeholders are likely to change as the project becomes more focused on implementation.

It's not uncommon for the designers who do detailed design and other build-phase activities to have different roles or to be on a different team from other designers. These designers may be more integrated with development and so may be positioned alongside the people working to bring the experience to life. If you're working with a process that has detailed design outside of the main design team, make sure to brief those doing the detailed design and to empower them with principles and rationales so that they can make informed decisions when the details require more significant changes.

If you're working as a designer on the detailed-design team, make sure you understand the thinking and the intentions of the design you'll be extending. This will guide you in understanding where you can experiment and where simple execution is required.

> *"The details are not the details; they make the product."*
>
> Charles and Ray Eames

Artifacts

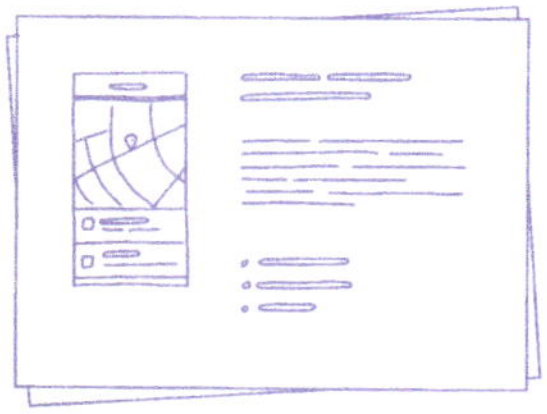

Level of detail and documentation will vary depending on the team.

Detailed design can be presented in multiple ways. For stakeholders requiring fewer details, you might show a single mock-up followed by its detailed-design states, or you might show the many detailed states of an interaction within a presentation of that scenario.

Individual detailed-design states and scenarios can be useful for communicating with developers, providing visuals for specific features and bugs in whatever project-management tool they're using. Detailed designs should also be integrated into living design documentation such as the flow diagram, design guidelines, and detailed documentation.

Where possible, use descriptions to reduce the amount of necessary work. For example, if the same detailed-design pattern is used in multiple places, mock it up once and use a written explanation to communicate how it applies to other parts of the design. Similarly, if a dialog box overlays multiple screens, you could mock it up

Definition of Done

Development teams often use a definition of done to determine when a product is ready for release. This definition has specific objective requirements that must be met. This technique can also be useful for design, ensuring that design work and communication are consistent in quality and in fidelity, regardless of the designer executing them.

without the screen underneath and reference it from multiple points of the flow diagram, denoting that it will always appear on top of the screen that led to it.

Observations Suite uses small flows to present specific detailed scenarios like adding a new chart, searching a list, and adding an employee. The detailed designs are done in the two weeks that precede development sprints, so that developers have everything they need in advance.

Detailed Design

Add a New Chart (mobile)

Related Stories

When I'm setting up Observations Suite, I add new charts to my dashboard, so it's easy to find the information that's most important to me.

After using Observations Suite for a few months, I update my dashboard with new charts, so I can continue to optimize my business.

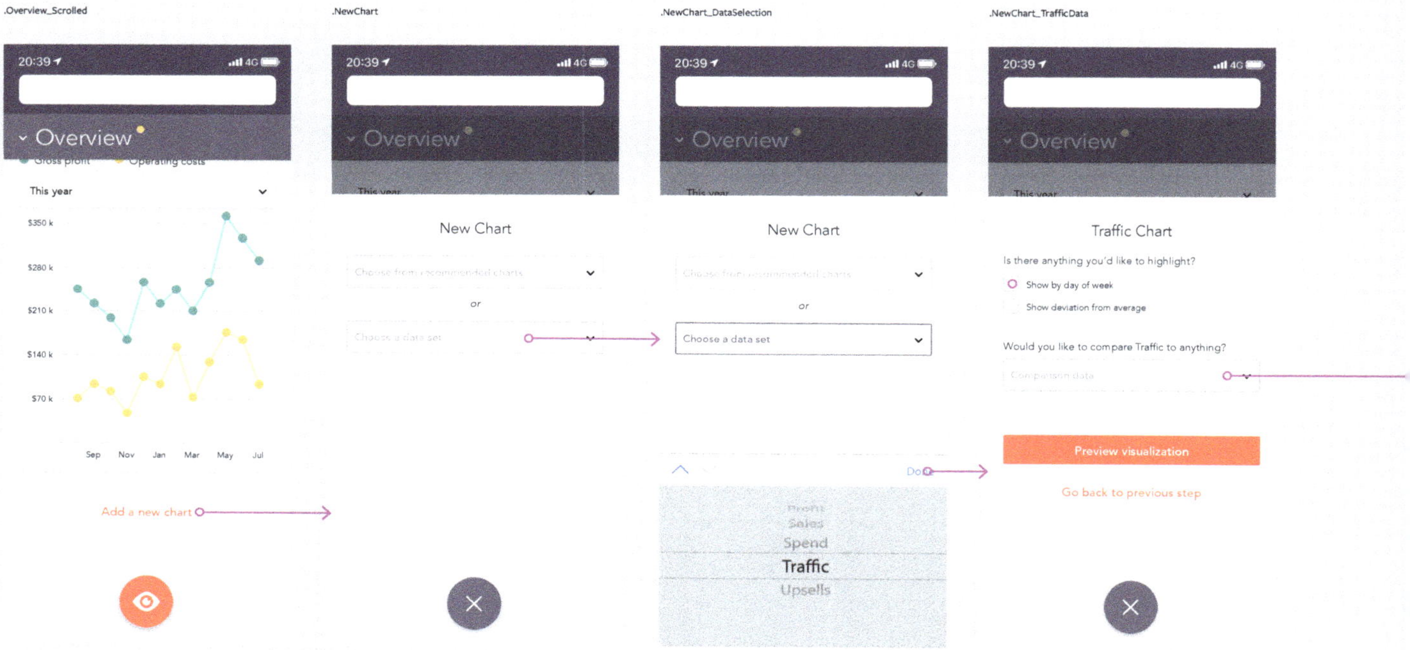

Use the built-in OS picker.

Advance to the next screen when the user taps the "Done" button.

These options will vary depending on the data set selected.

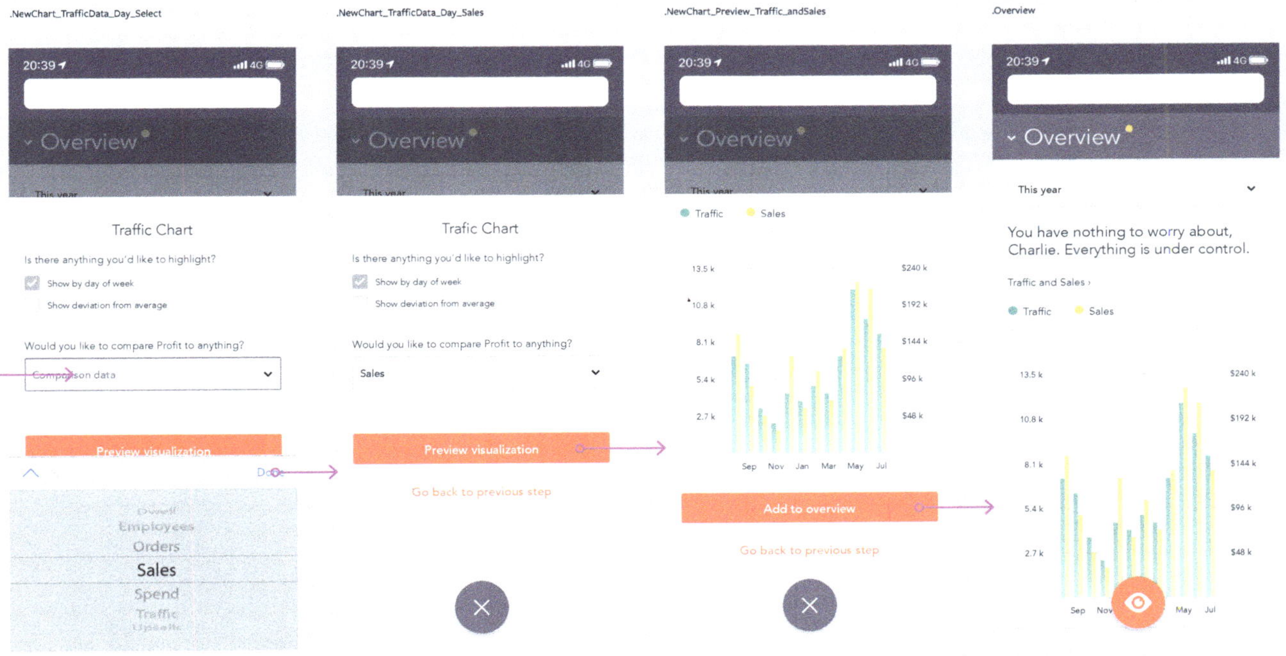

List should be curated to eliminate options that don't provide any value.

The chart preview should use the time resolution currently selected for the overview.

Employee Search (mobile)

Related Stories

When I need to access an individual employee's information, I search for the person in my directory, so I can find them more quickly.

When I forget an employee's last name, I search using their first name, so that I can find them more efficiently.

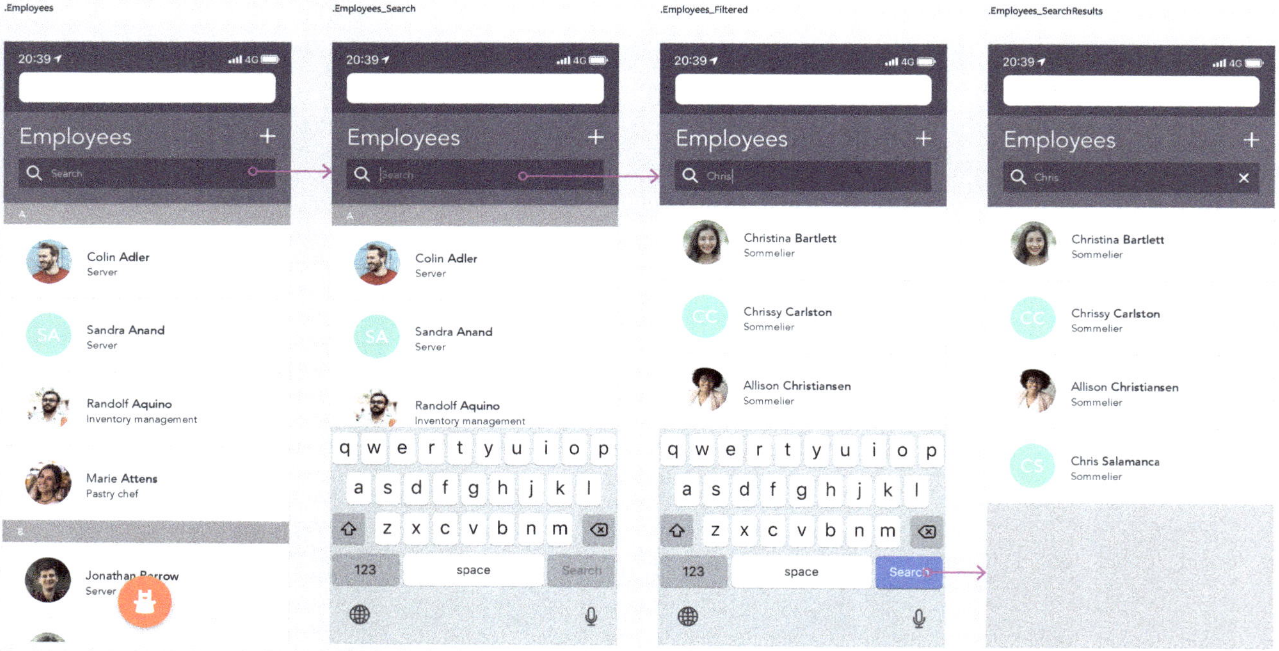

The first letter in the search should be capitalized (the keyboard should reflect this).

Results auto-update, filtering based on search input.

Add Employee (mobile)

Related Stories

When I hire a new employee, I enter their information into Observations Suite, so that I can track their performance.

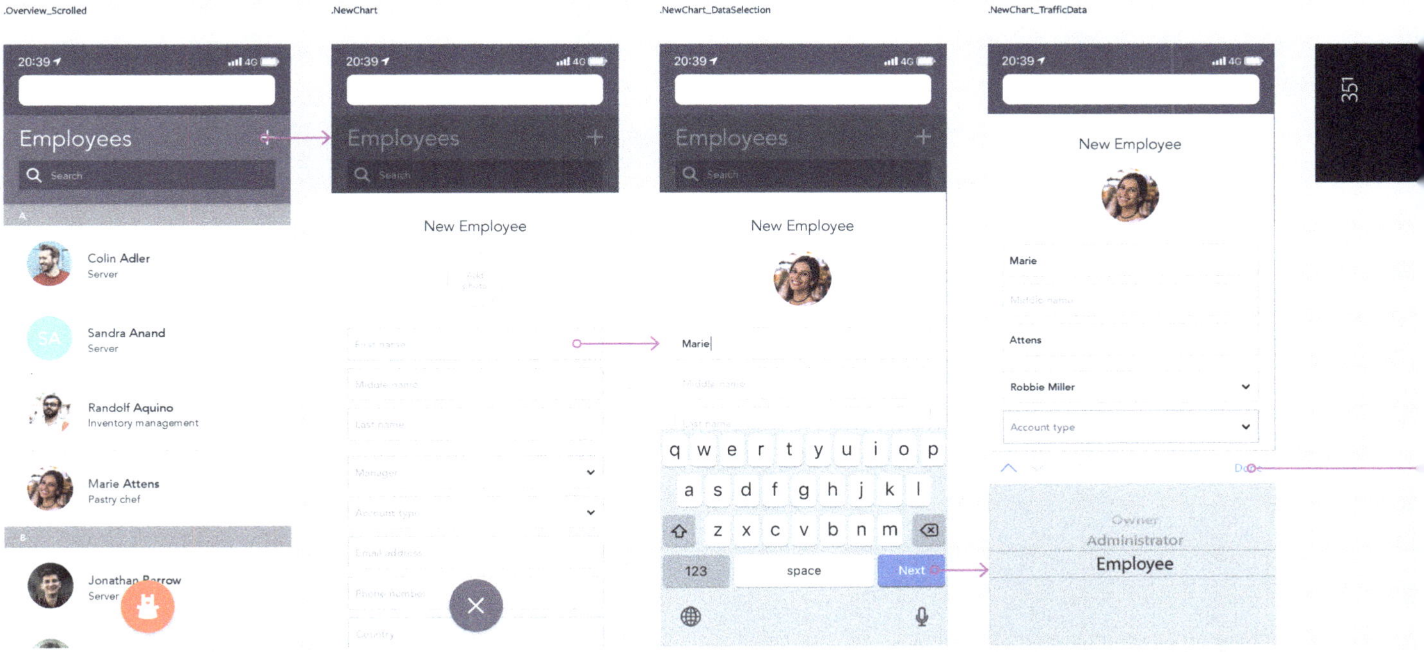

Add photo should use standard OS controls.

Capitalize the first letter of every field.

For error cases, see Employee Errors.

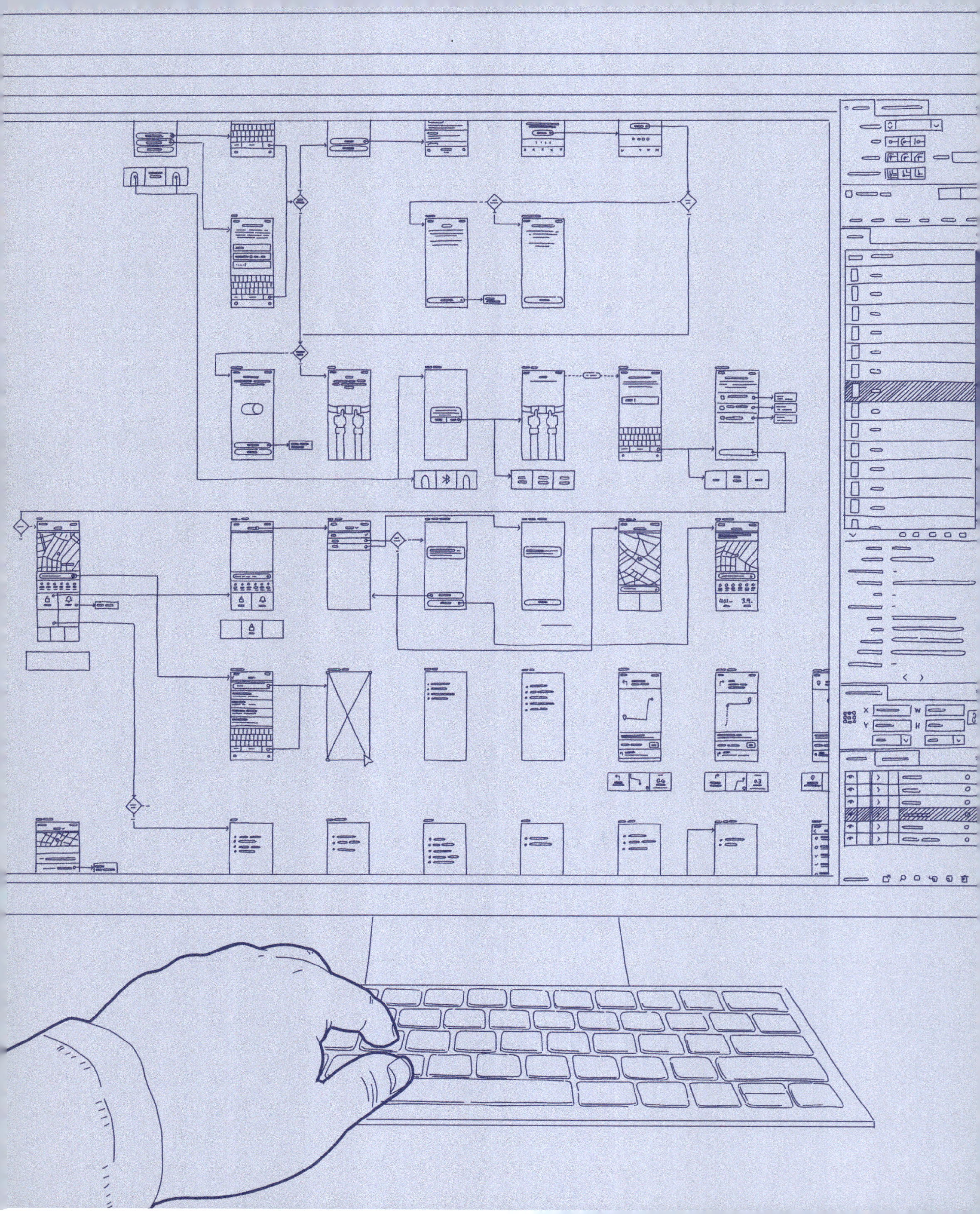

Flow Diagram

A flow diagram shows the relationship of states across an interactive experience. It uses mock-ups to capture these various states and documents how the user moves between them. Flow diagrams can vary in level of detail, layers of information, and even in comprehensiveness of the system. With careful organization, a flow diagram makes it easy for stakeholders to understand the overall structure of an experience and for developers to see the detailed relationships between elements. Meanwhile, the creation of the flow diagram can help designers identify and maintain patterns across complex design systems.

Not all products or services need a flow diagram, and not all experiences can be contained in a single flow. A simple product design that has only a handful of nonsequential states isn't complex enough to benefit from a flow diagram, while an experience that crosses many possible touchpoints over a lot of time likely needs one flow diagram per touchpoint. A conversational interface where inputs and responses are based on the endless variations of user input is probably too complex for a visual flow diagram, but the conversation could still be mapped using key words and responses.

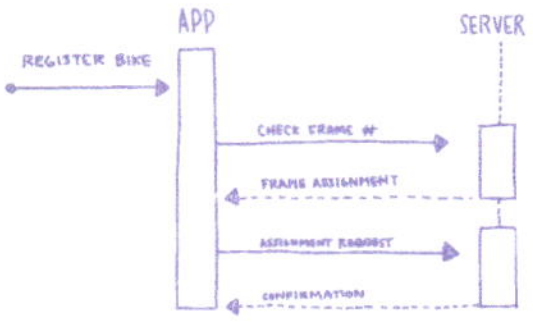

Sequence diagrams show objects interacting with each other.

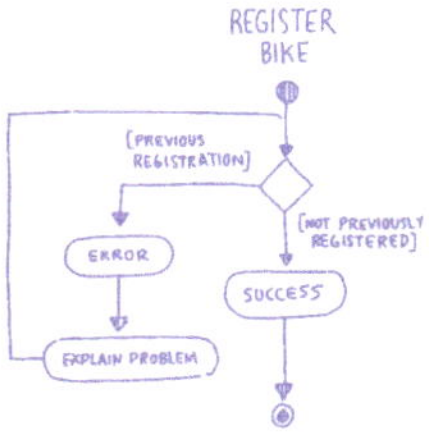

Activity diagrams capture flows with logic.

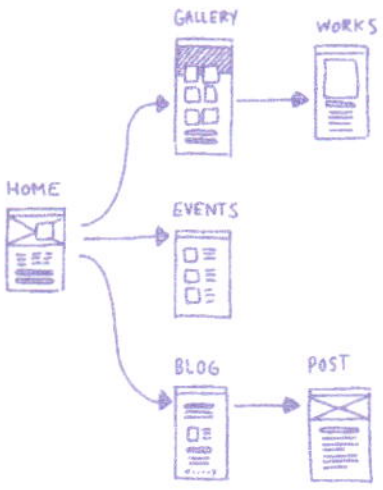

Site maps capture an entire design with some connection and hierarchy.

The flow diagram has its roots in technical documentation, pulling elements from sequence diagrams, activity diagrams, site maps, and decision trees. Understanding this history can help you design a diagram that communicates clearly with those implementing the design.

Sequence diagrams or event diagrams show how objects interact with each other over time. Each player (user, product, or service) is represented vertically, while the interactions between them are represented with lines and arrows. These diagrams have many limitations. They represent only a single possible flow of events, and their top-to-bottom format is restrictive for complex scenarios. But their use of solid lines and dotted lines is useful for conveying human action versus technological action.

Activity diagrams are aimed more toward capturing workflows. Unlike sequence diagrams, activity diagrams capture multiple possibilities using logic. This representation of logic is essential for creating a flow diagram where the user has choice or where certain criteria need to be met to move on. But these diagrams have one major drawback: actions are shown instead of states, making it difficult to represent digital- and physical-product states in a graphic way.

Site maps focus on capturing the architecture and hierarchy of a website in either a list or a graphic format. The priorities of a site map are similar to a flow diagram in that they capture the pages of a website and show their relationships to each other; however, they neither capture the many different states of a page nor show the interactions required to move from one page to the next.

Decision trees capture actions and consequences in a branching diagram. For experiences where the user is not presented with specific actions, the decision tree can help capture a broader range of possibilities. These sorts of diagrams tend to scale quickly, so it's important to establish a fidelity of information detail and visualization. A decision tree might be useful if you're working on a conversational interface, showing the different inputs and automated or customer service responses.

The flow diagram takes the best from these diagrams and combines them with mock-ups and detailed design to create an artifact that communicates the different possibilities of interaction in an intuitive way. Business stakeholders will be able to understand the overall system and trace individual user scenarios, while implementation stakeholders will have what they need to build out and test the product or service.

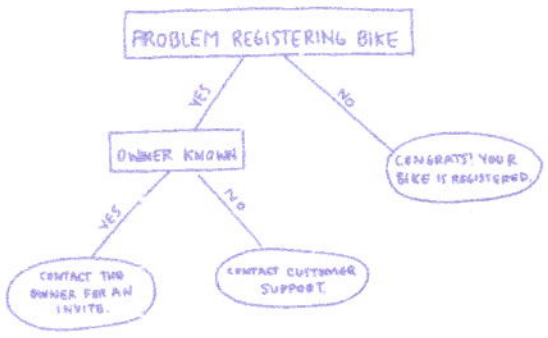

Decision trees capture actions and branch into consequences

Activities

While a flow diagram's primary purpose is to communicate how the user moves through a complex system, the exercise of creating it also forces deep consideration of how the user's many possible paths relate to the technology's many possible states. The process of creating a flow diagram is iterative and, especially in the case of digital and connected products, will likely span many versions of the design and development of the product. With this in mind, it's best to start the artifact as soon as you can and to revisit previous activities like concept generation, mock-ups, and detailed design to fill in or add new features to parts of the flow not yet considered.

Before you begin, make sure that you understand the overarching system and that you have designed the high-level product or service states. Artifacts like the information architecture or interaction model will guide the layout of your flow diagram, while mock-ups and detailed design will provide the content.

"Good design is a lot like clear thinking made visual."

Edward Tufte

Artifacts

A well-designed flow diagram will speak differently to different stakeholders. A business stakeholder will be able to understand the overall structure of the experience at a glance, while a development stakeholder will be able to discern the consequences of the user's many possible interactions. A designer will be able to see the user's different paths through the experience, and someone in quality assurance will be able to use the flow diagram to ensure that the built experience matches the designed experience.

As you begin your flow diagram, consider your audience. If you're designing for a close team where decisions are made as a group and developers and designers sit side by side, you may not need to capture every possible state; however, if you're working with a remote team of developers that you have rare contact with, your documentation will need to be more thorough. This is especially important for apps where screens can have dozens of variations. If you're having trouble deciding, consider the error states for a given screen. Will your team be able to extrapolate how different errors work from a single example, or will they need each and every possible error and combination of errors laid out in the flow diagram? Also consider the amount of time you have to create documentation, as the effort difference between these two fidelities of flow diagram can be significant.

If you're designing a complex flow diagram focused on a single touchpoint, avoid the urge to break it into multiple small flows. While this may be necessary in the end, it's important to start the diagram by showing the entire system of the product or service in one place. This ensures a foundation of consistency moving forward.

The first priority of the flow diagram is to communicate what the user experiences by capturing the different states of a digital or physical product. If you're working on an app, start by collecting all of the screens into a single document. If you're working on a physical product, gather the different states of the product (renderings or illustrations). For states you don't have visual representations for, use placeholders with text descriptions to complete the structure.

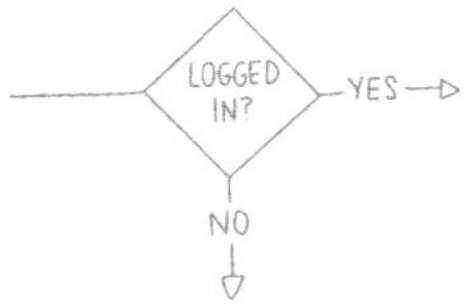

Use logic to show how different conditions affect the experience.

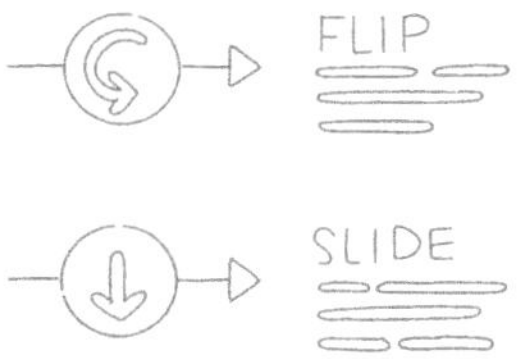

Pair the flow diagram with motion studies to communicate transitions.

Gather states into groups of common functionality, as defined in the interaction architecture, and lay them out on a grid within your document. In your layout consider the order that your user will experience states in as well as which states are most important. Typically, a flow diagram will show first use and setup in the first rows, followed by regular use states. Less frequented states like “Help” or “Settings” belong at the bottom. Sequences of states are positioned left to right. If your experience has a default or home state, this should be on the left, standing out so that stockholders can see easily where the user will typically start the experience.

As you lay out screens, respect the grid. The complexity of flow diagrams can often lead to confusion in reading them. By maintaining a grid system, you reduce the amount of chaos being presented.

If your experience has groups of functionalities, like connecting a product or creating an account, it might be worth calling these out by drawing boxes around the appropriate states and labeling them. This will help stakeholders find what’s important to them with minimal effort.

Once you’ve laid out the many states of your experience, give each a label. This will help create clarity in conversations between designers, developers, copywriters, and other stakeholders. State names should be consistent in capitalization and format and should be human readable. If your team already has a naming standard, use it. Otherwise, try the following: begin each state name with the platform followed by a period. Follow this with the top-level section name. For states within a section, add a hyphen followed by the substate name. For feedback states that occur within or overlaying another state, such as errors or confirmation dialog boxes add an underscore followed by the feedback state name. Some examples of state names might include the following:

iOS.Login
iOS.Login_IncorrectPassword
iOS.CreateAccount_PasswordTooShort_PasswordTooSimple

iOS.ConnectionConfirmed

SmartProduct.ConnectionConfirmed

With your flow diagram's structure in place and states consistently named, it's time to add the logic and connections between states. To ensure readability, choose a color that contrasts with your design. When the user interacts with a state, arrows draw connections between the target of that interaction (often a button) and the consequence of that interaction. In cases where the state changes without user interaction, a dashed-line arrow is drawn from one state to the next.

Start with the connections that represent the most frequented path through the experience. If you find that these paths are difficult to represent in simple, mostly linear ways, you may need to reconsider the overall structure of your diagram. Add logic to highlight whether certain conditions have been met. For example, logic might confirm that a user's phone is connected to their bike, or it could differentiate between uploading photo versus video content.

Adding detail in flows and in logic will likely raise new questions and highlight missing states. It's helpful to document these open issues in the flow diagram in a way that makes them easy to find and correct as you continue iterating.

If you're designing a flow diagram for an app with nonstandard transitions, it's likely that you'll want to communicate these, along with the relationships between states. Because transitions are often repeated throughout an experience, it's easiest to create a label or icon that represents each transition and then to add this to the appropriate connection arrow in the flow. This means your flow will need a legend so that your audience can easily reference the transitions. If you're doing motion studies, it's helpful to use the same system of names and icons at the start of each video, making sure that there's no confusion.

With all of these layers of information and complexity, it's easy to get overwhelmed with designing and maintaining the flow diagram. Try to establish a strong workflow up front to avoid having to do a lot of clean up later in the process. Rather than rebuilding or pasting mock-ups into your flow, try using a tool that allows linking to external files. This way states will automatically update in the flow diagram as you update them elsewhere. For extra efficiency, try laying out your working files for mock-ups and detailed design similarly to the flow diagram, reinforcing the structure in your mind and making it easier to move between the two.

When presenting the flow diagram, it's often most effective to print it at a large scale. This provides stakeholders with a view of the entire system, while also allowing them to zoom into individual moments. It also makes it easy to take notes, adding information or marking areas for improvement where necessary. Once a team is familiar with the flow diagram and its structure, digital artifacts can be easier to navigate.

Through the multiple iterations of the product or service, make sure that the flow diagram stays up to date so that decisions and revisions don't get lost in the process. With increased complexity, you may find that your flow diagram has grown unwieldy. Don't be afraid to reorganize everything when the flow just isn't working. Sometimes a big pain early in a project saves you from an even bigger pain later.

Excerpts from the flow diagram for CityBikes capture the states of the mobile app alongside the related states of the on-bike display. The diagram is relatively simple, avoiding the details of error states and transitions.

CityBike / **Connected Bicycle**

Flow Diagram

First Use

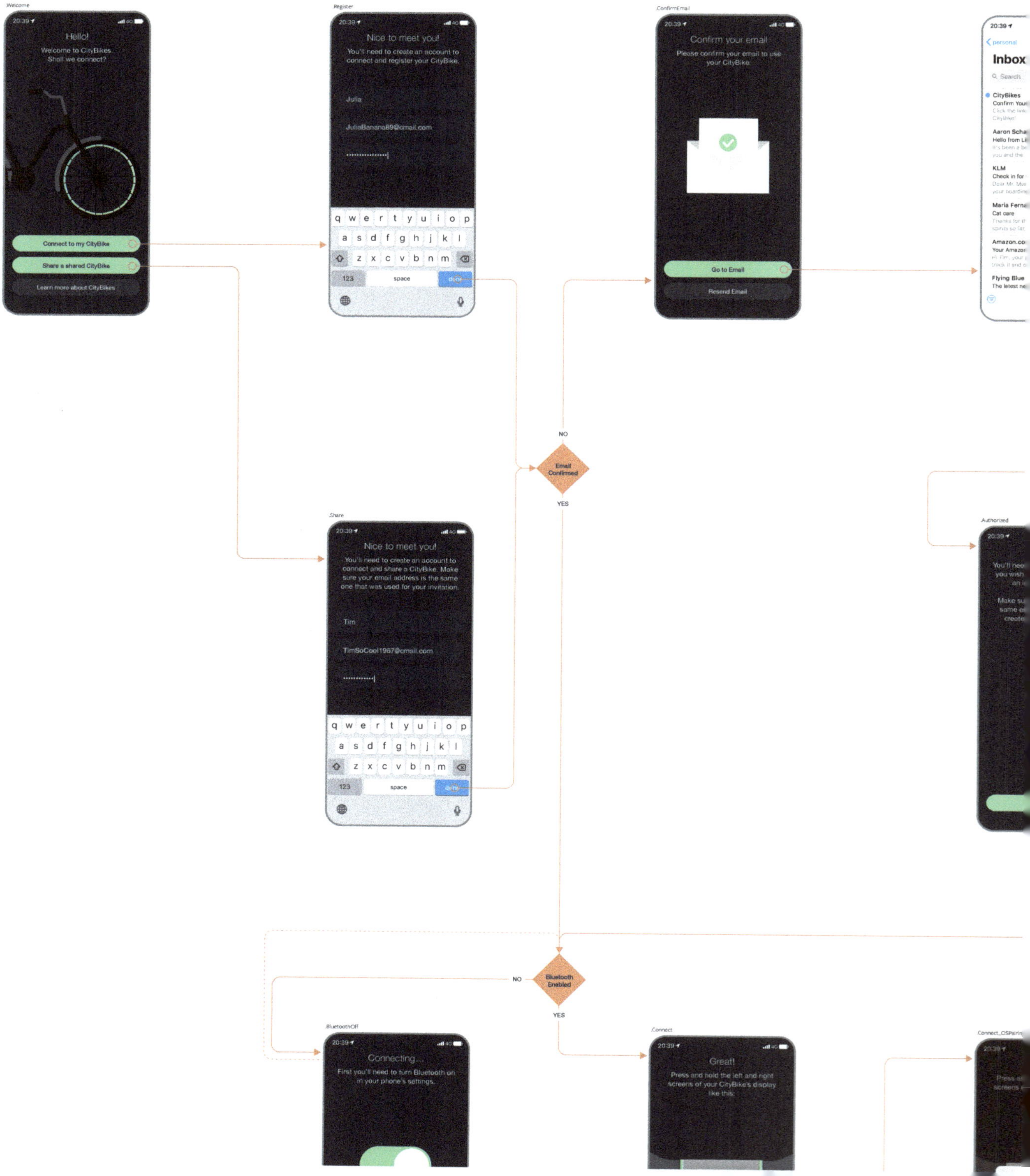

From: CityBike
Confirm Your Email
Welcome to CityBike
Just click the button below to confirm your email address and start riding!
Confirm Email
citybike.com
CITYBIKE
Your email has been confirmed and you're one step closer to riding!
Return to app
Subscribe to our newsletter to be the
YES
Email Authorized
NO
Primary User
AuthorizationRequired
You're authorized!
But before you can ride, you'll need to connect to the CityBike via Bluetooth.
You will need access to Sparrow's screen for this step.
Continue
Links to .Help_Sharing
Connect_Success
Great!
Your CityBike is connected!
2 seconds
BikeName
What's in a name?
Make your CityBike yours—give it a name. You can always rename it later if you change your mind.
GettingStarted
You're ready to ride!
Here are a few important things that might come in handy before you take off.
Learn about locking and unlocking

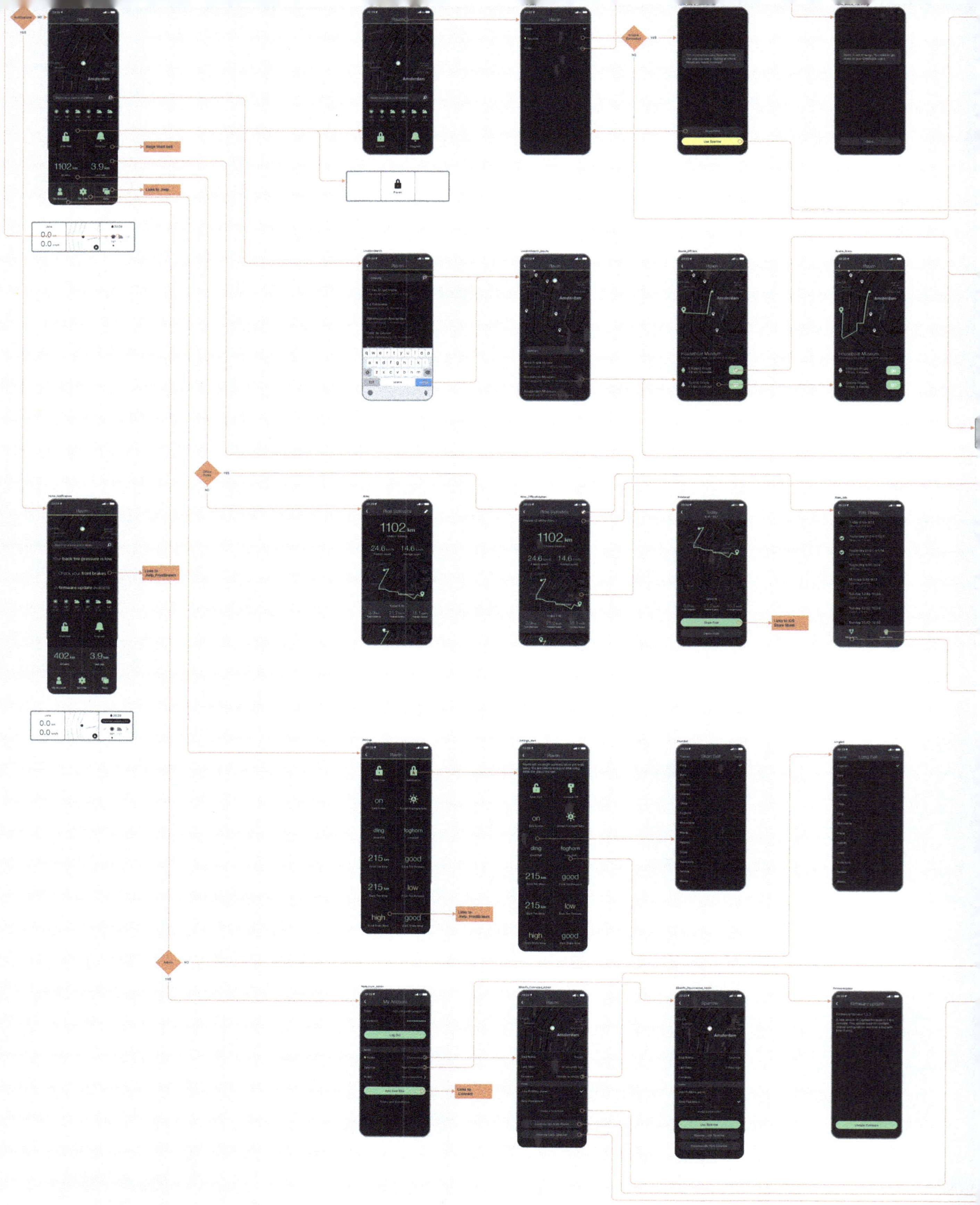

Amsterdam
1102 km
3.9 km
402 km
24.6
14.6
on
ding
foghorn
215 km
good
low
high

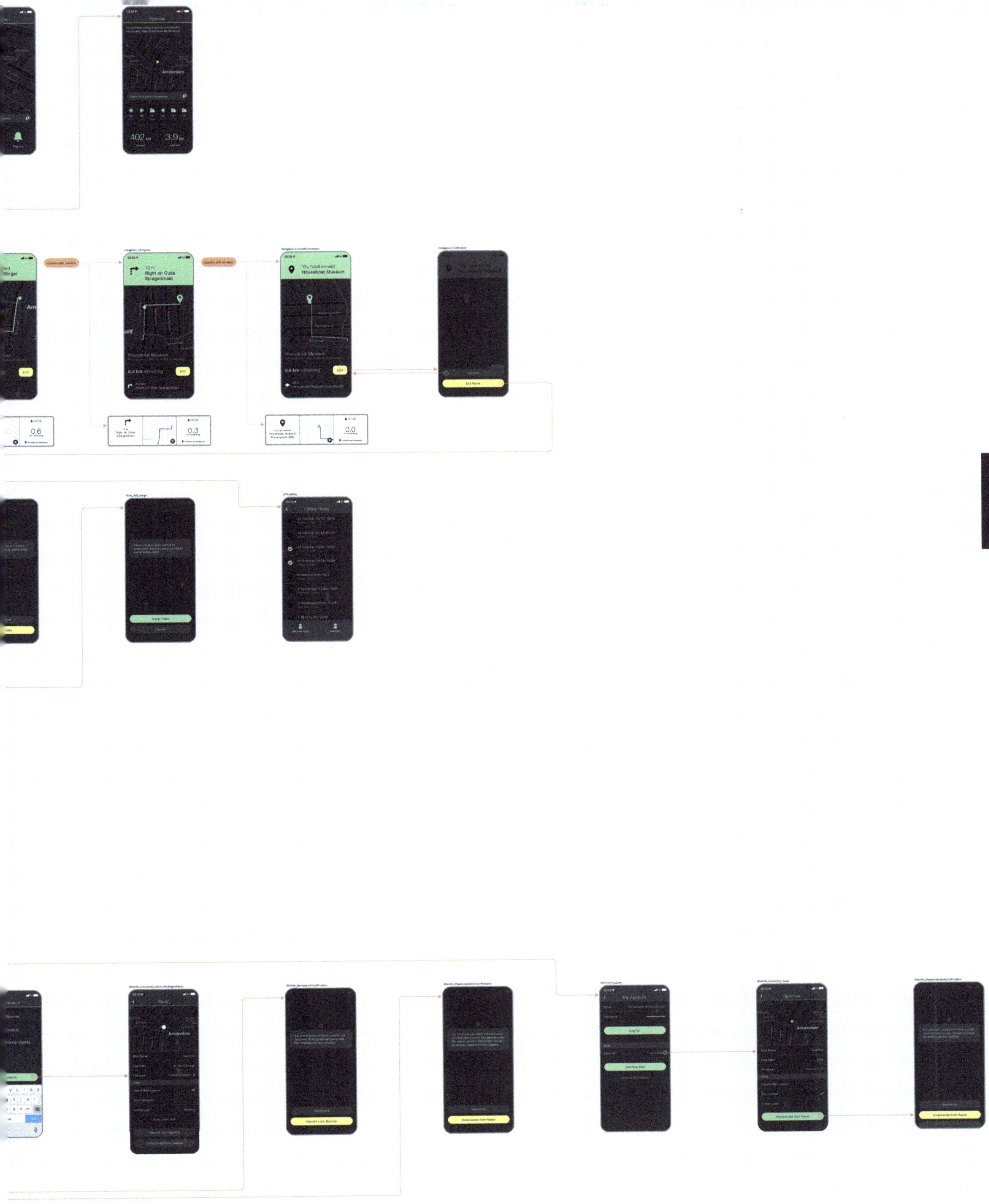

Flow Diagram

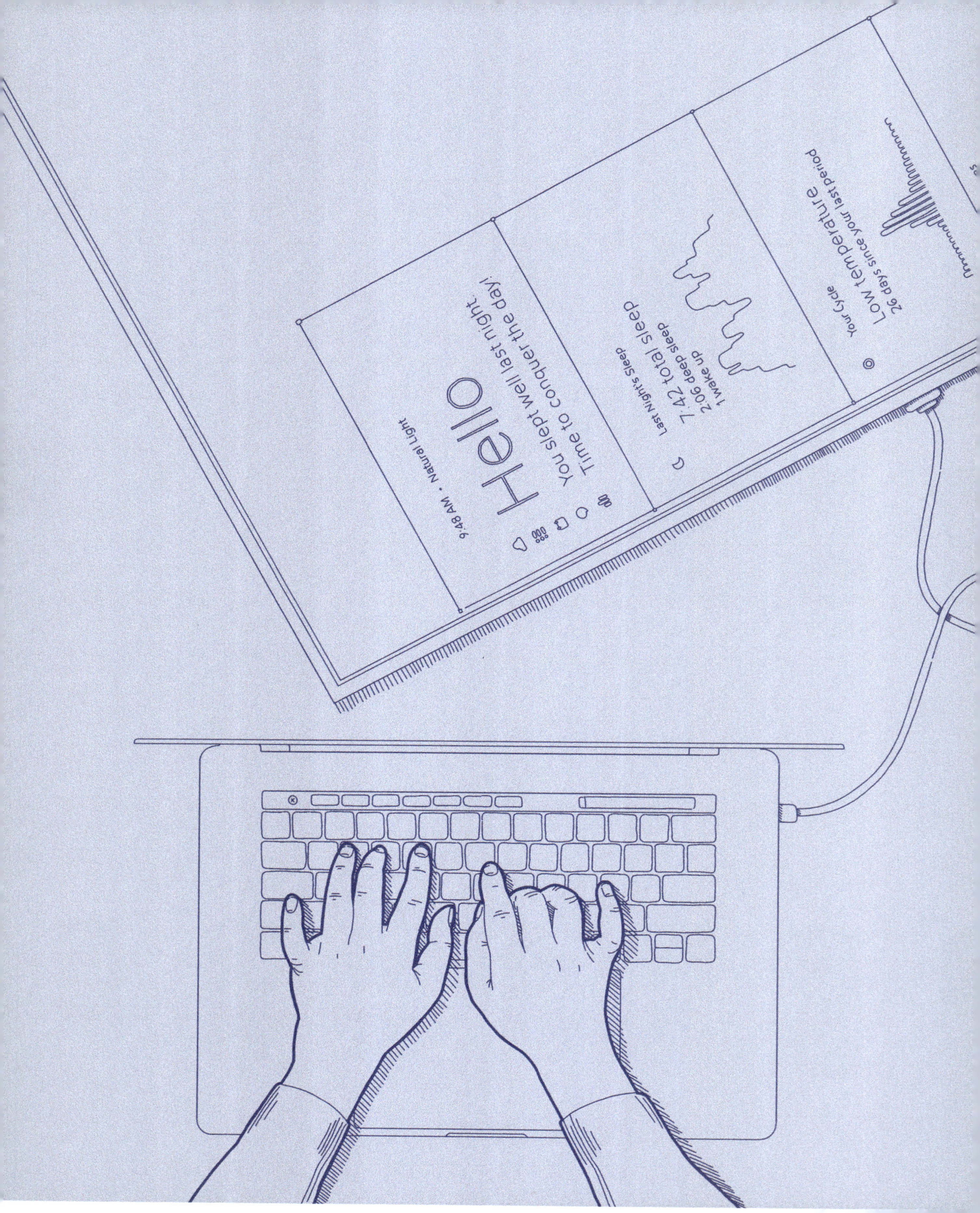
9:48 AM • Natural Light
Hello
You slept well last night.
Time to conquer the day!
Last Night's Sleep
7.42 total sleep
2.06 deep sleep
1 wake up
Your cycle
LOW temperature
26 days since your last period

Prototype

Prototypes are simulations of products or services that are created with the intention of communicating and learning without the full investment of development. While design teams are often able to refine their designs and make better decisions simply through the activity of building prototypes, the primary goal is usually to learn by sharing with stakeholders and doing user validation with your target audience.

Prototypes are most useful for testing innovative products and services and for ensuring that users understand novel interactions. They can range in fidelity from rough paper prototypes that the design team can produce quickly to full-fledged production prototypes that usually require coordination with developers or manufacturers. As the level of investment rises, typically so does the quality of the feedback. Choosing a prototype fidelity depends on how far along your project is and what you hope to learn from testing it.

Paper prototypes allow the user to step through a process with sketches or mock-ups.

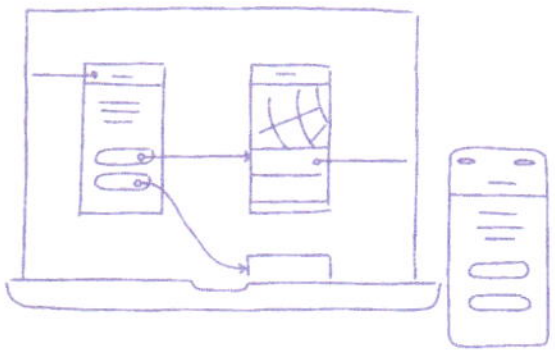

Simulation prototypes feel somewhat realistic but are still throwaways.

Proof-of-concept and production prototypes use actual manufacturing and development processes.

Activities

Building prototypes starts with understanding the goals of the prototype. Are you sharing with stakeholders or testing with users? What kind of feedback are you hoping for—general reactions, ergonomic, or usability? Does your project have any time or budget constraints that will affect the quality of the prototype you're able to build? With these answers in mind, define the scope of your prototype. Determine how much of the experience the prototype will encompass. Should it communicate a specific scenario in depth or provide a lightweight overview of the entire experience? Also consider fidelity. Does the user need merely to understand how it looks and functions, or should they experience how it feels with transitions and materials?

Once you have defined a scope, gather the inputs you'll need to help build the prototype. This could range from early artifacts like gestural designs and interaction models to more refined artifacts like mock-ups, detailed design, and assets. Based on your desired level of interaction, select a tool that fits your needs, and prepare your files. Because prototypes can grow and change, it's important to maintain organization throughout the process. Here are four types of prototypes you might build:

Paper Prototype

Because paper prototypes are easy to create and cheap to discard, they are useful in the early stages of the design process when you're rapidly testing and iterating on the design. Depending on what you're testing, your paper prototype could range anywhere from sketches to printed designs.

Paper prototypes can be helpful in conjunction with participatory design and can help you to discover not only what a user thinks of an interface but also how they might use it. While they are useful in gathering high-level feedback, paper prototypes are usually too low fidelity to be relied upon for user validation—unless of course the final product you're designing is made of paper!

Simulation Prototype

A simulation is a type of prototype that provides a closer-to-real-world experience to the user. Depending on its type and fidelity, simulation prototypes can also be cheap to create and easily iterated upon. A chat or voice interface might be simulated by having the user speak to an actual person with a script; a physical product might be 3-D printed to see how it looks on the shelf or how it feels in the user's hand; and a click-through prototype with high-fidelity screens and realistic transitions but no back end could represent an app.

Simulation prototypes are useful for getting feedback for how an experience looks and feels, for understanding how a user might engage with an experience, and for testing usability. Because simulation prototypes can require more effort, the hypotheses being tested often need to be more mature.

Proof of Concept

A proof-of-concept prototype focuses less on the fidelity of the experience and more on proving that the technology supporting the experience is viable. A proof of concept can also test whether users can use a thing as well as if they actually will use a thing—rather than if they enjoy using it. For example, if a company wants to see if users will spend more money if they can do it automatically with a wearable bracelet, they could equip users with proof-of-concept prototypes.

Proof-of-concept prototypes are often necessary in the product-development process, but they are not always used to learn from users. They require the input of developers and/or engineers and often require significant time and effort to develop. This type of prototype is rarely executed on a whim.

Production Prototype

A production prototype requires the most effort of all of the prototypes because it uses actual code or materials for the prototype. With code, there is the added benefit of potentially reusing the code. With physical products, manufacturing techniques can be perfected through iteration. Production prototypes are the most reliable for usability testing and can also help the design team understand whether their design is possible. They might even help to highlight the challenges of scaling.

Production prototypes often occur late in the process; require the support of developers, engineers, and manufacturers; and are used to test more detailed hypotheses. Despite many teams' discomfort with creating high-fidelity prototypes that might just be thrown away, this level of prototype can be more useful than others when understanding user behaviors, since it's something that users can take away from the testing context and use in real life.

As you build your prototype, test it. Ask team members to test it. If you can break your prototype, it's likely that stakeholders and users will also be able to break the prototype. If you're also creating detailed design and flow diagrams, make sure that the findings from prototyping are integrated into that documentation.

> *"If a picture is worth a thousand words, a prototype is worth a thousand meetings."*
>
> A saying at IDEO

Artifacts

Depending on how your project is structured, you might end up with one large prototype or many small prototypes. Make sure that you keep prototypes organized by their functionality and that you always know which prototype is the most recent. Keeping separate notes files can be useful for remembering goals and limitations when walking stakeholders or users through prototypes. If prototypes are used with any sort of user validation, you might also make sure that summary documents link to prototypes in case stakeholders have any questions.

CityBike uses a simulation prototype to validate the design with users. The prototype encompasses a subset of the app experience, ensuring that the user can navigate the experience to perform a key selection of activities.

Ambience Mirror uses multiple prototypes. A proof-of-concept prototype (not shown) is maintained throughout to confirm that all designs and integrations are possible. The mirror also relies on a simulation prototype for user validation, with a designer using a script to react to users' voice commands.

CityBike / **Connected Bicycle**

Prototype

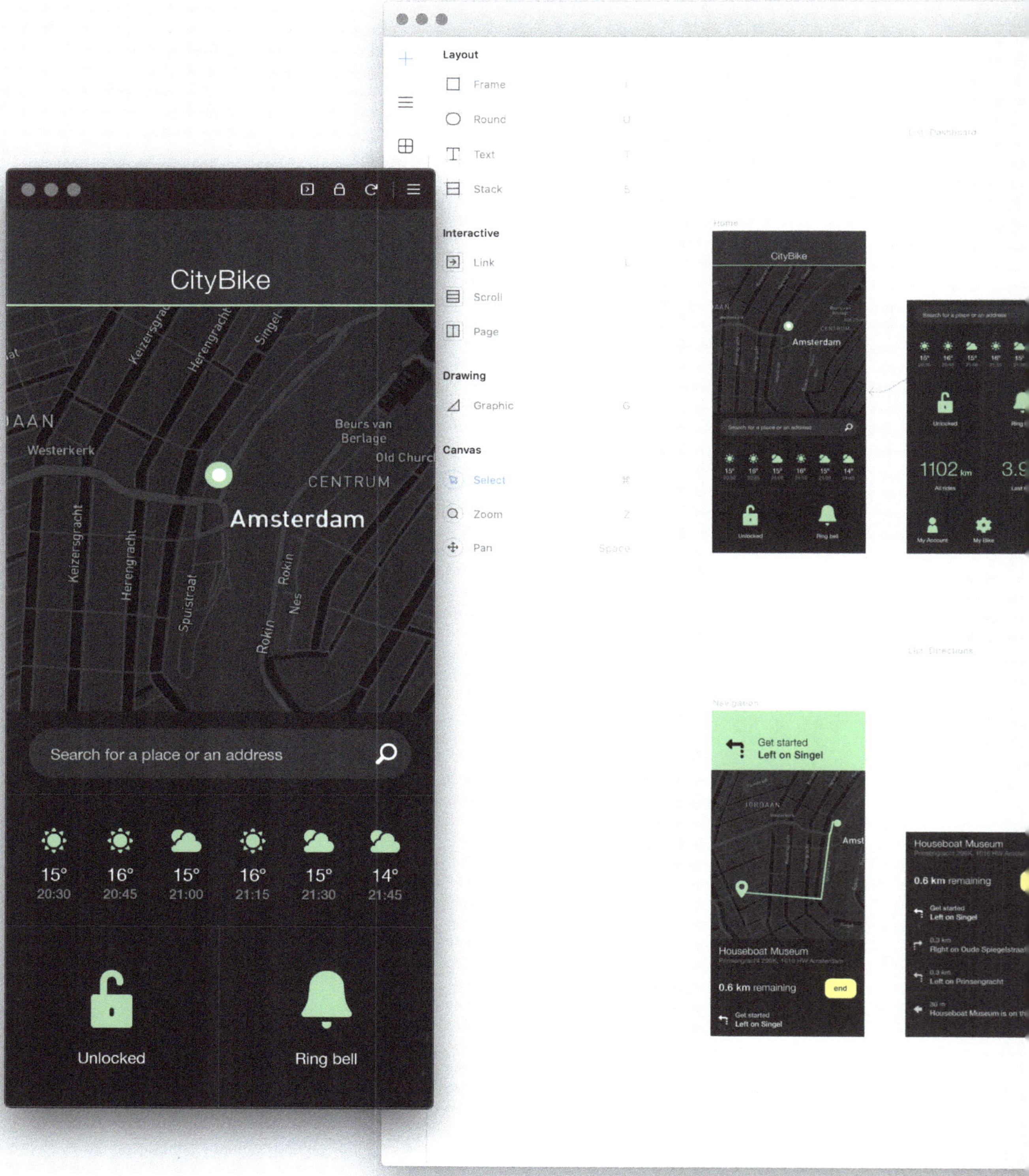

Used with the permission of Framer B.V.

prototype.framerx
Layout
Device
Apple iPhone XS
Orientation
Position
1050
0
Width
375
Fixed
Height
812
Fixed
Overflow
Hide
Opacity
100%
Rotation
0°
Radius
0
Link
Override
Fill
100%
Border
Shadows
Inner Shadows
Blur
Filters
CityBike
Anne Frank House
Houseboat Museum
Amsterdam Museum
Stedelijk Museum
MOCO
Rijksmuseum
Tulip Museum
Foam Fotografiemuseum
space
search
Amsterdam
Efficient Route
Scenic Route
go
Ride Statistics
1102 km
24.6 km/h
14.6 km/h
3.9 km
21.2 km/h
15.1 km/h
Today
Share Ride
Delete Ride
Resume
End Route

Prototype

Input and Response Test Script

Task: Take a few minutes to explore the different topics available to you via the Ambience Mirror: **weather**, **daily overview**, **calendar**, **social notifications**, and **data and statistics**.

Keywords: *weather, temperature, sun, rain, storm, umbrella, air, air quality, wind, thunder, snow, warm, cold, hot, freezing*

Weather

Hello <Name>

It's 64° and air quality is good.

Light rain is expected throughout the day.

Keywords: *my day, calendar, event, schedule, agenda, what's happening today, diary, meeting*

Calendar

Hello <Name>

You have 6 events today.

The first one is from 9:00–10:30 AM.

- calendar visualization

Keywords: *today, overview, information, summary, headlines*

Summary

Hello <Name>

You have a busy day ahead of you, but you're ready for it!

- hydration summary
- sickness summary
- event summary
- email summary

Keywords: *social, notifications, Twitter, Facebook, email, social network, friend, conversation, message*

Social

Hello <Name>

You have 21 notifications.

6 are from the past 8 hours.

- email
- Twitter

Keywords: *stat, data, chart, graph, visualization, statistic, step, workout, heart rate, weight*

Stats

Hello <Name>

Nice run this morning!

You were even faster than usual.

- run summary
- weight
- heart rate
- steps

Task: Modify what you see in the **“Data and Statistics”** view. Add a **sleep chart** and remove the **weight chart**.

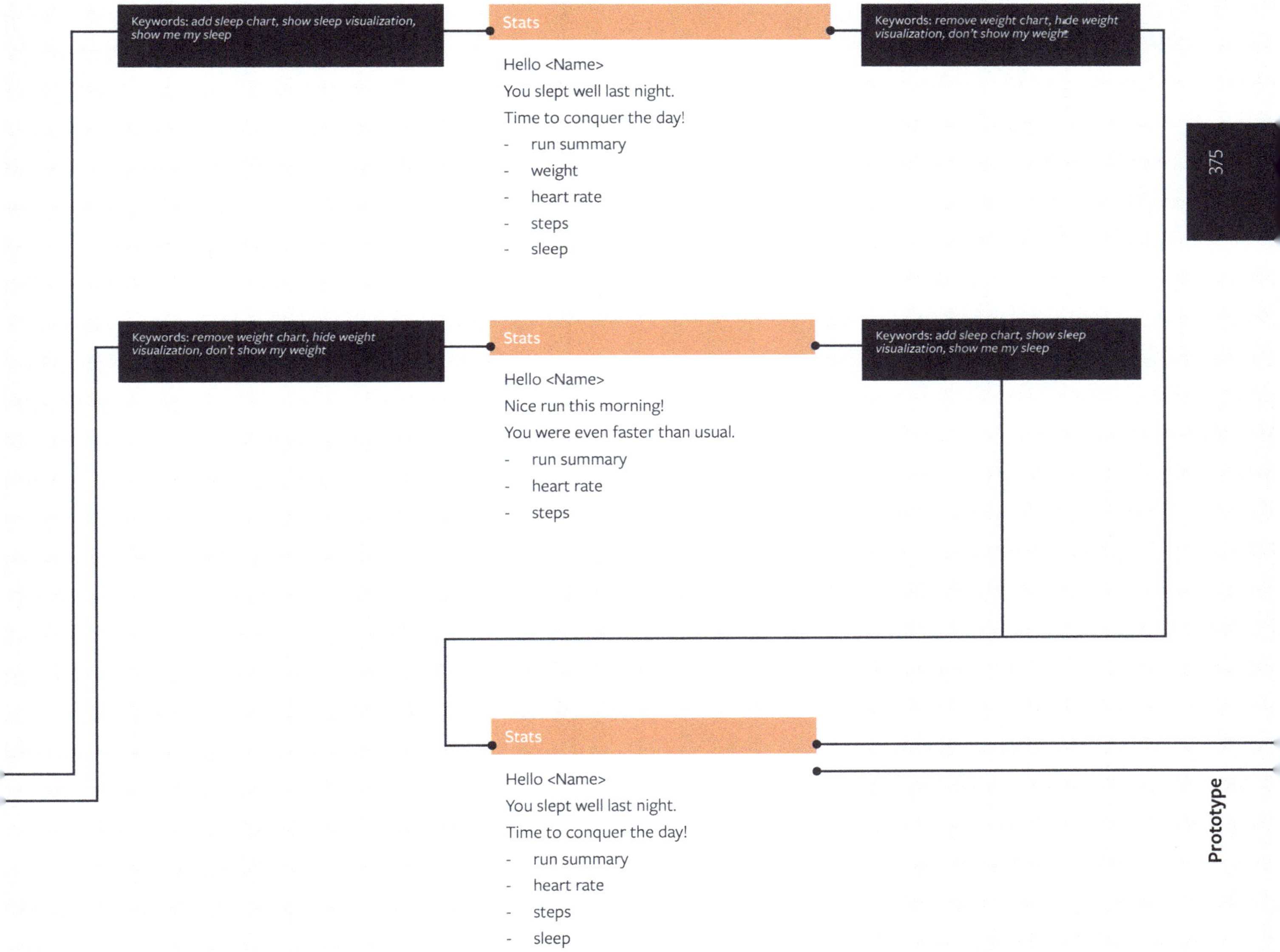

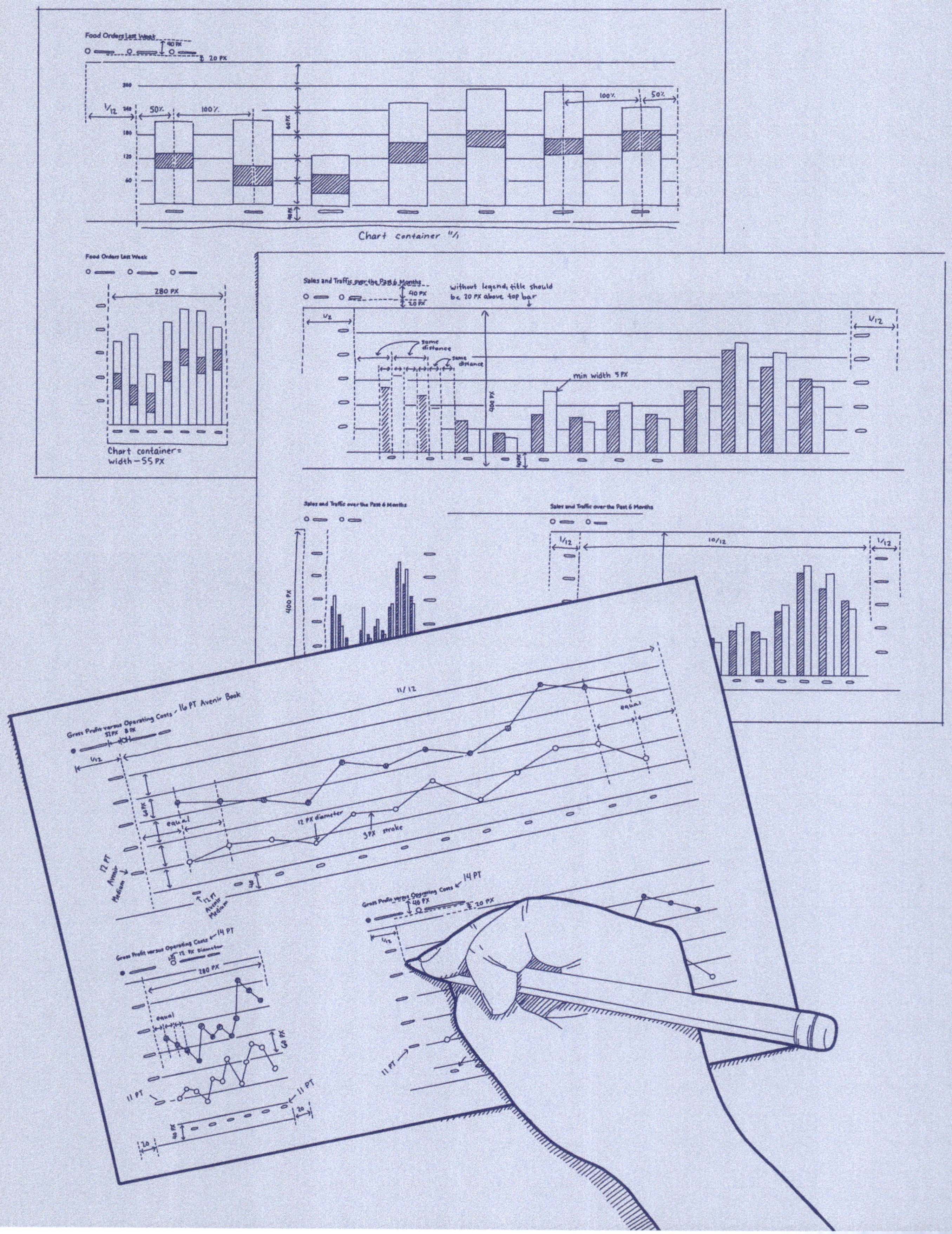
Food Orders Last Week
40 PX
20 PX
1/12
50%
100%
Chart container
Food Orders Last Week
280 PX
Chart container=
width−55 PX
Sales and Traffic over the Past 6 Months
40 PX
20 PX
without legend, title should
be 20 PX above top bar
1/12
same
distance
min width 5 PX
400 PX
Sales and Traffic over the Past 6 Months
400 PX
Sales and Traffic over the Past 6 Months
1/12
10/12
1/12
Gross Profit versus Operating Costs / 16 PT Avenir Book
11/12
equal
equal
12 PX diameter
3 PX stroke
12 PT
Avenir
Medium
Gross Profit versus Operating Costs 14 PT
20 PX
Gross Profit versus Operating Costs 14 PT
280 PX
equal
11 PT
11 PT
20
20
11 PT

Detailed Documentation

Communication is critical to seeing intentions preserved as designs are built into functioning products and services. Even with strong processes that have the design team communicating directly with developers, engineers, and manufacturers, decisions can easily slip through the cracks. Detailed documentation seeks to mitigate the risks of both good and bad communication by capturing the specifics about how a product or service should be built. This might include details around the dimensions, relationships, behaviors, and transitions of a design. Typically the less face-to-face communication a team has, the more detailed documentation will be required.

Detailed documentation has benefits aside from the documentation itself. It can help designers think through how the design will scale and adapt to different screens and scenarios. Even if the documentation itself is not required for the project, thinking through the questions a developer might have, the constraints an engineer might encounter, or how you would communicate requirements to a manufacturer will likely make the design stronger and more foolproof.

Activities

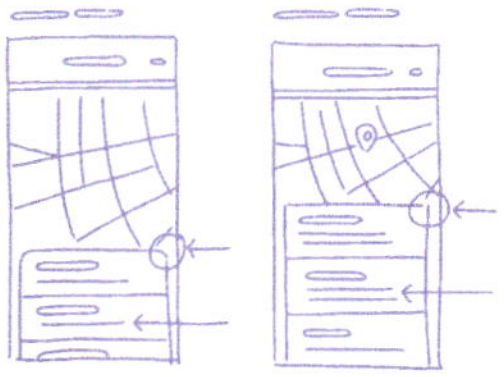

Check for consistency as you document the details.

Especially when designing large, complex experiences, specifying every detail can be tedious. Efficiency can be achieved by approaching specification in multiple layers. These layers will be somewhat familiar if you already created a component library.

First, inventory the foundational ingredients of your design such as colors, typography, and iconography. Check for consistency as you go. Next, look for elements of your design that appear more than once throughout the product or service. These may include controls like switches and fields or components like charts and content cards. Consider how these elements scale when there's no content versus too much content. While their appearances may be variable, items that adhere to a common layout with consistent behaviors only need to be specified once.

For digital experiences, inventory the different layouts or templates in your system. Maybe there are pages containing text, pages containing a combination of visual content and text, pages with forms, and pages with galleries of images. You only need to specify each template once so long as only the content changes.

Many tools will automatically generate detailed documentation using a similar breakdown of symbols and screens. While automation makes for easy production, it might be less efficient for consumption depending on the types of layouts you're designing. Check your work to make sure that elements are specified the same everywhere and that considerations like multiple screen sizes have been accommodated.

Whichever method you choose, work closely with your implementers to make sure that the format and approach of your documentation makes sense. Aligning on a small number of early specifications can be helpful so that you understand how much work detailing out the rest of the design will be. Perhaps most importantly, always check your work or have someone else check your work. Mistakes that are easily made in documentation are often much more difficult to correct once they've been built.

The Dangers of Duplication

If your project contains both design guidelines and design documentation, it's likely that some of the elements will be repeated in both. Avoid duplication. Maintaining two sets of documentation not only creates more work, but it also increases the risk of inconsistencies.

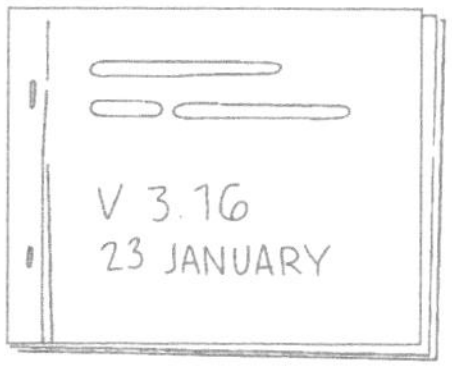

Use version numbers and dates to make sure nobody is using an old set of documentation.

Artifacts

Detailed documentation should aggregate all of the specifications from your product or service in one place, either online or in a document. The more complex the design, the more organization your documentation will need. Make sure to have a clear overarching structure and use naming conventions and consistent terminology so that implementers can search for specific terms and references within your document. When necessary, add links to relevant information. For example, if you reference a component when specifying a layout, link back to that component.

Be both internally and externally consistent in your documentation. Provide measurements appropriate to the platform that the experience is being developed upon, and work closely with the implementation team to ensure accuracy. When something specified in the detailed documentation changes as it is implemented, update the documentation. As you iterate, make sure that each version of the documentation is clearly marked with the date, the version number, or both. This will help your implementation team know which version to use and to ask if their version gets too out of date.

> “*The difference between the almost right word and the right word is really a large matter—’tis the difference between the lightning-bug and the lightning.*”
>
> **Mark Twain**

Samples from the detailed documentation for Observations Suite show how charts and content cards should be built to scale to multiple screen sizes using a combination of absolute values and proportions.

Omniscient / **Observations Suite Web App**

Detailed Documentation

Comparative Bar Chart (not mobile)

Title

Chart titles can wrap up to two lines.
They use the "Chart Title" style in Black.

Y-Axis Labels

A chart may have one or two y-axis labels. Label area is 1/12 the total width of the chart, with the remaining width left for the visualization.

Visualizations always use five Y-axis labels, dynamically generated based on the data set.

Axis labels use the "Chart Label" style in Black.

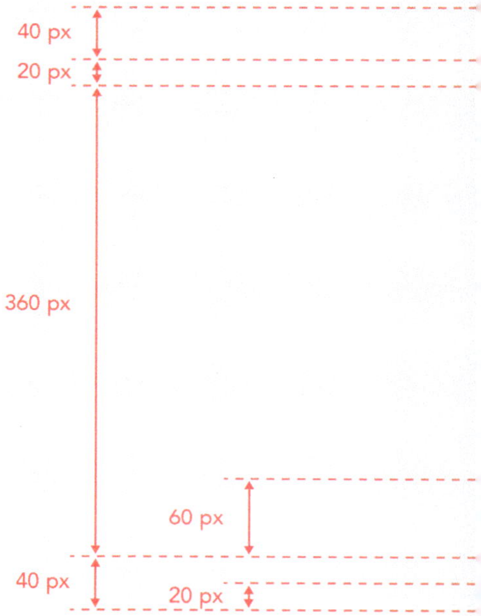

Legend

Only for charts visualizing multiple data sets, the legend adds 40 px. to the height of the chart.

Legend color dots have a 12 px. diameter. It's 8 px. from the color dot to the text, and 30 px. between items.

Typography is "Chart Legend" style in Black.

Visualizations

Visualizations should use Turquoise, then Yellow, and then Neutral palettes for visualizing multiple data types. They should not visualize more than three types of data.

Horizontal dividing lines are 1 px. solid Light Gray.

Bars are 80% opacity. Turquoise bars are Dark Turquoise at the top and Turquoise at the bottom.

Daffodil bars are Dark Daffodil at the top and Daffodil at the bottom.

Neutral bars are Darkest Gray at the top and Dark Gray at the bottom.

See Also

Line Charts >

Stacked Bar Charts >

Scatterplot Charts >

Mobile Translations >

100% of 12-column canvas grid
Sales and Traffic
Traffic
Sales
20 px
20 px
13.5 k
10.8 k
8.1 k
5.4 k
2.7 k
$240 k
$192 k
$144 k
$96 k
$48 k
evenly divided
Aug
Sep
Oct
Nov
Dec
Jan
Feb
Mar
Apr
May
Jun
Jul
evenly divided
1/12
10/12 total width
1/12

Reservation Card

Unassigned

Assigned, Upcoming (within 1 hour)

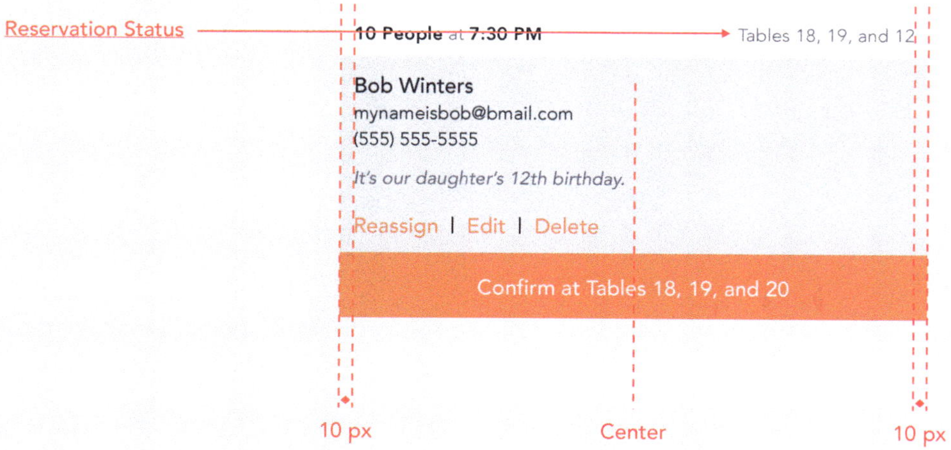

Assigned, Not Upcoming

Additional Details

Names are limited to one line before being truncated with an ellipsis.

Email and phone number are optional. Without name and phone number, distance to notes is 15 px. If there are no notes, distance to buttons is 20 px.

Notes can wrap up to four lines before being truncated with an ellipsis. If there are no notes, the distance between reservation information and text buttons is 20 px.

Cards are stacked vertically with 10 px. between them.

See Also

Restaurant Layout >

Text Buttons >

Notification Cards >

Overview
Overview
Overview
Overview
Overview
- alert dot is too far right
- search field has bad margins
- text for summary intro is WAY TOO big
- chart legend items have wrong spacing
- navigation button is
Safari UI;

Design Assurance

The process of bringing a product or service to market is long and iterative, and it's not uncommon for the design team to disengage before it's complete. Often the design team will move on to other projects after delivering documentation to a team of manufacturers or developers. When new constraints and opportunities arise, the team responsible for implementation makes decisions that were left to the design team before, often losing sight of the original intention.

Design assurance seeks to mitigate the risks of compromise by continuing to involve design throughout production. By providing a process with regular reviews and open channels of conversation, design assurance provides consistency when new opportunities are considered, when new constraints arise, and when existing designs need to be extended for new circumstances. It also ensures that what gets built matches the intention of the design team, not just the documentation.

Activities

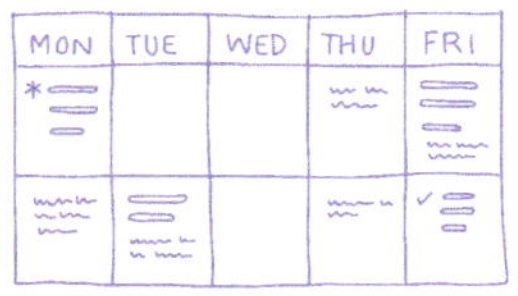

Make room in the development schedule for design assurance.

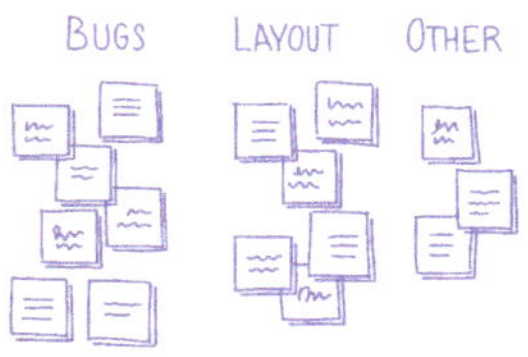

Review each iteration of the product or service, and gather feedback from the team.

Design assurance sets aside time in the implementation process for designers to engage with developers and manufacturers to ensure the quality of what's being built. This process is an iterative one, where first the team building the experience or feature takes a proposed solution and tries to build it. Along the way, they will likely uncover new constraints and considerations that affect how the design gets implemented. Here, the design team can offer support by reconsidering the solution and providing a more appropriate one.

Once built, the product or service is reviewed by the design team to ensure that it is faithful to the original intention. This might be kicked off with developers and engineers formally sharing what they've done, along with any known outstanding issues. This provides an opportunity for designers to ask questions before taking the build and comparing it to artifacts like detailed design and documentation. If there are issues, the execution needs to be revisited. If not, it's considered done, and the team can move on to the next iteration.

Especially for digital products and services, the process of implementation is likely to be broken into smaller pieces. For the design team, this provides an extra challenge, as adjusting the design for a problem in one part of the experience is likely to affect other parts of the experience, even those previously thought to be finished. Working alongside the development team in sprints also requires significant flexibility. It's likely that some weeks will require significant work and others minimal effort. A design backlog can be useful to avoid allowing quick fixes to pass for long-term solutions and for giving the design team a list of things to work on in less busy sprints.

> *"When I am working on a problem, I never think about beauty . . . but when I have finished, if the solution is not beautiful, I know it is wrong."*
>
> **Buckminster Fuller**

Because working with the development team often means working on their schedule, it's important to make sure that design assurance is considered from the start. The design team should be consistent in how they approach design assurance, keeping a checklist of their own or contributing to the development team's definition of done to ensure that the product or service meets the same standard throughout iterations. Make sure that there is time for the design team to receive and react to input, to review the execution, and to provide feedback. Agree on tools before beginning, and make sure that the design team can effectively use those tools to provide input to the development process.

It can also be helpful to have regular points to reflect on how the process is going and to adjust where necessary. If your team doesn't already have a formal process around this, try gathering team members into a room and asking everyone to write down what they thought went well and what could be improved. Stay focused on process and communication, as these are areas that can be improved. You might have a facilitator writing down everyone's thoughts, or you might have individuals place their notes on Post-its on a whiteboard. Someone from outside the project should facilitate a conversation around how to improve for next time.

Artifacts

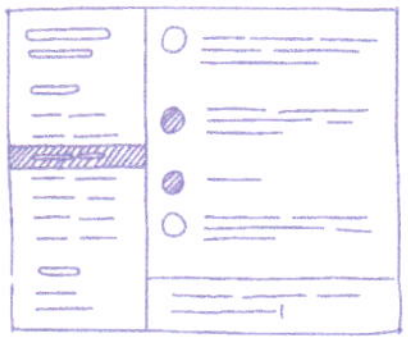

Design assurance may result in a lot of communication rather than an artifact.

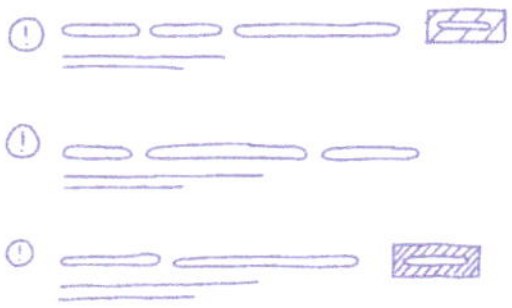

Developer tools can be useful for capturing and communicating feedback.

The most important artifact produced during design assurance is the communication that goes back and forth between the teams involved. In cases where teams are working closely with each other, this may not amount to an artifact at all. You might end up with little more than a series of bug reports, design versions, and email conversations, all supporting the most important artifact—the product or service.

In teams that don't have a close working relationship or that aren't colocated, you may end up with more meetings for sharing progress and providing feedback. If this is the case, then design assurance may be shared in a presentation highlighting where the implementation deviates from the original intention.

In addition to the regular back-and-forth between designers and developers or manufacturers, it can also be helpful to keep a log that captures the intentions and thinking behind decisions. Organized by screens or by features, the decision log might exist as part of the design guidelines or on a team wiki, ideally in a place that's both version controlled and accessible to all members of the team.

Once per sprint, the Observations Suite development team sits with the design team to review the build. The design team then focuses on the relevant features, providing detailed feedback to the development team about misalignments.

Omniscient / **Observations Suite Web App**

Design Assurance

Mobile Safari

.Overview

Design

Screenshot

Alert dot should be 5 px. from end of title text box.

Chevron icon should be 4 px. up from title text baseline.

Search box should have 20 px. margin above and 25 px. margin below.

Text should be 20 pt. with 26 pt. line height.

Legend items should have 30 px. between them.

Navigation button should be 20 px. from bottom of visible page.

.Overview_Navigation

Design

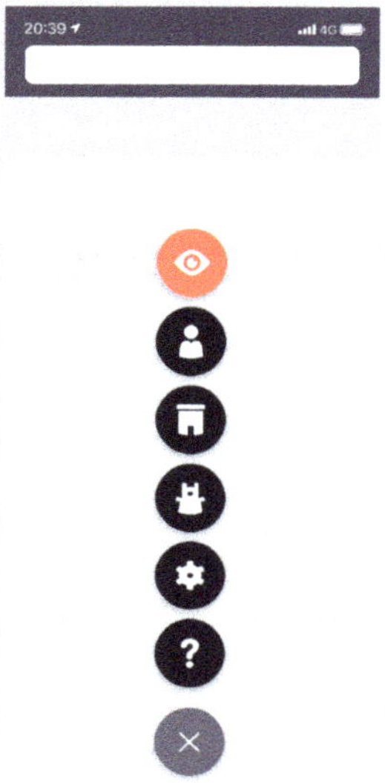

Screenshot

Buttons should have a drop shadow with a 2 px. *y* offset, 4 px. blur, and 30% opacity.

Navigation buttons and close button should have 20 px. margin between them.

Close navigation button should be 20 px. from bottom of visible page.

.Overview_Notifications

Design

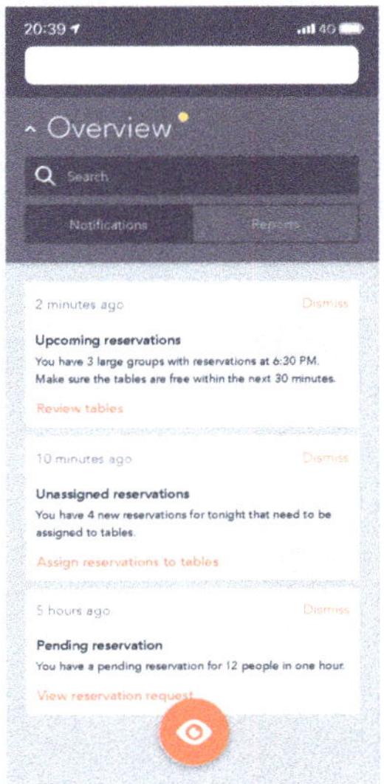

Screenshot

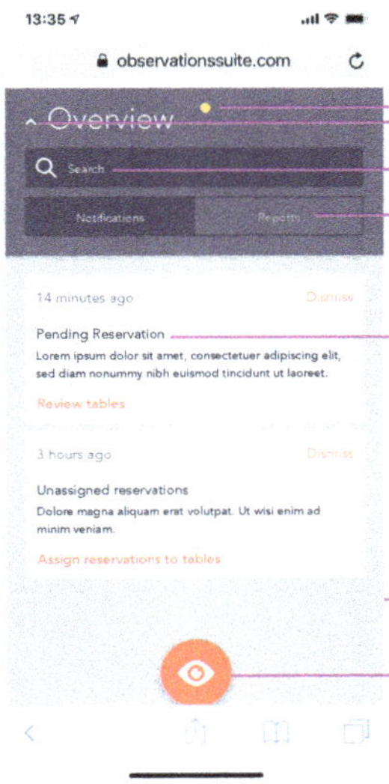

Alert dot should be 5 px. from end of title text box.

Chevron icon should be 4 px. up from title text baseline.

Text should be 14 pt.

Text should be medium weight.

Capitalization should be sentence case.

Background should be #D0CED5.

Navigation button should be 20 px. from bottom of visible page.

.Overview_Notifications_Empty

Design

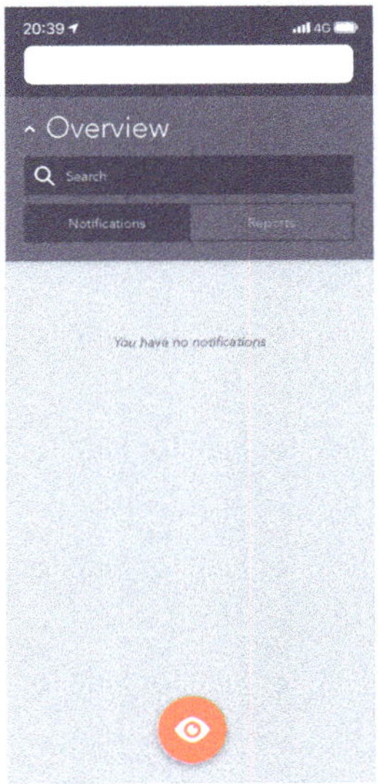

Screenshot

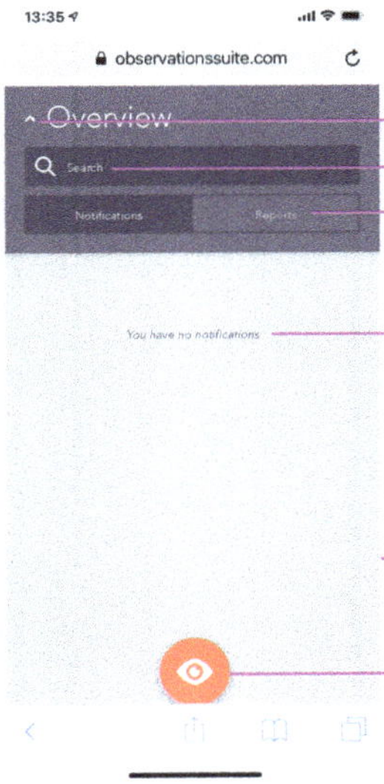

Chevron icon should be 4 px. up from title text baseline.

Text should be 14 pt.

Text should be 14 pt.

Background should be #D0CED5.

Navigation button should be 20 px. from bottom of visible page.

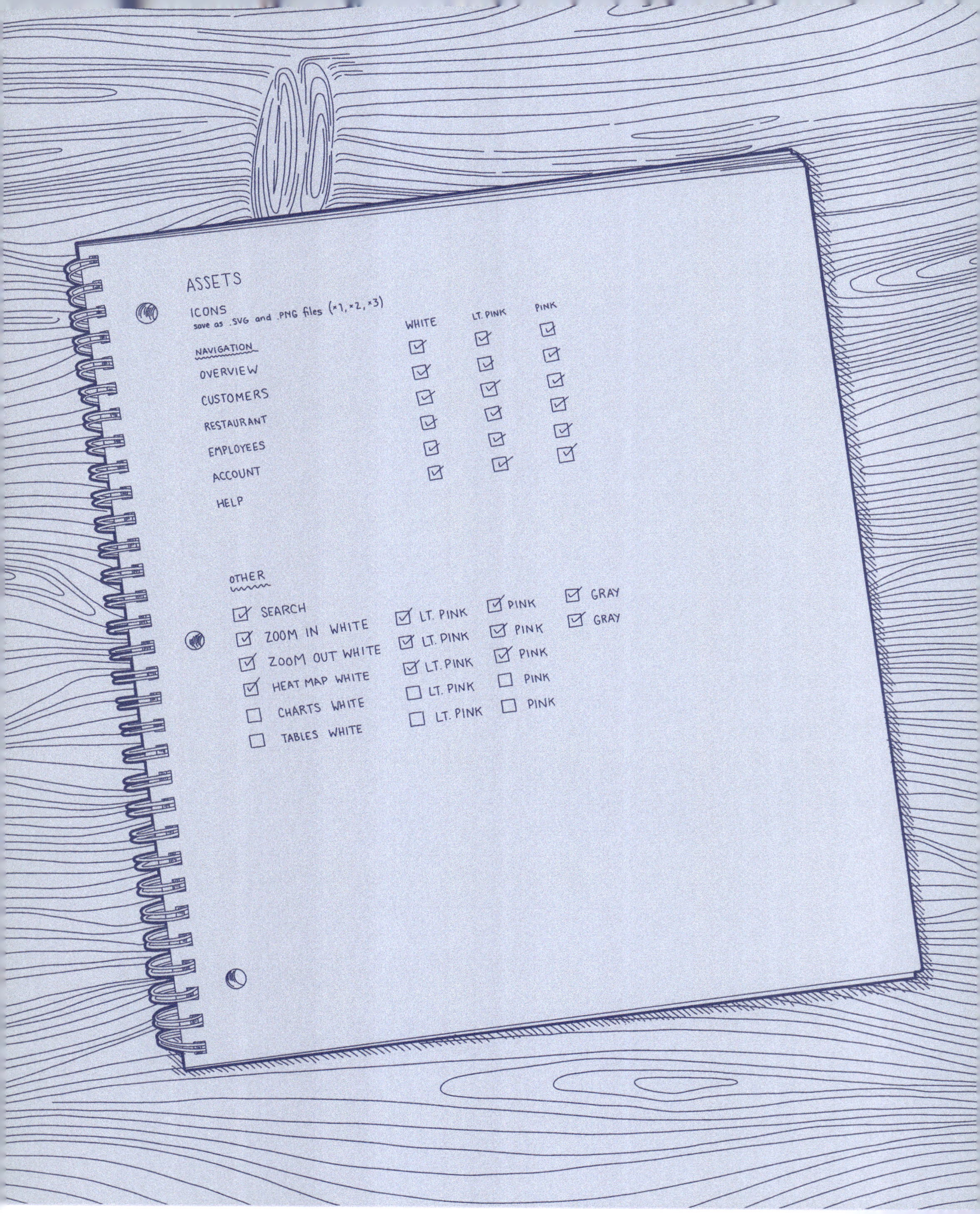
ASSETS
ICONS
save as .SVG and .PNG files (×1, ×2, ×3)
WHITE
LT. PINK
PINK
NAVIGATION
OVERVIEW
CUSTOMERS
RESTAURANT
EMPLOYEES
ACCOUNT
HELP
OTHER
SEARCH
ZOOM IN WHITE
ZOOM OUT WHITE
HEAT MAP WHITE
CHARTS WHITE
TABLES WHITE
LT. PINK
LT. PINK
LT. PINK
LT. PINK
LT. PINK
PINK
PINK
PINK
PINK
PINK
GRAY
GRAY

Assets

Assets are used in the production of a product or service. Format, fidelity, and quantity will change depending on the experience you're designing for. A physical experience will likely need one set of assets, while a digital experience will need many. Before diving into asset production, it's best to understand from developers, printers, and manufacturers what assets are necessary and how they should be delivered.

Even if you're not the designer creating assets, it's important to have an understanding of what parts of the design need to be assets as well as how formats can affect the final product. With this knowledge, you can better ensure the quality of the design throughout the production process.

Activities

Start by talking to developers to know what assets and formats they need.

The process of creating assets should always include enough time to check the design to ensure that it meets all of the requirements for production. Avoid the risk of making assumptions by talking to whoever will be using your assets. Then consider what's already been created by the design team. Does it use the right color space, or is it designed with the available inks in mind? Is it designed to accommodate the constraints of the process? Do the components consider and encompass all possible states? Assets often require some optimization before they're ready to be delivered and implemented.

Start by creating asset files in an organized way. Select the appropriate color space. If you're designing an experience that spans touchpoint and color spaces, create a separate file for each and label them accordingly. Digital assets will typically use the RGB (red, green, blue) color space and print assets the CMYK (cyan, magenta, yellow, black) color space. Some printers might use different inks, so confirming the technique before producing assets can save time later. For assets that are silk-screened or pad printed onto products, you'll need to create assets with specific spot colors, from systems such as Pantone or Toyo.

Next, start pulling in assets. If you created a component library, start by pulling elements like icons, illustrations, and logos into your assets file. If you didn't create a component library, review mock-ups and detailed designs to find these elements for your assets file.

Review each asset as you add it to the file. Make sure that minimum sizes and tolerances are respected. Ensure that assets not delivered in vector format have a high-enough resolution. For certain printing processes, your assets may need to accommodate multiple layers of printing to ensure that the design can withstand a slight offset. Get proofs before diving into production to ensure that you understand the constraints of the process.

While assets for physical products are usually straightforward, digital experiences often require more variation. An asset for a click interface or a remote interface will need regular, hover, and pressed states, while assets for touch interfaces will need only regular and pressed states. High-resolution displays and print media need higher-resolution assets, and most nonphoto assets can be done with vector rather than raster graphics to ensure fidelity at all scales. Some things that seem like assets, such as button shapes, can even be drawn using code rather than produced with design tools. In most cases, using code to generate forms is preferable, so work with developers to know their capabilities.

Before exporting and delivering assets, make sure that they are appropriately named. Every medium and platform has its own requirements in terms of both file format and naming conventions. Check with developers, printers, and manufacturers to understand the best way to deliver assets. If there is any ambiguity, it can be useful to do a process test run with assets and documentation to work out any issues before diving into full production or development.

Artifacts

Assets should be exported in the appropriate formats from whatever tool you're working in, organized into files, and then delivered to the implementation team or company. Make sure to communicate with development teams to ensure that what you deliver matches their workflow. Other artifacts such as detailed documentation might provide guidance by referencing which assets to implement where and how. If you're working on a project whose process will be repeated, consider creating process documentation for everyone to follow.

Observations Suite needs very few assets, and the ones needed are primarily for icons. Assets were created and exported in formats for both modern and legacy browsers.

Omniscient / **Observations Suite Web App**

Assets

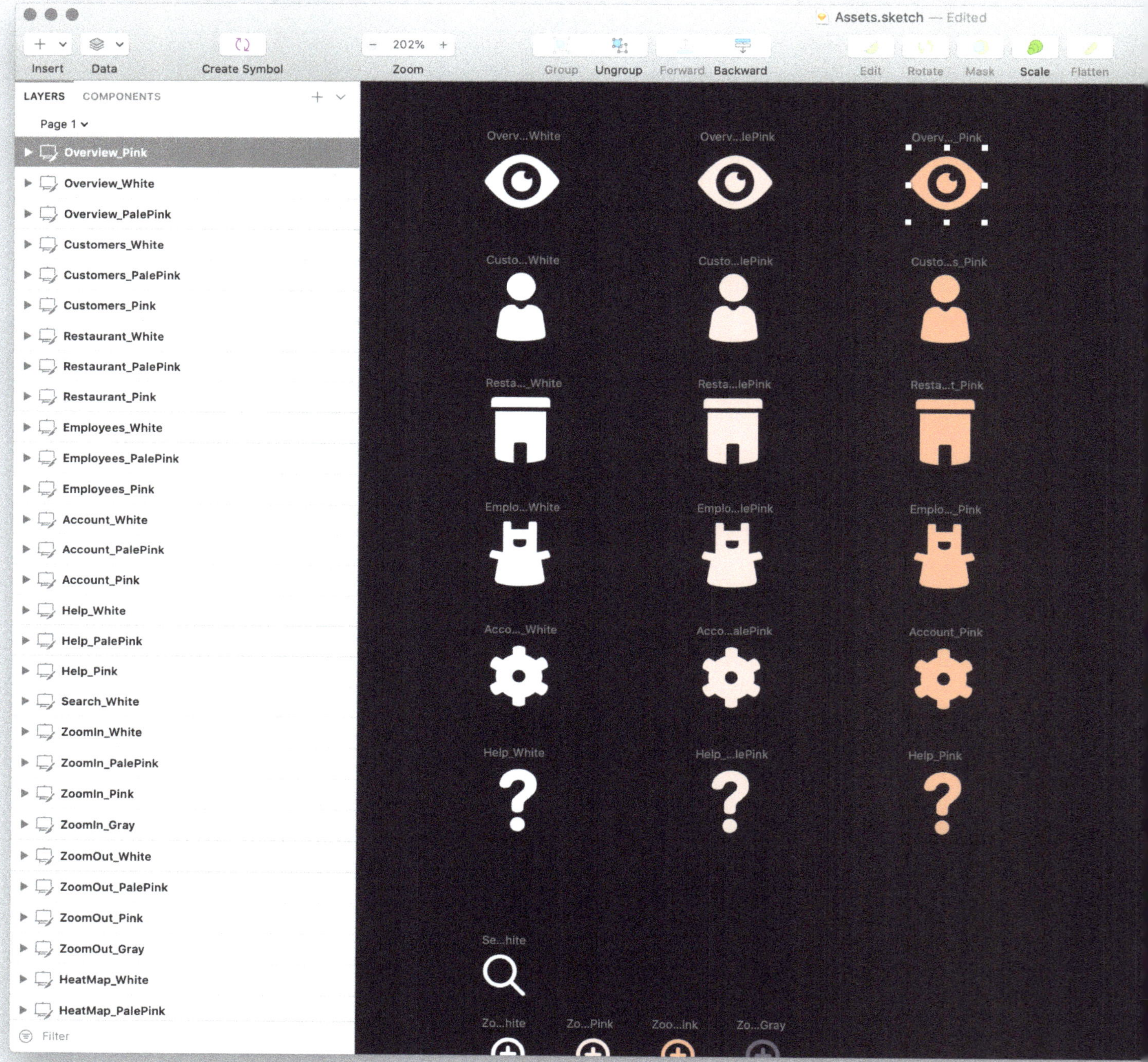

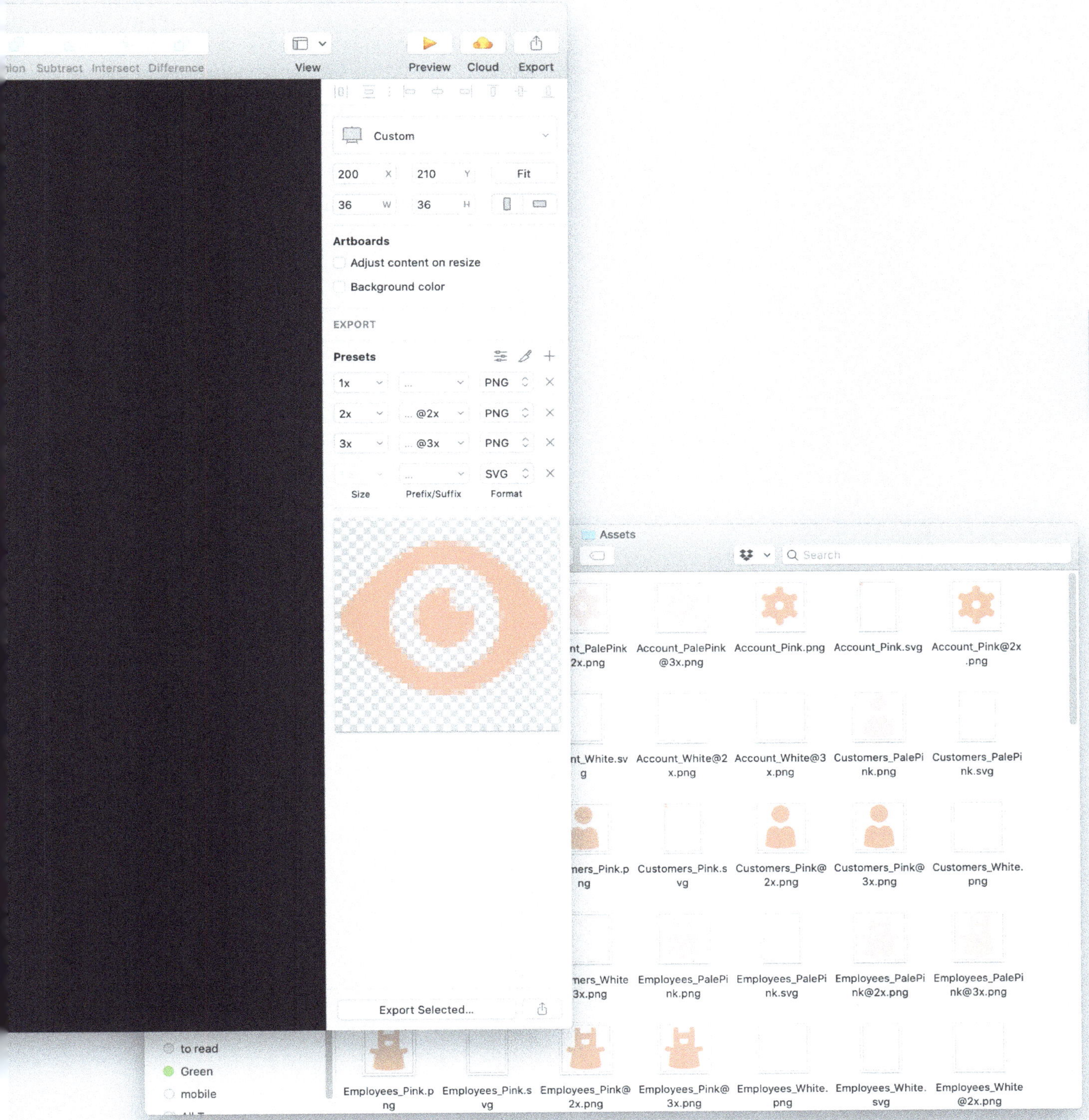

Subtract Intersect Difference
View
Preview
Cloud
Export
Custom
200 X
210 Y
Fit
36 W
36 H
Artboards
Adjust content on resize
Background color
EXPORT
Presets
1x ... PNG
2x ... @2x PNG
3x ... @3x PNG
... SVG
Size
Prefix/Suffix
Format
Export Selected...
Assets
Search
Account_PalePink@3x.png
Account_Pink.png
Account_Pink.svg
Account_Pink@2x.png
Account_White@2x.png
Account_White@3x.png
Customers_PalePink.png
Customers_PalePink.svg
Customers_Pink.svg
Customers_Pink@2x.png
Customers_Pink@3x.png
Customers_White.png
Employees_PalePink.png
Employees_PalePink.svg
Employees_PalePink@2x.png
Employees_PalePink@3x.png
Employees_Pink.png
Employees_Pink.svg
Employees_Pink@2x.png
Employees_Pink@3x.png
Employees_White.png
Employees_White.svg
Employees_White@2x.png
to read
Green
mobile

Raven
Unlocked
Autolock On
on
Bike Screen
Screen Backlight Auto
ding
Short Bell
215 km
Front Tire Wear

User Validation

User validation can be broken into two equally valuable buckets. The more formal ergonomics and usability testing seek to ensure that a design and execution are comfortable and intuitive to users. Less formally, a walk-through with users might seek to gather their feelings and thoughts as they experience a product or service. While usability testing might reveal that low-contrast buttons are affecting a user's ability to complete a goal, less quantitative approaches could reveal that users feel a color palette is too institutional for an in-home experience.

Because users don't have a stake in the product's success, they provide fresh perspectives and insights. When user validation is conducted before a product's launch, the input can help to prioritize features, refine executions, and create an experience with broader appeal. Perhaps most importantly, it mitigates the risk of shipping a product or service with embarrassing mistakes or oversights. By regularly integrating user validation into the design and implementation processes, a team ensures fewer surprises and dramatic changes in direction.

Activities

See how users perform specific tasks with facilitated testing.

Wizard of Oz testing simulates interaction with a human or artificial intelligence.

Get feedback from users in their natural context with in-home tests.

In order to do effective validation with users, you'll want to start by recruiting people who match your target audience. It's obvious that if you've designed a Spanish-speaking service, you'll want to recruit Spanish speakers, or if you've designed an app for soon-to-be mothers, you should recruit pregnant women. Similarly, if you're designing a product for commuter cyclists who can afford high-end bicycles, you'll want to make sure that you're using those specific people for validation. If your project has personas and marketing segments, consider using these as a starting point for the recruiting brief. While a few outliers might provide interesting, or possibly even inspiring, results, they won't provide an accurate picture of what to expect when you ship the experience.

You'll also need to decide what you're testing. If you want feedback about a specific aspect of the experience, optimize the test for that. You might have a prototype that requires facilitator support, or you might have a high-fidelity model or build that your users can take home and live with. The more fidelity and context you provide to users, the more meaningful the results will be. While what you are able to test depends mostly on what you are able to build, there are some clever techniques you can use to increase the fidelity of the experience without necessarily increasing the fidelity of the product or service.

Facilitated Testing Session

Facilitated testing sessions are useful when you have a prototype with limited functionality. The evaluator asks the user to accomplish very specific goals and observes the user's behavior. Throughout the process, the user will often be asked to talk through what they are doing and what they expect. In a facilitated testing session, the evaluator might follow up with a short survey about the experience.

Wizard of Oz Test

The Wizard of Oz method, named after the character behind the curtain in the popular movie and book, is especially useful if you need to test a product or service where the user interacts with some sort of human or artificial intelligence. In this method, the user interacts with the experience and the experience reacts to the user. The reactions are performed by someone on the team, but this is not revealed to the user taking part in the test.

In-Home Test

An in-home test requires that you have a high-fidelity experience or part of the experience that users can take out of the lab and into their homes for days at a time. This could be the entire experience of riding a commuter bike through the city, or it could be the specific experience of navigation while riding. With in-home tests, it's common to ask users to keep and then share notes or a diary of their experiences and then to answer a short survey when the test is over.

Alpha and Beta Testing

Alpha and beta testing are done when the product is nearing launch. With these tests, users often get a free version or trial of the product or service you're building with the agreement to provide feedback on their experience. If you have an existing product or service, alpha and beta testing can be used with a subset of existing customers to validate upcoming iterations. Digital products especially can survive in the beta phase for years, as the process of learning and iterating is never really complete.

Interpreting results can be a challenge. Even in situations where design is not directly responsible for user validation, it's important for designers to be present to observe and interpret sessions. Seeing users succeed and struggle firsthand can help designers see opportunities that they wouldn't with only a report from a testing agency. It's also important to remember the fidelity of the experience tested. Consider what feedback is relevant to the future of

Beta programs get user feedback on an unfinished version of the product.

the product or service and what feedback is relevant only to the test experience.

User validation is likely something you'll want to do multiple times as you build your experience, and it's likely that the tests will get closer and closer to the actual experience of the product or service as you near shipping. While you don't need to predict the execution of each test at the beginning of the build phase, you should make sure that time and budget are set aside for testing at regular intervals throughout.

> *"After you've worked on a site for even a few weeks, you can't see it freshly anymore. You know too much. The only way to find out if it really works is to test it."*
>
> **Steve Krug**

Artifacts

The goal of user validation is to get a preview of what parts of an experience users will struggle with and what they will enjoy. The resulting report should focus on these outcomes. Start by summarizing what you did and what you hoped to learn. For stakeholders who aren't aware of the process, highlight any particulars of the test that provide context and confidence in the results.

When presenting findings, prioritize the goals of the test. For example, if you were looking to confirm that users could navigate using an app, avoid extraneous information about how users interacted with settings. Highlight the issues users had as well as which solutions were validated. For tests with larger participant groups, use numbers to quantify how well different aspects of the experience performed. For smaller groups, use quotes and photos to support findings.

The presentation should also provide recommendations and next steps to improve on poorly performing areas of the experience. Recommendations might be shown within the context of photos or screenshots, highlighting issues with the existing design solution. For small issues, describe or mock up recommendations. For larger issues requiring further iteration and testing, outline next steps to get approval to move forward. In situations where user-validation testing has results that require dramatic rework, photos, videos, and quotes can be powerful tools for persuading high-level stakeholders.

For every sprint, CityBike conducted facilitated walk-through sessions using a prototype of the app to ensure that it was intuitive even to new users. The report documents areas for improvement along with suggestions.

Ambience Mirror used the Wizard of Oz approach to provide users with a realistic experience. The report documents outcomes, providing confidence that the final product should focus on information over interaction.

Omniscient uses alpha and beta testing to continually test new builds of Observations Suite. Each release focuses on a specific set of features, and feedback is given via forums. A community manager works with design to review and consolidate recommendations for future releases.

User Validation

Objective: Input the destination and select a route

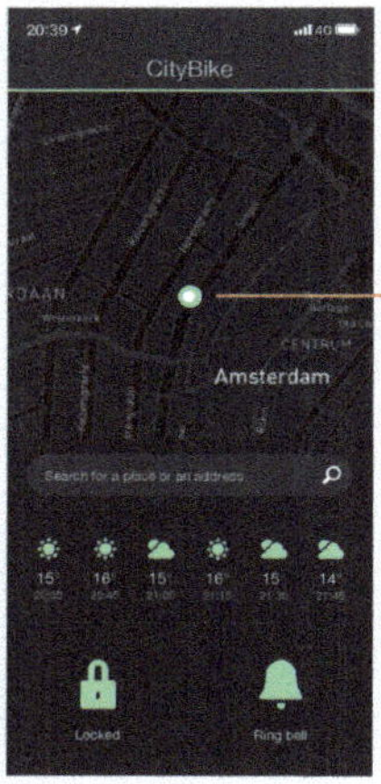

- Users weren't sure if the green dot was them or the bike.
  Try showing the user's location as well in this view.
- The address search was intuitive to all users.
- Many users commented on how useful the weather visualization was.
- One user mentioned that he would use the app just to check the weather!
- Half of the users didn't realize that they could scroll for more information.
  Try adding a peek of lower content to make this more obvious.

- One user mentioned wanting an easy way to clear all contents from the search field.
  Try replacing the "search" icon with an "x" seen on the next screen.
- Seventy-five percent of users tapped on the destination from this screen.

- Four users couldn't tell which was the starting point and which was the destination.
  Make the starting point more consistent with "current location" indicator from previous screens.
- Most users tried to switch routes.
- Two users complained that it wasn't obvious enough which route was selected.

Objective: Use directions to get to your destination

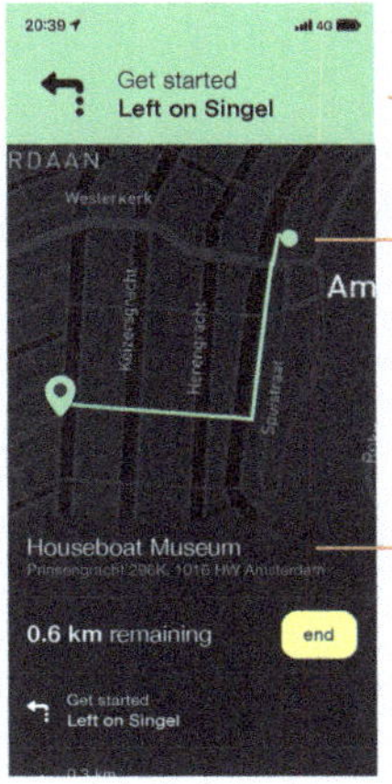

- One user suggested adding a way to minimize instructions without fully leaving the screen.
- Two users couldn't tell which dot was the current location and which was the destination.
- Many users had a diffiult time orienting at first.
  Try adding a point showing direction to the location dot.
- One user was frustrated that he couldn't change the route from this screen.
  Try adding a back button for the user to easily adjust his route.

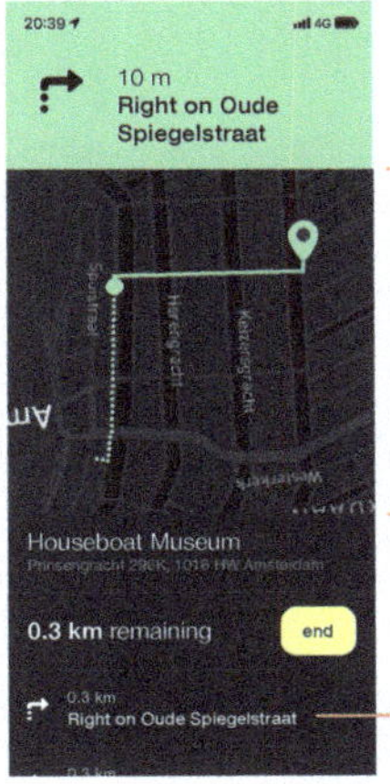

- Eight users were confused when the map rotated with their orientation.
- About half of users wanted a way to lock the map's orientation.
  Try adding a compass icon to show current direction and to lock direction (similar to other mapping tools).
- One user thought it was confusing to see nonupdating directions here.
- Two users wanted access to all of the directions, even after the trip had begun.

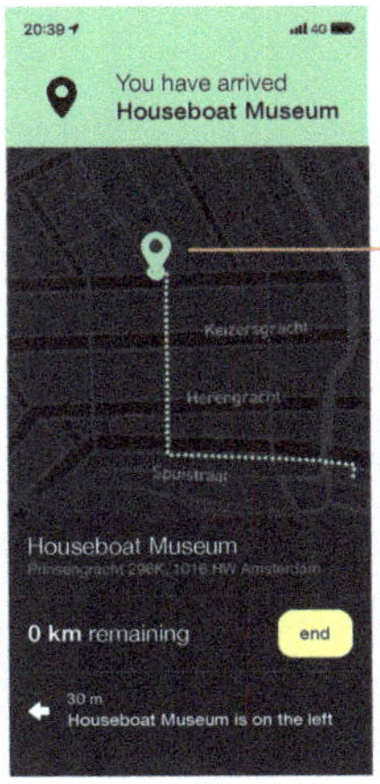

- Two users complained that it wasn't obvious enough when they'd reached their destination.
  Try changing color or adding an effect that shows when the user has reached their destination.
- Most users thought it was weird that they still needed to end directions after they'd reached their destination.
  Add a timeout after the user reaches their destination.

User Validation

Questions

How much interaction do users expect with a smart mirror?
What types of information do users want to interact with?

Approach

We tested the Ambience Mirror with forty-eight users. All users use or have used connected health products, and eighteen were existing Personal Intelligence or Ambience-product customers.

We gave users twenty minutes to use a mirror with a display behind, faking different visual and audio responses to the user's voice commands.

Findings

Ambience Mirror does not need to show details about friends' posts and comments on social media.

Of the 30% that tried to see more details from Facebook, only 4% were disappointed that they couldn't.

83% of users don't trust social networks in their bathrooms.

I really don't want Facebook in my bathroom.

– Eugene F.

Most users liked that they could see their email, but a majority did not want to read email in the bathroom.

Only 6 users tried to check their email.

I think I want to read my email all of the time, but I'm pretty sure that feeling goes against my well-being.

– Kurt G.

Most users don't find data that interesting, but those that do are likely to spend more money.

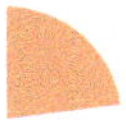

Only 23% cared about data visualization, and only 2 users wanted to see more detailed data.

I like to know everything about myself. You can tell by how many connected things I have!

– Hans T.

Users did want more information on news stories but preferred to have it read aloud to them instead of reading it on the mirror.

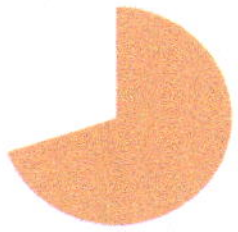

70% of users thought it would be nice to have the mirror read them details about news stories but not emails or social postings.

Calendar and weather were favorite features. Only a few users thought their calendars would be too complex to display in the current design.

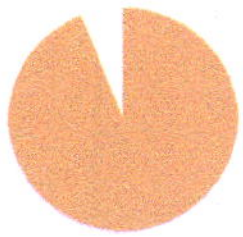

94% of users thought that the calendar offered plenty of information, though 3 users were worried that their calendars would be too complex to display.

I don't know how smart a mirror has to be to show my calendar and the weather. But that's all I need.

– Katie P.

Overall, most customers agreed that the mirror should not distract too much from everything else that happens in the bathroom.

The bathroom is one of the last places where I'd want to bring my phone. So why would I want a mirror that does all of the same things?

– Scott S.

I really only care about what the next day looks like. I probably wouldn't even use it at night.

– Carol L.

Omniscient / **Observations Suite Web App**

User Validation

Sprint 03 Summary

Group Size: Ten companies, twelve users

Feature Focus: See Movement in an Area, See Table Dwell Time, See Server Interactions

Positive Feedback:

"It's really nice that I have all of the same features available even on my phone. Most of the tools I use haven't had this, and it's always frustrating."

Jerome W., Veggie West

"Seeing which areas of my restaurant suffered as my employees moved around tables for large groups highlighted a lot of problems that we could feel, but not see."

Janine K., Café Apricot

"Having real-time heat map data helped us experiment in ways we hadn't before. We ended up adding three more tables, which means we can seat up to 20 percent more customers."

Roxanne M., Lali Lali

"It's helpful to see which employees are going the extra mile. It's definitely changed the way I'm staffing."

Juan B., La Cucina

"The integrations are really nice, so that I can keep using the same POS tools without retraining all of my staff."

Kevin D., Future Burger

Recommended Updates:

Pull in details of a customer's order for read-only purposes. Link to third-party tools only when the user needs to adjust an order.

"I should be able to see the orders I've taken in Observations as well as having a link to Toast."

"Sometimes I need to check on a customer's order, but I don't want to leave the Observations app. Maybe it's possible to pull in that information in the table-detail view?"

"There should be some warning that when I go into order details, I'll leave Observations Suite."

Highlight when a table is double-booked in the heat-map view.

"I can see when a table is overbooked in the table overview, but I can't from the heat map. Is this a mistake?"

"I keep accidentally double-booking tables from the heat map, but I can't see that it's a problem until I switch to a different view!"

Show the table-overview visualization when looking at a table's details from the heat map.

"I really like the heat-map view, and it's frustrating that I have to switch to the table overview to see when a table is booked."

"Why can't I see the table's timeline in the heat-map view?"

Make it easier to assign large group reservations to multiple tables.

"Small groups are fine, but when you get a group that needs two or three tables, it takes a lot more time to book those tables. It would be easier to just have a multiselect option, rather than having to remember and input multiple table numbers."

"Reservations that require multiple tables are a nightmare."

Make a table's individual seats interactive, showing a customer's information and order.

"How do I see information about the people sitting at the bar?"

"If I have a regular at a table, I want to see that person in a special way so that I can say hi and thank them for their loyalty."

"I really like the table info, but it feels too blunt. I want to see individual customers' orders. I also want to know when I'm dealing with a customer who's been in before."

Design more interaction into charts.
Document rules for summary messaging on dashboard.
TEST ALL CHARTS WITH SAMPLE DATA.
Test multiple report layouts and optimize.
BETTER LAYOUT FOR ORDER INFO ON CUSTOMER PAGE
Make table dwell viz more clear.
ake restaurant more recognizable.
TEST CUSTOMER SPEND PER VISIT WITH ACTUAL DATA.
Date navigation in table overview viz isn't obvious enough.
reservation isn't clear.
HIGHLIGHT MOST IMPORTANT INFO IN NOTIFICATIONS.
Hold PDS with users to design their ideal dashboard.
Test a version of the dashboard where time is built into charts.
TEST CHART SELECTION WITH USERS TO CONFIRM AVAILABLE SELECTION.
Make it more obvious when a table is double-booked.
DESIGN AND TEST A UNIVERSAL SEARCH OPTION.
Refine motion studies for
How do we accommodate international customer info?

Design Backlog

No matter how grand the project, there will always be things that require more time and resources than are available. Perhaps the design team wants to spend more time perfecting the transitions between states or to design and test different layouts with users. In the rush to produce a product or service, it's easy to lose track of the things that don't fit the schedule. The design backlog can be used to capture and prioritize these items, resulting in a shared list of actions that the design team will take on as time becomes available.

Depending on the working model, the design backlog can emerge at different points in a project. It might be used from the beginning of the refine phase as a means of organizing and prioritizing all of the work that needs to be done, or it might be created for use at the end of the first release, creating a series of ways to improve the product or service for subsequent versions.

“Embrace iteration as the road to improvement, but don’t let that lull you into rolling out poorly thought-out crap.”

Kate O’Neill

Start by holding a workshop to gather input from everyone.

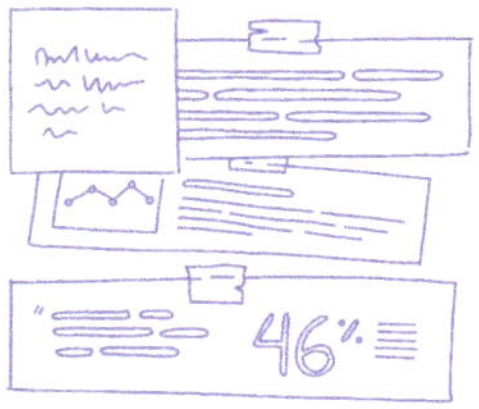

Reference findings from other activities to provide context to backlog items.

The design backlog originates from the product backlog, an artifact commonly used in software development. The product backlog is usually created as soon as features are established, creating a prioritization as well as capturing any issues that arise throughout the development process. Teams often collaborate to prioritize the product backlog into week- or sprint-sized chunks, making it easier to gauge progress.

The design backlog is similar, though less tactical than product backlogs. Rather than focusing on requirements for release, design backlogs seek to capture the activities that need to be performed in order to dispel the ambiguity around certain features. For the design team, keeping a backlog helps ensure that ideas are not forgotten, that explorations are accommodated when there is time, and that the team stays proactive rather than reactive.

Perhaps the most important outcome of the design backlog is that it keeps designers focused on finding quality solutions by deprioritizing less important items. It gives the team a place to park ideas and concerns that would otherwise distract, with the promise that they will be revisited.

Activities

As you move through the activities of creating mock-ups, detailed design, user validation, design assurance, and more, you will likely uncover problems that are worth exploring, hypotheses that need to be tested with users, and solutions that could be made better if only there were time. As these issues arise, capture them in a common place. This might be on pieces of paper, on a whiteboard, or in a shared spreadsheet. While everyone should be able to access and add to the design backlog, only one person should be responsible for organizing and prioritizing it.

If your project is already well underway and you haven't started a backlog, you might jump-start the process by holding a workshop to collect issues from everyone. You can also use this time to explain the purpose of a backlog and to help everyone understand how they can contribute. Formalizing critiques and reviews to include time for backlog contributions can also ensure that ideas and issues are captured for later consideration.

Maintaining a backlog requires ensuring that new items are added in the appropriate format, removing or updating the status of items as they are resolved, and reprioritizing as necessary. The keeper of the backlog should also make an effort to keep the team apprised of status and ensure alignment on both what's to be done and by when.

When adding items to the backlog, make sure to provide enough context. Backlogged items can be simple, or they can be rich, with references to findings from user validation, experience audits, and stakeholder feedback. Of course not everything in the backlog needs to be a reaction to negative input. New technologies and trends might also provide new design opportunities that weren't viable earlier in the process.

When prioritizing and estimating effort for the backlog, consider the processes of other teams. If there's an independent research team, make sure you understand how long it takes for them to recruit and test. If they already have a test plan and schedule, consider it while setting priorities for the design team. Regular check-ins with engineers and manufacturers are also

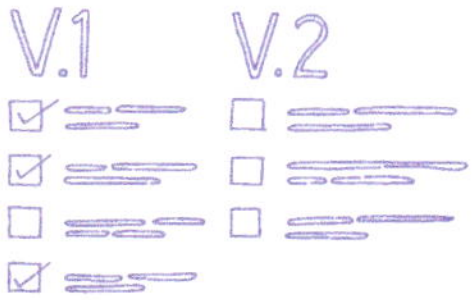

The backlog will live on through multiple versions of the product or service.

essential to ensure that the design artifacts feed into the execution schedule in an efficient way.

Backlogging is a process that has no end. By the time a product is manufactured and built, the design of the next version is probably already underway. Services and digital products continuously evolve and improve. With each new iteration, the design team has the opportunity to influence it through the priorities of the design backlog.

Artifacts

While the design backlog may begin less formally, it should be transitioned to a shareable format as soon as priorities are established. This living artifact might be a spreadsheet, a wiki, or some other project-tracking software.

Start by giving all backlog items similarly formatted descriptions. These might reference specific features, stories, or state names. Capture the actions that need to be taken in order to fulfill the backlog item. You might also link to related documentation or add relevant attachments. If your descriptions are long, create a title or summary that can be easily scanned. Give each issue a number so that they are easy to reference. Sequential numbering will also provide a sense of when the issue was added to the backlog.

Collaborating with the team and with relevant stakeholders, add priorities to backlog items. Estimate how much work will be needed to complete an item, and capture any deadlines for completion. If a backlog item requires a specific expertise, denote this or assign it to the appropriate team member. If prioritizing as a team, you might use a process to balance the value versus the effort, similar to those used in feature definition. Otherwise, a designated team member might be responsible for managing what items get tackled when.

Over time, the backlog will grow to have more items. At regular intervals, it should be reviewed to ensure that existing items are still relevant, that related items are grouped, and that the existing prioritization still stands. Individual backlog items will also need to be maintained with relevant notes, images, and links that provide additional insight and context as the experience evolves.

The design backlog for Observations Suite has a number of issues raised by multiple stakeholders. The list grows and evolves as high-priority issues are resolved and as new issues from beta testers are uncovered.

Omniscient / **Observations Suite Web App**

Design Backlog

#	Category	Title	Actions
013	Charts	**Design more interactive charts**	• Survey beta testers about what extra information would be useful • Design useful interactions for charts
022	Charts	**Refine Customer Spend chart with actual data**	• Gather multiple data sets, seeking outliers • Prototype chart using data sets • Refine the Customer Spend chart design
023	Charts	**Test chart selection with beta testers**	• Survey beta testers about what charts they need • Hold PDSs to design ideal charts with users • Add charts to current selection (ongoing)
031	Charts	**Review charts with outlier data**	• Seek feedback from users on chart visualizations • Revise as necessary
003	Dashboard	**Test time-specific charts on dashboard**	• Design an alternative dashboard option • Build the alternative dashboard • Test with users over a period of six weeks • Refine and implement best-performing option
004	Dashboard	**Define dashboard summary messaging**	• Work with experts to define specific rules • Bring in a copywriter to write samples and guidelines
041	Navigation	**Redesign Restaurant icon**	• Redesign Restaurant icon
048	Navigation	**Improve navigation transitions**	• Explore different options for motion • Work with development team to find an implementable solution
007	Search	**Explore universal search option**	• Design a universal search
014	Heat Map	**Improve table-dwell visualization**	• Explore multiple options for the table-dwell visualization • Test options with users to select one for implementation
015	Heat Map	**Make it clear when a table has a conflict**	• Design a way to show in the heat map when a table is double-booked
016	Table Overview	**Make conflicts more obvious**	• Redesign conflicts on the "Table Overview" page
005	Table Overview	**Add a Today button for table overview**	• Add a Today button to "Table Overview" page
062	Reservations	**Make multitable reservations easier**	• Observe customer behavior and collect feedback around assigning a reservation to multiple tables

Input	Effort	Priority
"Most competitors have some form of chart interaction to see specifics about the data." —Brad V.	Moderate	Medium
"The current visualization design makes too many guesses about how many times a guest visits a restaurant, how much they spend, etc." —Karen L.	Moderate	High
"The selection of charts we offer is based on competitive research and educated guesses, but not on user feedback. Work with users to make sure we're fulfilling their needs." —Brad V.	Unknown	Medium
"We're not sure how well our current chart designs will work with extreme and outlier data." —Maggie W. "We've tried to use realistic and extreme sample data to test, but haven't tested with any actual user data, so we should expect some issues on launch." —Paul M.	Low	Low
"Most competitors use charts with specific time frames, while we have a single time frame that applies to the entire dashboard. Consider trying and testing an alternative to our dashboard design with a subset of beta users." —Brad V.	High	Low
"Our current dashboard shows a message at the top, but no rules are defined and the copy is only a placeholder." —Malia S.	Moderate	High
"Several users have asked what the Restaurant icon is supposed to be." —Anne H.	Low	Low
"The current animation of the navigation on mobile is really choppy and awkward. We should work with developers to explore options." —Karen L.	Moderate	Medium
"The per-section search works well, but a lot of users expect to be able to search everything at once." —Anne H. "Some sections are already really complex, so we might have to limit the universal search to the dashboard (home) page." —Karen L.	Low	Low
"Users don't understand that the table-dwell visualization is showing them information. They need it explained and then it's fine." —Anne H.	Moderate	Medium
"Is there a way to tell when tables have a conflict? For example, when a party runs intoanother's reservation?" —Samantha M. "Not right now, but it's worth revisiting with the table-dwell visualization." —Paul M.	Low	Medium
"Users aren't seeing when there are conflicts in the 'Table Overview.' It should be more obvious at a glance." —Anne H.	Low	High
"Is there a quick way to get to Today when browsing through 'Table Overview' visualizations?" —Samantha M.	Low	Medium
"A lot of users complain about how complicated it is to assign a reservation to multiple tables. We should make it easier." —Anne H. "We already looked at a lot of options, and this was the simplest. It's already easier than all of our competitors." —Karen L.	Low	Medium

Glossary

Activity	A sometimes-collaborative action performed with certain goals or outcomes in mind
Artifact	The output of a process or processes that communicate outcomes to the team, to stakeholders, or to users
Channel	The medium through which the user interacts with a product or service
Component	A standard part of the design made using multiple ingredients and controls; often repeated throughout an experience
Concept	An idea for a feature, product, or service; the user's understanding of a feature, product, or service
Control	An element in an interactive experience that the user engages with
Customer	A user who intentionally engages with an experience
Design Language	A cohesive system of design decisions covering both the experiential and the aesthetic
Experience	Something a human interacts with, often spanning time
Feature	A distinct aspect of an experience
Framework	A way of structuring thinking that highlights patterns and anomalies
Generative	A type of activity done with the purpose of creating or exploring ideas or executions; the opposite of reductive

Edge Case	A situation predicted to be rare but still possible to encounter
Enabler	A tool or capability an organization will require to develop or operate a feature
Function	The tactical version of a feature, usually more specific than a feature, relating to a single user action
Hypothesis	A guess about how a design decision will affect the user's behavior; often needs validation
Ingredient	An element of a design language, such as typography or color
Phase	A segment of an overall design approach; phases are made of smaller, more specific activities and artifacts
Product	A physical or digital aspect of an experience
Project	A plan for executing a series of activities and delivering artifacts resulting in an outcome
Proposition	A description of the value a product or service will provide to its users
Provocation	A prompt in the form of a statement, question, or design shared with an audience to get a reaction or generate ideas
Reductive	A type of activity done to reduce or refine ideas or possible executions; the opposite of generative
Risk	Danger that a project will run over its planned time and budget

Scenario	A focused part of the user's experience, usually with specific goals and a single outcome
Service	An aspect of an experience where the user engages with a company over time
Stakeholder	A person who has an interest in and who provides input to a project
State	The position, condition, or status of an experience at a single point in time
Story	A single sentence that captures a user's interaction with an experience; could include the user's role, context, and desired outcome along with action taken
System	A set of consistent rules governing the design of a product or service
Touchpoint	The physical or digital location where a user interacts with a product, service, or channel
User	Anybody who encounters an experience; could be professional or consumer, intentional or not
Value Proposition	A statement that defines your users and describes what needs your product or service fulfills

Thanks

Many thanks are owed to the many people who helped in the production of this tome.

First and foremost, thanks to my partner, Hans. Together we ran The Artificial, the agency that would provide the foundation for this book, and the many conversations of our morning walks refined the content within its chapters. While I may have filled these pages with words, anyone who knows Hans will surely see his influence.

Thanks also to the many women of The Artificial who helped me refine my own practice and who taught me how to be a better teacher. Special thanks to Natalia, who worked with me to create many of the sample artifacts throughout this book.

And many more thank-yous to the clients who have trusted me as a partner when tackling challenges, to the collaborators who shaped my approach and my practice, and to the many, many people who use the power they have to help others learn and grow.

About the Author

Shannon E. Thomas is a design and strategy consultant with a passion for communication and mentorship. She has over twelve years of experience with experience design working for clients in North America, Europe, and Asia. For five years she ran The Artificial, a boutique UX agency in Amsterdam, providing experience design and strategy for a wide range of clients, from start-ups to corporations.

Lightning Source UK Ltd.
Milton Keynes UK
UKHW021157160421
382085UK00004B/41

9 789083 041407